JAGUAR
XK140/150

In Detail

JAGUAR
XK140/150

In Detail

BY ANDERS DITLEV CLAUSAGER

H&S

Herridge & Sons

Published in 2008 by
Herridge & Sons Ltd
Lower Forda, Shebbear,
Beaworthy, Devon EX21 5SY

© Copyright Jaguar Daimler Heritage Trust 2008

Designed by Ray Leaning
Special photography by Simon Clay, François Prins
and Karam Ram

ISBN 978-1-906133-07-8
Printed in China

Contents

Introduction

XK past

It was a dark and stormy night some years ago that my publisher Charles Herridge and I first discussed the idea of writing an "In Detail" title on the Jaguar XK. I said "We need to cover all of them" and he said, "No, we'll just do the XK 120" – and it was just as well that we did, since even the XK 120 book rather pushed the envelope in several directions. However, that book was sufficiently well received to re-visit the original idea, so here, two years later, is the follow-up volume on the later cars. In other words, this is "Volume 2"; "Volume 1" was my *XK 120 in Detail* published in 2006, and still available.

With the XK 120 book, I hope to have done those cars justice, much as I hope that the present volume does justice to the later XKs which are equally fine cars. However, while the original XK 120, despite its undoubted shortcomings, has been elevated to a remarkable status in the automotive Pantheon – as indeed it deserves to be – its successors have never quite scaled that pinnacle. I think that one important reason for this is that what in 1948 was a sensation, and in 1950 was still a world-beater, by 1955, never mind 1960, had become everyday and matter-of-course: familiarity does supposedly breed contempt. The celebrities who had once queued up to buy an XK 120, had transferred their always fickle allegiance elsewhere, perhaps to a gull-wing Mercedes-Benz, or a Ferrari.

The development of the original styling was always controversial. Let me be honest about this, I do feel that the later cars lost much of the litheness and simple elegance of the XK 120. No doubt in 1954 it was quite sensible of Jaguar to put bigger bumpers on a car whose main market was the USA, but the XK 140 grille was a poor effort. The XK 150 was criticised openly in some quarters as being yesterday's left-overs warmed up, and by the end of production the styling was best described as traditional – but still good-looking.

On the mechanical front, there was a great deal of progress. The XK 140 was given much better rack-and-pinion steering, and overdrive became available, while the XK 150 put a stop to the oft-encountered brake problems by adopting Dunlop disc brakes. For those who wanted it, from 1956 there was also the option of an automatic gearbox. Engines grew steadily more powerful, as they needed to be to keep pace with the increasing weight of the cars; the final XK 150 3.8-litre S was the fastest ever production XK. Its engine went on to power the early E-type, which in 1961 was the answer to those who had criticised the XK as being out-of-date, and which restored Jaguar to the position of leadership in the sports car market.

Another reason for the different perceptions of the XK 120, and the 140/150 models, is that the XK 120 was without any doubt a sports car, and earned its laurels in competition. The two later cars were always seen more as GT cars and were less likely to be used in racing or rallying.

This picture must have been taken in early 1956, as it shows the then-new 2.4 litre saloon together with the Mark VIIM, as well as a D-type and all three versions of the XK 140. The central figure is the newly knighted Sir William Lyons. (JDHT)

As I explain later on in this book, there were good reasons for this. While I may have accumulated a surprising number of cases where the cars were raced or rallied, it was more a question of taking part, than of having any realistic chance of winning something important. As much as anything else, this lack of worthwhile competition results has tended to dull the image of the later XKs; one benefit however is that since the cars were mostly active in amateur and club racing, then as now they gave enormous pleasure to their owners, and on this level of motor sport they were and are fully competitive.

As Jaguar went on to the next generation with the E-type, the shadows fell over the XKs. Through most of the 1960s, values continued to fall, and many cars were scrapped when repair costs exceeded their potential value. Who wanted an XK, when after a few years you could get a second-hand E-type, with its higher performance and more glamorous image, for

very little more money? – never mind the fact that there were actually more E-types around.

However, some die-hard enthusiasts continued to cherish their XKs, and no doubt cherry-picked the best bargains out of the classified advertisements in *Motor Sport*. In 1967, the XK register of the Jaguar Drivers' Club was founded, with a very young Paul Skilleter as one of its driving forces. In 1975, he wrote the book *Jaguar Sports Cars* which contained the first well-researched, serious study of the XKs and others, and which even more than thirty years later remains a useful standard reference work. Paul won't mind me quoting the opening paragraph of his introduction:

"While I've been engaged on this book, more than one person has asked me if I really thought there was room for *another* work on Jaguars, knowing as I did that there have been five or six published already. My answer was, of course, an unequivocal 'yes'."

A sentiment I fully echo… even if nowadays I guess it is more like five or six hundred books on Jaguar! – but I hope there is still room for more…

With increased interest, nurtured within the clubs, and nourished by books such as Paul's, during the 1970s the classic car movement got under way in earnest. As even the E-type got to be "old hat" some sort of parity was eventually established between the two generations of Jaguar sports cars, and of course after 1974 there was for a long time no more open Jaguars. The XJ-S of the day was simply too expensive to buy and run for most enthusiasts, besides which it had a very different, and somehow "wrong" image.

Ever since, the XKs have gone from strength to strength in the classic car world, and have been the subject of much research and many more publications. I was personally involved as a classic car owner and enthusiast from around 1970 onwards, but XKs were rather rare in Denmark at the time (this was before the import boom got under way), and I recall very few encounters with XKs in those early days. For many years afterwards, my main professional interest was in other makes such as MG and Austin-Healey, and I only became more involved with the XKs, and other Jaguars, when I joined the Jaguar Daimler Heritage Trust in 2000.

It became part of my duties to look after the original Jaguar production records which are in our care in the Trust's archive, and to use these to provide information to owners and enthusiasts. It occurred to me that it would be useful to convert the information from the original records to databases. This took about three years, but it has helped to unlock a great deal of previously unavailable information, which I have used in my two books on the XKs. I hope that the result will be of interest to the reader, whether he or she is a relative newcomer to the XK world, or an established respected "pro".

In the process of writing such a book as this, inevitably one uses a variety of sources which apart from original records and contemporary material will include many other published works, books as well as magazine articles, and there has been an awful lot of material published on the XKs in the last thirty-odd years. Apart from including a bibliography, I have as far as possible tried to identify indi-

vidual sources in footnotes. In this day and age there are naturally many references to material found on the internet, most of which I hope will continue to be there when you, the reader, follow my lead and look up the web page in question! No doubt fellow historians will continue to gather information and will publish their results; I know there are already a few other XK titles in the pipeline, which I look forward to, as I believe that all of these books complement each other, and we can all learn something new.

This book has been about two years in the writing, really from the time that I finished *XK 120 in Detail*. A great number of people have been very helpful and supportive throughout this period. My thanks are first and foremost due to John Maries, executive director of the Jaguar Daimler Heritage Trust, and Roger Putnam, chairman of our board of trustees, together with my colleagues and our volunteers at the JDHT, in particular Karam Ram who as our photographic archivist again helped me find and scan appropriate images in our archive.

Outside our own organisation, I am particularly grateful to David Bentley, the registrar of the XK Club, to John Elmgreen and Terry McGrath, the two great XK experts in Australia, and to Paul Skilleter whom I quoted above; these four gentlemen all read part or all of the typescript, and gave me the benefit of their comments. Terry especially provided much information on elusive special-bodied cars. Paul has also provided many rare photos for this book, as he did for the previous volume. I have included a fuller list in the appendix, and would like to thank everybody for their kind assistance.

Thanks are also due to my publishers, Charles, Bridgid and Ed Herridge, not least for the friendship and hospitality they have extended to David and myself; and again to my partner David, who this time read most of the typescript, and I actually think he quite enjoyed it…

Anders Ditlev Clausager
Birmingham and Coventry – 1 April 2008

Chapter One

Success breeds... success

Conditions really were appalling during most of the 1954 24-hour race. This is the Rolt/Hamilton Jaguar D-type which came so close to beating the Ferrari. (JDHT)

It is Sunday afternoon, 13 June 1954. The place is Le Mans, France. The clock is ticking away to the hour of 4pm. The twenty-first 24-hour sports car race nears its climax. There are still twenty cars of the 54 starters running in a race which has been almost continuously dampened by anything from a drizzle to a downpour. Excitement is running high and there is much nail-biting in the grandstand and the pits. The race leader, the 5-litre Ferrari of Gonzales and Trintignant, has been delayed by a lengthy pit stop, but now it is back on the track and everyone is enjoying a rare spell of sunshine. As the road surface dries out, the big

Ferrari has the edge thanks to its power and superior acceleration. Still, close behind is the 3.4-litre Jaguar D-type of Hamilton and Rolt. Less than two minutes separate the two cars. Gonzales has not slept for 24 hours, he is exhausted, his Ferrari is ailing, and his lap times are now being consistently bettered by Hamilton in the Jaguar. The flame of hope burns bright that the British car may yet overtake the leader.

No, Duncan Hamilton did not quite make it, but his second place in the D-type in its debut race, a minute and a half and two-and-a-half miles behind the Ferrari, was the closest one-two finish since 1933 and nothing like it would be seen until 1966 in this most famous of all motor races. The 1954 race was, in the words of *Motor Sport*, "A Battle between Brute Force and Science": the brute force, Ferrari; the science, Jaguar. Jaguar lost, but lost with honour, its reputation intact, even enhanced in this David versus Goliath battle.[1]

Now, fifty-odd years later, it is curious to look back and reflect that at the time both Ferrari and Jaguar were relative newcomers. The Italian marque was a post-war phenomenon, even if *il Commendatore*, Enzo Ferrari himself, had a distinguished pre-war career racing with Alfa Romeo. Thus Ferrari set out with a pedigree, it was a brand born out of racing, and it had the distinction of having won the Le Mans race at its first attempt, in 1949. And Jaguar? Jaguar had the longer but humbler history. By 1954 its antecedents stretched 32 years into the past, and its history could be compartmentalised in a series of neat steps – from motorcycle sidecars to special coachwork, through its own brand of stylish but affordable motorcar, then increasingly gaining respectability by offering above-average performance and finally arriving at a unique identity, underpinned by the adoption of the name Jaguar on its own in 1945.

Yet even in 1945, Jaguar was but one of many British upmarket brands. Undoubtedly, it stood out in the marketplace, offering a near-unique combination of style and performance at almost bargain prices. Its success so far owed everything to the remarkable personality of William Lyons, the company's founder, largest shareholder, chairman and managing director, who also most unusually directed the styling of the cars that his company produced. As well as being a gifted designer, Lyons was an astute and ambitious businessman who had a very clear idea of where he wanted his company to go, and had at an early stage expressed his aim to build one of the finest luxury cars in the world.[2]

Lyons saw high performance as the key to achieving this goal. Already the 3½-litre version of his pre-war Jaguar saloon had a top speed of around 92mph (148km/h),[3] yet sold for a paltry £445 before the war – which due to inflation and the imposition of Purchase Tax had risen to £991 after the war and to £1263 by 1948, although this was then still a very reasonable figure for what the car offered. But Lyons's future plans called for a full-size luxury saloon capable of 100mph (161km/h), which would need at least 160bhp rather than the 125bhp of the current six-cylinder engine.[4] The solution which he thrashed out with a small group of engineers during the final years of the Second World War was to use two overhead camshafts rather than the traditional pushrod-operated overhead valves. The key members of staff were chief engineer William Heynes, engine designer Claude Baily and development engineer Walter Hassan. By 1948, their new engine was well advanced and nearly ready for production, and had been given the "XK" designation, where the X originally indicated experimental and XK was the last in a sequence that had started with XF, if not earlier. The final version was of 83x106mm bore and stroke, with a capacity of 3442cc (210cu.in), and with a compression ratio of 8:1 delivered 160bhp at 5000rpm.

The secret of Jaguar's performance advantage in the 1950s – and beyond – was the twin overhead camshaft layout of the XK engine, here laid bare, but I need to add that this particular engine is from a Mark VII saloon. (JDHT)

It is difficult to overstate the enormity of such a small company as Jaguar even contemplating making this incredibly advanced and powerful engine. Today we are completely blasé about twin overhead cam engines, but before the Second World War they had been very rare outside the world of motor racing and were mostly familiar to enthusiasts from expensive and exotic cars of the stamp of the Alfa Romeo and the Bugatti. Such engines were often of semi-racing type, were temperamental, and difficult to service. Furthermore, Jaguar had until recently relied on the supply of all its engines from the Coventry-based Standard company which had originally supplied S.S. chassis complete. Only during the war had Standard unexpectedly offered to sell its six-cylinder engine production facility to Jaguar; Lyons, typically, negotiated a bargain price of £6000.[5]

The company now had the facilities and the design to manufacture a new potentially world-beating engine. The factory at Foleshill in Coventry had been extended in stages, starting in 1938-39 on the strength of a promise of a Ministry contract for aircraft work in wartime, with further expansions following during the war so that by 1944, production capacity had doubled.[6] On the other hand, one of Lyons's ambitious schemes had come to nothing: on the eve of war he had bought the adjacent factory of Motor Panels, already a supplier to SS Cars, presumably with a view to extending the company's body making facilities, yet had felt obliged to sell the company on to Rubery Owen in 1943, to reduce his bank overdraft.[7] The early post-war Jaguar bodies continued to be put together in the factory from a variety of smaller, mainly bought-in, panels. However, for the all-new saloon car which was intended to have an all-steel body of modern full-width styling, Jaguar decided to buy in the bodies complete from the Pressed Steel Company at Cowley, at that time Britain's largest independent maker of all-steel coachwork and a supplier to most of the leading car manufacturers.

Then there was a series of delays; at the time, PSC was struggling to keep up with demand, and a relatively small contract from a new client may have got shuffled to the back of the queue. There was nothing for it but to delay the introduction of the planned MkVII saloon, and instead launch an interim car with a body built in-house of traditional style, with the old pushrod engine, but at least using the new chassis with independent front suspension and hydraulic brakes that Heynes and Hassan had also been busy on. This became the Mark V, launched in time for the first post-war Earls Court Motor Show in London in October 1948.

Lyons was loath not to use this important occasion as the launch platform for his new engine, and made the bold decision to introduce the XK engine in a new "Super Sports" model which was tentatively named the XK 120, from the engine designation coupled with the hoped-for top speed of the car of 120mph (193km/h). Also planned, but quickly dropped, was a second model, the XK 100 with the same chassis and body but a four-cylinder 2-litre engine of similar basic design. After the briefest of press previews, the new sports car was unveiled to the public when the Motor Show opened its doors on 27 October 1948. The XK 120 was an immediate sensation, offering a stunning combination of advanced engineering, beautiful styling, and high performance, all at a basic price of £988 or £1263 including Purchase Tax – the same as the new Mark V 3½-litre saloon.[8]

The XK 120 may have been intended just as a limited-production car, in the same way that SS had only made 309 SS Jaguar 100 sports cars between 1935 and 1939, but this was 1948 and the British motor industry was making every effort to sell its products abroad, especially in the USA to earn Dollars. Jaguar had appointed two distributors in this market, Max Hoffman in New York and Charles Hornburg in Los Angeles, with the Mississippi river as the border between their territories, and there was the nucleus of a dealer network. From his trip to the USA in early 1948 when he visited both coasts, Lyons was well aware of the growing demand for British sports cars in the USA and the enthusiasm that had greeted the arrival of the MG Midget. The gratifying result was that both American distributors placed large orders for the new Jaguar sports car as soon as it was launched. This however left Jaguar with the headache of how to make more of them than had, originally, been planned.

A first series of XK 120s was put in hand, using the hand-built aluminium body as intended, but even so it was into the summer of 1949 before the first production cars began to trickle out of the factory. At an early stage, it had been decided to re-tool the bodywork in steel, and the Pressed Steel Company stepped in and offered to supply the body panels. After some 240 aluminium-bodied cars had been made, the steel-bodied version followed with little fanfare in the spring of 1950. By then the XK 120 had already earned its spurs and put the doubting Thomases in their place. In May 1949, a prototype car had set up a speed record of 132.6mph (213.4km/h) in front of a press party at the Jabbeke highway in Belgium, while a few months later three XK 120s were entered in the first sports car race at Silverstone, and two of them finished first and second. Six cars were specially prepared for motor sport, the most successful being the car rallied by Ian Appleyard who won the Alpine Rally and the RAC Rally, while Stirling Moss drove another of these cars to victory in the first post-war Tourist Trophy race in 1950.

This year also saw the first appearance of the XK 120s in a major international race, the feared and famed 24-hour race at Le Mans. This had initially been founded as an event to test the stamina and endurance of touring cars, but by 1950 the race had come to be increasingly contested by rather more special types of sports-racing cars euphemistically called "prototypes", and the three Jaguars were at a disadvantage by being very close to the standard catalogue specification. Nevertheless, they did not disgrace themselves as two of them finished in twelfth and fifteenth places, one of the cars having been at times as high as eighth in the field. There were two consequences of the competitions programme undertaken with the early XK 120s: the first was that the few shortcomings of the car were high-lighted, the worst being the brakes which were not sufficiently powerful and were particularly prone to fade. The other consequence was that chief engineer Heynes realised that if Jaguar developed a specialised light-weight racing model with the XK engine, it might stand a chance of winning at Le Mans, "given reasonable luck".[9]

Work was soon under way on both fronts. The racing car project bore fruit in 1951. This derivative of the XK 120 was initially called the XK 120 "C" – C for Competition – but became universally known as the C-type. It had a tuned XK engine giving around 180bhp in a tubular chassis frame clothed in a tightly-fitting aluminium skin designed, or as some would have it, calculated, by the aerodynamicist Malcolm Sayer who had joined Jaguar from the Bristol aircraft company. Three of the new cars were ready in time for the race at Le Mans in June 1951, they were driven out to France under their own power, entered the race, and one of them won it. If none of their other achievements had established Jaguar's credentials as a leading sports car manufacturer, this victory in the debut race for the new model certainly did.

At the same time, Jaguar began to co-operate with the Dunlop company on the development of the disc brake. The idea was not new, having been used nearly 50 years before on a Lanchester car, and had latterly been taken up by Dunlop for use on aircraft – no doubt a very sensible notion in view of the rather higher landing speeds of the new jet-powered planes. In the USA, Chrysler also toyed briefly with the idea. Jaguar believed that the more efficient and less fade-prone disc brake would give them an edge in motor racing, even when competing against more powerful cars, and much of the development work was carried out on the C-type. In 1952 one of the early C-types was fitted with disc brakes and Stirling Moss raced it at the Goodwood Easter meeting, while soon after Moss and Jaguar test driver Norman Dewis entered the Mille Miglia with the same car but retired. Later in the season, the first victory for a disc-braked C-type came in the sports car race at Reims, Moss again being the driver. In 1953 the entire Jaguar works team at Le Mans had C-types with disc brakes, and took first, second

and fourth places.

The C-type, and the disc brakes, had an enormous influence on the Jaguar production cars which were to follow. Special tuning modifications for the XK 120 were announced by Jaguar and the parts became available in the summer of 1951, while a higher-tuned model, the XK 120 SE (or "Special Equipment") became part of the

The XK 120 had created a sensation on its debut in 1948. Over the following years, Jaguar added fixed-head and drophead coupé versions. (JDHT)

This is the actual C-type which won the 1951 Le Mans race, chassis XKC 003, at the factory before being driven out to Le Mans. (JDHT)

The Mark VII was launched in 1950, and was the luxury saloon for which the XK engine had always been intended. (JDHT)

Jaguars would be powered by this engine, remarkable not least for its adaptability and ubiquity. In motor sport, the only field that Jaguar did not enter was Grand Prix racing, and this may have been the only disadvantage of the company to Ferrari and the few other road car makers who did make single-seater racing cars as well.

Otherwise, in the 1950s the world was Jaguar's oyster. The original works team was only active in the brief period from 1949 to 1956, and afterwards Jaguar instead handed the torch to selected privateers. Jaguar's target was always Le Mans, the most famous motor race in the world, and between 1951 and 1957 their sports-racing cars won five times – while their record in other races was patchy. At one time, British saloon car races were almost Jaguar benefits, while in rallying there were wins in the RAC and the Alpine Rallies, together with several good places in the Monte Carlo including an extraordinarily close second in 1953, and finally, in 1956, a win.

However, to return to 1954. The XK 120 range had been extended with additional body styles, a fixed-head coupé in 1951 and a drop-head coupé in 1953. The model was actually at the peak of its popularity, with more cars being made in 1953 than in any other year, and a similar rate of production was maintained until production ended in August 1954. Jaguar now had a replacement ready, the XK 140 which was launched at the Earls Court Motor Show in London in October. This was in many ways changed from the XK 120. The standard engine was now to the specification that had been

normal production range a year later, and in 1953 a full-blown C-type cylinder head was offered by Jaguar to convert XK 120s. It should be noted by the way that the solidly-constructed XK engine had proved itself to be completely docile and reliable, and capable of withstanding a great deal of tuning.

Indeed, Jaguar was still only at the start of the development process that this engine would continue to undergo in the quest for higher performance until well into the 1960s. And of course, at the 1950 Motor Show Jaguar had finally launched the new saloon model with the XK engine, the 100mph (161km/h) Mark VII which went on to carve a niche for itself in the international luxury car market. For the next twenty years, from racing cars to limousines, all

Photographed at Wappenbury Hall together with an XK 140 fixed-head in the spring of 1955, the proposal for a new sports car is so low that it must have been completely impractical, if built on an XK chassis. (JDHT)

found on the XK 120 SE with 180bhp, while alternatively, a 210bhp engine with the C-type cylinder head was a regular option. Overdrive was offered as an optional extra, there was rack-and-pinion steering, and improvements to the brakes. Externally there was a new radiator grille and much stronger bumpers. As the engine was mounted further forward than on the XK 120 it became possible to fit occasional rear seats on the two coupé models. The fixed-head had other more extensive changes to its bodywork for the same reason, while the two-seater and drophead bodies were less changed. At the same time as the XK 140 was introduced, the Mark VII was given the 180bhp engine and became the Mark VIIM.

The XK 140 was destined for a shorter production life than its predecessor, of little more than two years until January 1957. During its production life, the most important change was that in 1956, the coupé models became available with an automatic gearbox, at first only for the American market. Together with the other changes made to the XK 140, this development underscored the fact that the XK was now seen as more of a GT car than as an out-and-out sports car, both by its makers and by the public. There was also the consideration that automatic transmission was a necessity in the

American market, especially since the Jaguar's most important competitors, the Chevrolet Corvette and the Ford Thunderbird, were both available in automatic form.

Behind the scenes, Jaguar was looking forward to an eventual successor to the XK. In April 1955, a remarkably low-slung sports car mock-up was photographed at Lyons's home, Wappenbury Hall. This would have been totally unfeasible if it were to be built on the existing XK chassis, and I must tentatively conclude that

In the rear three-quarter view we can see experiments with two different bumper sections, standard XK 140 rear lamps and a neat solution for the number plate surround. (JDHT)

The mock-up had an XK 120 radiator grille, and "bug-eye" headlamps. (JDHT)

Taken a little later at the Jaguar sports field, a slightly modified mock-up with alternative windscreen, and a contrast-colour spat, still with the XK 140 for comparison. (JDHT)

it was intended to use some form of unitary or semi-unitary construction. Other mock-ups seem to have been short-wheelbase coupé or convertible versions based on the new 2.4-litre model. Malcolm Sayer was working on a project for a sports-racing car which was to some extent derived from the D-type, as it had a similar semi-unitary form of construction. Initially it was fitted with the 2.4-litre engine, to allow the car to compete in the prototype category at Le Mans. This project eventually metamorphosed into the E2A prototype which did race at Le Mans in 1960, and later formed the basis for the E-type production car of 1961. However, the more immediate replacement for the XK 140 was introduced in the spring of 1957 as the XK 150, which compared to the earlier XKs featured a more radically redesigned body, while the new disc brakes were the major mechanical

change. It was obviously still a lineal descendant of the original XK 120, using an otherwise little modified chassis, while the most important change to the engine was that the 210bhp specification was now standard.

At first launched only with a choice of the two coupé body styles, the XK 150 in a sense completed the transition from sports car to GT; it took nearly another year for a two-seater to reappear, aimed more than ever at the American market, and that was then accompanied by the S version with a more highly-tuned three-carburettor engine. In September 1959, the 3.8-litre version of the XK engine, introduced a year earlier in the Mark IX saloon, found its way under the bonnet of the XK 150, in both standard and S forms. As production of the XK 150 was run down towards the end of 1960, the basic design was beginning to feel its twelve-year age, yet the model was still more than competitive with later and more sophisticated high-powered sports and GT cars. To the end of its life, the XK offered that traditional unbeatable Jaguar combination of style and performance at a remarkably low price. Its successor, the E-type was waiting in the wings to make its bow at the 1961 Geneva Motor Show; it would uphold and reinforce these qualities.

Despite the other Jaguar models in the future, including the Mark II of 1959, the E-type which became an icon of the 1960s, the remarkable first XJ of 1968, and the V12 engined cars of the

This is the other sports car mock-up which was under consideration around 1954-55, but which is more likely to have been derived from the new compact 2.4-litre saloon. Note XK 120-style grille and front bumpers. (JDHT)

1970s and beyond – never mind other more recent introductions – I would argue that the 1950s were Jaguar's "golden decade", certainly in the sports car field, whether on road or track. Just look at the following list of the company's achievements from 1948 to 1959 – barely a year went by without some milestone event, whether a new model introduction, or a major competitive success:

And of course, the expansion of the company

1948:	Launch of XK 100/120 and Mark V
1949:	"Mark IV" discontinued, XK 120 and Mark V go into production
1950:	Steel-bodied XK 120; first Tourist Trophy win; Mark VII saloon
1951:	XK 120 fixed-head coupé; C-type; first Le Mans win; second Tourist Trophy win
1952:	Move to new factory at Browns Lane completed
1953:	Mark VII automatic; XK 120 drophead coupé; second Le Mans win
1954:	Mark VII with overdrive; D-type; XK 140; Mark VIIM
1955:	Third Le Mans win; 2.4-litre saloon
1956:	XK 140 automatic; Monte Carlo win; fourth Le Mans win; Mark VIII
1957:	XK-SS; 3.4-litre saloon; XK 150 fixed-head and drophead coupés; fifth Le Mans win
1958:	XK 150 two-seater and XK 150 S; Mark IX
1959:	XK 150 3.8 and 3.8 S; Mark II

could be measured in the almost ever-growing production figures, which quadrupled in less than ten years:

Amazingly, in 1955, the proportion of sports

	Total production	Saloons	Sports cars	% of saloons	% of sports
1949	4190	4093	97	97.7%	2.3%
1950	7206	5687	1519	78.9%	21.1%
1951	6496	5167	1329	79.5%	20.5%
1952	8968	5966	3002	66.5%	33.5%
1953	10,099	6694	3405	66.3%	33.7%
1954	9894	6454	3440	65.2%	34.8%
1955	10,868	6119	4749	56.3%	43.7%
1956	13,205	9888	3317	74.9%	25.1%
1957	13,676	12,173	1503	89.0%	11.0%
1958	19,456	14,857	4599	76.4%	23.6%
1959	18,509	16,308	2201	88.1%	11.9%
1960	22,449	21,090	1359	93.9%	6.1%
Total	**145,016**	**114,496**	**30,520**	**79.0%**	**21.0%**

car production reached its zenith; even when the E-type was at its most popular in the American market in the late 1960s (while at the same time the old saloon models were falling out of favour) the sports car output stayed just under 40 per cent of production (1968: 38.7 per cent, 1969: 39.1 per cent). From 1956 with the new compact saloon car in production, the balance shifted away from sports cars, as it would do when the XJ range got into its stride from 1969 onwards.

So, the original XK range was of huge importance to Jaguar. From being only another small British specialist producer, thanks to the XKs and their derivatives, within a few short years Jaguar had become a household name around the world, and a force to be reckoned with in the sports and prestige car market.

The compact saloon launched in 1955 completed the Jaguar range. Here William Lyons and William Heynes show off their new baby, together with a distant ancestor. The early 2.4 litre had a grille very like the XK 140. (JDHT)

1. *Motor Sport* Jul 1954
2. Paper by WM Heynes published in 1960, quoted in Porter and Skilleter *Sir William Lyons* p.55; Heynes remembered Lyons making this statement in 1935
3. *The Motor* 31 May 1938
4 WM Heynes "The Jaguar Engine", published in *The Autocar* 24 Apr 1953, *The Motor* 15 and 22 Apr 1953
5. SS Cars Ltd board minutes 1 Oct 1942; letter from Lyons "Gold Medal" paper, quoted in Skilleter *Jaguar Sports Cars* p.50; Porter and Skilleter p.87
6. Whyte *Jaguar* (first edition) p.111; Lyons's statement at the 1944 AGM quoted in Porter and Skilleter p.87
7. Whyte pp.111, 115; Porter and Skilleter pp.64, 81, 86-87
8. For a detailed discussion of the circumstances surrounding the birth of the XK 120, see my *Jaguar XK 120 in Detail* chapters 1 to 4
9. Skilleter *Jaguar Sports Cars* p.88; Whyte *Jaguar Sports Racing and Works Competition Cars to 1953*, p.98

The 2.4 was followed in 1957 by this 3.4-litre model. In profile, there is a clear family resemblance to the XK 150, and the grilles were also similar. (JDHT)

Chapter Two

The XK 140

The new model which was launched in time for the 1954 Earls Court Motor Show in London featured a considerable number of changes, some of which had undoubtedly been inspired by customer feedback from the American market. While some of the changes were worthwhile improvements, others were of dubious merit, and some might even be said to detract from the original simple elegance and purity of line of the XK 120.

The chassis frame had been changed, mostly to allow the engine to be moved 3in (76mm) forward to improve legroom. The wheelbase was unchanged at 102in (2591mm). The penalty came in the form of a forwards weight transfer, from 47.5 to 50.3 per cent of unladen weight on the front wheels.[1] While this enhanced straight-line stability, the XK 140 was always more of an understeerer than the XK 120. At the front of the chassis, the upwards extensions for mounting the XK 120 bumper bars were deleted, but there was an additional wraparound panel, partly closed off at the bottom by a shield protecting the radiator hoses. The front cross member was slightly shorter, front to rear. The chassis central cross member was moved rearwards and was reshaped, to allow for the installation of an optional Laycock de Normanville overdrive unit, which had proved very popular on the Mark VII saloon since it was first offered in January 1954. Another change to this cross member was to provide two holes for the full dual exhaust

In the front view the XK 140 was immediately identifiable from its predecessor, thanks to the new grille, the bumpers which were massive compared to those of an XK 120, and the separate flashing indicator lamps. The headlamps now had a central "J" medallion.

This was undoubtedly a Jaguar XK, and although most observers find that the changes did detract from the appearance of the car, the XK 140 was still handsome. TNK 745 was the second car of this type to be made, and there were only 74 two-seaters with right-hand drive altogether.

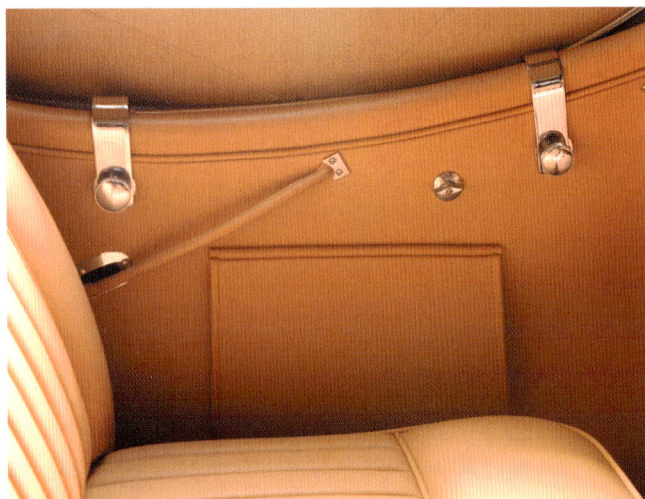

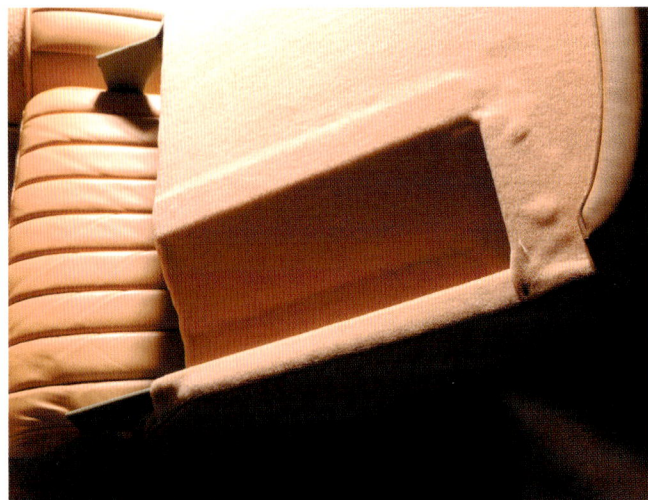

The side screen lugs fitted on to these threaded brackets on the door trim, and the screen was then held in place by tightening the knurled knobs.

This recess or pocket in the back of the seat of the two-seater was necessary to clear the hood frame when the hood was folded.

At the rear there were for the first time proper bumpers, of the quarter type with over riders, flanking the rear number plate. The number plate lamp was a standard Lucas type, with a reversing lamp in the same housing. The boot lid finished above the number plate, and on the boot lid was a central chrome strip matching that found on the bonnet.

Like the XK 120, the hood still had this narrow chrome-framed rear window, fitted in a zip-out section attached with lift-the-dot fasteners at the bottom.

On each side of the hood were press-stud fasteners. The side screens had chrome finishers around the Perspex windows, and a flap for hand signalling or getting at the internal door release strap.

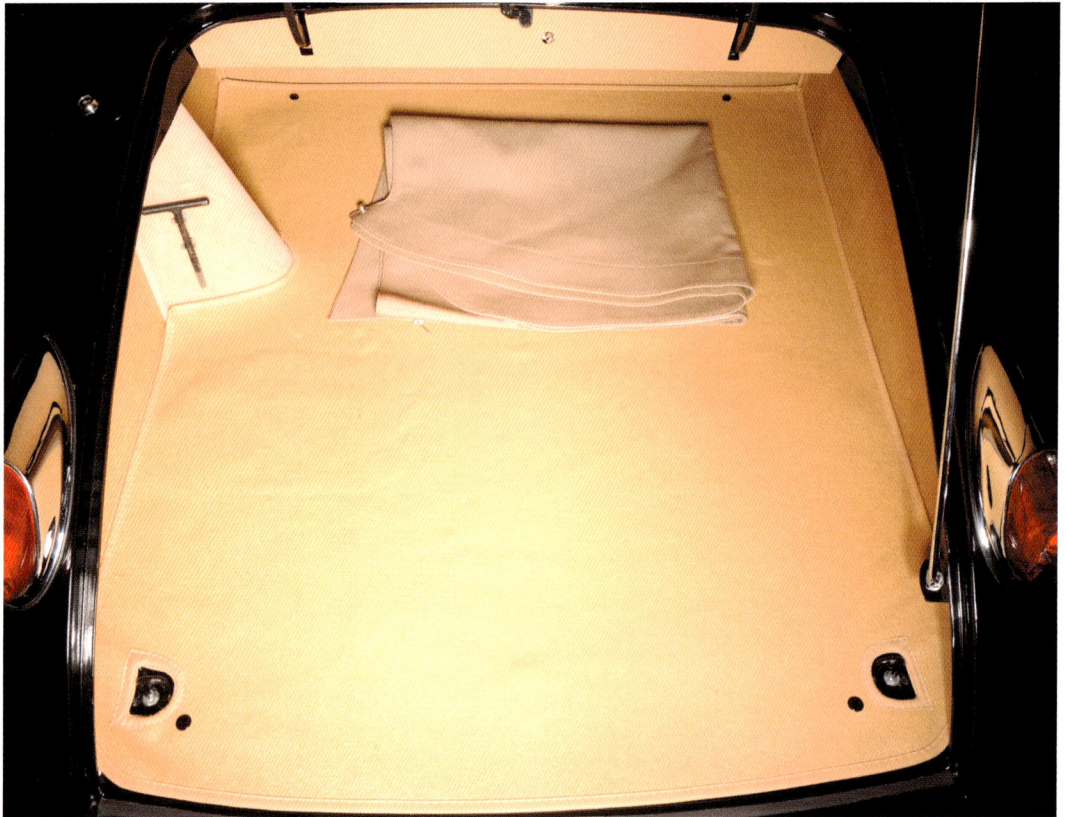

The boot was fully trimmed on cars to Special Equipment specification. The coach key mounted on the trim around the fuel filler was for unlocking the plywood false floor over the spare wheel well. The tonneau cover was standard equipment on the two-seater model.

The boot lid badge proclaimed Jaguar's success as winner of the Le Mans race in 1951 and 1953. The badge remained unchanged during XK 140 production, although Jaguar was to win this race twice again (1955 and 1956) before the model went out of production.

The pedal arrangement was basically similar on all XKs but with an astonishing number of detail variations. The foot dip switch mounted on the tunnel can just be seen on the left.

Here the false floor has been lifted to show the jack with its ratchet handle and the grease gun clipped to its underside, and the spare wheel below. The hammer for the wheel spinners and the tool roll were originally stored loose in this compartment.

This detail shot of the inlet manifold shows the cast-in number C 7462 which is actually the part number of this part. Many Jaguar parts have such cast-in numbers which are helpful in determining their origin and application.

On right-hand drive cars, the Trico windscreen washer bottle was mounted on the left-hand side (nearside) of the engine, and here we can also see the rather inaccessible battery fitted inside the front wing.

The actual XK 140 chassis frame was little modified from the XK 120, but there was a new U-shaped wrap-around extension at the front, and changes to the cross members as well as the mounting points for the rear shock absorbers. (JDHT)

system now found on the SE models.

The cross member above the rear axle was moved rearwards and incorporated mounting points for new rear shock absorbers which were of the Girling telescopic type in place of the lever-arm type. The front suspension torsion bars were 1/16in (1.6mm) thicker, and the spring rate went up from 128 lb/in to 154 lb/in; these stiffer torsion bars which were similar to those found on the Special Equipment version of the XK 120 helped to counteract the additional weight on the front wheels. The brake system now used a normal single Lockheed hydraulic master cylinder instead of the tandem type of the XK 120, and the handbrake was initially of the conventional type although in 1956, a return was made to the fly-off type as found on the XK 120.

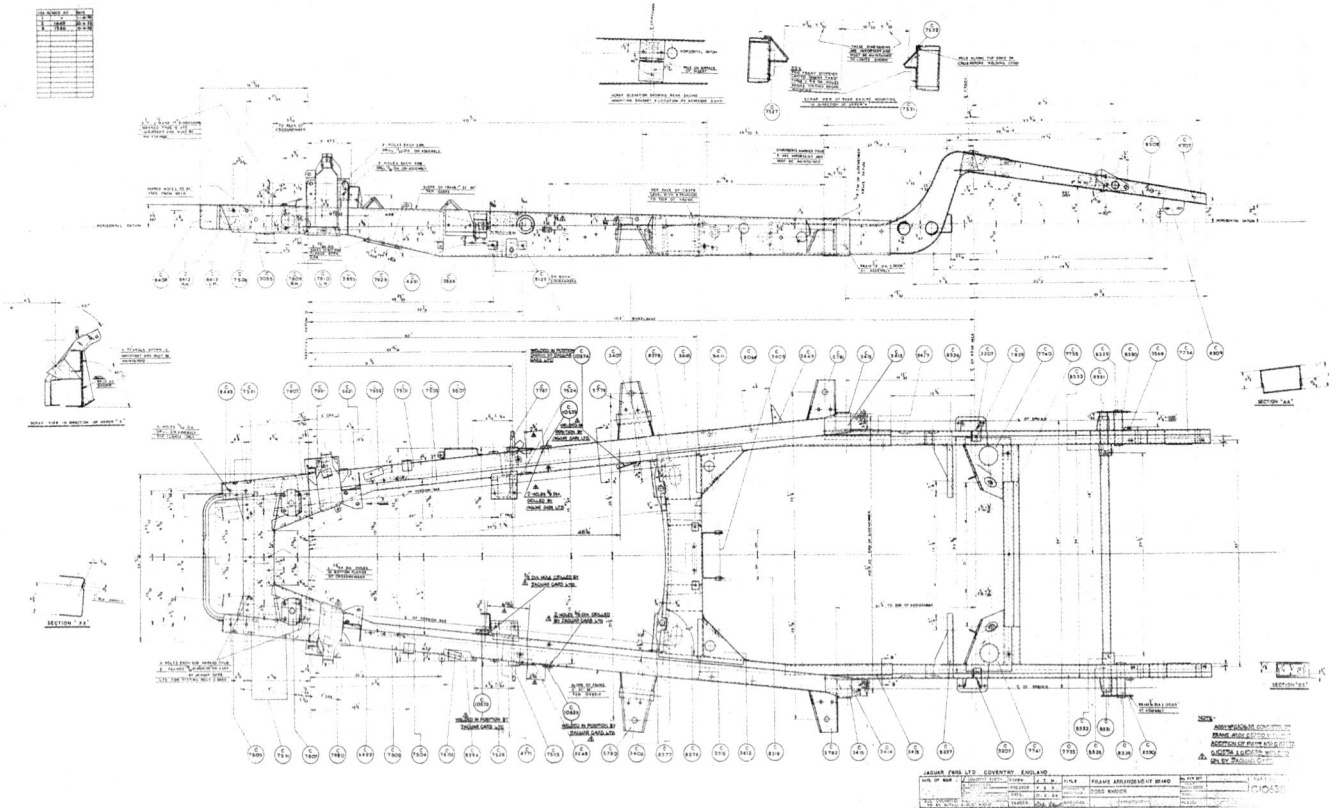

Seen from below, the new extension to the front end of the chassis is apparent, together with the front end of the torsion bars and the bottom radiator bose. (JDHT)

Here is the rear anchor point for the torsion bar, and the fuel pump can just be seen on the outside of the chassis side member. (JDHT)

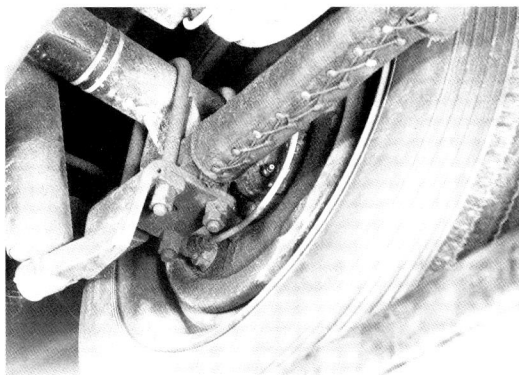

The rear springs were fitted with these leather gaiters. (JDHT)

For some reason this car has a different less elaborate type of gaiter, but note the grease nipples. (JDHT)

More importantly, following the example of the C-type and D-type, the old re-circulating ball steering box was replaced by a rack-and-pinion system, supplied by Alford and Alder. To minimise road shocks being transmitted back through the steering, the steering rack housing was mounted on pads with rubber bonded between metal plates. The steering column was now in two sections, with universal joints at both ends of the lower section, which was shorter on fixed-head coupé models. The steering wheel resembled that of the late-model XK 120 with a flat horn push and was of 17in (432mm) diameter; a 16in (407mm) wheel was quoted as an option in the *Spare Parts Catalogue* but was rarely if ever seen. The steering wheel was more angled from vertical than on the XK 120. There was around 2.75 turns lock to lock, and the turning circle went up to 33ft (10.06m). The new steering was more precise than that of the XK 120, but was more prone to kick-back, which is why Jaguar reduced the castor angle during the XK 140 production run.

The XK engine could now be considered a well-proven design, with more than 30,000 such engines having been made. For the XK 140, it was designated as the type G (the later XK 120 engine had been type F) and a number of modifications were made to increase the power output. The high-lift camshafts with 0.375in (9.53mm) lift from the Special Equipment version of the XK 120 were standardised – the normal XK 120 had a camshaft with 0.3125in (7.94mm) lift – and the cylinder head was modified in detail to improve breathing. The standard compression ratio for most markets was 8:1, and while 7:1 remained available I reckon there were less than 80 cars with the lower compression. These included around ten cars fitted with the C-type head (see below). Similarly, there

This photo of the chassis was taken on the XK 140 production line, and shows the Girling telescopic shock absorbers which were new on this model. The car is a standard model, as it has the disc wheel hubs. (JDHT)

The front view of the same chassis shows the rack-and-pinion steering as well as the detail of the front suspension. (JDHT)

The classic Jaguar XK engine, in a rendering much used in contemporary brochure material and for publicity purposes. (JDHT)

were only 80-odd cars fitted with the optional 9:1 compression ratio; except half-a-dozen, these all had the C-type head.

Power output was now quoted as 190bhp at 5500rpm for the standard engine with 8:1 compression. The cast aluminium sump of the XK 120 was replaced by a pressed steel sump with a small step at the front. There were a number of other smaller changes to the engine, and a Lucas oil-filled ignition coil was fitted. For subsequent changes to the engine during production, please refer to the list of change points in the appendix. To accommodate the

The dip stick was at the rear of the engine on the left-hand side. We can also see the enamelled exhaust manifold, and since this is a left-hand drive car, the brake fluid reservoir, and on the right, the throttle linkage running across the bulkhead behind the engine. (JDHT)

An XK engine on its trolley awaiting installation in the chassis. (JDHT)

This chap is obligingly holding up the bonnet so that we can see the bonnet lock and safety catch. (JDHT)

The complete XK 140 chassis with engine on the trolley which moved it down the production line. This left-hand drive car is an SE model with wire wheels and the C-type cylinder head but no overdrive; it is probably destined to become a two-seater as it has the straight gear lever. (JDHT)

Still under the bonnet, this is the correct position for the washer bottle on a left-hand drive car. The air filter is further confirmation that this is an SE model. It is also a good illustration of the voltage regulator and fuse box. (JDHT)

Under the bonnet of an XK 140, on the scuttle behind the engine was the unhandy water valve for the inefficient heater, while the rev counter cable is coming out of the back of the cylinder head in the foreground. (JDHT)

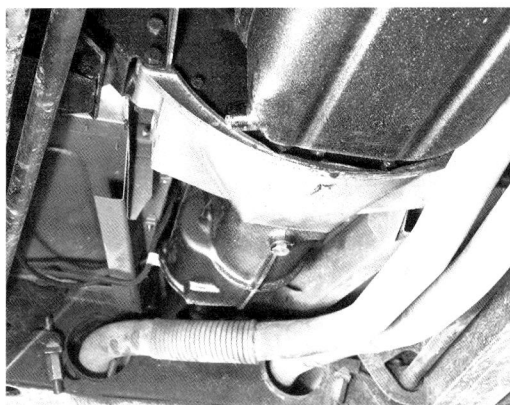

On the special equipment models there was a complete dual exhaust system, and therefore two large holes in the central cross member. (JDHT)

forward-mounted engine and to have clearance to the steering rack below it, the radiator was also moved forward and was inclined towards the rear. The 16in (406mm) diameter fan now had eight blades and was housed in a u-shaped cowl.

In addition to the normal engine, there was a more highly-tuned engine available, fitted with a cylinder head of the design found on the C-type. On this head, the throat diameter of the inlet ports was increased from 1.375in (34.9mm) to 1.5in (38.1mm) diameter, although the inlet valve diameter was still 1.75in (44.5mm). The exhaust valve diameter was increased from 1.4375in (36.5mm) to 1.625in (41.3mm), and the exhaust port throat size was 1.375in (34.9mm), up from 1.25in (31.8mm).[2] This C-type cylinder was painted red, as opposed to unpainted aluminium for the standard head, there was a cast letter "C" in the centre of the plug valley, and each cam cover had a little badge with the legend "Jaguar Type C" on a red background, although it seems that not all of these features were found on the earliest engines with the C-type head.[3] Cars with this type of engine had a dual exhaust system, and power went up to a quoted 210bhp at 5750rpm. On cars fitted with this engine, the chassis number was prefixed with the letter S, and the engine number had a suffix letter S after the compression ratio. These cars were designated as "SE" or Special Equipment models, and were commonly referred to in

The two carburettors were fed through this air manifold, which in turn drew air from the large cylindrical air cleaner below. Note also the automatic starting carburettor just to the right of centre of the manifold. For some reason this car has a black ignition coil which may be more typical of the XK 120. (JDHT)

North America as the XK 140 "MC" (see below).

For both the normal and the C-type head engine, the carburettors remained the SU H6 type of 1.75in (44.5mm), only with different needles. However, on cars with the C-type head 2in (50.8mm) carburettors type SU H8 were available to special order; these had sand-cast dashpots of a noticeably different shape. On standard engines, there was a single cylindrical air filter fitted below the carburettors and feeding these through an aluminium manifold,

With the hood down, the XK 140 two-seater looks even better. From this angle, the "foreshortening" achieved by the inwards curve to rear wing in plan view is particularly evident.

The most important difference on the SE model was undoubtedly the more highly-tuned engine with the C-type cylinder head (when fitted), which was painted red and had the small "Jaguar Type C" badges on the cam covers. This is the second type of XK 140 radiator with its fluted header tank.

The small individual pancake air filters for each carburettor of the SE engine can be seen here, while on this car the washer bottle with its vacuum bowl is mounted on the offside (right-hand side) of the engine – on the left in this photo.

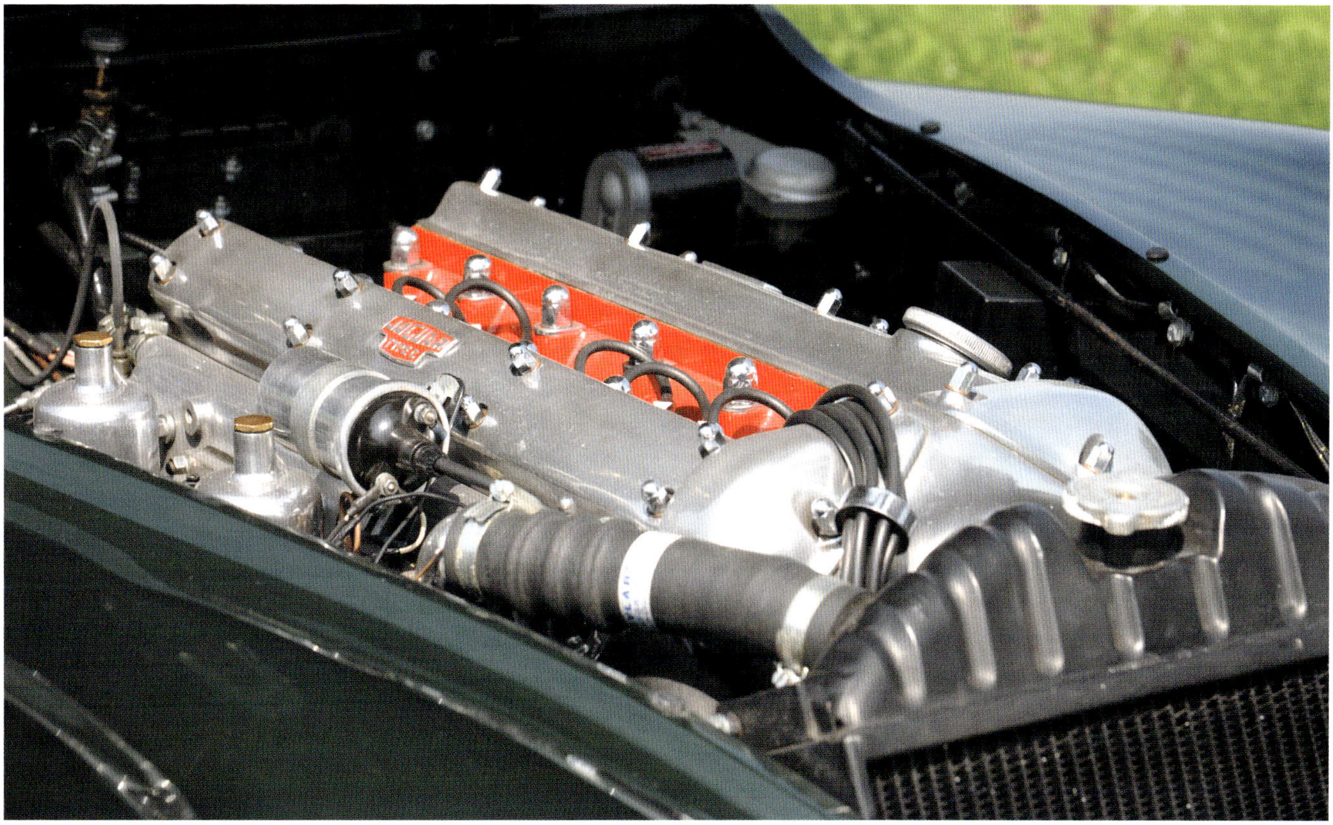

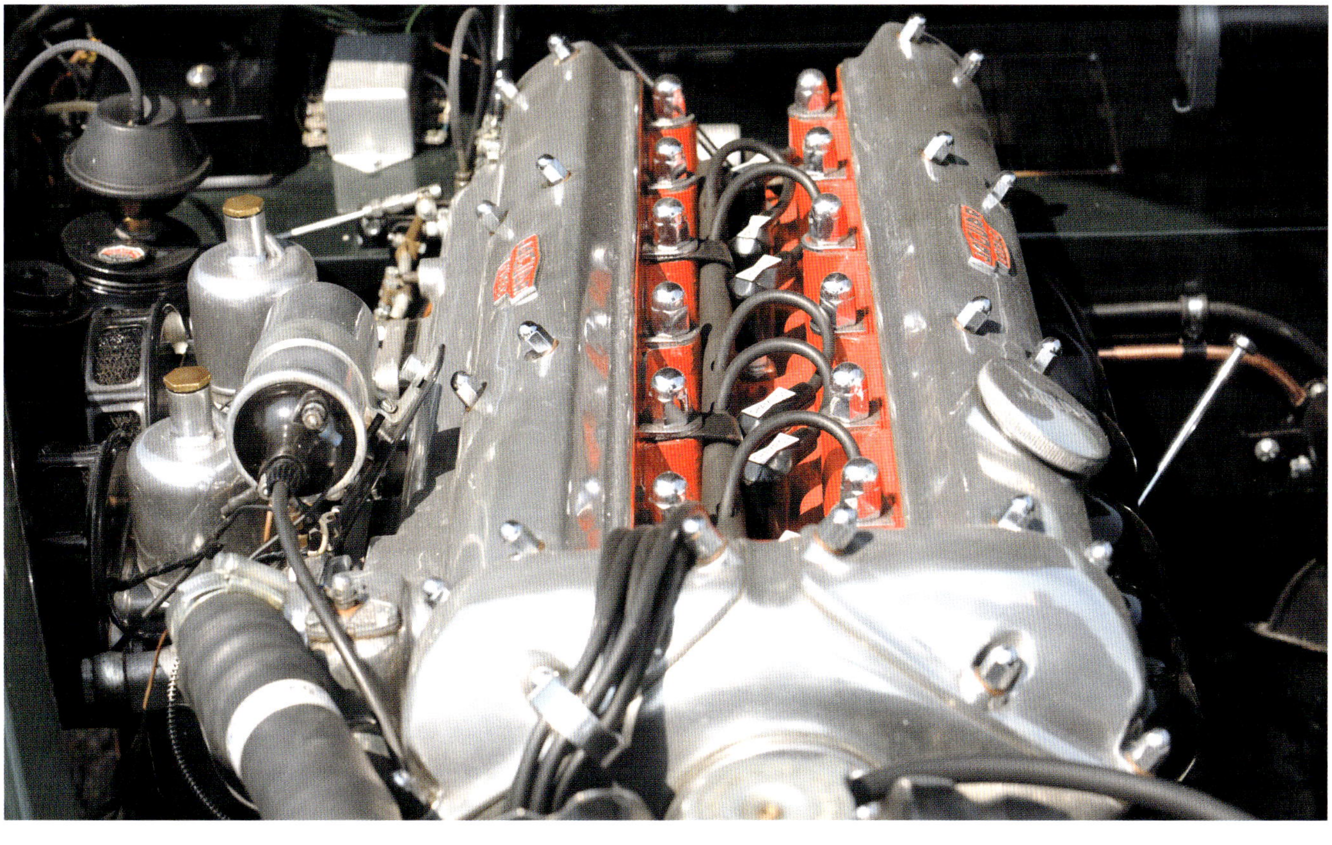

*The door trims on two-
seaters had pockets
covered by a flap held in
place by a fastener. The
small turn button above the
pocket is for locking the
door, whatever point there
is in that on an open car.
The strap, of course, is for
opening the door.*

**The colour scheme of
British Racing Green with
Tan trim is a perennial
favourite on Jaguars. The
registration mark by the
way is original; this car
was sold to a first owner in
Northern Ireland in 1955.**

The layout of the interior and the dashboard was the same on all XK 140 two-seaters, and indeed the dash was virtually the same as on the later XK 120s. A detail difference was that the vertical edges of the centre panel were now curved slightly inwards towards the bottom. The dash was covered in leather to match the rest of the interior.

A detail difference on the XK 140 compared to most XK 120s was the flat horn push, which in fact had been introduced near the end of XK 120 production.

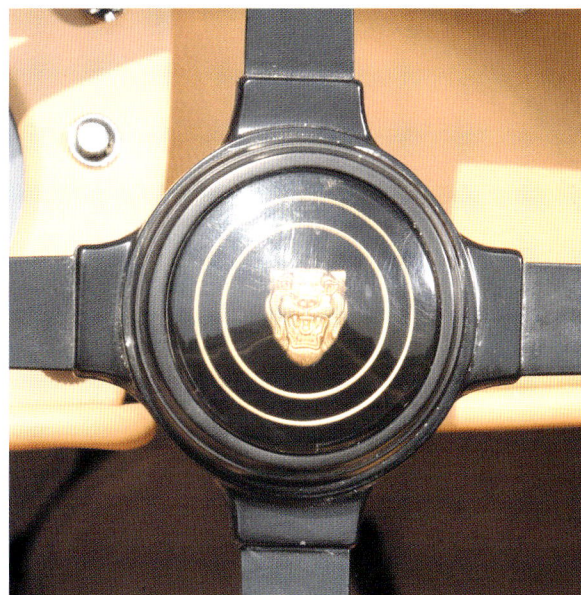

The switchgear and instruments were of a common style. The rev counter and speedometer are, so to speak, counter-rotating: the rev counter anti-clockwise, the speedometer clockwise. The gear lever here is probably in neutral; in first and third, it leans forward at an even greater angle. The handbrake was chrome-plated, whether of the normal or the fly-off type

The hood frame on the two-seater is plainly visible from the inside as the hood is not lined, unlike the much more elaborate hood on the drophead model. The grey-painted frame really is this simple. It is attached on either side behind the doors but can be removed quite easily.

Behind the seats of the two-seater is this shelf which may accommodate hand luggage, at least when the hood is up; when folded the hood takes up most of this space. The full-width panel above the shelf forms the bulkhead of the boot and hinges forwards and downwards to allow long items of (shallow) luggage to be carried. Above this again is the compartment for stowing the side screens.

The one-piece cast construction of the radiator grille is evident here. The badge now quoted the model name, with full stops in "X.K.140". The hexagon shape around the central Jaguar name had a long tradition in the company's history, dating right back to the SS cars of the early 1930s.

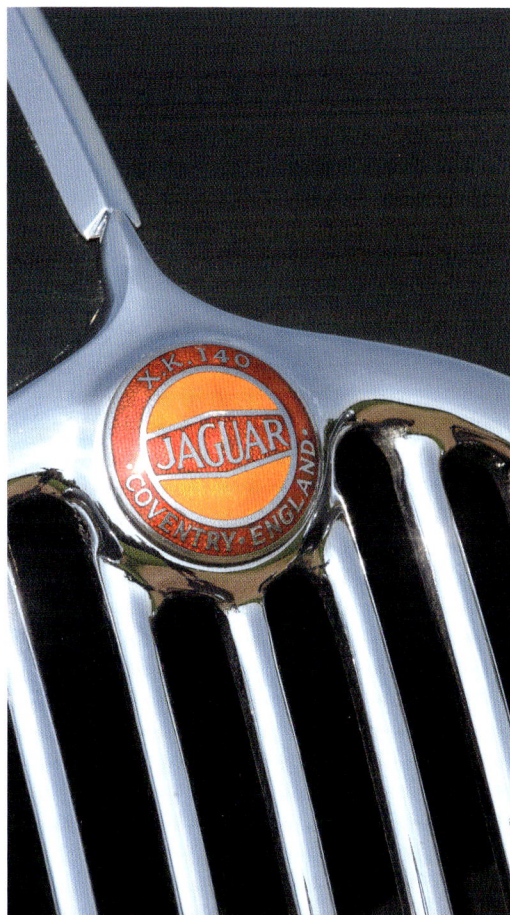

Without the air manifold we can see the carburettors in greater detail, and the more normal bright-finish coil with the words "fluid cooled" on the Lucas label. (JDHT)

whereas on engines with the C-type head, each carburettor had a small pancake-type air filter, of a slightly different type on cars with the 2in carburettors. When the 2in carburettors were fitted, there was a manual choke rather than the normal thermostatic electric choke.

Like its predecessor, the XK 140 could be fitted with two slightly different types of gear-boxes, the JL and the SL series; in practice the latter had a gearbox number prefix OSL and the suffix letter B to the number. Similar to the later

XK 120 'boxes, both were of the short main shaft type, but the SL type had a countershaft with a one-piece gear cluster and the JL series had a built-up countershaft with individual gear-wheels. According to the *Spare Parts Catalogue*, both were available with normal ratio gears and with close-ratio gears. In practice, it appears that the tell-tale suffix letters CR (or, more rarely, MS, for Moss-shaved close ratio gears[1]) are only found on JL gearboxes, but the OSL 'box may have changed from normal to close ratios during the production run, or as is perhaps more likely, they may all have had close-ratio gears. The standard ratios were: first and reverse, 3.375:1, second, 1.982:1; third, 1.367:1. The close ratios were: first and reverse, 2.98:1; second, 1.74:1; third, 1.21:1. Both gear sets had direct drive in top. On the open two-seater and the drophead coupé, a short straight gearlever was used, while on the fixed-head coupé with its more forward seating position the lever was longer and cranked.

Then there was the overdrive box. Since it was based on the JL series, it became the JLE type, and was similarly available with normal and close-ratio gears; interestingly, most JLE gearbox numbers with the CR suffix occur in the *Car Record Books* from the autumn of 1955 onwards, and through 1956 the close ratio gears

This left-hand drive two-seater has the normal width brake pedal, and note the position of the foot-operated dip switch. The bonnet release can be seen under the dashboard on the right. The heel pad here is the D-shape. (JDHT)

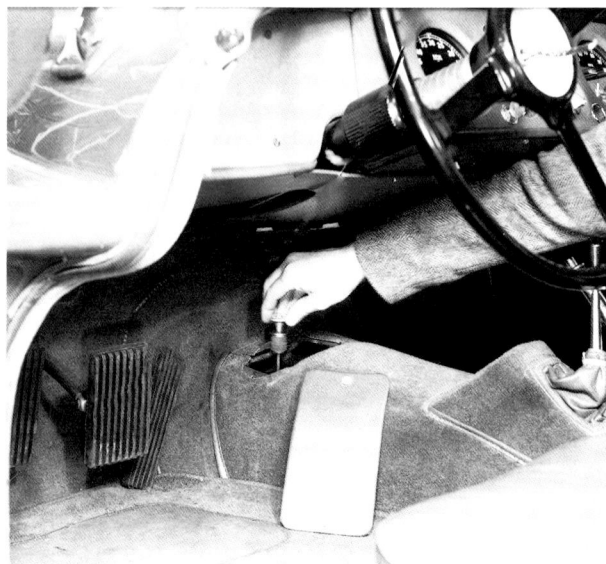

By contrast, this car has an unusually wide brake pedal, and a rectangular heel pad in the carpet. The cover at the front of the transmission tunnel gave access to the gearbox dip stick. (JDHT)

This XK 140 gearbox has overdrive, so it is of the JLE type, here upended on the bellhousing ready to be attached to an engine. (JDHT)

The Salisbury 4HA rear axle was carried over from the later XK 120s, and was found on all XK 140s and 150s. The fuel tank drain plug can be seen on the right. (JDHT)

On the dashboard of this right-hand drive two-seater we can see the position of both the indicator switch and the overdrive switch next to each other, to the right of the steering column. The rear view mirror is missing. (JDHT)

increasingly come to predominate on overdrive cars. The actual overdrive unit was a Laycock de Normanville type 28/1390 with a reduction ratio of 28 per cent. The overdrive was electrically engaged by a switch outboard of the steering column on the dashboard, and operated on top gear only. With overdrive, a shorter prop shaft was fitted, and the rear axle ratio was lowered from 3.54:1 to 4.09:1. As far as I can determine, 2543 XK 140 cars of all types had the overdrive gearbox. All cars had the Salisbury 4HA axle, and ratios of 3.31:1 and 4.27:1 were also available.

In January 1956 the XK 140 became available with an automatic gearbox. This was only fitted to the two coupé models, not to the open two-seater, and it was at first offered only on left-hand drive cars, mostly for the USA; right-

hand drive cars with the automatic gearbox became available later in 1956. The installation was similar to that found on the Mark VII M saloon. The auto 'box was the Borg-Warner type DG.250/MJ (the earlier type DG.200 was only fitted on the Mark VII until November 1954[5]), with a torque converter and three forward speeds – low, intermediate and direct drive. The selector rod was fitted above the steering column – with the control lever on the right-hand side on left-hand drive cars, left-hand side on right-hand drive cars – and the quadrant positions were P-N-D-L-R. It seems that there were 830 XK 140s with the automatic gearbox, of which incidentally nearly 500 were SE models with the C-type cylinder head.[6] It needs to be added that eighteen of these cars lack the BW suffix to the chassis number in the *Car Record*

The side view clearly demonstrates the shorter bonnet and longer cabin in comparison to the other two XK 140 body styles. Compared to the XK 120 fixed-head, the side window area was much larger.

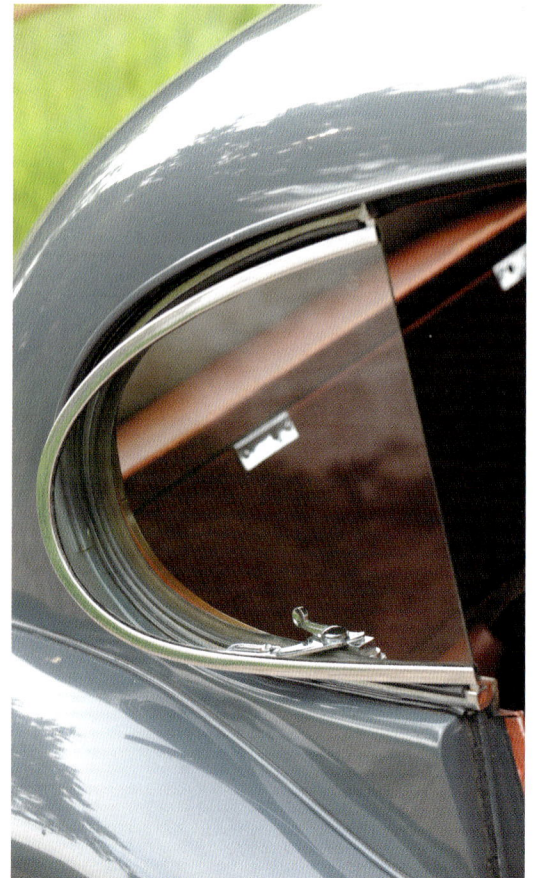

The spats on disc-wheeled standard cars were held in place by a budget or coachwork lock at the top. The door handles were rather similar to the boot lid handle.

The XK 140 fixed-head coupé front view is perhaps not so flattering, as the vertical side windows and consequent lack of tumble-home give a slightly top-heavy appearance to the greenhouse. This is an early 1955 car, in Battleship Grey, sold in Monmouthshire, and wonderfully original. As it is a standard model, it has no fog lamps. This badge bar is probably an after-market accessory.

The front quarter lights in the doors opened for ventilation. They were matched by these opening rear quarter lights; note the lack of a frame to the front edge.

The two-piece V-shape windscreen was fitted in a chrome-plated surround. Note the original Jaguar sticker in the bottom corner, and the tax disc opposite which expired in 1970. This standard car lacks the windscreen washer but has small chrome plugs where the nozzles would be.

This is a standard XK 140 engine, so the cylinder head is not painted, and the cam covers lack the "Type C" badges. The exhaust manifolds still display the original enamel finish, pitted though it is.

This rear end detail shows the standard Lucas rear lamps on their plinths – they incorporated reflectors and flashing indicators. The boot lid handle has an external key lock and push-button release. These features were common to all three body styles. Standard models only had a single exhaust system, unlike the dual system of the SE models.

The boot on the standard model is less well trimmed than on the SE, with no trim pieces for the boot sides, the fuel filler or the hinge panel. This car has the small strap on the boot lid trim to hold up the boot floor when it is lifted to give access to the spare wheel.

On the standard engine there is a single remote air filter, and this unusually shaped distribution manifold for the two carburettors; the cylindrical air filter is fitted below this. The ID plate on this car is mounted on the other side of the engine compartment.

The disc wheels were finished in body colour and were fitted with these hub caps with the hexagonal Jaguar logo. On the XK 140 they were often fully chromed, unlike those of the XK 120 which were partly finished in body colour over the chrome plating.

This car has the early type of XK 140 radiator with the smooth header tank. It is not entirely obvious in this shot that the radiator is angled rearwards. Note the bonnet lock right at the bottom. This car by the way seems to have been fitted with a radiator blind.

Compared to the two-seater, the fixed-head and drophead coupé models had a much more luxurious interior, with the dashboard in walnut, which was also used for the door garnish rails and the trim fillets around the windows and windscreen. On the windscreen rail above the instrument panel were no less than two ashtrays, flanking the central indicator switch. The rear view mirror on all XK 140s was below the windscreen.

The coupé door trims were very simple, with a sliding release to open the door, a window winder and a pocket which is so shallow that it is pretty useless. On the garnish rail there is a finger grip for pulling the door shut. Quite obviously there are no door checks, an omission frequently complained about in contemporary road tests.

The seats were similar on all XK 140s, but were mounted further forward on the fixed head coupé, which also had a greater range of seat adjustment on the longitudinal runners. These seats are just about broken in with the most wonderful patina.

This is an early XK 140 rev counter red-lined at 5200rpm; this was later raised to 5500rpm.

The overdrive on XK 140s thus equipped was operated by this switch, fitted to the dash panel outboard of the steering column.

Below the instruments was this small drawer, but if a radio was fitted it would occupy the drawer space.

These were the "occasional" seats found on XK 140 coupés, which were just about suitable for children but not very comfortable. The roof lining was of high-quality cloth, and the fixed-head had two roof lamps built into recesses in the rear quarter pillars.

As on the two-seater, the boot bulkhead folds down to extend the luggage space.

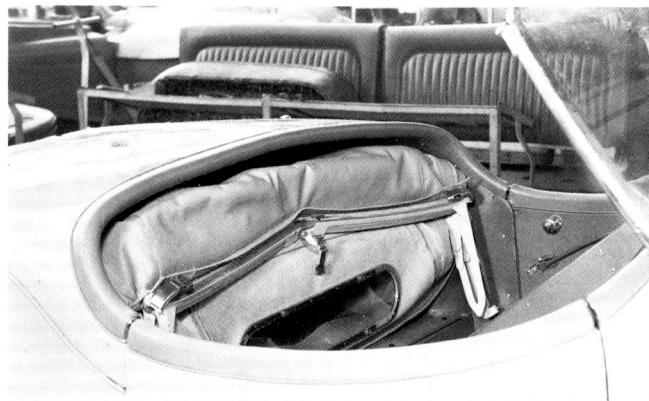

The two-seater hood was simpler and easier to fold than that of the drophead. The second photo shows it stowed behind the seats, with the centre catch and both side catches clearly seen. Note also the chrome-framed rear window in its zip-out section. (JDHT)

Below: The interior of a brand-new left-hand drive two-seater. Below right: Possibly the same car but note the protective covering on the steering wheel, and the differently adjusted seats.

Books, but their gearbox numbers appear to be of automatic gearboxes. Of these, 390 were LHD fixed-heads and 429 LHD dropheads. Of the RHD cars, there were only seven fixed-heads and four dropheads with automatic 'boxes; the RHD cars may have had the intermediate speed hold facility which was introduced on the Mark VIII in late 1956 and on the XK 150 the following year.

The body changes on the XK 140 were perhaps rather more important – and certainly more obvious – than the mechanical changes. The importance of these changes was that they turned the coupé models into two-plus-twos which made them more of grand tourers than their predecessors had been, even if the rear seats were only for small children or for very occasional use by a single adult. However, the open two-seater remained just that, and retained its loose sidescreens. On this model, the basic bodyshell was little changed, but the forward-mounted engine allowed deeper footwells and longer seat runners for a greater range of adjustment. The scuttle with the dashboard and steering wheel was raised by 1in (25mm) which

also helped to give more room for a long-legged driver. The two 6-volt batteries had been moved from behind the seat and were replaced by a single 12-volt battery mounted inside the front wing – left-hand side on right-hand drive cars and vice versa – where it could only be reached, somewhat inconveniently, through a trapdoor at the rear of the wheel arch. This gave more room for hood stowage or luggage in the tonneau area, and there was now a hinged flap in the boot bulkhead so longer items of luggage could be stowed.

The drophead coupé was similarly changed, but on this car the extra room behind the front seats was used for occasional seats, with a small cushion on the floor on either side of the prop shaft tunnel and an even smaller pad acting as support for the lower back; these backrests stopped just below the boot access panel. The hood was made longer to allow headroom above the rear seats – rear seat legroom was another matter altogether – and had a larger rear window. One distinction that Jaguar continued to make between the open two-seater and the two coupé models was that the former had the

The drophead hood was fastened to the windscreen frame with a catch either side. I am not sure that it was quite as effortless to lower or raise the hood by the central handle as this chap is demonstrating; note also the elaborate hood lining ...

leather-covered dashboard and instrument panel, where the coupés had a full wood veneer dash, wood cappings on the doors and windscreen pillars, as well as around the windows on the fixed-head. The drophead even had wood cappings on those edges on the hood which surrounded the door windows.

Changes to the fixed-head were much more extensive. Firstly the front bulkhead was wrapped around the rear of the engine, pushing the footwells even further forward. As a knock-on effect, with this body style there was a 6-volt battery in each front wing. Next, the scuttle and windscreen were moved forward, and the bonnet was in consequence shorter. The doors were wider by 5.5in (140mm) than on the 120 fixed-head, and with the front seats further forward than on the drophead there was at least a little bit more room for those occasional rear seats – but not much. The roof was longer, extended at the front and by 6.75in (171mm) at the rear, and there was more headroom. The rear quarter-lights were larger and of a different shape, with a vertical line to the front.

Oddly enough, at the launch of the XK 140

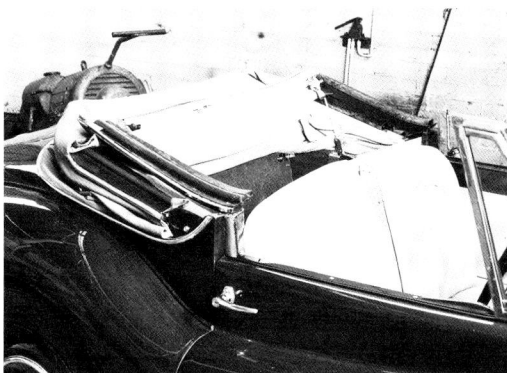

The folded hood was held down by two rods latching on to the hood catches, one can be seen here on the far side ...

... and was then fitted with a separate hood cover.

The final shot gives a glimpse of the rear seat and shows the boot bulkhead opened. (JDHT)

When the XK 140 was launched, Jaguar published this completely misleading rendering of the fixed-head: basically an XK 120 with the new grille, front bumpers, and indicator lamps. (JDHT)

45

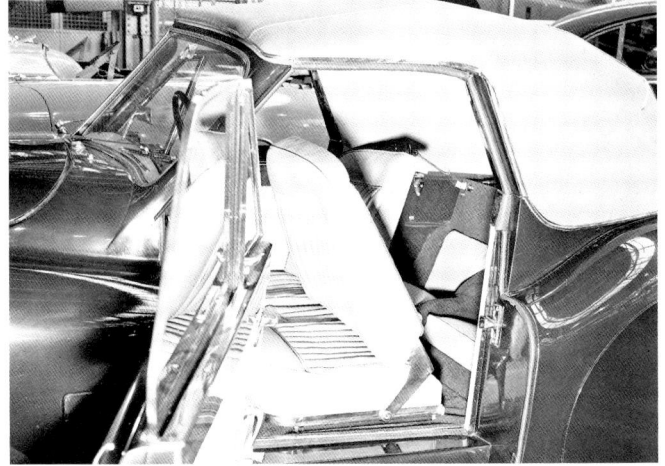

Above: The interior of a factory-fresh right-hand drive drophead, with an unusual contrast between the colours of seats and carpet. This shot was used in the XK 140 brochure....
Above right: Probably the same drophead, with the hood up and rear wheel spat in place. (JDHT)

This is an XK 140 fixed-head prototype, not chassis 804001 which had an XK 120 body, but it could possibly be chassis number 804002. Note the XK 120 style door handles, grille and headlamps, the part-painted hub caps and the slope to the rear of the door window frame. (JDHT)

Jaguar released a picture of a fixed-head which was based on a much-retouched photo of an XK 120, merely with the new bumpers and grille, and this was published for instance in *The Motor* whereas *The Autocar* had photos of the real thing, although their cut-away drawing still had an inclined line to the rear quarter-light. Both magazines showed higher backrests for the rear seats, attached to the folding bulkhead by press-studs, which Jaguar had experimented with.[7]

Common to all three body styles on the XK 140 chassis were a number of changes to the external body trim. That lovely grille of the XK 120 had been replaced by a one-piece cast grille with seven thicker bars; this change can only have been made to save money, unless the idea was to use similar-looking grilles on the XK and the new compact saloon which was a year in the future. The grille incorporated a new circular enamel badge with the word "Jaguar" in

And here is the same car with the XK 140 grille being offered up to see what it will look like – a typical example of Lyons's styling methods. (JDHT)

I don't suppose this was too seriously meant but it could have been a rough and ready way to check out how much the windscreen could be moved forward, compared to the XK 120 fixed-head. (JDHT)

This is another intriguing photo of an XK 140 fixed-head prototype. The rear window here is XK 120 style. There is a full-width bumper and a very unusual number plate plinth. (JDHT)

With the boot lid open, we can see that this prototype had rubbing strips to the boot floor. Incidentally note the location: the building in the background was later replaced by the JDHT Museum, and to the right of this is the old Browns Lane gate and gatehouse. (JDHT)

a central flattened hexagon. In response to pleas from the American market, the delicate XK bumpers were replaced by much stouter items, with a section like that found on the Mark VIIM saloon, and with similar overriders. The front bumper was full width and had a valance bridging the gap to the bodywork, while at the rear there were quarter bumpers hugging the body contour closely and with the number plate mounted on a plinth on the lower body panel between them. The new bumpers pushed up overall length by 3in (76mm) to 14ft 8in (4470mm).

Other dimensions were unchanged from the XK 120, but the question of weight remains.

This is probably the same car modified. The bumper is still full-width but the number plate plinth has gone to be replaced by two brackets, but the number plate would then partly cover the boot handle. The rear window is now the proper XK 140 type and size. (JDHT)

The interior of the prototype fixed-head had cushions but not yet backrests for the rear seats. Note the extraordinary opening angle of the door, and the hand-held flash gun in the foreground! (JDHT)

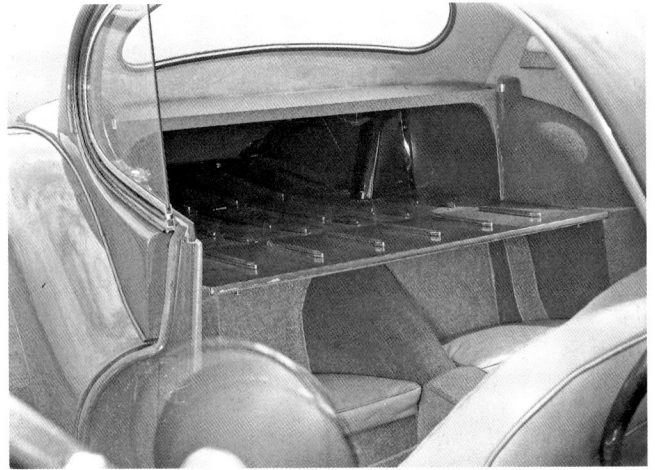

With the boot bulkhead opened on the prototype, we can see that this, too, had rubbing strips. There is that flash gun again... (JDHT)

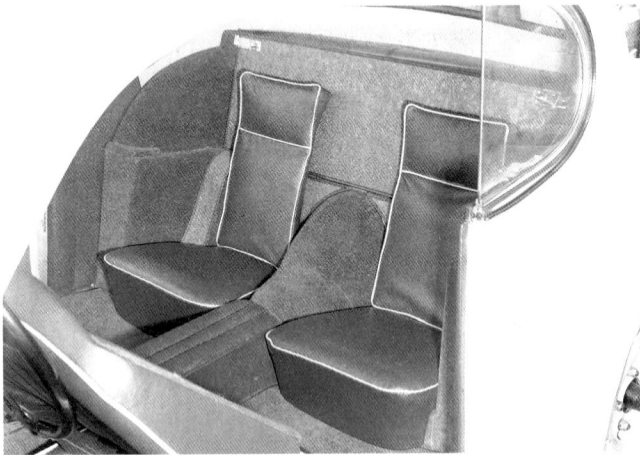

This poor guy is probably not enjoying sitting crosswise in the back, even if he has the second loose backrest behind him. By the way the model is Jaguar's publicity manager, Ernest "Bill" Rankin. (JDHT)

There was some experimenting with the rear seats. One idea was to use these higher loose backrests, which could then be moved around to suit. (JDHT)

This is an extraordinary photo. The car is probably the XK 140 fixed-head prototype which was the subject of the rear seat experiments. Behind it is a row of Mark VIIMs, which had started production in August 1954, and the car in the middle has a label in the windscreen with a body number L22677 (possibly not legible here) dating it to late September, yet the stillages are full of XK 120 bodies, including some fixed-heads, which had stopped production earlier! Oh and there is a D-type on the right... (JDHT)

These two youngsters seem altogether happier! Note the door handle which is still not of the final production type. It is a left-hand drive car, possibly chassis 814001. (JDHT)

When the boot bulkhead was opened, these taller backrests would willy-nilly have to be folded in half. On this later prototype, the boot trim is more or less as on production cars. (JDHT)

This XK 140 drophead is a low mileage, remarkably original car which was recently awoken from a long slumber. It had less than 30,500 miles on the odometer in the summer of 2008.

Some XK 140s did have their hub caps partly painted.

This standard car has no fog lamps, and in this case we can be absolutely sure that the side lamp tell-tales are facing the right way – vertical at the front, slope towards the rear.

These tools may never have been out of the car; well, perhaps the owner wielded the grease gun now and then! The wheel brace is particularly important since this was only supplied with standard cars on disc wheels.

As we can see here, on the drophead the window frame is attached to the glass and is lowered with it.

The exhaust system is a bit of a puzzle – as a standard model it should have a single exhaust, and the system here is somewhat different from the Jaguar dual system on SE models. The 1950s GB plate with an AA logo is rather splendid.

How many cars, fifty-plus years later, still have their original hood? This is what the drophead hood should look like, disregarding the cracks in the fabric and the discoloured rear window.

There was a single interior lamp on the drophead, actually mounted in the headlining as seen here. There is a hook on either side to hold the folded hood in place; needless to say we did not attempt to fold the hood on this car. Note the wood fillets in the hood around the side window.

The XK 140 – and 150 – radiator was mounted at this rather acute angle, to allow for the forward-mounted engine and for the steering rack to be mounted below and behind the radiator.

Under the bonnet the main items to point out as non-original are the top hose and the battery which can just be seen above the oil filler cap, while I am told that the inlet manifold and water gallery also had to be replaced.

The side view looks exactly like the Jaguar rendering of the time, with the correct outline of the hood.

The drophead dashboard and interior are in principle the same as on the fixed-head model but note the bracket for stiffening the scuttle, below the steering column on the far side. Just in front of this is the loudspeaker for the Radiomobile period radio.

The boot of the standard model did not have any trim to the sides, around the fuel filler, or to the hinge panel at the front of the boot. With the mat folded back, the top of this false boot floor appears to be body-coloured. (JDHT)

This is a great picture since it shows the tools on a standard model with disc wheels, including the wheel brace. The tool roll is lying on top of the spare wheel. (JDHT)

Source	Condition	OTS	FHC	DHC
Sales brochure "Advance Particulars"	Dry weight	24.5cwt (1246kg)	25.5cwt (1297kg)	26.5cwt (1347kg)
Main sales brochure	Dry weight	24.5cwt (1246kg)	25.75cwt (1309kg)	26.75cwt (1360kg)
Handbook	Dry weight	25.5cwt (1297kg)	25.75cwt (1309kg)	26cwt (1322kg)
RAC recognition form	With fuel	26.25cwt (1335kg)	27cwt (1373kg)	27.5cwt (1398kg)
Ditto, for automatic	With fuel	n/a	29 cwt (1475kg)	29 cwt (1475kg)
The Autocar				
15 Oct 1954	With 17 gallons (77 litres) fuel	26.25cwt (1335kg)	27.5cwt (1398kg)	27.5cwt (1398kg)
The Motor				
13 Oct 1954	Dry weight	24cwt (1220kg)	25.5cwt (1297kg)	26.5cwt (1347kg)

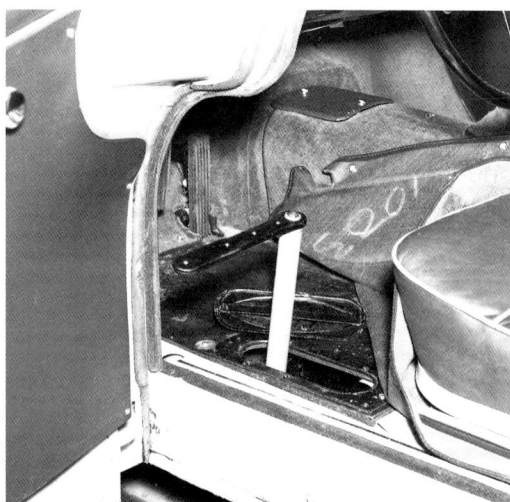

The jack was inserted through an aperture in the floor. By the way I think that must be the body number scrawled on the underside of the carpet. This car has contrast-colour trim piping. (JDHT)

Realistically an XK 120 steel-bodied open two-seater weighed in the region of 2884 lb (1309kg).[8] Jaguar themselves displayed some uncertainty and quoted different weights in the XK 140 sales literature and the handbook.

The figures quoted by *The Autocar* are odd since they also quoted the fuel tank capacity as 14 gallons (64 litres). Some of these figures were plainly too low. In the USA, it seems that more realistic figures prevailed. *Sports Car Illustrated* quoted 3040 lb (1380kg) for a two-seater "MC" model[9] while *Road & Track* quoted the "curb weight" of 3135 lb (1423kg) in their road test of a similar car.[10] By contrast the near-identical figure in *The Autocar*'s road test of a fixed-head SE model of 28cwt (3136 lb or 1424kg), with 5

The coach key is used to unlock the spat at the top, this can then be lowered and lifted off its retaining pegs, allowing the photographer's assistant to remove the hub cap with the wheel brace. (JDHT)

gallons (23 litres) of fuel, seems too low.[11] *Autosport* who tested the very same car gave its weight as a remarkable 26.5cwt (2968 lb or 1347kg).[12] In the absence of precise knowledge of the conditions in which road test cars were weighed and of whether the journals always did their own weighing, it is difficult to draw a conclusion, but I suspect that the dry weight of an open two-seater was more like 26cwt (2912 lb or 1322kg), of the fixed-head possibly 27cwt (3024 lb or 1373kg) and the drophead possibly as much as 28cwt (3136 lb or 1424kg). Overdrive cars were a little heavier, and the automatic gearbox clearly added 1.5-2cwt (76 to 102kg).

As on the later XK 120s, the bodyshell was made of steel. To save a little weight aluminium continued to be used for the bonnet, the boot lid, and for the roadster doors, although coupé doors changed to all-steel construction in mid-1956.[13] Both the bonnet and the boot lid had a central chrome strip; that on the boot lid incorporated a medallion proclaiming Jaguar's Le Mans victories in 1951 and 1953. At least one contemporary commentator expressed his dislike for this "gooking-up ... with fancy medallions and chrome strips."[14] Even worse some early cars had a chrome-plated raised centre section to the bonnet, tapering from 2in (51mm) at the front to 4in (102mm) at the rear. At the rear, the boot lid stopped above the level of the bumpers and number plate, and access to the spare wheel compartment was therefore through a hinged trapdoor in the boot floor.

The XK 140 was fitted with flashing direction indicators as standard for all markets. At the front these were sensibly large circular units mounted towards the bottom of the front wings separate from the side lamps, while at the rear they were combined with the tail and stop lamps, and a reflector, in standard Lucas units – as found, for instance, on the Morris Minor – mounted on chrome-plated plinths. The headlamps on home market cars were of the Lucas J700 type, with a small "J" medallion at the centre, while some export cars had PF700 "Le Mans" type headlamps and cars for the USA continued to have the mandatory sealed beam units. The semi-trumpet type horns of the XK 120 were replaced by flat-fronted diaphragm horns. There was a two-speed motor for the wipers. The inefficient XK 120 heater was found on open cars, but an improved heater was fitted to the fixed-head – where arguably it was least necessary!

The C-type engine is discussed above, but there were in fact three different versions of each XK 140 model. The standard cars had the 190bhp engine, single exhaust system and disc wheels, with spats over the rear wheels. Next came a Special Equipment model with the same engine, but with a full dual exhaust system and painted wire wheels – and therefore no spats, but see below. This model also had twin fog lamps, a windscreen washer, and upgraded trim in the boot. A Special Equipment model with the standard 190bhp engine had a chassis number prefix letter A, and in the *Car Record Books* such cars are invariably marked "less C-type engine". This version became known in the USA as the XK 140 "M". Finally there was the Special Equipment model with the C-type

210bhp engine, known in the USA as the XK 140 "MC", and with a prefix letter S to the chassis number, as well as a suffix letter S to the engine number. It was the intention to supply the SE model with the 190bhp engine only for export and fit all home market SE models with the C-type engine, but in practice there were a few exceptions. The best split between the three types for each body style that I can provide is as follows:

	Standard	SE less C-type engine	SE with C-type engine	Total
OTS RHD	36	2	36	74
OTS LHD	732	522	2028	3282
FHC RHD	637	7	199	843
FHC LHD	311	366	1289	1966
DHC RHD	393	5	82	480
DHC LHD	532	291	1488	2311
Total	2641	1193	5122	8956

This has to be hedged about with the usual provisos of errors in the records, as well as anomalies where a car may have an S suffix engine but not an S prefix chassis, or vice versa. However what is quite clear is that the SE model with the C-type engine was by far the most popular version in export markets, but the opposite prevailed in the home market. The SE model without the C-type engine was rare in the home market where sales amounted to one two-seater, five fixed-heads and three drophead coupés.

The distinctions between the various models were blurred by the fact that some of the SE equipment was offered also as optional extras, including the windscreen washer, the Lucas SFT.576 fog lamps, and wire wheels. The latter could be fully painted which was standard on SE models, or could have chrome-plated spokes with a painted rim, or could be fully chrome-plated. Other extras included Dunlop racing tyres, Dunlop whitewall tyres, rimbellishers for disc wheels, and a luggage rack for the boot lid. Intriguingly, the *Spare Parts Catalogue* lists special rear wheel covers for use with wire wheels (part nos. BD.11267/11268), these covers must have been of the cut-away type to clear the wire wheel wing nuts, and were fitted with Dzus fasteners.

Also available were three different HMV radios, wing mirrors, Dunlop Road Speed white-wall tyres and a 16in (406mm) steering wheel, as well as a range of items for those owners who wanted to improve performance or race

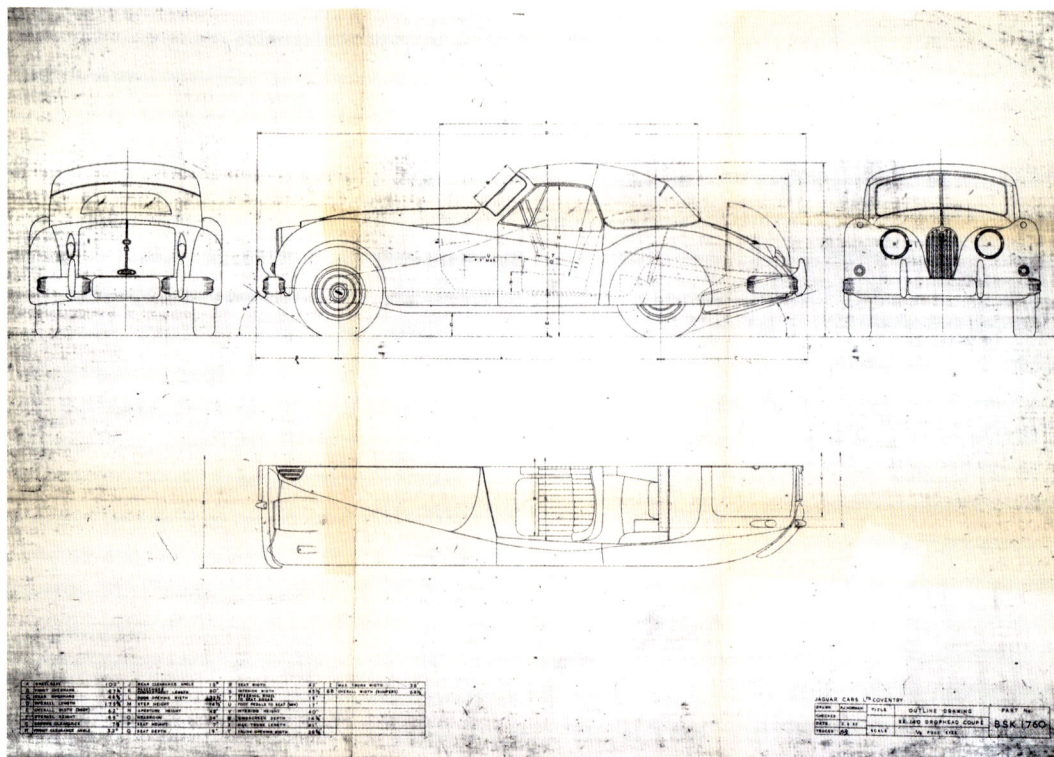

An XK 140 drophead general arrangement drawing.

These renderings were prepared by Rearsden, the commercial artists, for the XK 140 sales brochure. (JDHT)

their cars. These included pistons for the compression ratio of 9:1, a crankshaft damper, lead-indium main and con rod bearings, a racing clutch and competition bucket seats; and for the two-seater, racing screens which were supplied with cowls for the rear view mirror and for the redundant windscreen pillar apertures.

At launch in October 1954, the home market factory prices of the standard XK 140 coupé models were fixed at the same as the XK 120 models, except that the two-seater was actually £2.10.0 cheaper. The SE models (with the C-type engine) were however more expensive, to the tune of £106.5.0 extra on the basic prices and in round figures £50 more than SE versions of the XK 120, which clearly reflected the higher cost of the C-type cylinder head – this as a matter of interest had been quoted at £60 if supplied for an XK 120. While Jaguar kept the basic factory prices to the same figures throughout the XK 140 production run, in October 1955 the Purchase Tax was increased from 50 to 60 per cent on the wholesale price of a car, resulting in an increase of the total retail prices. The following table quotes both the early and the late prices for the various models:

Body style	Model	Basic price	Purchase Tax to Oct 1955	Total to Oct 1955	Purchase Tax from Oct 1955	Total from Oct 1955
OTS	Standard	£1127.10.0	£470.18.4	£1598.8.4	£565.2.0	£1692.12.0
	SE	£1233.15.0	£515.3.9	£1748.18.9	£618.4.6	£1851.19.6
FHC	Standard	£1140.0.0	£476.2.6	£1616.2.6	£571.7.0	£1711.7.0
	SE	£1246.5.0	£520.7.11	£1766.12.11	£624.9.6	£1870.14.6
DHC	Standard	£1160.0.0	£484.9.2	£1644.9.2	£581.7.0	£1741.7.0
	SE	£1266.5.0	£528.14.7	£1794.19.7	£634.9.6	£1900.14.6

Incidentally, from this table it is possible to calculate that the wholesale price of a Jaguar was around 83.5 per cent of its retail price, so the company gave its distributors a discount of 16.5 per cent. Of the extras, overdrive was £45 and the automatic gearbox £128. On a standard model a set of painted wire wheels cost £20, the part-chromed wires £46.5.0 (£26.5.0 on an SE) and the fully-chromed version £62.10.0 (£42.10.0 on an SE). Purchase Tax would have to be added to all of these prices, as it would be to any other factory-fitted extra.

Prices in the USA were originally advertised as follows, at "Port of Entry", not including transportation charges within the USA, or any local sales tax, but inclusive of shipping charges and US import duty.[15]

In June 1955, *Road and Track* quoted $3745 for a two-seater to "MC" specification and in March 1957, the two-seater was quoted as $3510 for the basic model, $3805 for the "MC" model, in *Sports Car Illustrated*; they also quoted $160 for the overdrive and $150 for chromed wire wheels, if replacing painted wire wheels. The cost of an automatic gearbox to a US customer was probably in the region of $450, although one American magazine quoted only $240 but this was probably for the Mark VII saloon.[16] At the rate of $2.80 to the £, this meant that American Port of Entry prices were typically £100 more than the home market basic factory price.

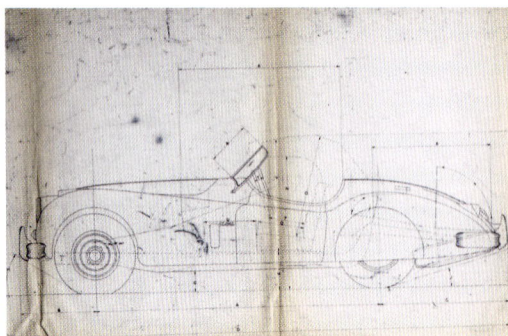

The XK 140 two-seater general arrangement drawing.

	Standard	"M" (i.e. SE less C-type engine)	"MC" (i.e. SE with C-typeengine)
OTS	$3465	$3610	$3760
FHC &			
DHC	$3810	$3955	$4105

1. Comparison applies to the fixed-head coupé model; see *The Autocar* 9 Dec 1955; according to *Road & Track*, weight on the front axle for an open two-seater went up from 48 per cent to 49.6 per cent. However, *The Autocar* on 15 Oct 1954 also quoted 51.7 per cent on the front wheels for coupé models and 52.3 per cent for the open two-seater. Clearly this depends on the condition in which the car was weighed, e.g. whether with an empty or a full fuel tank.
2. As quoted in *The Autocar* 15 Oct 1954
3. Information courtesy of Terry McGrath
4. Jaguar *Service Bulletin* no.196, Sep 1956
5. Jaguar *Service Bulletin* no.155B, Nov 1954
6. I have been tremendously encouraged to discover that Montagu in *Jaguar – a Biography* (first ed.) quoted a very close figure of 827 cars; Whyte *Jaguar* gives a figure of only 781 cars which is disappointingly inaccurate
7. *The Motor* 13 Oct 1954; *The Autocar* 15 Oct 1954
8. Clausager *XK 120 in Detail* p.86

9. *Sports Car Illustrated* Mar 1957
10. *Road & Track* Jun 1955
11. *The Autocar* 9 Dec 1955
12. *Autosport* 4 Nov 1955
13. Jaguar *Service Bulletin* no.198 issued Oct 1956; Porter *Original Jaguar XK* p.30 quotes early coupés as having aluminium skins on part-wooden frames and steel skins from mid-1956, with possibly some late cars having all-steel doors; Terry McGrath believes coupé doors had steel skins from the start and changed to all-steel construction in 1956
14. John Bentley in *Sports Illustrated* Apr 1955
15. *Motor Life* Jul 1956 for coupé prices
16. *Auto Age* May 1955 at a time when the automatic gearbox was not yet available on the XK 140; confusingly the same article quoted a list price only $185 higher for an automatic Mark VII than for the standard model

Chapter Three

The XK 150

In the process of evolution from XK 120 to XK 140, the car had become more of a *Gran Turismo* than a sports car, and the next model would continue this process. Indeed, when the XK 150 was launched in May 1957, at first only fixed-head and drophead coupé models were available. It took ten months for Jaguar to introduce the complementary open-two-seater which appeared in March 1958, and then this car was aimed at the American market, even more so than its predecessors.

The big story at the introduction of the XK 150 was that the car had disc brakes on all four wheels. Already at this point, it is necessary to digress a little in an attempt to clarify matters. When the model was launched, Jaguar at first referred only to the disc brakes and the 210bhp engine with the B-type head which was also used on the Mark VIII and 3.4-litre saloon models.[1] This was echoed in the magazine articles which suggested that the car was available only with these features.[2] Both in Jaguar's own literature and in the press it was originally stated that there would be two versions of the XK 150: a standard car with disc wheels, and a Special Equipment model with wire wheels, as well as a dual exhaust system, fog lamps and a windscreen washer – in other words a similar distinction in terms of equipment as had existed between the standard and SE models of the XK 140. Both versions were available with all three types of transmission – manual, manual with

There were only 93 XK 150 two-seaters with right-hand drive altogether and only 24 were of the 3.8 S version. This 1959 British Racing Green car with Suede Green trim is the very first of those. The registration mark, although highly appropriate, is not original.

Uniquely among the XKs, not to say Jaguar sports cars, the XK 150 could be fitted with the famous mascot as an optional extra. It was the same type as fitted on contemporary saloons. I should not wonder that these days, it is more popular than it was at the time; it is rarely seen in contemporary photos.

The only distinguishing mark of the S models is this discreet badge fitted on the doors.

The later XK 150s had these larger rear lamp clusters, set on rather monolithic chrome-plated plinths, but they were undoubtedly more practical than the smaller earlier type, inherited from the XK 140.

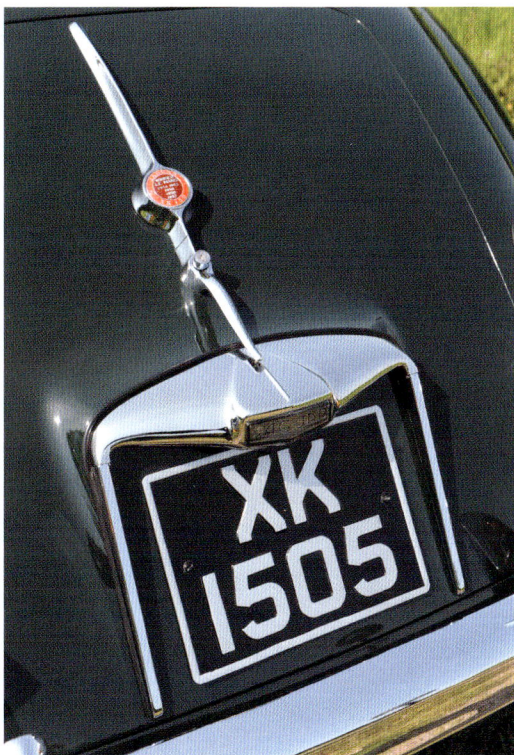

This is the revised boot lid found on the two-seater and generally introduced on all XK 150 models in early 1958, with the more forward-leaning number plate plinth and the boot handle finishing on the chrome housing for the number plate lamp.

Wire wheels were virtually standard on the XK 150, only a handful of cars had the disc wheels. The 60-spoke type seen here was introduced in 1958, replacing the earlier 54-spoke type. This all-chrome finish is nowadays probably the most popular choice.

All XK two-seaters look best with the hood down, but the XK 150 has perhaps the least gawky-looking hood when raised, and the rear window was usefully larger than on previous models, besides being of soft Vybak plastic that would fold with the hood.

The S engines had this gold-painted cylinder head, and the three carburettors are another instant identification point.

This S two-seater is fitted with the mechanical overdrive control, in front of the gear lever, and still has the handbrake lever on the passenger side, while the arm rests on the doors are the later type which doubled as pull handles. The total absence of ashtrays is odd.

From some time in 1957 onwards, the boot lid medallion on the later models could claim no less than five Le Mans wins.

The main difference in the XK 150 boot compared to earlier cars is that the boot lamp was deleted, instead there was this cut-out in the boot lid trim to allow the number plate lamp to illuminate the boot. This car has a manual boot prop; earlier XK 150s had an automatic telescopic prop, while on later cars the prop was deleted altogether and the lid was held open by improved spring-loaded hinges.

In principle all XK 150s had the instrument panel in the centre of the dash covered in light grey leather regardless of trim colour. The only exceptions were the early drophead coupés which had a patterned aluminium panel. The instruments and layout are rather different from earlier XKs, more like the "Mark I" saloons, and the rev counter now sweeps clockwise. Note the later type of heater control, above the central ammeter.

This is the general design of seat on all the XK 150s, and for that matter the XK 140s; the seat backs were noticeably flatter from side to side than on the XK 120s. Behind the seats is the short tonneau cover or pelmet which covers the folded hood.

Built into the number plate lamp housing was this reversing lamp, with the Jaguar name in the glass and still a suggestion of the hexagonal shape.

overdrive and automatic. When the two-seater appeared in March 1958, there was also the S version – some times called, amusingly, the "S-type" – of which more later.

By the time a second edition of the XK 150 brochure was printed in June 1957, the story had changed. Jaguar now stated that the "Standard" model, apart from disc wheels, was equipped with drum brakes and the 190bhp engine, and since the company's price lists (see below) consistently listed the Standard models at basic prices of £117 less that the Special Equipment versions, this probably confirms that these Standard cars were indeed supposed to have the drum brakes and 190bhp engine. The first mentions that I have found in the press of the Standard model built to such a specification are from 1958, in *The Autocar*'s road test of an XK 150, and later when the two-seater was launched.[5]

The question is whether there ever was such a thing as a Standard XK 150. The matter even caused some confusion within Jaguar, and in June 1957 "Lofty" England wrote a memo to Sir William Lyons, pointing out that "none of the literature which has been issued, the engineering schedules or engineering memos give any information on the subject, apart from the

letter put out by the Sales Department" which suggests that the Standard model was an invention by the sales staff.[4] One would expect the difference between a 190bhp engine and the 210bhp type to lie in the cylinder head and the valves. The *Spare Parts Catalogue* for the XK 150 lists only one type of cylinder head for the non-S 3.4-litre XK 150, apart from the slightly revised head introduced in May 1959 when the original mechanical rev counter was replaced by an electronic instrument. Furthermore, the same valves were used throughout, on all versions of the XK 150 engines. I think this indicates that there were no XK 150 cars fitted with a 190bhp engine. Similarly, there is no mention in the *Spare Parts Catalogue* of drum brakes. Again, my conclusion must be that all XK 150 cars did indeed have disc brakes.

Continuing this investigation, there is reference to a single exhaust system, but only for manual gearbox cars, with or without overdrive, while all automatic cars had the dual exhaust system. In practice the single system is rarely if ever seen. From the parts catalogue, it would appear that the windscreen washer was fitted to all cars. However, the catalogue also lists the fog lamps without qualification, when it is clear that many XK 150s did not have them, and the bumper plinth panels were not always drilled to accept them; in fact fog lamps were sold by Jaguar as accessories. Finally, the *Spare Parts Catalogue* does obligingly list disc wheels and state that wire spoke wheels were "supplied to special order only". The appropriate different types of front and rear hubs are also listed, as are the rear wheel spats, and different rear wings to accept them.

My belief is that there was no such thing as a 190bhp, drum-braked XK 150, but we do know from the *Car Record Books* that a small number of cars had disc wheels, and from the same source we know that a small number of cars did not have the S prefix to the chassis number, which would traditionally denote a "Special Equipment" car. The numbers involved are so small that it is worth listing all of these cars individually here. The first table is of those thirteen or fourteen cars which do not have a chassis prefix letter in the *Car Record Books* but which are not marked to show whether they had disc wheels. It must be remembered that the omission of a prefix letter might simply be a clerical error.[5]

Chassis no	Engine no	Date	Registration mark	Type	Remarks
832097 DN	VS 2087-8	17/08/1959	Export France	3.4 S OTS LHD	
832098	V 7299-8	24/08/1959	Export France	3.4 OTS LHD	For American customer
824903 DN	V 6892-8	15/05/1959	541 HPP	3.4 FHC RHD	Car exists, later owners quote S prefix
836227	V 6896-9	28/05/1959	Export USA	3.4 FHC LHD	
836937 DN	VA 2061-8	06/09/1960	Export USA	3.8 FHC LHD	
836963 DN	VA 2118-8	20/09/1960	7585 DU	3.8 FHC LHD	PED car, for USA
827378 DN	V 6930-8	21/05/1959	Not recorded	3.4 DHC RHD	Car exists; S prefix quoted in 1998 XK register
827380 DN	V 6954-8	22/05/1959	WYN 623	3.4 DHC RHD	Car exists
827509 DN	V 7468-8	09/02/1960	777 OFM	3.4 DHC RHD	
837443	V 3781-8	16/05/1958	Export USA	3.4 DHC LHD	Two entries in records, with and without S
838263 DN	V 6897-8	14/05/1959	Export Canada	3.4 DHC LHD	
838270 BW	V 7116-8	26/06/1959	Export Switzerland	3.4 DHC LHD	Car exists; owner quotes S prefix
838271	V 7097-8	26/06/1959	Export USA	3.4 DHC LHD	
838967	VA 2131-9	22/09/1960	Export USA	3.8 DHC LHD	Car exists

The next list is of those ten cars which are marked in the book as having disc wheels, but which do have prefix letters to their chassis numbers:

Chassis no	Engine no	Date	Registration mark	Type	Remarks
T 832109 DN	VS 2088-8	20/11/1959	Export Jordan	3.4 S OTS LHD	Possibly intended for HM King Hussein?
S 825125	V 7451-8	18/12/1959	LDJ 768	3.4 FHC RHD	
S 825133 BW	VA 1595-9	09/02/1960	Export Jamaica	3.8 FHC RHD	
S 825149 BW	V 7456-7	17/02/1960	Export Trinidad	3.4 FHC RHD	
S 825213 DN	VA 1729-8	12/04/1960	Export Singapore	3.8 FHC RHD	
S 825218	V 7512-8	20/04/1960	OVG 399	3.4 FHC RHD	In Australia by 1984[6]
S 825245 DN	VA 1796-8	16/05/1960	616 MVT	3.8 FHC RHD	
S 827524 DN	V 7467-8	15/02/1960	PO 7	3.4 DHC RHD	
S 827535 DN	V 7477-8	04/03/1960	144 ETT	3.4 DHC RHD	
T 838705 DN	VAS 1098-9	18/02/1960	Export Canada	3.8 S DHC LHD	Car exists

The final list is of those cars which are known from various observations and reports to have disc wheels but which are not so marked in the books:

Chassis no	Engine no	Date	Registration mark	Type	Remarks
S 820088 DN	VA 1895-8	04/07/1960	1050 LG	3.8 OTS RHD	Car exists; was JW 165
S 824075 DN	V 1779-8	08/10/1957	Export New Zealand	3.4 FHC RHD	Information from John Elmgreen
S 824114	V 1927-8	07/11/1957	UXR271	3.4 FHC RHD	Information from Terry McGrath
S 824174 DN	V 2293-8	07/01/1958	SVM 779	3.4 FHC RHD	Car exists
S 824200	V 2728-8	31/01/1958	150 CRO	3.4 FHC RHD	Information from Terry McGrath
S 824512 BW	V 4462-8	24/06/1958	Export Singapore	3.4 FHC RHD	As above
S 824529 BW	V 3970-8	02/07/1958	Export Australia	3.4 FHC RHD	In Australia in 1984[7]
S 824783 DN	V 6543-8	09/02/1959	150 DYB	3.4 FHC RHD	Car exists[8]
S 824795	V 6442-8	20/02/1959	9494 BP	3.4 FHC RHD	Car exists; disc wheels may not be original
S 825131 DN	V 7364-8	08/02/1960	586 AOP	3.4 FHC RHD	Car exists; has cut-away spats[9]
S 827026 DN	V 3048-8	04/03/1958	LDY 819	3.4 DHC RHD	Car exists but no longer has disc wheels[10]
S 827125	V 4175-8	17/06/1958	791 or 793 DKE	3.4 DHC RHD	Car exists
S 827270	V 6082-8	17/12/1958	900 GMB	3.4 DHC RHD	Car exists
S 827639 BW	V 7610-8	24/08/1960	Was 1 BGG, later 832 HYV, now 786 JAG	3.4 DHC RHD	Car exists but no longer has disc wheels[11]

This fixed-head, OVG 399, was one of the very few XK 150s to have disc wheels, here photographed with a wire-wheeled car for contrast. (JDHT)

A splendid recent colour photo of the all-white XK 150 two-seater registered 1050 LG on its original disc wheels. (Photo courtesy of Bill Leaby)

Some of these cars, including 1050 LG and OVG 399, have been illustrated in a number of books and magazine articles to show examples of disc-wheeled XK 150s.[12] I have indicated which of the cars I believe to be in existence, in part based on JDHT certificates issued over the years; needless to say, further information or confirmation from present-day owners would be most welcome. To me, the most intriguing are the two or three S models that may have had disc wheels. Another mystery concerns the peculiar cut-away spats that were quoted in the XK 140 parts list (see chapter 2) but not in the XK 150 parts list, although it is known from photos that Jaguar fitted at least one wire-wheeled fixed-head car with similar spats. Of the cars listed above, 586 AOP and 9494 BP are fitted with these spats, yet there seems to be no good reason for fitting them to cars with disc wheels.[13]

In fairness I need to mention a claimed sighting of a "RHD 150 S FHC on disc wheels and drum brakes (but no spats)!" by Jeremy Wade who unfortunately did not record the chassis number.[14] Paul Skilleter also refers to a green cylinder head being found on a standard XK 150 engine with 190bhp.[15] Even if such engines existed, there is no distinctive prefix letter to the engine number, and no other identification of them in the records.

The question that is now begging for an

This must be described as an XK 150 prototype: a fixed-head with wire wheels but these strange cut-away spats, which had been offered on the XK 140. It also has a non-standard frame for the windscreen. It is a left-hand drive car, but it can't be chassis S 834001, as that was Claret (dark red), and from other photos we know that the car seen here was cream or light grey. It has also been claimed to be the first XK 150 S. (JDHT)

The biggest novelty on the XK 150 was that disc brakes were fitted to all four wheels. This is one of the front discs, with the original type caliper. (JDHT)

Here it is installed on the car with a slightly different type caliper, but still of the early type which did not allow quick pad changes. (JDHT)

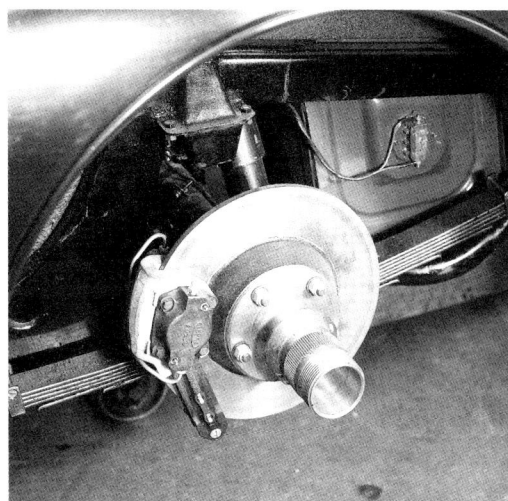

In this view of the XK 150 rear hub and disc, we can see both the handbrake caliper and above it the main caliper for the foot brake. Behind is the sender unit for the fuel gauge on the side of the petrol tank. (JDHT)

answer, is why did Jaguar persist in quoting a somewhat fictitious "standard" model XK 150, if no such car was made? – in much the same way that for quite some time, they quoted a "standard" model of the 2.4-litre saloon. The only reason that I can think of would be a desire to keep the quoted list price down. When the 3.8 litre model was introduced in 1959, there was no mention of a "standard" version of this.

However, to return to the XK 150 as it was made and sold. As discussed in chapter 1, since 1950, Jaguar and Dunlop had co-operated on the development of disc brakes for motor vehicles. They were at first fitted to some of the C-types, and the D-types of 1954-56 had disc brakes. By 1957 Jaguar was obviously satisfied that the system was sufficiently well developed and proven to be offered as standard equipment on a normal production road car. In the meantime, four-wheel Dunlop disc brakes had been fitted to the limited-production Austin-Healey 100 S of 1955, and had appeared on the Jensen 541 de luxe at the 1956 Motor Show. The abortive HRG twin-cam of 1955 had a rather different type of disc brake. Citroën fitted disc brakes on the front wheels of the DS 19 in October 1955 and at the end of 1956 the Triumph TR3 had Girling front discs, but most of the credit for pioneering the system on production cars must still go to Dunlop and Jaguar.[16]

Jaguar paid a price for being pioneers, since the XK 150 disc brakes suffered from teething troubles and were the subject of many modifications, of which a particularly important change was to bridge-type calipers with square pads in late 1958 which greatly simplified brake pad changes;[17] for further details, please see the list of change points elsewhere in the present volume. A perennial problem with disc brakes is how to arrange the handbrake. On the XK 150, the fly-off handbrake worked on separate calipers on the rear brake discs, which was not a terribly effective solution. Another problem was the loss of the self-servo effect of twin leading shoe drum brakes so to reduce pedal effort, Jaguar fitted a Lockheed vacuum servo. Incidentally, in 1958 a servo kit was made available for retro-fitting to XK 140 cars.[18]

There were far fewer changes to the rest of the XK 150 chassis compared to its predecessor. The actual frame was changed mostly in respect of sundry mounting brackets, including those for the radiator, while the curved front member was deleted. The wheel hubs were changed to suit the brake discs, there was a new rubber-

In the front view, the wider grille of the XK 150 shows up well, together with the curved one-piece windscreen. There is generally a more muscular feel to the look of this car compared to the earlier XKs.

You may wonder what colour this car is, and so did I, so I should explain that the car started life in 1960 in Cornish Grey with Red interior trim. The closest Jaguar offered to this colour was Indigo Blue which is rather purply; there were also Imperial Maroon and Claret, although neither of these colours were found on any of the right-hand drive two-seaters.

Contrasting studies of the two-seater with hood up or down.

The arrangement in the tonneau area behind the seats is similar to the XK 140 two-seater with the folding boot bulkhead, except the XK 150 does not have the compartment for stowing side screens. There is now a strap either side to help hold the folded hood in place. At top right is one of the two stiffeners which swing out to hold the hood cover pelmet rigid

As well as showing the
ashtray and the
mechanical overdrive
lever just in front of it,
this late XK 150 has
the handbrake lever
on the driver's side.

The two important
innovations on the XK
150 two-seater were
the wind-down door
windows, with the
chrome-plated channel
frame fitted to the
glass, and the external
door handles.

A period radio is a wonderful addition to any
classic car, and this HMV medium and long-
wave radio looks perfect in the XK 150.

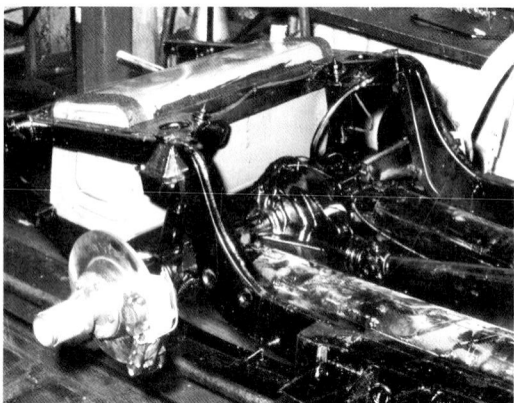

Taken on the rudimentary XK chassis assembly line, this photo shows the rear end of an XK 150 chassis, not much changed from earlier models except for the disc brake. (JDHT)

Another photo from the chassis line, now with the petrol tank installed. (JDHT)

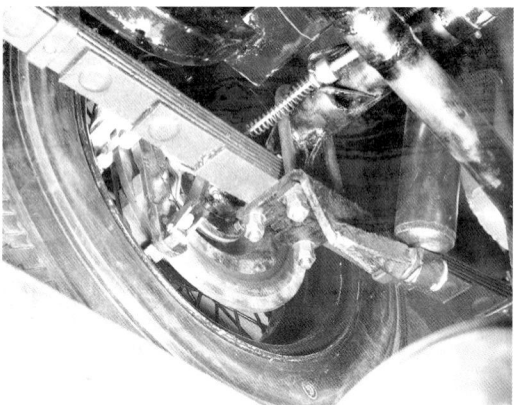

No gaiters for the XK 150 rear springs. This view also shows the brake disc and the some times troublesome handbrake caliper, with its mechanical actuation. (JDHT)

angle was increased from 30 degrees to 45 degrees, already used for the exhaust valve seats, and the inlet valves themselves had convex faces. The claimed maximum power of 210bhp (or 190bhp net) and torque of 216 lb.ft were similar to those of the XK 140 engine with a C-type head but were developed at lower engine speeds, especially noticeable for the maximum torque which was now available at 3000 rather than 4000rpm, so the engine was more flexible and acceleration was improved. The XK 150 3.4-litre engine was designated as the V type. The carburettors were the latest SU HD6 diaphragm type. An immediate identification feature was that there was a new inlet manifold where the water outlet pipe from the cylinder head was separate, and had a new design of thermostat housing and outlet at the front. A new radiator was fitted, with the filler cap in a rearwards extension of the header tank, and a 12-blade fan which was completely encircled in a two-piece cowl.

In September 1959, Jaguar introduced the 3.8-litre size of the XK engine in the XK 150. This was bored out from 83mm to 87mm for a capacity of 3781cc. With the bigger bore it became necessary to fit dry liners to the cylinder block. From then on, the XK 150 was offered with a choice of the two engine sizes, both in standard and in S form. The standard 3.8-litre engine was designated type VA, and was claimed to develop 220bhp. The normal compression ratio for both engine sizes was 8:1, and less than forty cars (mostly 3.4-litre models) had the optional 7:1 ratio. On the other hand, around 650 cars had the 9:1 compression ratio, not including the S models.

There are several ways of identifying the various XK engines, although it has to be said that none is totally fool-proof. There is the engine number prefix, the part number usually cast into the cylinder block, and the colour of the cylinder head. In the table opposite, these are all quoted, as well as the cylinder head part numbers.[20]

Apart from the wide interchangeability of XK engines in general, some of these cylinder blocks or heads, and thus their part numbers, were shared with Mark VII, Mark VIII and 3.4-litre saloon cars; or, for the 3.8-litre, the Mark IX, Mark II 3.8 or E-type 3.8. The cylinder block part number is typically cast in on the right-hand side of the block, at top centre. The part

mounted steering column, and during 1958 the wire wheels were changed from the 54-spoke type to the 60-spoke type (the 3.4-litre saloon adopted 72-spoke wheels a little later). In early 1959, wire-wheeled cars for Germany and possibly other markets were fitted with special hub caps (spinners) with shorter lugs.[19]

The major change to the engine was that, as mentioned above, the XK 150 engine adopted the B-type cylinder head with exhaust valves of 1.625in (41.3mm) diameter. The inlet valve seat

	Eng. no. prefix	Cyl. block part no.	Cyl. head colour	Cyl. head part no.
XK 120 1948-50	W	C.2331 or C.2331/1 to eng. no. W 2011	Unpainted	C.2242 to eng. no. W 1880/W 2483, C.2242/1 from then onwards
XK 120 1950-54	W to 1953, then F; S suffix on SE engines	C.4820 from eng. no. W 2012 on, and on all F engines	Unpainted	C.2242/1 to eng. no. W 4690; C.6733 from eng. no. W 4691, and on all F engines
XK 140	G	C.4820 to eng. no. G 1907; C.8610 from G 1908 to G 4410/4430; C.8610/1 from G 4410/4430 on	Unpainted	C.6733 to eng. no. G 6911; C.6733/1 from G 6912 on
XK 140 SE with C-type head	G, with S suffix	As XK 140	Red, with cast-in letter "C"	C.7707 to eng. no G 6406; C.7707/1 from eng. no G 6407 on
XK 150 3.4	V	C.8610/1 to eng. no. V 6860; C.15951 from V 6861 on; C.17568*	Light blue/green (turquoise)	C.12500 (mechanical rev. counter) or C.14956 (electronic ditto)
XK 150 3.4 S	VS	C.8610/1 to approx. eng. no. VS 2000; C.15951 from then on; C.17568*	Pumpkin orange (old gold)	C.12600 (mechanical rev. counter) or C.14957 (electronic ditto)
XK 150 3.8	VA	C.16020; C.17212 from eng. no. VA 2053; later C.17212/1*	Dark metallic blue	C.14958 (also found on Mark IX and Mark II 3.8)
XK 150 3.8 S	VAS	C.16020; C.17212 from eng. no. VAS 1285; later C.17212/1*	Pumpkin orange (old gold)	C.14957 (also found on E-type 3.8)

* C.17568 and C.17212/1 on very late engines and/or replacement units only. In practice, other block numbers have been found on 3.8-litre engines including C.13790 and C.17200 (as on Mark IX), both are genuine Jaguar 3.8-litre block part numbers; information courtesy of Terry McGrath

number of the head may only be cast in on the underside of the head, in a central recess on the left-hand side. The actual engine number should be stamped on both the block and the head (see also the appendix concerning identification).

The XK 150 transmission was similar in principle to that of the XK 140, with the time-honoured manual Moss gearbox which could be fitted with an optional overdrive working on top gear, or the alternative of an automatic Borg-Warner 'box. The commonest type of manual gearbox was designated the JL, and was effectively the same as the JL gearbox on the XK 140. It had either close ratio ground gears, with a suffix CR to the gearbox number, or normal ratio Jaguar shaved gears, with suffix JS. The close ratios were the same as on the XK 140 but the ratios on gearboxes with the JS suffix were now as follows: first and reverse, 3.378:1; second, 1.86:1; third, 1.283:1; and top, direct.[21] The SL type gearbox with its one-piece gear cluster was replaced on the XK 150 by the M type gearbox with Moss shaved gears, also with the one-piece cluster, now always with close ratio gears.

When fitted with overdrive, the gearbox became type JLS, again available with either a normal or a close ratio gear set. The overdrive

was electrically operated, by a switch mounted at the outboard end of the facia on the driver's side. Overdrive was standard on the S model and in January 1959, the S was fitted with a mechanically engaged overdrive, which then also became available to special order on the non-S model. This was operated, perhaps less conveniently, by a small lever next to the gear lever. According to the parts list, the mechanical overdrive could be fitted only to the JLS-JS gearbox with Jaguar-shaved normal ratio gears.

Since a standard 3.8-litre XK 150 was not photographed for this book, we have included this photo to show the dark metallic blue colour found on the cylinder head of this engine, here installed in a Mark IX saloon.

The windscreen glass is the same on all the XK 150 body styles. This car has been fitted with an external mirror attached to the front quarter light frame, a period accessory. The registration mark also looks period but is in fact an "age-related" mark issued later: many XKs have been re-registered a number of times.

For the first time on an XK, the side windows were angled slightly inwards, effectively giving a bit of tumble-home to the greenhouse, which gave a much improved and more modern look to the car. Both front and rear quarter lights still opened.

Here is the door-mounted S badge again, with the subtle difference that the arrow of the horizontal flash points forwards which may be more correct.

This is the third and final configuration for the rear view of the XK 150s, with the over riders mounted closer together, and the new larger lamp units introduced afterwards. The over riders were moved to avoid obscuring the lamps.

On XK 150s from early 1958 with the more forward-sloping number plate, the boot handle ended on the number plate lamp housing, with a rubber pad in between.

The profile of the XK 150 fixed-head coupé is quite different from the earlier fixed-head models. The proportions are similar to the XK 140, but the new wing line and larger window areas gave it a distinctive look.

A view from the exhaust side of the "gold-top" three-carburettor S engine, with the enamelled exhaust manifolds. On this car, the windscreen washer (in the foreground) is of the electric pump rather than the vacuum-operated type.

The XK 150 grille was very much like the grille of the 3.4-litre saloon, probably intentional, in the same way that the XK 140 grille had been like that of the 2.4-litre model. It reverted to the built-up construction of the XK 120 grille but was much wider, with sixteen bars.

Compared to the XK 140 fixed-head, the opening panel in the boot bulkhead was shallower and probably of less practical value. With the rear quarter pillars so much narrower, there was now only a single interior lamp, fitted centrally. And there really was no legroom for the poor rear seat passengers.

This is where the coach key is inserted in one of the two locks of the false boot floor which covers the spare wheel compartment.

As is common on the XKs, the back of the front seats were covered in moquette.

This fixed-head interior is typical of the later XK 150s, with the ashtray on the tunnel and the handbrake on the driver's side, although this car has the more common electrically operated overdrive, rather than the mechanically operated version.

The switch for the electric overdrive was mounted outboard of the driver's cubby hole. Below is the warning light for brake fluid and handbrake which was introduced towards the end of production. On this car, the radio loudspeaker has been fitted in the cubby hole.

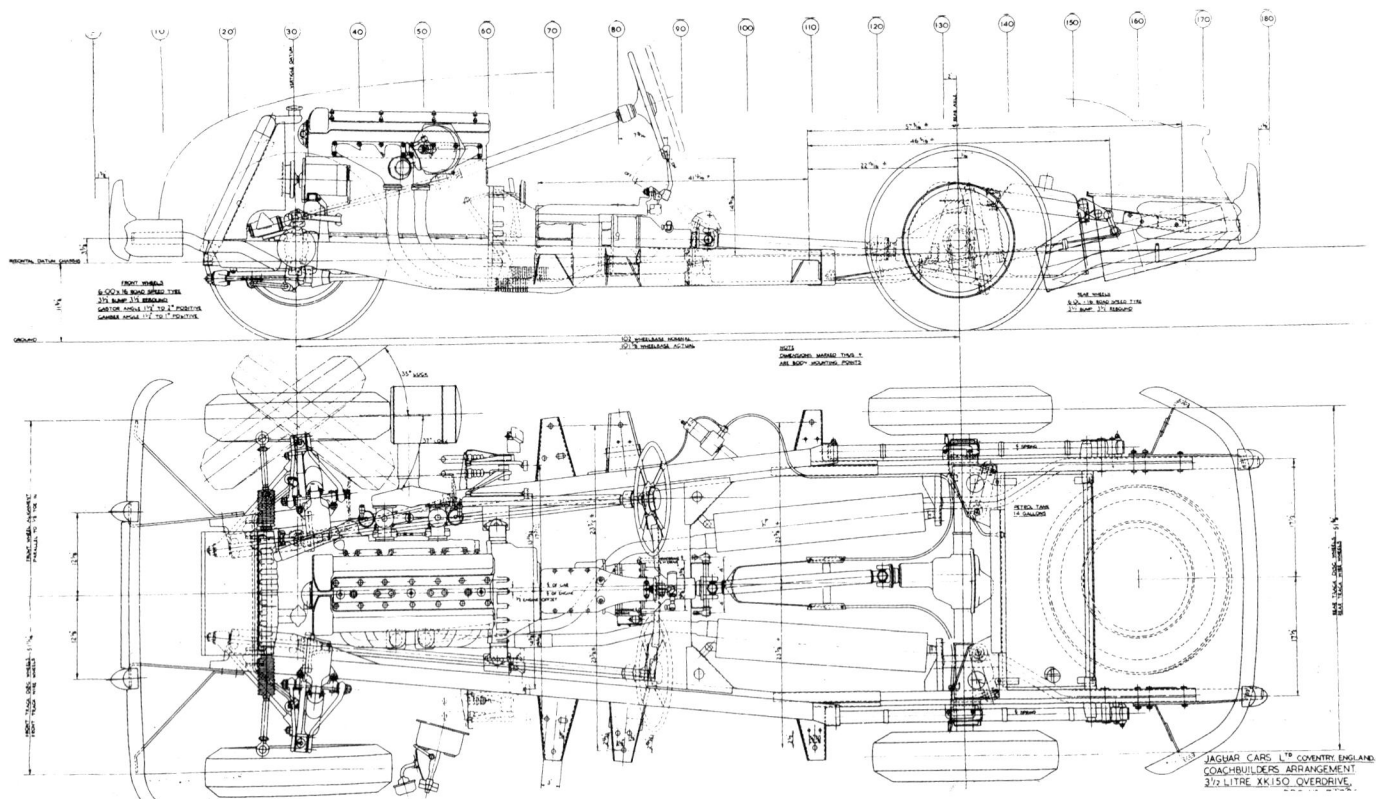

This is the "Coachbuilder's Arrangement" Drawing of the XK 150 chassis. (JDHT)

This is confirmed by the *Car Record Books*; while they show that more than 225 S models had CR suffixes to their gearbox numbers, with two exceptions these were all 3.4 models made not later than January 1959. Altogether there were almost exactly 5000 XK 150s with overdrive, making this the most common type of transmission on the model. Apart from the S models from January 1959 onwards which are supposed always to have the mechanical overdrive, it is not possible to state from the records whether a car had an electric or a mechanical overdrive.[22] Several slightly different overdrive units were used during XK 150 production, but they all had the 28 per cent reduction ratio.

The automatic gearbox was now also available on the open two-seater model although of the 1600 or so automatic cars, only seventy were open two-seaters. The Borg-Warner DG.250 'box was similar to that found on the XK 140. During 1958, the original American-made automatic gearboxes were gradually replaced by 'boxes made by Borg-Warner in the UK, and the British-made boxes can be identified by prefix codes starting with the letter J – one presumes for Jaguar. JBX is the normal and most common

prefix for an XK 150 auto 'box, found on over 600 of the approximately 800 cars with British-made 'boxes.[23] There were two important changes to the automatic XK 150s compared to the XK 140s: firstly, the useful intermediate speed hold became a standard feature, and secondly, the selector lever was moved from the steering column to below the centre of the instrument panel where it moved in the horizontal plane, still with the P-N-D-L-R positions. This location was similar to that adopted for the 2.4 and 3.4-litre saloons and had the advantage that it was the same on both right-hand and left-hand drive cars. The lever was connected to the gearbox by cable rather than rods. The auto 'box was never offered on the S versions.

The only other change to the transmission was that a Thornton Powr-Lok limited slip differential was fitted on 3.8-litre cars except for those exported to North America; it was available to special order on North American cars, and on 3.4-litre cars. The rear axle was still the Salisbury 4HA type with the 3.54:1 ratio, except on overdrive cars which had 4.09:1, with alternative ratios of 3.31:1 and 4.27:1, and all ratios could be found on either the normal or the

I think this left-hand drive drophead may have been a prototype or very early car, photographed even before it had its interior trimmed. (JDHT)

limited slip differential. The *Car Record Books* do not indicate whether or not individual cars had the limited slip differential, but each rear axle with this differential was fitted with a metal tag stamped "P/L" adjacent to the bolt carrying the ratio tag.[21]

Apart from the disc brakes, the biggest change on the XK 150 was that the body was almost completely restyled. While the basic shape was similar to the XK 120 and 140, the scuttle and the front wing line were raised, the side windows were pushed outwards to improve interior width, there was a new wider grille and bonnet, while the front windscreen was of the curved one-piece type, although shallower than on earlier models – together with many other smaller or less obvious changes. Undoubtedly the car looked more modern by 1957 standards, but some of the original elegance had been lost, which is why the XK 150 styling is still considered controversial. Another point to bear in mind is that the centre of gravity was raised slightly, arguably to the detriment of handling and road holding.

Both the fixed-head and the drophead now had a shorter bonnet as first seen on the XK 140 fixed-head, and there was a no doubt welcome degree of standardization of many of the lower body panels between the two body styles, such as front wings, dash assembly, doors, rear wings and boot lid. Both bodies therefore also had the wider doors and roomier cockpit of the XK 140 fixed-head, and naturally occasional rear seats were still fitted. The fixed-head greenhouse was given a much bigger rear window and the side window shapes were changed. Similarly, there

Conceivably the same car, showing the original arrangement of the boot lid, rear lamps and bumper over riders. (JDHT)

The number plate UWK 36 was issued to a Personal Export Delivery car in July 1958, but I do not think that it was the correct number for an XK 150 drophead! (JDHT)

For the XK 150 brochures, Jaguar no longer used elaborate colour renderings but simply took black-and-white photos which were then heavily airbrushed and retouched, as seen here. (JDHT)

A well-known view of an early XK 150 two-seater taken in the Service Department at Browns Lane. The point to note is the boot lid of the early type with the more upright number plate, which was found only on the very earliest two-seaters. (JDHT)

The reason why this XK 150 two-seater was photographed on a lift was that this photo, cropped and doctored, was used on the cover of the brochure for this model. (JDHT)

Here this car, or another very early two-seater, has been taken out of the factory to be photographed against a more attractive background, with the hood down. (JDHT)

And this is the resulting brochure cover. (JDHT)

The first photo in this series shows the hood catches on the two-seater – this car has not even had its dashboard installed yet – and then three stages in folding the hood, which is stowed behind the seats. The short tonneau cover stays in place, but the stiffeners are moved to allow it to fold out of the way when the hood is raised or lowered. (JDHT)

I am not sure why this two-seater was photographed without headlamps, which was the condition in which cars were typically exported to the USA, as they were fitted with American sealed-beam headlamps on arrival. (JDHT)

was a bigger rear window in the hood of the drophead, although this model lacked the rear quarter lights, and the shape of the drop glasses in the doors was different from the fixed-head.

The open two-seater followed in the spring of 1958. The reason given for the delayed appearance for this body style was the fire which had devastated a part of the Jaguar factory in February 1957.[25] At first the model was made only with left-hand drive and reserved for the Dollar areas – USA and Canada, with a few cars going to Mexico. The first car had been made in September 1957, with production beginning to build up from January 1958, and the model was launched to the American public at the 1958 New York Motor Show, together with the S version. Export sales to Europe started in August, while right-hand drive cars for home and export followed in October-November but were always rare, and only 93 RHD open two-seaters were to be made.

The "roadster" as it was also known still had more or less the original length of bonnet, about 4in (102mm) longer than coupé models, so the scuttle and windscreen were set further back. However, the two-seater had the same front wings and door sills as the coupés which gave the benefit of doors that were just as wide, at the cost of a rather ugly step in the front shut-line of the door, to bring it back to the line of the windscreen. The windscreen glass was the

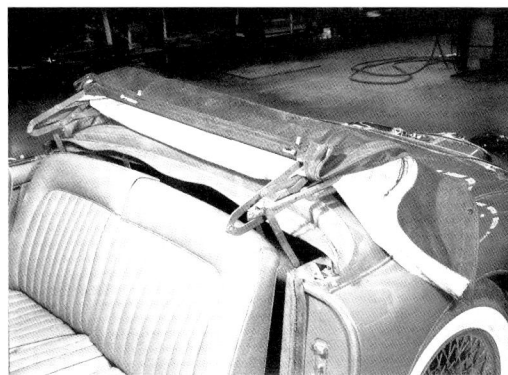

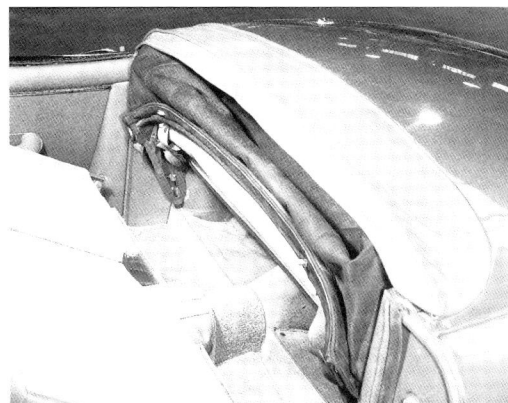

The tonneau cover was standard equipment on two-seaters; note the way in which it is attached to the front of the "short" tonneau cover. On this light-coloured car, the "step" in the front door shutline shows up well. (JDHT)

On this left-hand drive 1958 car, the ashtrays are in the doors. It is also worth noting that the handbrake lever is on the passenger side, therefore on the right-hand side of the tunnel on a left-hand drive car

same on all three cars, but the frames were different. Two major improvements on this body style – at the time still very unusual on a sports roadster – were the exterior push-button door handles and the wind-down door windows. The front seats were in the same location as on the coupé models but as rear seats were not required, the tonneau panel behind the cockpit was brought forward to the seat backs and was much deeper than on the coupés; the boot lid was the same on all body styles.

The wider radiator grille found on all XK 150s was of a style pioneered on the 3.4-litre saloon in early 1957 and later also adopted for the 2.4-litre model. No longer of the cast one-piece construction found on the XK 140, it had 16 narrow bars and a plastic badge with the "growler" motif inset at the top. The front bumper had a central dip following the grille outline. The horizontal plinth or valance panels behind the bumper were supplied in two forms, either with or without holes for fog lamps. The

A Jaguar publicity shot of the two-seater with the hood up, but side windows wound down, photographed at Compton Verney. Also taken at Compton Verney, now with the hood down. (JDHT)

A study of the rear view of the early two-seater, if against a less elegant background at the factory. Quite possibly the same car taken at the same time in an adjacent factory location, with the door open to give a glimpse of the interior. (JDHT)

bonnet had a 4in (102mm) wide raised centre section with a centre chrome strip, which could be fitted with the leaping Jaguar mascot, quoted as an option: most unusual for a Jaguar sports car! It is also curious that the introduction of the mascot on the XK more or less coincided with the first bans on dangerous mascots in some European countries...

At the rear, the bumper was of the full-width type, and the number plate had migrated to a square plinth pressed into the boot lid itself. On the early cars this plinth was at a less forward angle than the surrounding boot lid, but it later adopted a similar angle. This has proved to be a difficult change to pinpoint, but I believe it occurred in January 1958 coinciding with the start of production of the open two-seater in LHD form. I accept that early factory photos of a two-seater show the original type boot lid but I believe these to be of the prototype, 830001, which had been built some months earlier (see chapters 8 and 9). That the two-seater always had the second type of boot lid but the coupé models changed, is borne out by the fact that the *Spare Parts Catalogue* in the "Body Fittings" sections for the fixed-head and drophead state that "The first type of Lid with near-vertical Number Plate is no longer available" but no similar note is included in the two-seater section.[26]

On the revised boot lid, the handle finished

on the chrome housing for the number plate lamp and reversing lamp rather than on the plinth itself. Two other better documented changes to the appearance of the rear end were, firstly, that the rear bumper overriders were moved closer together in September 1958, and secondly, that in October 1959 the original XK 140 rear lamps were replaced by larger Mark II-type lamp units which had separate indicator lenses and circular reflectors mounted below the actual lamps. The central chrome strip on the boot lid incorporated a medallion proclaiming Jaguar's Le Mans victories, amended some time after June 1957 to include the fifth win!

Lighting at the front was identical to the XK 140, with the large front indicators, small side lamps and the J-medallion headlamps. All body versions of the XK 150 had two 6-volt batteries, one in each front wing. Other electrical equipment was broadly speaking similar to the earlier models, but the heater carried over from XK 140 fixed-head coupé was replaced with a more efficient fresh-air type heater in 1958, shortly after the heater controls on the instrument panel had been moved.

The most obvious change to the interior concerned the facia and instrument panel. The coupé models no longer had the wood facia and door trims, instead all models had the facia covered in leather to match the trim colour of the car, but the central instrument panel was

The drophead hood should fold down rather lower than is the case here, and the cars were supplied with a hood cover to fit over the fully folded hood.

This is the 3.4 litre two-carburettor engine which was standard on the XK 150. I am however not too sure about the cylinder head colour: this should originally have been a solid light turquoise green colour rather than this pale gold seen here.

The outline with the hood raised is still harmonious. The drophead doors were now as wide as those on the fixed-head. As is the case on the two-seater, the drop glasses in the door windows have frames fitted to the glass.

The inlet manifold and water gallery was of this new design on the XK 150. On the left, coming out of the back of the cylinder head, is the cable for the mechanical rev counter, not found on the later cars with an electronic instrument.

This drophead coupé is another car which has been re-registered, and as it some times happens, it has been issued with a 1963-style A suffix registration; in fact the car dates to 1958.

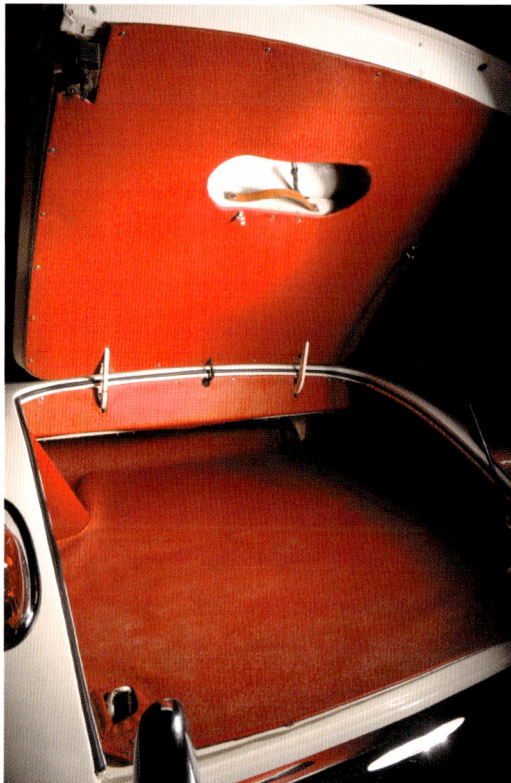

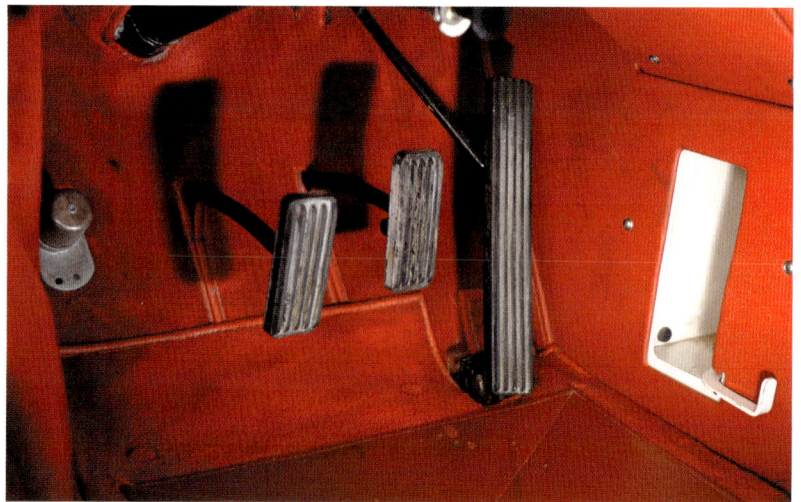

The boot was fully trimmed on all XK 150 models. This car has the manual prop. The strap for holding the false floor up is here inside the aperture in the trim panel allowing light through from the number plate lamp.

As the car was wider, there was more room around the pedals than on the XK 140, but the pedals were more off-set to the outside of the car, and there was room for the dip switch on the toe board. The air vent to the side of the foot well was conveniently adjusted by the lever seen here.

The drophead interior was very similar to the other body styles, the only significant difference to the trim was that the seat backs were slightly different on this body. This car I feel should have the ashtrays mounted in the doors; presumably the present-day owner has no need for them!

Early dropheads had an instrument panel in patterned aluminium, but by June 1958 this panel covered in grey leather had been introduced also on this body style. Just visible is the slide lever for the heater, centrally above the panel. This car has another period-looking radio. The mechanical rev counter has little red arrows as indicator tell-tales, and a different clock compared to the later electronic instrument

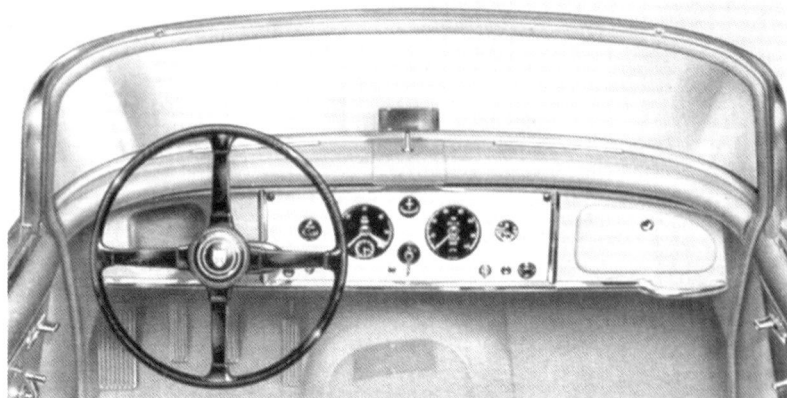

This illustration of the dashboard of a left-hand drive two-seater was used in the brochure, and shows the driver's left foot rest well. (JDHT)

covered in grey leather regardless of trim colour. The deletion of the wood trim was largely welcomed by contemporary commentators, not least in the USA: "No longer is there any varnished wood trim which needs refinishing in six weeks" – ouch![27] The only exception was the drophead which until June 1958 had an instrument panel covered in patterned aluminium. The layout of the central panel was changed to the style found on the 2.4 and 3.4-litre saloons, with the two large instruments closer together, the ammeter between them above the ignition and light switch, the fuel gauge on the extreme left, and the combined oil pressure and water temperature gauge on the extreme right. During the production run the direction indicator switch was replaced by a lever on the steering column, and as a final change during production, a

handbrake and brake fluid warning light was fitted.

All cars, even the open two-seater, had two door-mounted ashtrays, although these were later replaced by a single ashtray mounted on the gearbox tunnel. There were armrests on the doors, at first of a solid type, later replaced by combined armrests and door pulls. The seats were similar in style to the earlier models but were wider and featured tubular construction for the back rests. A wider choice of trim colours was available (see the appendix on colour schemes), all of them single colours, while carpet colours – which are not quoted in most of the literature – were apparently Black, Dark Blue, Green, Red, or Tan, broadly speaking to match the trim colour. The *Spare Parts Catalogue* lists three different carpet qualities, of which the final (type 1201) introduced in early 1960 had straight-cut rather than curly pile.[28]

Overall length of the XK 150 had crept up by another inch (25mm) to 14ft 9in (4496mm) but other dimensions were unchanged. As for the XK 140 (see chapter 2), there is a question mark over how much the cars actually weighed, with conflicting figures being quoted by Jaguar. A sudden inexplicable weight increase occurred in 1960, and there were other inconsistencies in the company's published figures.

The dry weights originally quoted were unrealistically low. *The Autocar* later quoted

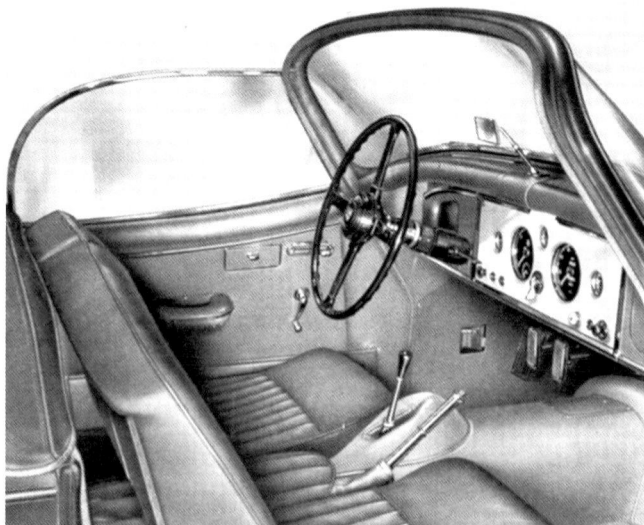

The general interior view was another brochure illustration, of a car with the door-mounted ashtrays. (JDHT)

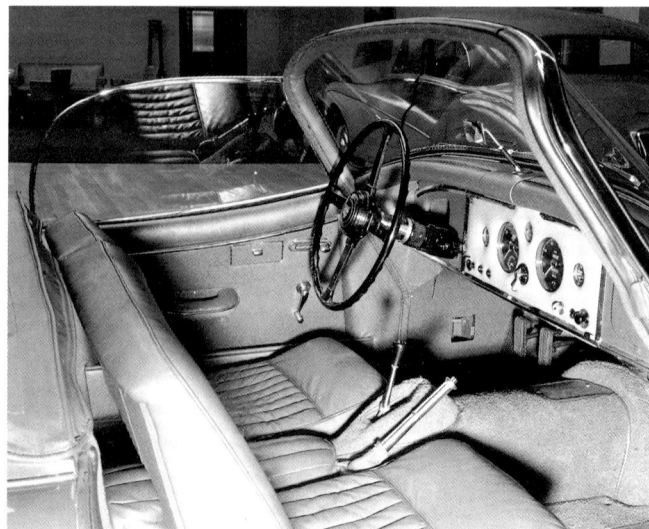

Just for interest, this seems to be the actual photo that the brochure illustration was based on. (JDHT)

Source	Condition	OTS	FHC	DHC
Brochures 1957-59; handbook; *The Motor* 22 May 1957	Dry weight	n/a	26cwt (1322kg)	26.75cwt (1360kg)
The Autocar 24 May 1957	Dry weight	n/a	2900 lb (1318kg)	3000 lb (1364kg)
1960 sales brochure	Dry weight	n/a	27.5cwt (1398kg)	27.5cwt (1398kg)
OTS *The Autocar* 21 Mar 1958	Kerb weight	3190 lb (1447kg)	n/a	n/a
OTS *The Motor* 26 Mar 1958	Dry weight	27.75cwt (1411kg)	n/a	n/a
OTS sales brochure	Kerb weight	28.5cwt (1449kg)	n/a	n/a
Jaguar internal memo	Dry weight	27.5cwt (1398kg)	27.75cwt (1411kg)	27.75cwt (1411kg)
Jaguar internal memo	Kerb weight	28.75cwt (1462kg)	29.5cwt (1500kg)	29.5cwt (1500kg)
RAC recognition form	With fuel	27cwt (1373kg)	27cwt (1373kg)	27.5cwt (1398kg)
Ditto, for automatic	With fuel	27.5cwt (1398kg)	29cwt (1475kg)	29cwt (1475kg)
FIA homologation form	With water and oil, less fuel	3.8: 1400kg 3.8 S:1400kg	3.8 S: 1384kg	3.8 S: 1445 kg

3226 lb (28.8cwt or 1465kg) with 5 gallons (23 litres) of fuel for a fixed-head with overdrive and *The Motor* 29 cwt (3248 lb or 1475kg) for a 3.4 S fixed-head in a similar condition.[29] American road tests quoted 3160-3190 lb (1435-1448kg) kerb weights for the 3.4 S two-seater.[30] I suspect that all models had put on about 2cwt (224 lb or 102kg) compared to the XK 140, giving dry weights for the three body styles of in round figures 28cwt, 29cwt and 30cwt (1424kg, 1475kg and 1525kg). The automatic gearbox would add to these figures, and I expect the S models were in reality also slightly heavier.

The XK 150 fixed-head general arrangement drawing. (JDHT)

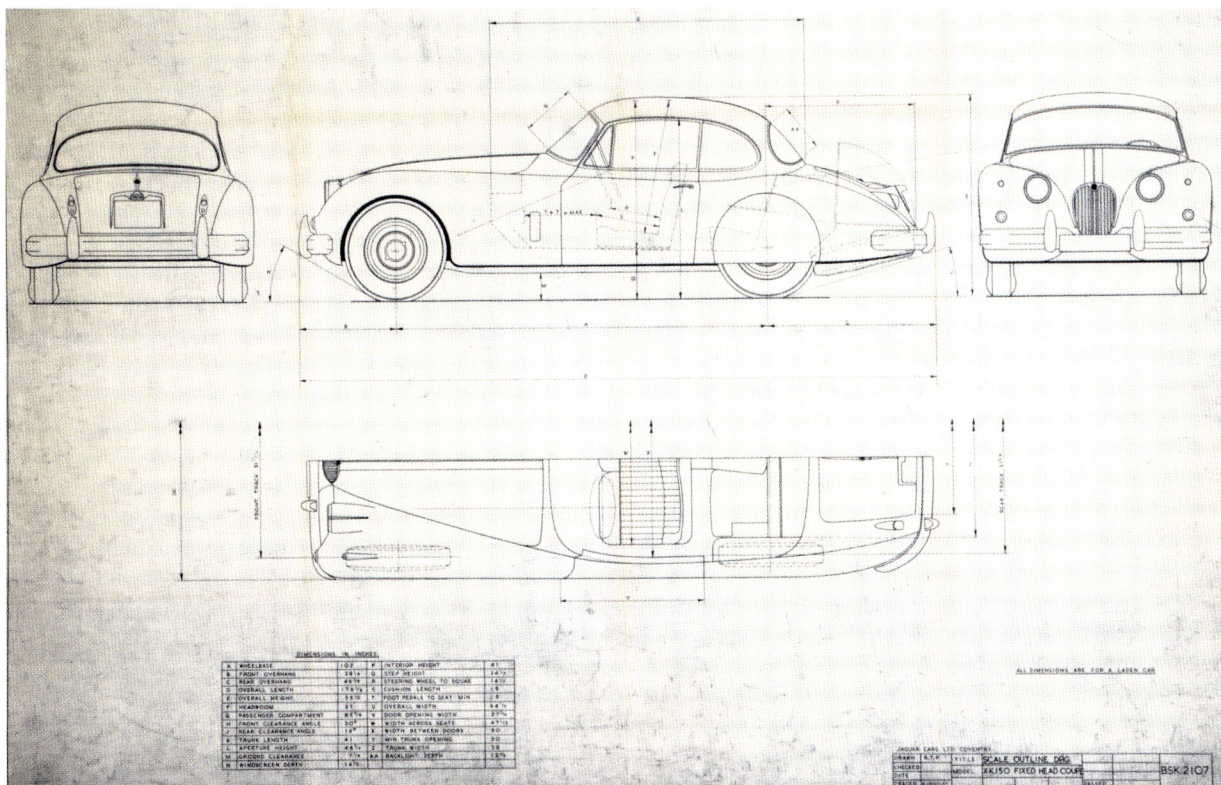

The XK 150 S and 3.8-litre S

The main *raison d'être* for the "S" version of the XK 150 was increased competition in the vital American export market, where by 1957 the "horsepower race" was in full swing. Mid-range family sedans were routinely available with engines up to 7 litres and claimed outputs of over 300bhp (SAE); in the 1958 Mercury range there was even a 400bhp unit, described as "America's most powerful car". More importantly from Jaguar's point of view, the second-generation Chevrolet Corvette was now fitted with a 4.6-litre V8 engine which in its most powerful fuel injection form yielded 290bhp, giving the car an estimated top speed of 200-220km/h (125-135mph). This was now America's only domestic sports car, as the Ford Thunderbird for 1958 had grown into a bigger, heavier four-seater model, but still with an estimated top speed for its most powerful 300bhp version of 190km/h (nearly 120mph).[31] In Europe, the most formidable competitor remained the Mercedes-Benz 300 SL, an example of which Jaguar had on assessment at MIRA in early 1957.[32]

There was as yet plenty of mileage in Jaguar's XK engine, but the 210bhp from the normal 3.4-litre unit of the XK 150 began to look less impressive against the American competition, although road tests of a 3.4-litre non-S fixed-head with overdrive measured a top speed of around 125mph (201km/h) – which was slower

The complete S engine with three carburettors, first introduced in 3.4-litre form in the spring of 1958. (JDHT)

than the XK 140, even if acceleration was improved, thanks to the better torque characteristics of the engine.[33] Already in early 1957, Claude Baily had compiled an outline specification for two different three-carburettor versions, both with the straight-port cylinder head. One had H6 carburettors, the other had HD8 carburettors and a 9:1 compression ratio, and this became the eventual production specification.[34]

In June 1957, Peter Whitehead wrote to "Lofty" England enquiring about having a car specially prepared for him and his brother Graham to enter in the Tour de France in September. Peter already had an XK 150 fixed-head on order. The upshot was that this car, chassis S 824021, registered VDU 358, was fitted with engine number V 1001-8 at the end of August 1957. This engine had come from the first left-hand drive fixed-head S 834001 and was now fitted with a prototype S cylinder head, with its part number already then quoted as C.12600, and three SU HD8 carburettors, as well as other modifications.[35]

It has also been claimed that the first prototype fitted with a three-carburettor engine was the fixed-head with cut-away spats (see above) but that this car "had an accident shortly after being put on the road and in December 1957 was fitted with a new body."[36] I have not been able to identify this car but it may have been S 834001. Another car with a claim to being an S prototype is the left-hand drive drophead S 837003 DN built in May 1957 and registered WWK 468 which was rebuilt with an S engine and an open two-seater body, and appeared in this form at the Guild of Motoring Writers' Test Day in 1958.[37] This car still exists.

In March 1958, when Jaguar launched the delayed open two-seater version (see above), together with this there was the production 3.4-litre S model with a quoted 250bhp. The so-called "straight port" type cylinder head had less curved inlet ports than the normal head, and a new inlet manifold with three SU HD8 2in carburettors, drawing air through a common air box with three wire-mesh filters, later replaced by a single paper element. The cylinder head was finished in a gold colour. It was not, however, the "35/40" or wide-angle head from the later D-type, despite what was said in one American magazine.[38] Pistons with the 9:1 compression ratio were standard – a few cars were in fact supplied with 8:1 – as were Cham-

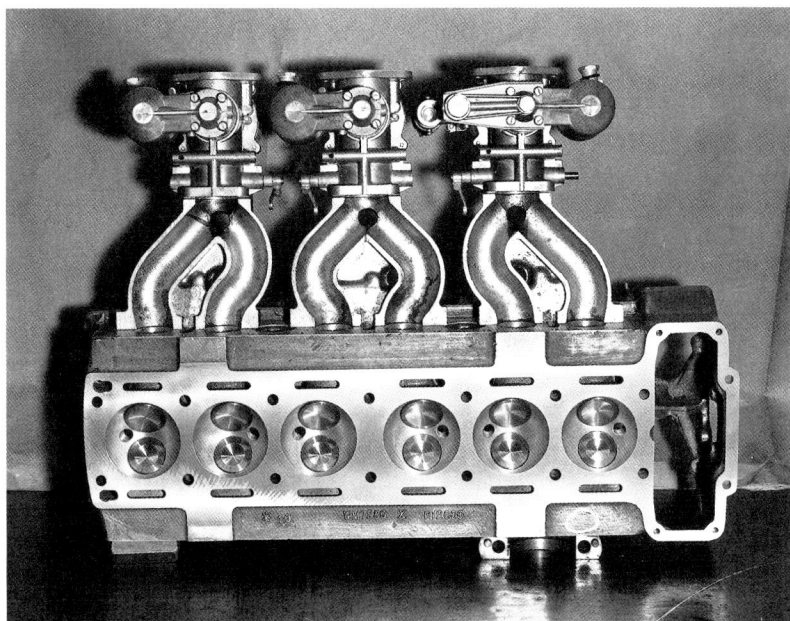

This is the 3.4 S cylinder head with the mechanical rev counter (part number C 12600, which is cast-in on the right-hand side of the central recess at the bottom of the photo). The inlet ports may have been straighter than on the non-S head, but the inlet manifold tracts, here cut open, were very curvy to be effectively of equal length. (JDHT)

A handy photo showing the three different types of XK 150 pistons together, from left to right flat-top 7:1 (which was rare by now), the normal 8:1 and the high-dome 9:1 for the S model. (JDHT)

These photos were taken for the purpose of the homologation form for the XK 150 S model, showing the cylinder head part number C 14957 – the later type for the electronic rev. counter – and the exhaust and inlet manifolds. (JDHT)

pion N5 spark plugs. Jaguar advised that the higher compression ratio required the use of 98 octane (RON) fuel. Main and big-end bearings were of the lead-bronze type (in March 1959, lead-indium bearings were introduced on the non-S engine).

Twin SU electric fuel pumps were fitted, and the bracket for the second pump was now found on all XK 150 chassis. The only type of transmission offered on the S was manual with the electrically-operated overdrive on fourth gear, with a stronger clutch than on the normal XK 150, and a final drive ratio of 4.09:1. The manually-operated overdrive (discussed above) was only introduced in January 1959. Wire wheels were standard, although a few S cars may have been fitted with disc wheels (see above), and the disc brakes featured quick-change rectangular pads, which were introduced on other XK 150 models in November 1958, and on the new Mark IX model. The only external identifier was the arrowed S found towards the front at the top of each door; even this was in fact not found on the early cars.

Initially, like the two-seater generally, the S was offered only for export. The first two cars, 830073 in Black and 830074 in Cotswold Blue, were built at the beginning of March 1958 and were shipped out for the New York Motor Show, which saw the official debut of the new model. Both of these cars still exist. It then took

This XK 150 S engine was lovingly sectioned as a display unit. The overdrive unit is unaccountably missing. (JDHT)

Here is the sectioned engine in a glass case at the Motor Show, without gearbox, so the missing overdrive did not matter! I think this photo is from the 1960 Show, but this engine seems to have been at several Motor Shows. (JDHT)

headache for American owners and mechanics, and after the 3.8-litre model had been introduced in late 1959 this became the preferred engine in the American market; it may only have had 220bhp but was probably not so very much slower than a 3.4 S. Together with the 3.8, in September 1959 Jaguar also launched an S version with this engine size for which no less than 265bhp was claimed, and which was the fastest of all XKs, with a top speed of 136.3mph (219.4km/h).[39] The 3.8 S was also the most expensive of the range, costing around £2200 in the home market.

It would seem that the 3.8 S model remained somewhat of a special order item. One wonders whether Jaguar felt that the performance of the 3.8 S was at the upper limit of what the chassis could cope with. It is interesting that only 30 3.8 S cars were exported to the USA, all of them fixed-heads or dropheads, while the home market took no less than 196 cars altogether. The *Car Record Books* list a total of 283 cars with the 3.8-litre S engine. One of these was an earlier 3.4 S which was converted with a 3.8 S engine around January 1960, possibly by Jaguar's service department, whereas one of the last cars, a left-hand drive drophead, was converted to right-hand drive and was fitted with a 3.4 engine. Then on the other hand, a left-hand drive fixed-head 3.8 became a right-hand drive 3.8 S, and a few other cars were converted to 3.8 S specification! I have settled for a final figure of 282 3.8 S cars. All of the 3.8 S cars are listed in the appendix of this book, with the most important details from the *Car Record Books*.

In one sense, rather more important than the 3.8 S car was the engine which was bequeathed

some time before regular production got under way, as the next S was 830336 in the last week of April. Until August 1958, all cars produced went to North America, including a few to Canada and Mexico, but the S then also began to filter through to European and other export markets. The first right-hand drive home market car was 820003, built at the beginning of October. The first fixed-head, with LHD, 835897, followed in November, and the RHD version with 824789 in February 1959. The first drophead, again a LHD car, was 837993 at the start of January 1959, while the RHD drophead only appeared with 827336 in April.

During 1958 the 3.4 S accounted for just over one-third of open two-seater sales in the USA (661 of 1817 cars). However, I suspect that the three-carburettor set-up proved somewhat of a

JAGUAR CARS LTD. COVENTRY.
6 CYLINDER. 83M/M BORE × 106 M/M
CAPACITY = 3442 C.C.S.
COMPRESSION RATIO = 8 : 1
XK.3584.

MARK 2 & X 15 .

JAGUAR CARS LTD. COVENTRY.
6 CYLINDER 87M/M BORE × 106M/M
CAPACITY = 3781 C.C.S.
COMPRESSION RATIO = 8 : 1
XK.3024

3·8 LITRE MARK IX.
MARK 2 & XK150.

JAGUAR CARS LTD. COVENTRY.
9 TO I COMPRESSION RATIO
XK.3583

XK 150 S. MODELS.

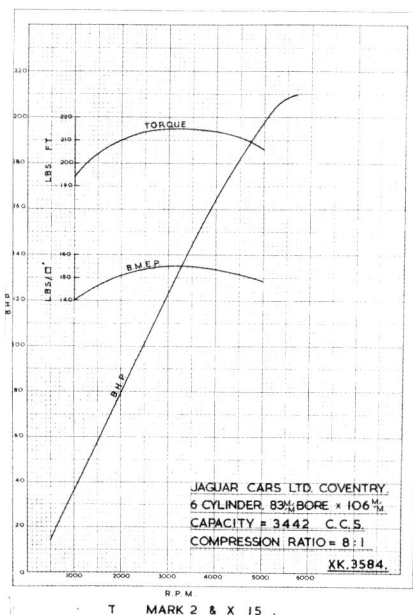

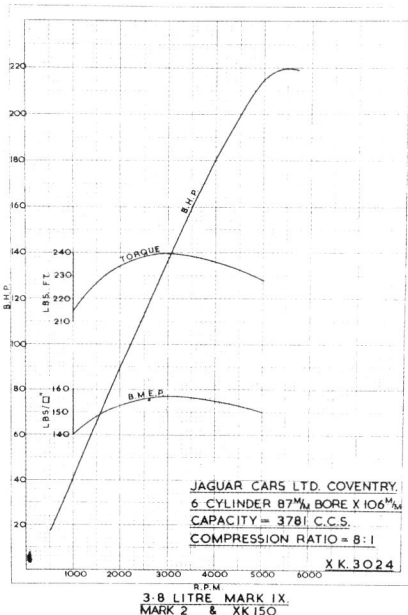

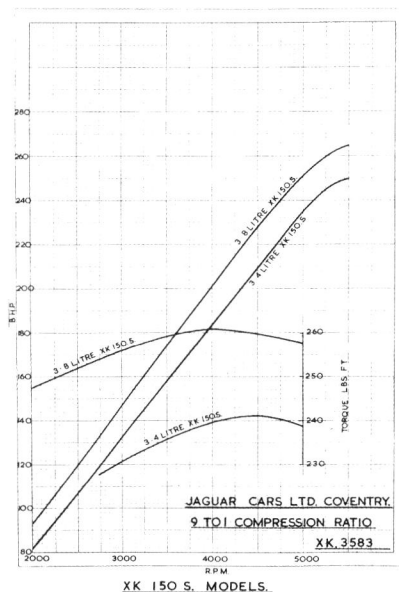

to the E-type which followed in 1961, and for that matter to the Mark X saloon. Two of the E-type prototypes including the first fixed-head 885001 (9600 HP) were fitted with XK 150 3.8-litre S engines.

Production figures of the different versions of the XK 150 were as follows:

These are the comparative power curves for different XK 150 engines. The 3.4-litre engine had 210bhp while the 3.8-litre devloped 220bhp, and the two S engines were even more powerful with 250bhp and 265bhp respectively – if you believe Jaguar's figures. All the power curves peaked at around 5500rpm. (JDHT)

	OTS RHD	OTS LHD	FHC RHD	FHC LHD	DHC RHD	DHC LHD	Total
3.4	23	1278	1074	2375	501	1389	6640
3.4 S	44	846	86	108	37	68	1189
3.8	2	36	94	564	56	533	1285
3.8 S	24	14	115	41	69	19	282
Total	93	2174	1369	3088*	663	2009*	9396*

NB Figures include the nine chassis only deliveries (two FHC RHD, seven FHC LHD).
*after subtraction of late cars converted to RHD, including 1 FHC LHD and 7 DHC LHD,
of which one 3.8 S DHC LHD became a 3.4 DHC RHD.

With the plethora of models which gradually became available between 1957 and 1959, the pricing structure of the XK 150 range became quite complicated. At launch, the XK 150s were £50-60 more expensive than the cars they replaced, comparing the SE models, so customers got the disc brakes for this extra amount. It is interesting that the two-seater and the fixed-head now cost the same. Jaguar managed to keep the factory prices at the same level from 1957 to 1960-

61, but the rate of Purchase Tax was reduced from 60 to 50 per cent in 1959. Disregarding the probably fictitious 3.4-litre "standard" model (which was quoted in price lists to the end of production), the XK 150 price range in 1959-60 was from £1831 to £2204. At that time a Mark IX saloon with automatic gearbox cost £2043, while in 1961 the E-types were introduced at £2098 for the two-seater and £2197 for the fixed-head.

Of the extras, the overdrive was listed at £45

Body style	Model	Basic price	Purchase Tax to Apr 1959	Total to Apr 1959	Purchase Tax from Apr 1959	Total from Apr 1959
OTS	3.4 "Standard"	£1175.0.0	£588.17.0	£1763.17.0	£490.14.2	£1665.14.2
	3.4 "SE"	£1292.0.0	£647.7.0	£1939.7.0	£539.9.2	£1831.9.2
	3.4 S incl. o/d	£1457.0.0	£729.17.0	£2186.17.0	£608.4.2	£2065.4.2
FHC	3.4 "Standard"	£1175.0.0	£588.17.0	£1763.17.0	£490.14.2	£1665.14.2
	3.4 "SE"	£1292.0.0	£647.7.0	£1939.7.0	£539.9.2	£1831.9.2
	3.4 S incl. o/d	£1457.0.0			£608.4.2	£2065.4.2
DHC	3.4 "Standard"	£1195.0.0	£598.17.0	£1793.17.0	£499.0.10	£1694.0.10
	3.4 "SE"	£1312.0.0	£657.7.0	£1969.7.0	£547.15.0	£1859.15.10
	3.4 S incl. o/d	£1477.0.0.			£616.10.10	£2093.10.10
OTS	3.8	£1370.0.0			£571.19.2	£1941.19.2
	3.8 S incl. o/d	£1535.0.0			£640.14.2	£2175.14.2
FHC	3.8	£1370.0.0			£571.19.2	£1941.19.2
	3.8 S incl. o/d	£1535.0.0			£640.14.2	£2175.14.2
DHC	3.8	£1390.0.0			£580.5.10	£1970.5.10
	3.8 S incl. o/d	£1555.0.0			£649.0.10	£2204.0.10

(standard on S models), automatic transmission at £128 (not available on S models) and the Powr-Lok differential at £30 on the 3.4-litre S cars; it was standard on all 3.8-litre models. All of these are basic prices and also attracted Purchase Tax. Other extras listed in the *Spare Parts Catalogue* included various radios and associated parts, bucket seats, a sump guard, a pair of wing mirrors, a set of four rimbellishers (for the disc wheels), racing tyres or whitewall tyres, anti-glare windscreen glass (of the tinted Sundym type), and the Jaguar bonnet mascot.[40]

Some of these items were also available as "accessories" as were a fire extinguisher, a passenger grab rail, fog lamps, a badge bar, the windscreen washer and a luggage carrier. Also listed were a wood-rim steering wheel, a Weathershields sliding sunroof for the fixed-head, instrument panel in leather to match the interior, a tonneau cover for the drophead coupé

(it was standard on the two-seater), Le Mans type headlamps, a pair of fitted suitcases, two-tone colour scheme (never found in practice; see the appendix on colour schemes), and a radiator blind.[41] The advantage of fitting accessories after you had bought the car, rather than having optional extras factory-fitted, is that you did not then have to pay Purchase Tax on such items. Many of the items listed were rare. A few cars are known to have had a white steering wheel.

In the USA, the fixed-head was quoted at $4530 (without extras) at launch, and prices for the two-seater were $4660 (SE model, with overdrive) and $5020 (S model, ditto), although this seems to have increased almost immediately to $5095 or even $5150; the latter figure included the limited-slip differential which was then said to be standard on the S model in the USA.[42]

1. Jaguar *Service Bulletin* no.215, May 1957; first edition of the XK 150 sales brochure, May 1957
2. *The Motor* 22 May 1957; *Autosport* 24 May 1957; *The Autocar* 24 May 1957
3. *The Autocar* 21 Feb 1958, 21 Mar 1958; *The Motor* 26 Mar 1958
4. Skilleter *Norman Dewis* p.251
5. Supplementary information courtesy of John Elmgreen
6. Elmgreen & McGrath *The Jaguar XK in Australia* p.135
7. *Ibid.* p.126
8. Jeremy Wade in *XK Gazette* no.5 Feb 1998; *XK Gazette* no.70 Jul 2003; information courtesy of Terry McGrath
9. Barry Dixon in *XK Gazette* no.71 Aug 2003; *Jaguar Enthusiast* Jun 2003
10. *Jaguar World* vol.9 no.5 May/Jun 1997
11. Chris Harvey "Carbohydrate Cat" in *Car* Dec 1983; information courtesy of David Bentley
12. Boyce *Jaguar XK Series* p.66; Elmgreen & McGrath p.135; Skilleter *The Jaguar XKs A Collector's Guide* p.66; Skilleter "Carnival Queen" in *Jaguar World* May 2007
13. Information on 9494 BP courtesy of owner, and *XK Gazette* Jan 2008; for the car photographed by Jaguar with cut-away spats, see Skilleter *Collector's Guide* p.75; Skilleter *Dewis* p.252; *Jaguar World* vol.9 no.5 May/Jun 1997; this is also claimed to have been a prototype for the three-carburettor S model but this can not be verified and the car has defied identification, unless it is S 834001
14. *XK Gazette* no.5 Feb 1998; there have been a couple of other claimed sightings
15. Skilleter *Collector's Guide* p.127
16. For a succinct outline of the history of disc brakes from Lanchester (1902) onwards, see Newcomb & Spurr *A Technical History of the Motor Car* pp.349-50; for HRG see Dussek *H.R.G. The Sportsman's Ideal* p.141ff
17. Porter *Original Jaguar XK* pp.127-28 and other sources
18. Jaguar *Service Bulletin* no.235, Jan 1958
19. Jaguar *Service Bulletin* no.263, Apr 1959
20. Based in part on Viart *Jaguar XK – Le Grand Livre* pp.74, 76-77, 330-31 *et passim*; also Porter p.94
21. Jaguar *Service Bulletin* no.214, May 1957
22. Some experts, including Terry McGrath, believe that only small numbers of S models had the mechanical overdrive
23. Jaguar *Service Bulletin* no.233, Nov 1957
24. Jaguar *Service Bulletin* no.243, Apr 1958
25. *The Autocar* 21 Mar 1958; *The Motor* 26 Mar 1958
26. Jaguar XK *Spare Parts Catalogue* vol.2 "Body Items" pp.53, 142, 225
27. *Road & Track* Sep 1958; oddly enough, mentioned in a road test of an open two-seater which never had wood trim
28. Carpet colours listed in *Spares Bulletin* P.27 Nov 1960
29. *The Autocar* 21 Feb 1958; *The Motor* 19 Aug 1959
30. *Sports Car Illustrated* Aug 1958; *Road & Track* Sep 1958
31. Data for American cars from *Automobil Revue Katalog-Nummer* 1958
32. Skilleter *Dewis* pp.252-54
33. E.g. *The Autocar* 21 Feb 1958 and other sources; see also chapter 5
34. Skilleter *Dewis* p.251
35. Information courtesy of Terry McGrath who now owns this car; see also chapters 7 and 9
36. Skilleter *Dewis* p.252; *Jaguar World* vol.9 no.5 May/Jun 1997
37. *Autosport* 7 Nov 1958; see also chapter 5
38. *Speed Age*, Oct 1958
39. John Bolster road testing a 3.8 S fixed head, YHP 791 in *Autosport* 17 Jun 1960
40. Vol.1, pp.434-38
41. Porter pp.136-37
42. *Road & Track* Nov 1957 Sep 1958; *Sports Car Illustrated* Aug 1958

Chapter Four

Production and sales

The 1950s were a period of tremendous growth and expansion for Jaguar. After having completed the move to the Browns Lane factory in late 1952, in 1953 for the first time calendar year production passed the magical 10,000 barrier. Thanks to the introduction of the new compact sports saloons – the 2.4 and 3.4-litre, followed by the Mark II in 1959 – in 1960 more than 23,000 cars were made, of which over 17,500 were Mark IIs. Although outside the scope of the present volume, it must then be recorded that Jaguar production stag-

nated for much of the 1960s, until given a similar lift by the introduction of the XJ6 in 1968.

Neither the XK 140 nor the XK 150 would match the total production figure of 12,059 cars reached by the XK 120, but since the XK 120 had been in production effectively for just over five years and the production periods for its successors were shorter – little more than two years for the XK 140, three-and-half years for the XK 150 – the later models in their best years would both comfortably beat the highest annual figure achieved by the XK 120 of 3420 cars in

1953. No less than 4738 XK 140s were made in 1955, and in 1958 4539 XK 150s were made. The table below sets out the annual production figures for each type of body, and is split in right-hand drive and left-hand drive cars.

In May 1957, when the factory had been rebuilt and after the fire, a series of photos were taken of the production lines. Saloons dominate but there are also quite a few XK 150s, then just going into production. (JDHT)

Total production by body type and year:

	XK 140					XK 150				
	1954	1955	1956	1957	Total	1957	1958	1959	1960	Total
OTS RHD	8	54	12	0	**74**	0	19	47	27	**93**
OTS LHD	617	1370	1134	161	**3282**	1	1922	190	61	**2174**
FHC RHD	6	585	252	0	**843**	166	578	382	243	**1369**
FHC LHD	3	1265	693	5	**1966**	984	979	690	435*	**3088***
DHC RHD	6	336	137	1	**480**	1	271	233	158	**663**
DHC LHD	111	1128	1065	7	**2311**	213	770	629	397**	**2009***
Total by year	751	4738	3293	174	**8956**	1365	4539	2171	1321	**9396**

*after conversion of seven cars to RHD with new chassis numbers

**after conversion of one car to RHD with a new chassis number

During the production period of the XK 140 and XK 150 from 1954 to 1960, the biggest threat to Jaguar production was the factory fire of 12 February 1957 which devastated large parts of the Browns Lane complex and resulted in the loss of over 200 cars, including some D-type and XK-SS cars. Amazingly, within days a truncated production line was up and running, and within a few months the worst affected parts of the factory had been completely rebuilt.[1] Nothing daunted, two weeks after the fire Jaguar launched the new 3.4-litre saloon, and followed this with the XK 150 in May 1957. Since the fire had occurred in the lull between the end of XK 140 production and the start of the XK 150, only eight XK 140s awaiting despatch were destroyed, although the fire was blamed for the delay in the introduction of the XK 150 open two-seater which appeared only in March 1958, when it was launched to the public, together with the S version, typically at the New York Motor Show – reflecting the importance of

An XK 150 progressing down the chassis line. Scrawled on the front cross member are some letters including "LOD" which I take it indicates that this left-hand drive car will be fitted with an overdrive gearbox. (JDHT)

Undoubtedly a posed shot, but the XK bodies did need a lot of hand finishing. And then the lead-loaders would get busy afterwards. (JDHT)

Here an XK 150 fixed-head is going through the paint tunnel which was installed when Jaguar moved to Browns Lane in 1952. (JDHT)

These chaps are trimming the top windscreen frame of a drophead. The hood frame is attached, but the hood has yet to be made around it. We can also see the actual back panel for the instruments, before the dashboard and outer instrument panel are fitted. (JDHT)

this market to Jaguar, to the XK and above all to this body style.

The export business, especially to the USA, was now very much Jaguar's game. The reason given for William Lyons being knighted in the New Year's Honours List in 1956, was his services to exports.[2] In 1958, in a series of articles commissioned for a special issue of *The Motor* magazine under the heading "Pipelines to Prosperity", Sir William (or may be his PR man "Bill" Rankin!) wrote a piece about Jaguar in America.[3]

Before the Second World War, export sales had been of little relevance to Jaguar, and had only amounted to 7.4 per cent of all sales from 1931 to 1940. Under Government direction this changed radically after 1945, and in the best season, 1951-52, 89 per cent of all Jaguars were exported. This level could not be maintained and from 1953 to 1960 export sales varied between 50 and 56 per cent of total production. Combined with the steady increase in overall production and the popularity of the new

The drophead hoods at least were built up in situ on the cars, and were liberally padded with horsehair, before the final outer mohair covering was fitted. (JDHT)

It seems to be the same car as in the previous photo, and the same blokes still trimming the windscreen frame, yet the car behind has a fully-trimmed hood. Behind that there is fixed-head model. (JDHT)

saloon models, this meant that a lot more Jaguars became available in the home market, and UK sales rose from just 1000 in 1951-52 to more than 10,000 in 1958-59.[4]

Once the XK 120 had established itself in the USA, this became Jaguar's best export market and remained so. From 1950 to 1953 more Jaguars were sold in the USA than in the home market. However, throughout the 1950s and 1960s Jaguar's sports cars sold much better in the USA than their saloons. Before the XJ6 the

only Jaguar saloons selling consistently in significant volumes in the USA were the 3.4-litre and the Mark II 3.8, between 1957 and 1962.[5] Still, the early success of the XK 120 meant that in 1953 around 4000 Jaguars were sold in the USA and in 1959 this figure rose to a peak of nearly 6000 American sales.[6]

The American market was a glittering prize for the British motor industry, but it was also a rough ride. The early 1950s sales of small British family cars were gradually eclipsed by the rise

The XK 150 trim line, mostly it seems with fixed-heads. (JDHT)

Intense peering under the bonnet of this XK 150; presumably final adjustment of the carburettors? (JDHT)

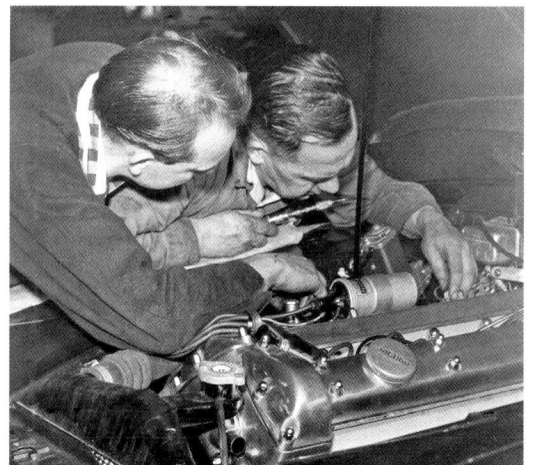

I am not quite sure what is going on here but I feel it is likely to be a repair job to an accident-damaged car in the Service Department, since I am sure the body was all welded up before the windscreen and dashboard were fitted; but at least we get to see the detail of the door pillar construction of this XK 140 fixed-head. (JDHT)

Not all XK 150s were tested in the water splash at the MIRA test track at Nuneaton. It may be Jaguar chief tester Norman Dewis in the passenger seat, for a change. (JDHT)

of the German Volkswagen from 1954 onwards, although British sales generally held up very well, in part thanks to increasing numbers of sports cars. In 1959 the USA took 209,333 British cars but, due to a recession in the USA and because of the launch of the domestic compact cars, British exports fell to 132,492 cars in 1960 and a near-disastrous 30,519 cars in 1961 – and would never recover to their pre-1960 level.[7] The only two significant makes of imported cars to survive the 1960-61 set-back relatively unscathed were Volkswagen, and Jaguar; Jaguar's lowest American sales figure of this period was around 4000 cars in 1961.

As far as the XKs are concerned, in total the USA had taken 9096 of the 12,059 XK 120s made, or just over 75 per cent. The actual figures for the XK 140 and XK 150 were lower, but the percentage of XK 140s exported to the USA at nearly 76 per cent was slightly better than even for the XK 120 and only dropped for the XK 150, to 63.5 per cent. The best year for the XK 150 in the USA was 1958, as exports to this market fell by two-thirds in 1959 and were lower still in 1960. There is evidence in the *Car Record Books* – which occasionally quote delivery dates to retail customers – that some of the later XK150s took a long time to sell out of American showrooms. As can be seen, the reduced demand for the XK in the USA had a clear impact on overall production.

Actual exports to the USA by body type and year:

	XK 140					**XK 150**				
	1954	**1955**	**1956**	**1957**	**Total**	**1957**	**1958**	**1959**	**1960**	**Total**
OTS RHD	0	0	0	0	**0**	0	0	0	0	**0**
OTS LHD	601	1293	1087	140	**3121**	1	1817	101	27	**1946**
FHC RHD	0	2	1	0	**3**	0	1	0	0	**1**
FHC LHD	2	1075	548	3	**1628**	912	702	465	327	**2406**
DHC RHD	0	2	0	0	**2**	0	0	0	0	**0**
DHC LHD	104	964	966	7	**2041**	197	628	487	302	**1614**
Total by year	**707**	**3336**	**2602**	**150**	**6795**	**1110**	**3148**	**1053**	**656**	**5967**

This XK 140 two-seater has been crated for export, with bumpers and windscreen probably stowed inside the car under the tonneau cover. There is unfortunately no indication of its intended destination. (JDHT)

This is not a recent barn-find but a shed full of new XK 140 two-seaters awaiting export, probably to the USA. Clearly the car in the foreground has not only whitewall tyres but chrome wire wheels. They are probably missing headlamps, but most have fog lamps. (JDHT)

By contrast, an un-crated XK 140 waiting on the dockside to be loaded on board ship, together with a Mark VIIM. Both have their bumpers and presumably other chrome parts covered for protection. (JDHT)

Of the different body styles, the open two-seater version was by now virtually a special for the USA. It was the best-selling XK 140 in this market, and the come-back of a two-seater in the XK 150 range in 1958 led to a substantial increase in sales of the range overall, but it was a short-lived fillip. Towards the end of production, American customers bought more of the coupé models, a trend witnessed in other markets already for the XK 120 in 1953-54.

It was during the XK 140 production period that Jaguar set up a subsidiary company in New York. The immediate reason for doing this was

the company's unhappiness with their previous East Coast importer, Max Hoffman.[8] Hoffman lost the franchise at the end of 1955 and from then on had no further involvement with Jaguar. In the following year the West Coast importer, Charles Hornburg of Los Angeles, lost the importer status but the company remains an important Jaguar distributor to this day.[9] From then on and until the merger with BMC and Leyland, Jaguar's distribution in the USA was handled by Jaguar Cars Inc under the direction of Jo Eerdmans, with a very traditionally-decorated showroom on East 57th Street in New

From left to right Johannes Eerdmans who ran Jaguar cars in New York; William Lyons; and Bruce Cunningham, the racing team owner whose business interests included a Jaguar dealership. (JDHT)

In 1958, Lyons paid another visit to New York, this time with the whole family – here he is, with Lady Lyons on the right, and Pat and Mary, by the XK 150 "Roadster" at the motor show. The young lady in the centre must have been one of the stand personnel! (JDHT)

The extraordinarily ornate Jaguar showroom in New York, 1955. (JDHT)

cars, so even in the pre-Leyland days it was quite normal to find Jaguars sharing showrooms with Austin-Healey, MG or Triumph. It is incidentally amusing to note that between 1959 and 1961, Jaguar Cars Inc handled Leyland commercial vehicles in the USA, with no great success, while on the other hand Eerdmans and Sir William Lyons turned down an opportunity to sell Rover cars and Land Rovers.[11]

The home market was the second-biggest market for the XKs. Here, Henlys in London was the biggest distributor by far. Their association with Lyons and Jaguar went back to the early Austin Swallow days when they signed up as the first distributor for Swallow-bodied cars, and in return got a territory comprising all of England south-east of a line drawn from the Bristol Channel to the Wash, as well as a higher discount than other distributors. "Bertie" Henly became a close personal friend of William Lyons. In addition, Henlys had a branch in Manchester which was an important Jaguar distributorship in its own right. Henlys in London handled 631 XK 140s and 1068 XK 150s, the Manchester branch respectively 90 and 136 cars, while Henlys in London also delivered 32 XK 140s and 77 XK 150s of those cars which were sold tax-free for Personal Export. If you lived anywhere from Cornwall to Norfolk and bought a Jaguar from a local dealership, a small commission would go into the coffers of Henlys. Well over half of all home market XKs were consigned to Henlys.

York City which had originally been built for the pre-war Rolls-Royce importer, JS Inskip, while the offices were on the twelfth floor above. Jaguar put in place resident service engineers sent out from the factory, established a school for mechanics and had a 15,000 square feet (1350 square metres) parts depot in Long Island.[10]

For logistical reasons, cars continued to be shipped into different Ports of Entry on both coasts. Most of Jaguar's retail outlets in the USA still sold a mixture of imported brands, but many tended to concentrate on British sports

Tinker, tailor, soldier, sailor... or rather pilot, doctor etc: An American 1956 advertisement for the Jaguar range. (JDHT)

their home distributors handled Standard-Triumph products as well, including PJ Evans in Birmingham and SH Newsome in Coventry, a connection going back to the early S.S. days. Also quite common were agencies for Nuffield (Morris etc) and Rover; for instance, Appleyard in Leeds handled the Nuffield marques, while Henlys sold Rovers. Some Jaguar distributors sold Vauxhalls but there were far fewer shared outlets with Austin, while Rootes and Ford tended to have separate dealer networks; Ford indeed had been a pioneer of appointing dealers who agreed to handle only their products.[12] The only Jaguar distributor which handled a major foreign brand was Ritchie in Glasgow with Fiat, and Ritchie's long-standing Fiat connection is thought to have been the catalyst for the Swallow-bodied Fiat 509A in 1929.[13]

Below the first tier of distributors who enjoyed the maximum discount on factory prices, there were the various tiers of retail dealers who obtained cars through distributors at lower rates of discount, including quite a few motor traders who would proclaim "any make of new car supplied." The whole dealer network would only undergo radical change during the British Leyland period when it was pruned and rationalised, the distinction between distributors and dealers was removed, and everybody ordered cars directly from the manufacturer at identical discounts. BL dealerships became fewer and bigger, and some took on the entire range from Mini to Daimler, but stopped selling other manufacturers' products. Only from 1984 onwards did the present-day exclusive Jaguar dealerships begin to emerge.

Home market conditions improved greatly during the early years of the XK. In 1952, the Government gradually abolished both the home market quota system and the "Covenant" scheme which prohibited the re-sale of new cars less than two years old. New car sales in the UK shot up to (in round figures) 300,000 in 1953, 400,000 in 1954 and topped 500,000 in 1955.[14] Waiting lists disappeared, and used car values tumbled. From then on, the only regulatory mechanisms imposed by the Government were occasional adjustments to the rate of Purchase Tax and, from 1952 onwards, to the minimum percentage required for the deposit when a car was bought on Hire Purchase.[15]

By 1955, the British home market therefore

Apart from Henlys there were two dozen distributors in the British Isles, including two in Scotland, one each in Wales, Northern Ireland, the Isle of Man and the Channel Islands, and the rest in England, from the Midlands northwards. Most of these had been Jaguar agents since pre-war days, and remained into the Leyland years. The big dealer chains were still in the future, but Henlys had many retail outlets and garages in the South of England, while Rossleigh of Edinburgh had branches elsewhere in Scotland, and in Newcastle upon Tyne.

In those days virtually all motor traders, whether distributors or merely retail dealers, had multiple agencies. In the 1950s there was no such thing as a "solus" dealership, least of all for a small company such as Jaguar. Nearly half of

Contemporary American publicity for the XK 150 two-seater. The poor animal on the right seems reluctant to get dragged into the picture. (JDHT)

had returned to a state of normality not experienced since 1939. Jaguar clearly benefited from these more relaxed conditions. The best year for XK 120 home sales had been 1953 with 318 cars but this was to be exceeded by the XK 140 in 1955 with no less than 852 cars, and by the XK 150 from 1958 to 1960. The figures probably demonstrate that in 1955 and later, any UK motorist who wanted an XK and could afford it, could buy one easily enough. In the home market, the most popular body style was the fixed-head coupé which outsold even the drophead by a factor of nearly two to one, and the open two-seater was almost an irrelevance, as will be clear from the following table. The detailed figures for sales by model and distributor may be found in the following section.

Looking finally at other export markets,

Home market sales by body type and year:

	XK 140					XK 150				
	1954	1955	1956	1957	Total	1957	1958	1959	1960	Total
OTS RHD	8	31	6	0	**45**	0	14	41	22	**77**
OTS LHD	0	1**	0	0	**1**	0	0	0	0	**0**
FHC RHD	6	514	218	0	**738**	138	504	345	214	**1201**
FHC LHD	1*	0	0	0	**1**	1*	0	0	0	**1**
DHC RHD	6	305	117	0	**428**	1	249	220	149	**619**
DHC LHD	0	1**	0	0	**1**	1*	0	0	0	**1**
Total by year	**21**	**852**	**341**	**0**	**1214**	**141**	**767**	**606**	**385**	**1899**

* To Jaguar Experimental Department

** Converted to RHD and sold second-hand

The Jaguar stand at the 1955 Geneva Motor Show, with fixed-head and drophead versions of the XK 140 on display. The stand here was organised by the local importer, Marcel Fleury of Grand Garage Place de la Claparede. (JDHT)

Canada was the most important and took a total of 562 XK 140s and XK 150s. During the 1950s, the Jaguar organisation in Canada underwent a shake-up similar to that which had taken place in the USA, and Jaguar established its own subsidiary company in Montreal which took over from the independent importers spread across the country. A parallel development could be observed in Australia where gradually, Bryson of Melbourne and Sydney handled more sales at the expense of distributors elsewhere, but with a total of 111 XK 140 and XK 150 cars, Australia was now a much less significant market for Jaguar than it had been before the first tariff barriers came down in 1952, while in 1956 further restrictions on imported cars were introduced.

Other good markets, all in Europe, were France with a total of 345 cars, Germany with 214 cars, Belgium with 163 cars, and Switzerland with 109 cars. Apart from Canada and Australia, the traditional British Empire or Commonwealth markets barely registered; New Zealand had currency difficulties, South Africa import restrictions, and the best other market in this category was Malaya still including Singapore with a mere thirty-four cars. The gradual process of giving independence to former colonies had obvious implications for sales of British cars in these emerging nation states. Oil-rich Venezuela was now the best market for Jaguars in South America, taking forty-five cars.

The number of tax-free Personal Export Delivery cars sold in the UK was no less than 240, many of them to US service personnel stationed here. There was a special UK Exchange Service

scheme operated through the US Forces Post Exchange which facilitated sales to US service personnel who paid for their cars in US Dollars[16] and this accounted for forty-six cars, while many cars were sold through Henlys (see above), through other UK distributors, or by Jaguar direct. At least 149 XK 140 and 473 XK 150 PED cars were originally registered by Jaguar in Coventry but they included many cars which had been ordered through the overseas agents.[17] Sales to US service personnel stationed abroad must also have accounted for substantial numbers of the sales recorded as exports to France, Germany, Italy and Japan, apart from other perhaps less expected locations.

As was the case for home market distributors, many importers had other agencies apart from Jaguar, and the one that must really have riled Sir William Lyons was Charles Delecroix in Paris who also sold Mercedes-Benz which accounts for the frequent proximity of Jaguar and Mercedes-Benz stands at the Paris Motor Show.[18] The main business for Emil Frey in Zürich was importing Austins, while Fattori & Montani in Rome handled the Nuffield range and Sommer in Denmark had a Volvo dealership. No doubt there were many similar examples. The following table includes the most important of foreign markets, and adds the US and UK sales to arrive at the total sales. It will be noticed that some markets such as Switzerland took a mixture of left-hand and right-hand drive cars, while Japan and Sweden who both drove on the left, took mostly LHD cars.

Similarly, at the Amsterdam Motor Show the local importer, Messrs. Lagerwij's of Den Haag, was in charge. I think this must be the 1958 show. Two XK 150s on the Jaguar stand was more than you ever got at Earls Court! (JDHT)

Important export markets, all body styles combined:

	XK 140 RHD	XK 140 LHD	Total	XK 150 RHD	XK 150 LHD	Total	Grand total
Algeria	0	5	5	0	15	15	20
Australia	59	1	60	50	1	51	111
Belgium	2	53	55	3	105	108	163
Canada	2	202	204	0	358	358	562
France	10	151	161	3	181	184	345
Germany	2	113	115	1	98	99	214
Holland	1	15	16	1	22	23	39
Hong Kong	7	0	7	12	0	12	19
Italy	1	8	9	1	37	38	47
Japan incl. Okinawa	2	7	9	2	36	38	47
Lebanon	1	12	13	0	24	24	37
Malaya	15	0	15	17	2	19	34
Morocco (combined)	0	22	22	0	30	30	52
New Zealand	11	0	11	18	0	18	29
PED in UK	18	62	80	30	130	160	240
Portugal	0	6	6	0	12	12	18
Rhodesia	15	1	16	8	1	9	25
South Africa	1	0	1	22	2	24	25
Sweden	2	7	9	3	5	8	17
Switzerland	8	12	20	9	80	89	109
USA	5	6790	6795	1	5966	5967	12,762
Venezuela	0	21	21	0	24	24	45
All other export sales	23	59	82	47	137	184	267
Misc. (scrapped or not known, see below)	1	9	10	0	3	3	13
Total	186	7556	7742	228	7269	7497	15,240
Plus home sales	1211	3	1214	1897	2	1899	3112
GRAND TOTAL	**1397**	**7559**	**8956**	**2125**	**7271**	**9396**	**18,352**

The following two tables give an overview of the split between the home market, the USA and all the other export markets combined, by respectively type of body and calendar year. From these figures it becomes clear how much of a "US special" the open two-seater was, and also how much more American sales declined in 1959-60 than sales in the home and other markets.

Comparison between sales to different markets by body type for all years:

	Home	Percentage	USA	Percentage	Other export	Percentage	Misc.	Total
XK 140 OTS	46	1.37%	3121	93.00%	181	5.39%	8	**3356**
XK 140 FHC	739	26.31%	1631	58.06%	438	15.59%	1	**2809**
XK 140 DHC	429	15.37%	2043	73.20%	318	11.39%	1	**2791**
All XK 140	1214	13.56%	6795	75.87%	937	10.46%	10	**8956**
XK 150 OTS	77	3.40%	1946	85.84%	243	10.72%	1	**2267**
XK 150 FHC	1202	26.97%	2407	54.00%	846	18.98%	2	**4457**
XK 150 DHC	620	23.20%	1614	60.40%	438	16.39%		**2672**
All XK 150	1899	20.21%	5967	63.51%	1527	16.25%	3	**9396**

Comparison between sales to different markets by year for all body types:

	Home	Percentage	USA	Percentage	Other export	Percentage	Misc.	Total
XK 140 1954	21	2.80%	707	94.14%	23	3.06%		**751**
XK 140 1955	852	17.98%	3336	70.41%	549	11.59%	1	**4738**
XK 140 1956	341	10.36%	2602	79.02%	349	10.60%	1	**3293**
XK 140 1957	0	0.00%	150	86.21%	16	13.79%	8	**174**
All XK 140	1214	13.56%	6795	75.87%	937	10.46%	10	**8956**
XK 150 1957	141	10.33%	1110	81.32%	114	8.35%		**1365**
XK 150 1958	767	16.90%	3148	69.35%	621	13.68%	3	**4539**
XK 150 1959	606	27.91%	1053	48.50%	512	23.58%		**2171**
XK 150 1960	385	29.14%	656	49.66%	280	21.20%		**1321**
All XK 150	1899	20.21%	5967	63.51%	1527	16.25%	3	**9396**

The "miscellaneous" cars in the three tables above are accounted for as follows:
Eight XK 140 OTS LHD cars built in January 1957 which were destroyed in the factory fire
One XK 140 DHC LHD S 818129 built in 1955 which was damaged on delivery and scrapped
One XK 140 FHC RHD S 804650 chassis only built in 1956 for which there is no destination in the records
One XK 150 OTS LHD T 831455 DN built in 1958 which was damaged on delivery and scrapped
Two XK 150 FHC LHD S 835203 and S 835381 (chassis only) built in 1958 for which there are no destinations in the records

The figures quoted have been adjusted for cars converted from LHD to RHD as follows:
XK 140 OTS LHD 811101 built in the Experimental Department in 1955 was converted to RHD but kept the same chassis number; it was possibly registered RHP 574 and was sold second-hand to Duncan Hamilton
XK 140 DHC LHD S 817378 built in 1955 was rebuilt with RHD by Jaguar but kept the same chassis number; it was registered RWK 700 and was sold second-hand
Eight late XK 150 cars including seven FHC and one DHC which were all converted from LHD to RHD but were given new chassis numbers and except for one car were sold in the UK:
    S 847039 BW converted to S 825369 BW (3.8 engine)
    S 847041 BW converted to S 825365 DN (3.8 engine)
    S 847042 converted to T 825363 DN (3.8 engine changed to 3.8 S engine)
    S 847048 BW converted to T 825364 DN (3.8 engine changed to 3.8 S engine)
    S 847062 BW converted to S 825367 BW (3.8 engine changed to 3.4 engine)
    S 847067 BW converted to S 825366 DN (3.8 engine changed to 3.4 engine)
    S 847070 BW converted to S 825368 DN (3.8 engine; exported to Hong Kong)
    T 838974 DN converted to S 827663 DN (3.8 S engine changed to 3.4 engine)
Some of these cars also had changes to the transmission.
Three LHD cars have been counted as home sales as they went to Jaguar's experimental department:
XK 140 FHC LHD 814001 chassis only built in 1954
XK 150 FHC LHD S 834001 and DHC LHD S 837003 DN built in 1957

The XK 150 S

In view of the special interest in this model, it is worth giving a similar breakdown of production between the different versions. The first table below gives the split between the two different engines, by year, body style and by RHD/LHD.

Total production:

	3.4 S				3.8 S		
	1958	1959	1960	Total	1959	1960	Total
OTS RHD	9	35	0	**44**	7	17	**24**
OTS LHD	711	134	1	**846**	2	12	**14**
FHC RHD	0	71	15	**86**	32	83	**115**
FHC LHD	2	99	7	**108**	18	23	**41**
DHC RHD	0	35	2	**37**	12	57	**69**
DHC LHD*	0	66	2	**68**	4	15	**19**
Total by year	**722**	**440**	**27**	**1189**	**75**	**207**	**282**

Several cars were converted from one specification to another, and generally speaking, the above figures are post conversions, as follows:
Non-S cars to either 3.4 S or 3.8 S:
    3.8 OTS RHD S 820073 to 3.8 S
    3.4 DHC RHD T 827370 DN to 3.4 S
    3.4 OTS LHD S 831657 DN to 3.4 S
    3.8 FHC LHD S 847042 to 3.8 S FHC RHD T 825363 DN
    3.8 FHC LHD S 847048 BW to 3.4 S FHC RHD T 825364 DN
3.4 S to 3.8 S:
    3.4 S FHC RHD T 825211 DN to 3.8 S
    3.4 S DHC RHD T 827461 DN to 3.8 S
    3.4 S DHC RHD T 827482 DN to 3.8 S
    3.4 S DHC RHD T 827556 DN to 3.8 S
    3.4 S FHC LHD T 836237 DN to 3.8 S; a later conversion for the owner in Service Department
    3.4 S FHC LHD T 836448 DN to 3.8 S
    3.4 S FHC LHD T 836450 DN to 3.8 S
3.8 S to 3.4 S:
    3.8 S DHC LHD T 838701 DN to 3.4 S
3.4 S LHD to 3.4 S RHD:
    3.4 S OTS LHD T 832016 DN 3.4 S to 3.4 S OTS RHD S 820046 DN; a second OTS LHD car with chassis number S 832016 DN was subsequently built but this had a 3.4 engine
3.8 S LHD to 3.4 RHD:
    3.8 S DHC LHD S 838974 DN built in 1960 to 3.4 DHC RHD S 827663 DN, the only instance of an S model becoming a non-S model

Clearly, in 1958 the 3.4 S was intended for the American export market, which is confirmed by the separate figures for sales in the USA. Originally, in the USA in 1958, the S engine was available only with the two-seater body and accounted for more than one-third of American OTS sales that year but the engine was offered in other body styles in 1959. Equally clearly the 3.8 S was a *rara avis* in the USA and was presumably available to special order only; not a single two-seater with this engine was exported there, although a few such cars were supplied to American customers in other territories. Towards the end of production, it is probable that the 3.8 non-S model was preferred by American customers. It is curious that one American customer in 1960 (a Mrs Wernick) obviously insisted on having a 3.4 S DHC LHD; in fact this was a PED car registered 5747 DU in Coventry. May be she intended to take the car to a country which taxed cars by engine size!

Actual exports to the USA by body type and year:

	3.4 S				3.8 S		
	1958	1959	1960	Total	1959	1960	Total
OTS LHD*	661	72	0	**733**	0	0	**0**
FHC LHD	2	65	0	**67**	8	12	**20**
DHC LHD	0	44	1	**45**	3	7	**10**
Total	**663**	**181**	**1**	**845**	**11**	**19**	**30**

*not including T 831455 DN built in 1958 for the USA but damaged on its way to the docks and scrapped

The second-biggest market for the S models with either engine size was the UK, with a total of 342 home sales, of which two-thirds went through Henlys. Then in descending order came Canada, France, PED sales in the UK and Germany. After the 3.8 S had appeared in October 1959, there was much less interest in the 3.4 S version with only 65 such cars being built between August and December 1959, except possibly in markets where the extra capacity meant higher tax, but even the home market took 15 of the 27 3.4 S cars made in 1960.

Sales by market, all body styles combined:

	3.4 S RHD	3.4 S LHD	Total	3.8 S RHD	3.8 S LHD	Total	Grand total
Algeria	0	7	7	0	1	1	**8**
Australia	8	0	8	7	0	7	**15**
Austria	0	3	3	0	0	0	**3**
Belgium	0	11	11	0	5	5	**16**
Brazil	0	1	1	0	2	2	**3**
Canada	0	63	63	0	6	6	**69**
France	0	26	26	0	4	4	**30**
Germany	0	14	14	0	7	7	**21**
Guatemala	0	1	1	0	2	2	**3**
Italy	0	4	4	0	1	1	**5**
Japan (incl Okinawa)	0	6	6	0	1	1	**7**
Lebanon	0	9	9	0	3	3	**12**
Mexico	0	3	3	0	0	0	**3**
Morocco	0	2	2	0	1	1	**3**
New Zealand	0	0	0	3	0	3	**3**
PED in UK	5	10	15	2	6	8	**23**
Portugal	0	2	2	0	1	1	**3**
Switzerland	1	4	5	0	2	2	**7**
USA	0	845	845	0	30	30	**875**
Venezuela	0	4	4	0	0	0	**4**
Other export markets	4	6	10	1	1	2	**12**
Henlys (London and Manchester)	94	0	94	135	0	135	**229**
Other UK distributors	53	0	53	59	0	59	**112**
Jaguar direct*	2	0	2	1	1	2	**4**
Misc**	0	1	1	0	0	0	**1**
Total	**167**	**1022**	**1189**	**208**	**74**	**282**	**1471**

* 3.4 S: OTS RHD S 820046 DN converted from OTS LHD T 832016 DN registered YDU 455 second-hand sale to Coombs, Guildford, and FHC RHD T 824803 DN registered XDU 984 ex-press and demo car second-hand staff sale; 3.8 S: FHC RHD T 825028 DN registered YHP 791 ex-press car second-hand sale to Henlys, London, and DHC LHD T 838915 DN sold direct to the Shell petroleum company
**OTS LHD T 831455 DN intended for the USA but damaged on its way to the docks and scrapped

1. Montagu of Beaulieu *Jaguar A Biography* (first ed.) pp.161-62; Porter and Skilleter *Sir William Lyons* p.149; Whyte *Jaguar* (first ed.) pp.148-50
2. Porter and Skilleter p.144
3. *The Motor* 14 May 1958 pp.563-64
4. Porter and Skilleter tables pp.280-81
5. Based on export sales statistics, JDHT archive
6. Dugdale *Jaguar in America* (second ed.) table p.142
7. Clausager "The Swinging Sixties" in *Britain's Motor Industry* p.151; Dugdale table p.117
8. Porter and Skilleter pp.136-37
9. Now owned by the British Pendragon group which also owns the Stratstone Jaguar dealer chain; www.homburg.com, www.pendragonplc.com
10. Dugdale p.89; *The Motor* 14 May 1958 p.563
11. Porter and Skilleter p.164
12. Based on a not very scientific study of AA and RAC handbooks, and Bellamy's *Who's Who in the Motor Industry*, various years
13. Whyte p.189
14. Robson *Cars in the UK* Vol. 1 1945-1970 pp.41, 46, 54, 59 and 223
15. *Ibid.*; also Dunnett *The Decline of the British Motor Industry* pp.88-89 tables
16. *News Exchange*, Nuffield Exports magazine, Jan 1950 p.2, Feb 1950 p.21
17. Information substantiated by Coventry registration records in the Coventry Transport Museum archive, courtesy of Lizzie Hazlehurst
18. Porter and Skilleter p.194, John Morgan's reminiscences showing Lyons's antipathy to Mercedes-Benz

Tables of sales by agent

Table 1: XK 140 sales by agent, home market

Location	Distributor	OTS Std	SE	SE/C	FHC Std	SE	SE/C	DHC Std	SE	SE/C	Total
Birmingham	PJ Evans (1)	1			45		4	21		2	73
Belfast	Victor	1		1	5		1	1			9
Bolton	Parkers	1			19		4	11		2	37
Cardiff	Exclusive Cars				3						3
Cardiff	Norton				2		1				3
Carlisle	Scottish Motor Traction				7			3			10
Coventry	SH Newsome				9		4	3		2	18
Derby	Sanderson & Holmes				1		1	1			3
Douglas, I.o.M.	WH Shimmin				1		1				2
Edinburgh	Rossleigh	1			22		5	8			36
Glasgow	Ritchies	1		1	13		6	6		3	30
Grimsby	Roland C Bellamy				11		4	1		1	17
Harrogate	Glovers of Ripon	1			7		6	5		1	20
Hull	WL Thompson				7		2	3			12
Jersey, C.I.	St Helier Garage				2		4	2			8
Leeds	Appleyard				18		11	17		8	54
Leicester	Walter E Sturgess	2		1	10		3	5			21
London	Henlys (2)	12		8	281	5	72	214	2	37	631
Malvern	Rothwell & Millbourne			1	6		2			1	10
Manchester	Henlys	1	1	3	38		15	24		8	90
Newcastle	Rossleigh				2			1			3
Nottingham	CH Truman				12		1	2			15
Preston	Ashton Preston				2		1	4			7
Sheffield	Ernest W Hatfield				13		2	3			18
Shrewsbury	Wales & Edwards				1			1			2
Stoke-on-Trent	Byatts of Fenton	1		1	8		1	6		1	18
Wolverhampton	Charles Attwood	2			14		9	6	1	3	35
Miscellaneous	Jaguar Cars etc	1		3	12		2	7		1	26
Total RHD home		**25**	**1**	**19**	**571**	**5**	**162**	**355**	**3**	**70**	**1211**
Total for body style, home		**45**			**738**			**428**			
Plus RHD export		11	1	17	66	2	36	38	2	12	185
Total for body style, export		**29**			**104**			**52**			**185**
Not recorded	Not recorded (3)						1				1
Total all RHD by body style		**74**			**843**			**480**			**1397**

Notes to table 1: (1) a.k.a. Broad Street Motors; (2) incl. one OTS SE/C chassis only; (3) S 804650 chassis only which can not be accounted for

Table 2: XK 140 RHD sales by agent, export

Location	Distributor	OTS			FHC			DHC			Total
		Std	SE	SE/C	Std	SE	SE/C	Std	SE	SE/C	
Australia	Bryson	2		2	24		8	5		2	43
Australia, Adelaide	Dominion Motors				2		3				5
Australia, Brisbane	Andersons				5		2	1			8
Australia, Perth	Brooking				2			1			3
Belgium, Bruxelles	Belgian Motor Co					1	1				2
Burma, Rangoon	Autocars Ltd	1									1
Canada, Montreal	Budd & Dyer			1						1	2
Cyprus, Nicosia	PM Tseriotis				1						1
Eire, Dublin	Frank Cavey				1						1
France, Paris	Delecroix (1)			3	2		1	2		2	10
Germany, Frankfurt	RM Overseas	1						1			2
Ghana, Accra	Berberi & Malek							2			2
Holland, The Hague	Lagerwij's							1			1
Hong Kong	Gilman & Co	2				1	2	1		1	7
India, Bombay	BD Garware						1			1	2
India, Calcutta	French Motor Car Co							1			1
India, New Delhi	Pearley Lal			1							1
Italy, Milano	CGA						1				1
Jamaica, Kingston	Daytona Sales						1	1			2
Japan, Tokyo	Jidosha			2							2
Kenya, Nairobi	Lowis & Hodgkiss				1			1			2
Lebanon, Beirut	Robert M Trad						1				1
Malaya, Singapore	Cycle & Carriage	2		4	6			3			15
New Zealand, Auckland	Shorters							1			1
New Zealand, Christchurch	Archibald			2	1		2			1	6
New Zealand, Wellington	Independent						2	1		1	4
Nigeria, Lagos	Mandilas & Karaberis				2		1				3
Rhodesia, Bulawayo	Sagers	1			6		5	3			15
South Africa, Cape Town	Robb Motors									1	1
Sudan, Khartoum	Geo. Djerdjian								1		1
Sweden, Stockholm	Fredlund						2				2
Switzerland, Geneva	Claparede				2			3			5
Switzerland, Zurich	Emil Frey				1			1			2
Switzerland	Erwin Lutz		1								1
Thailand, Bangkok	Assia	1		1				2			4
USA, Los Angeles	Hornburg				1						1
USA, New York	Hoffman						1		1	1	3
USA, New York	Jaguar Cars Inc						1				1
London	Crown Agents							1			1
PED, direct sales	Jaguar	1			2			1			4
PED, London	Henlys				7		1	5		1	14
Misc	Hommond (?)			1							1
Total RHD export		**11**	**1**	**17**	**66**	**2**	**36**	**38**	**2**	**12**	**185**
Total for body style		**29**			**104**			**52**			**185**

Notes to table 2: (1) incl. one FHC SE/C chassis only

Table 3: XK 140 LHD sales by agent, export

Location	Distributor	OTS			FHC			DHC			Total
		Std	SE	SE/C	Std	SE	SE/C	Std	SE	SE/C	
Aden	Besse & Co							1			1
Algeria, Algiers	Anglo-American Garage						1	1			2
Algeria, Algiers	Malglaive				1						1
Algeria, Algiers	SAPIVA						1	1			2
Argentina, Buenos Aires	Ehlert Motors									1	1
Australia	Bryson (PED)			1							1
Austria, Vienna	Georg Hans Koch		1	1						1	3
Bahamas, Nassau	Commission Merchants							1			1
Bahrain	M & A Kooheji	1		1	1		1	1		1	6
Belgium, Bruxelles	Belgian Motor Co	1		1	23	5	9	8	3	3	53
Brazil, Rio de Janeiro	Goodwin Cocozza				1						1

Location	Dealer										Total
Canada, Montreal	Budd & Dyer	13	1	4	21		4	13	2	4	62
Canada, Ottawa	Waverley Motors			1	10		1	3			15
Canada, Newfoundland	MJ Duff				1		2			1	4
Canada, Toronto	James L Cooke	12		7	21	2	6	18	1	5	72
Canada, Vancouver	Oxford Motors	2		4	12		6	8	1	2	35
Canada (thro' New York)	Jaguar Cars Inc	3	5	4	1		1				14
Cuba, Havana	Auto Jaguar			1							1
Cuba. Havana	Frank Seiglie						1				1
Curacao	Kusters			1							1
Denmark, Copenhagen	Sommer							1			1
Dominican Republic	Dominican Motors									1	1
Egypt, Cairo	Universal Motor Co							1			1
El Salvador	Import. Salvadorena			1				1		1	3
Equador, Guayaquil	Alviles Alfaro				1						1
Finland, Tampere	SM Kauppa						1	1			2
France, Paris	Delecroix (1)	4		5	15	30	25	26	33	13	151
Germany, Frankfurt	RM Overseas	38	5	9	22	6	7	14	3	2	106
Germany, Hamburg	Fendler & Luedemann				2		1	2		2	7
Gibraltar	Alfred Bassadone				1			2			3
Greece, Athens	CD Coulentianos			1	1					1	3
Guatemala	Juhan				1						1
Haiti	Haiti Motors									1	1
Holland, The Hague	Lagerwij's				3			10	1	1	15
Iran. Teheran	Abolhassan Diba				1		1			2	4
Italy, Milano	CGA				1			1		3	5
Italy, Rome	Fattori & Montani			1				1		1	3
Japan, Tokyo	Jidosha	3			2	1					6
Kuwait	Vehedi Brothers						2				2
Lebanon, Beirut	Saad			1						1	2
Lebanon, Beirut	Robert M Trad (2)				4		2	4			10
Libya, Tripoli	Godon Woodroffe									1	1
Madagascar, Tananarive	Weinberger			1	1						2
Malta, Gzira	Muscat's Garage	1									1
Morocco, Casablanca	Moto Maroc				11		2	4		4	21
Morocco, Tangier	Bendelac							1			1
Norway. Oslo	Standard Autos					2				1	3
Okinawa	Island Enterprises				1						1
Philippines, Manila	Products Inc	3						3			6
Portugal, Lisbon	Martins & Almeida (3)	1					1	3		1	6
Puerto Rico, San Juan	HV Grosch				1						1
Rhodesia, Bulawayo	Sagers							1			1
Spain, Madrid	Salamanca				1						1
Sweden, Stockholm	Fredlund				3		2	1		1	7
Switzerland, Geneva	Claparede	1			3		1	2			7
Switzerland, Zurich	Emil Frey				2		1	1			4
Switzerland	Erwin Lutz (4)							1			1
Taiwan, Taipei	Taiwan Trading Corp.	1						1			2
Uruguay, Montevideo	Pablo Aicardi				2			2			4
USA, Los Angeles	Hornburg	131	214	758	17	236	613	44	117	465	2595
USA, New York	Hoffman (5)	181	255	451	30	39	275	72	62	318	1683
USA, New York	Jaguar Cars Inc	328	41	762	87	41	290	263	65	635	2512
Venezuela, Caracas	CAMAV				3	1	13	1	1	2	21
PED, direct sales	Jaguar (6)					1	8	4	1	6	20
PED, Glasgow	Ritchies						1	1			2
PED. Leeds	Appleyard				1						1
PED, London	Henlys	1		3	2	1	4	4	1	2	18
PED, Wolverhampton	Attwood							1			1
PED, UK Exchange		2		2	2	1	5	4		3	19
Misc	(7)	1			1					2	4
Destroyed by 1957 fire		4		4							8
Total		**732**	**522**	**2028**	**311**	**366**	**1289**	**532**	**291**	**1488**	**7559**
Total for body style		**3282**			**1966**			**2311**			**7559**

Notes to table 3: (1) incl. one OTS std chassis only; (2) incl. two chassis only; (3) one FHC SE chassis only; (4) one FHC SE/C chassis only; (5) incl. one FHC SE chassis only; (6) incl. one FHC SE chassis only; (7) OTS 811101 converted to RHD by Jaguar Experimental Dept but kept the same chassis number; FHC chassis only 814001 for Jaguar Experimental Dept; DHC S 817378 was rebuilt with RHD by Jaguar but kept the same chassis number; DHC S 818129 was scrapped

Table 4: XK 150 sales by agent, home market

Location	Distributor	OTS 3.4	3.4 S	3.8	3.8 S	FHC 3.4	3.4 S	3.8	3.8 S	DHC 3.4	3.4 S	3.8	3.8 S	Total
Birmingham	PJ Evans				1	50	8	4	13	23	5	1	2	107
Belfast	Victor				1	8	1	1		3			1	15
Bolton	Parkers					31	1	4	2	8	1	2		49
Cardiff	Norton	1				3		1		1	1			7
Carlisle	Scottish Motor Traction					4				3				7
Coventry	SH Newsome					14	5			8			1	28
Derby	Sanderson & Holmes					9	2		3	1				15
Douglas, I.o.M.	WH Shimmin													0
Edinburgh	Rossleigh (1)					34		1	2	12			2	51
Glasgow	Ritchies		1			36	2	5		10		3	3	60
Grimsby	Roland C Bellamy					17		1	4	3	1	1	1	28
Harrogate	Glovers of Ripon					18	2	2	2	5	2		1	32
Hull	WL Thompson		1			8		1		5				15
Jersey, C.I.	St Helier Garage	3	1			8	1	3		1		1		18
Leeds	Appleyard		2		1	47		5	4	11		3	3	76
Leicester	Walter E Sturgess				2	10	4	1		2		1	1	21
London	Henlys (2)	9	27		15	468	36	32	64	319	19	32	47	1068
Malvern	Rothwell & Millbourne					6	1	1	1	1				10
Manchester	Henlys	1	4	1	1	67	7	12	4	29	1	5	4	136
Newcastle	Rossleigh		2		1	18				4				25
Nottingham	CH Truman					9		1		3		1		14
Preston	Ashton Preston					10	1		1				1	13
Sheffield	Ernest W Hatfield					22	1	3		3	1	2		32
Shrewsbury	Kennings					2	1							3
Shrewsbury	Wales & Edwards					3								3
Stoke-on-Trent	Byatts of Fenton					11	2	1	2	5				21
Wolverhampton	Charles Attwood	1				19	3	3	2	5	1	1	1	36
Miscellaneous	(Jaguar Cars etc)		1			3	1			1		1		7
Total home		15	39	1	22	935	78	83	105	466	32	53	68	1897
Total for body style, home		77				1201				619				
Plus RHD export		8	5	1	2	139	8	11	10	35	5	3	1	228
Total for body style, export		16				168				44				228
Total all RHD by body style		93				1369				663				2125

Notes to table 4: (1) incl. Aberdeen, Dundee, Kirkcaldy; (2) incl. one 3.4 FHC chassis only

In the front view the XK 140 was immediately identifiable from its predecessor, In side view, these differences are less obvious, and the basic body was indeed externally largely unchanged from the XK 120 two-seater.

Table 5: XK 150 RHD sales by agent, export

Location	Distributor	OTS 3.4	3.4 S	3.8	3.8 S	FHC 3.4	3.4 S	3.8	3.8 S	DHC 3.4	3.4 S	3.8	3.8 S	Total
Aden	Besse & Co									2				2
Australia	Bryson		1		1	26	6	1	4	2	1			42
Australia, Adelaide	Dominion Motors					3								3
Australia, Brisbane	Andersons					3		2						5
Bahamas. Nassau	East Bay Services		1											1
Barbados, Bridgetown	City Garages					1								1
Belgium, Bruxelles	Belgian Motor Co					2				1				3
Columbia, Bogota (?)	Auto Motores									1				1
Cyprus, Nicosia	PM Tseriotis					1								1
Denmark, Copenhagen	Sommer	1												1
Eire, Dublin	Frank Cavey		1							1				2
Fiji, Lakota	Burns Philp					1								1
France, Paris	Delecroix (1)					3								3
Germany, Frankfurt	RM Overseas					1								1
Ghana, Accra	Berberi & Malek			1										1
Holland, The Hague	Lagerwij's					1								1
Hong Kong	Gilman & Co	2				3		1		5		1		12
India, Calcutta	French Motor Car Co					1								1
India, New Delhi	Pearey Lal									1				1
Indonesia, Bogor	Sunda Motors					1								1
Indonesia, Djakarta	Govaars					1								1
Iraq, Baghdad	Rafidain Developments					1								1
Italy, Rome	Fattori & Montani					1								1
Jamaica, Kingston	Daytona Sales	1				1	1							3
Japan, Tokyo	Jidosha					1	1							2
Kenya, Nairobi	Lowis & Hodgkiss					7				1				8
Kuwait	Latif Supplies					1								1
Malaya, Singapore	Cycle & Carriage	3				11		1		1		1		17
Malta, Gzira	Muscat's Garage		1							1				2
Mozambique, Lourenco Marques	Africa Motores					2	1	1						4
New Zealand, Auckland	Shorters					5				1				6
New Zealand, Christchurch	Archibald					2	3							5
New Zealand, Wellington	Independent				1	3			2	1				7
Nigeria, Lagos	Mandilas & Karaberis		1			1		1		2		1		6
Norway, Oslo	Skoyen Bilservice									1				1
Nyasaland, Blantyre	Hay's Garage					1				1				2
Rhodesia, Bulawayo	Sagers					8								8
Sierra Leone	KATEMA					1								1
South Africa, Cape Town	Robb Motors					5				1				6
South Africa, Durban	Maxwell Campbell					3								3
South Africa, East London	Orient					3								3
South Africa, Johannesburg	John B Clarke					7								7
South Africa, Kimberley	Brook					2								2
South Africa, Windhoek	Terry's					1								1
Sweden, Stockholm	Fredlund					2				1				3
Switzerland, Geneva	Claparede									1	1			2
Switzerland, Zurich	Emil Frey					6				1				7
Tanganyika, Dar-es-Salaam	Marston Motors					1								1
Trinidad, Port of Spain	Engineering Ltd					1				1				2
USA, New York	Jaguar Cars Inc					1								1
PED, direct sales	Jaguar					5				3	1		1	10
PED, London	Henlys	1				7	2	1	1	5	2			19
PED, Jersey	St Helier Garage					1								1
Total RHD export		**8**	**5**	**1**	**2**	**139**	**8**	**11**	**10**	**35**	**5**	**3**	**1**	**228**
Total for body style		**16**				**168**				**44**				**228**

Notes to table 5: (1) incl. one FHC RHD 3.4 chassis only

Table 6: XK 150 LHD sales by agent, export

Location	Distributor	OTS 3.4	3.4 S	3.8	3.8 S	FHC 3.4	3.4 S	3.8	3.8 S	DHC 3.4	3.4 S	3.8	3.8 S	Total
Aden	Besse & Co	1										1		2
Algeria, Algiers	CAPIMA					3	6					1		10
Algeria, Algiers	SAPIVA		1			3				1				5
Argentina, Buenos Aires	Millet & Cia	2		2		3		2		2		3		14
Australia	Bryson (PED)					1								1
Austria, Vienna	Georg Hans Koch		2			2		1		2	1			8
Bahamas, Nassau	Commission Merchants									1				1
Bahamas, Nassau	East Bay Service									2				2
Bahrain	M & A Kooheji					4	1			1				6
Belgium, Bruxelles	Belgian Motor Co	2	7		2	60	2	4	2	18	2	5	1	105
Brazil, Rio de Janeiro	SAMDACO		1			3			2					6
Canada, Montreal	Jaguar of E. Canada	37	41		1	114	8	31	1	66	14	25	4	342
Canada, Vancouver	Oxford Motors					12				1				13
Canada (through New York)	Jaguar Cars Inc					2				1				3
Canary Islands, Las Palmas	Domingo Alonso									2				2
Chile, Santiago	Importadora Fisk						1							1
Colombia, Bogota (?)	Auto Motores					1	1			1				3
Colombia	Maquinarias									1				1
Cuba, Havana	Distrbuidora Jaguar					1								1
Denmark, Copenhagen	Sommer					5				2		2		9
Eire, Dublin	Frank Cavey (PED)	1												1
Equador, Guayaquil	Alviles Alfaro		1											1
France, Paris	Delecroix (1)	6	14			81	9	7	3	53	3	4	1	181
Germany, Frankfurt	RM Overseas (2)	7	10	1		30	2	8	4	10	1	7		80
Germany, Hamburg	Fendler & Luedemann		1		3	10		1		1		2		18
Gibraltar	Alfred Bassadone	1								1		2		4
Greece, Athens	CD Coulentianos					2				2				4
Greece, Athens	ETEMA							1		3				4
Guatemala	Juhan	1				1	1		2	1				6
Haiti	Agence Nationale		1											1
Holland, The Hague	Lagerwij's	3				12		2		2		3		22
Iceland, Reykjavik	ORKA	1								2				3
Iran. Teheran	Abolhassan Diba					1								1
Iraq, Baghdad	Rafidain Developments									1				1
Italy, Milano	CGA (3)	1	1			2		1	1					6
Italy, Milano	Metaucol (4)					2								2
Italy, Rome	Fattori & Montani	1	1	1		15	2	2		5		2		29
Kenya, Nairobi	Lowis & Hodgkiss					1								1
Jamaica, Kingston	Daytona Sales		1											1
Japan, Tokyo	Jidosha	5	1	1		5	3	4		11		2		32
Jordan, Amman	Tabbaa & Salameh		1		1									2
Kuwait	Latif Supplies					1				4				5
Lebanon, Beirut	Robert M Trad	2	5		3	7	3			3	1			24
Libya, Tripoli	Gordon Woodroffe							1		3				4
Malaya, Singapore	Cycle & Carriage							2						2
Mexico, Mexico City	Jaguar de Mexico	3	2			8								13
Mexico, Mexico City	JC Automotriz		1											1
Monaco	Albion Sales	3		2		1				3				9
Morocco, Casablanca	DIFMA		1			4			1					6
Morocco, Casablanca	Moto Maroc		1			10				3				14
Moroco, Tangier	Bendelac		1			6				4				10
Mozambique, Lourenco Marques	Gundle		1											1
Nicaragua, Managua	Nicaragua Machinery Co					1								1
Norway. Oslo	Skoyen Bilservice					1								1
Okinawa	Baxter Trading Co			1			1							2

Location	Dealer													Total
Okinawa	Island Enterprises		1			1								2
Panama	Motores SA	1		1										2
Philippines, Manila	Products Inc					1								1
Portugal, Lisbon	Martins & Almeida		2		1	7				2				12
Qatar, Doha	Darwish Automobiles					1								1
Rhodesia, Bulawayo	Sagers							1						1
Saudi Arabia, Jeddah	Binzagr	1								1				2
South Africa, Cape Town	Robb Motors					1								1
South Africa, Durban	Maxwell Campbell					1								1
Spain, Madrid	Salamanca			1		3				1				5
Sweden, Stockholm	Fredlund					3		2						5
Switzerland, Geneva	Claparede (5)		1			11	1	3		2				18
Switzerland, Zurich	Emil Frey	5	1			33	1	4	2	15		1		62
Tanganyika, Dar-es-Salaam	Benbros Motors					1								1
Turkey, Istanbul	Otokar Ticaret											2		2
USA, New York	Jaguar Cars Inc	1186	733	27		1840	67	479	20	1092	45	467	10	5966
Venezuela, Caracas	CAMAV		4			13				7				24
Virgin Islands	Island Imports	2												2
PED, direct sales	Jaguar	1	1	1	1	12	1	1		22	1		2	43
PED, Derby	Sanderson & Holmes								1					1
PED. Cardiff	Tom Norton									1				1
PED, London	Henlys (6)	1	5		1	17		4	1	27		3		59
PED, UK Exchange		3	2			12		1	1	6		1		26
Jaguar Experimental Dept						1				1				2
Destroyed T 831455 DN			1											1
n/r	(7)					2								2
Converted to RHD								7					1	8
Total LHD export		**1277**	**846**	**37**	**14**	**2375**	**108**	**571**	**41**	**1390**	**68**	**532**	**20**	**7279**
Total for body style		**2174**				**3095**				**2010**				**7279**

Notes to table 6: (1) incl. one FHC 3.4 chassis only; (2) incl. one FHC 3.4 chassis only; (3) incl. one FHC 3.4 chassis only; (4) incl. two FHC 3.4 chassis only; (5) incl. one FHC 3.4 chassis only; (6) of which possibly one to three home sales; (7) incl. one FHC 3.4 chassis only;

This 1958 drophead coupé rear view shows the tail lamp units fitted to the early XK 150s, which were the same as those found on the XK 140.

Chapter Five

"How do they make them for the money?"

RHP 576 was the solitary XK 140 press car, here displaying its engine. (JDHT)

This is the question so often asked in the press about Jaguars, and one which at least John Bolster of *Autosport* (quoted below) decided was unanswerable. The theme of the amazing value for money offered by the XKs, indeed by many Jaguars before or since, continued to intrigue the press and the public. By the second half of the 1950s there were other series production cars which would match the performance of the XKs, but none which did so at the price (see chapter 6). If Jaguars were built down to a price, there was very little sign of it,

and the cars continued to rate highly in terms of luxury and comfort, apart from performance. Only a few minor aspects of the cars merited serious criticism, and they could easily be overlooked in the context of their many outstanding qualities. Even after the passage of more than ten years, there was very little wrong with the basic design, and the engine continued to be one of the most remarkable in the world.

Whether by accident or design, the road tests of both the XK 140 and XK 150 in British journals were all of fixed-head coupés with overdrive. One can not overlook the very obvious possibility that Jaguar felt that this body style would be the biggest seller in the home market, as indeed it turned out to be. In today's world it seems rather strange that Jaguar apparently had just one XK 140 demonstrator to lend to the press, and that the first road tests of this car only appeared more than one year after the model had been introduced. The car in question was S 804132 DN, which was Battleship Grey and was registered RHP 576.

At the time, Britain had two heavy-weight weekly motoring journals. *The Autocar* published by Iliffe appeared on Fridays and *The Motor* published by Temple Press appeared on Wednesdays. In addition, since 1950 there was also *Autosport*, a rather more specialised publication aimed at the sporting fraternity which appeared on Fridays. The most important monthly was *Motor Sport* edited by Bill Boddy who was famous for speaking his mind, where

the two leading weeklies were more diplomatic. Apart from Boddy, amongst the best-known journalists were John Bolster of *Autosport* with his trademark deerstalker and Laurence Pomeroy junior of *The Motor*, son of a famous engineer and a *bon vivant* of impressively rotund appearance complete with monocle whose prose style belied his status as technical editor, but who was equally erudite when it came to his designated province.

Of these magazines, both *Autosport* and *The Autocar* published full road tests of RHP 576. Curiously, *The Motor* did not, but "Bill" Rankin, Jaguar's press officer, did lend the car to "Pom" who used it for his trip to the Frankfurt Motor Show in September 1955 and subsequently wrote this up for the magazine. Disregarding the column inches devoted to sundry hostelries and *haute cuisine*, never mind the writer's fondness for obscure quotations, what comes across is Pomeroy's liking for the XK 140, which he felt could only be improved by a close-ratio gearbox – which indeed this car did not have – and better seats. He found the car utterly controllable and responsive, with little roll on corners and brakes well up to some quick laps of the Nürburgring. No specific performance figures were quoted but acceleration to 100mph (161km/h) – which was reached in third – was described as astonishingly rapid, and he got 22-23mpg (12.8-12.3 l/100km) when cruising in overdrive.[1]

John Bolster of *Autosport* was the first to get

into print with a full road test of the same car. Strangely, there was a difference of nearly 8mph (12.5km/h) in the top speeds as measured by the two published road tests, with *The Autocar* getting very close to 130mph (208.2km/h) and Bolster only managing a shade under 122mph (195.7km/h); on the other hand, he measured better acceleration times, but also the worse fuel consumption figures. Bolster found that compared with the XK 120, the XK 140 was "a great improvement in every important respect", especially as regards driving position, steering and brakes. He noted that the suspension had been revised and that the XK 140 was "quite firmly sprung... all the 'float' of the XK 120 has gone." Bolster mused that "compared with some more complicated and much more expensive cars, the Jaguar does perhaps spin its wheels a little more when getting off the mark... Nevertheless, the Jaguar is far easier to drive than some Continental cars with independent rear ends" which suggests that he had the Mercedes-Benz 300 SL in his sights: a car which he had tested earlier.[2] In summing up, he felt that the appeal of the XK 140 was its combination of docility with potential for high-speed Continental touring, and had "long ago given up wondering how they make them for the money..."[3]

The Autocar seems to have been at the back of the queue for having a go in RHP 576. Like Pomeroy of *The Motor* they took the car to the Continent, their route taking in a Belgian motorway – possibly the Jabbeke autoroute – where the top speed was measured, before they went on to another famous place in Jaguar geography, Le Mans. They praised the quietness of the car while running at high speeds, with very little wind noise. They were very positive about the revised weight distribution which "has eliminated the oversteer noticeable in the earlier XK 120" and had also "improved cornering ability. It results in a controlled degree of drift…" Similarly, they found very little to criticize in the braking department: "The brakes proved entirely adequate for the high speed involved… they did not fade or grab" but they did squeal and since pedal pressure was on the high side, *The Autocar* would have welcomed servo assistance.

The gear change merited the epithet "satisfactory" – which may have meant "adequate". "First gear is desirable for starting from rest", so no more party tricks of measuring acceleration from standstill in top gear, as had been the case for the XK 120. This implied that the higher-tuned engine was not quite as flexible, despite direct fourth being lower at 4.09:1 than the 3.64:1 of the XK 120. *The Autocar*, however, had no trouble accelerating cleanly, and quickly, from 10mph (16km/h) in top. One interesting aspect of the test is that it was mostly carried out on Dunlop racing tyres, and *The Autocar* found that these caused the speedometer to be highly inaccurate: a speedometer reading of 100mph (161km/h) equalled a true speed of 92mph (148km/h). When they re-checked the car on normal Road Speed tyres the inaccuracy was reduced but was still there: a speedo reading of 100mph now equalled an actual speed of 95mph (153km/h). In conclusion, the comfort and safety of the XK 140 merited the word "superlative" and "When these qualities are related to its price, there is no other car which can approach it in the high performance sphere…"[4]

One lucky gentleman of the press, Michael Brown, associate editor of *The Autocar*, had the good fortune to enjoy an XK 140 as his "company car": SLU 927, chassis 804622 DN, a black fixed-head, was bought by Iliffe, the publishers of his magazine, in April 1956. Brown wrote up his impressions after 8000 miles, a 1950s equivalent of a long-term test which included an extended Continental trip to cover the Tulip Rally. Oddly enough his article

opened with a discussion of the "recirculating ball steering" of the XK 140 compared to the rack-and-pinion of his previous car, a Riley, when as we know the XK 140 also had rack-and-pinion. He summed up the car as "ferociously docile", with a dual nature, gentle, or fully capable of showing its fangs. He described the shape as "harmonious in the extreme and oh so logically a descendant of those impossibly long-bonneted S.S. models of so many years ago!"[5]

One curiosity is that Mike Hawthorn did a road test of an XK 140 fixed-head SE with overdrive for the *Sunday Express* and probably this was RHP 576 again. The article was rather full of superlatives and there was "never a grumble" about the gearbox; steering was "finger light" and "superb", the suspension "almost perfect", the brakes "faultless", the engine was a "lion heart" and the car "as quiet as a mouse on velvet." He quoted top speed as a remarkable 133mph (214km/h) and a 0-100mph (0-161km/h) time of 28.2sec. The conclusion was, "In a phrase: There are few sports cars in the world to compare with it. There are none within hundreds of Pounds of the price."[6]

In late 1956, it was presumably the hard-worked press car RHP 576 which was given a final outing by the now-defunct Scottish journal *The Motor World*. It may be type-casting to highlight the fact that they considered the car had "unusual economy for such high power" and was "as easily controlled as any 10hp saloon" with which their core readership could possibly claim greater familiarity. Whilst not casting doubts on the veracity of their "Scottish Road Test", many of their remarks bear an uncanny similarity to the reports which had appeared earlier in other journals, and the fact that they said of the handbrake that "A fly-off lever would be an advantage" betrays unfamiliarity with the development of the XK 140 on which that amenity had been introduced in July 1956 well before the date of their test, although presumably RHP 576 retained its conventional handbrake.[7]

An interesting addendum to the official road tests appeared later in *The Motor* under the title "An Innocent and an XK 140". This piece was written by John Eyles who had bought a second-hand fixed-head registered MAW 377, a black 1955 standard model with overdrive, chassis 804036 DN. The point of his article was that he indeed came to XK 140 ownership as an "innocent", as a layman who had no previous experience of fast cars, yet he found it surprisingly easy to handle, even when cruising on German *Autobahnen* at three-figure speeds, when the car behaved perfectly, and was overtaken only by a curious motorcyclist. Interestingly, we learn that Mr Eyles ran his car on Michelin X radial tyres. He summed up his XK 140 with the one word "purposeful".[8]

There is one road test of an XK 140 that I wonder a little about. This was carried out in Australia and the car in question was a fixed-head standard model without overdrive, chassis 804150, engine G 3471-7, imported to Melbourne by Brysons, and which had already been sold to Robert Kneale in August 1955. The article was written by one Bruce Kneale. The top speed of this car was measured to no less than 131.85mph (212.2km/h), except for Hawthorn's figure (see above) the highest I have found quoted for an XK 140, the 0-100mph (0-161km/h) acceleration time of 26sec was the best published figure, and the 0-60mph (0-97km/h) sprint was accomplished in 8.9sec, only beaten by *Road & Track* in their test of an XK 140 MC two-seater. The writer invited the readers to be sceptical: "If you regard these figures are unduly optimistic, so did the test crew at the time and they were checked and rechecked", followed by detailed explanations. Could a standard car with 7:1 compression and no overdrive really out-perform all the SE models road tested in Britain and the USA, or had Mr Kneale's car been breathed upon?[9]

There were at least three road tests of the XK 140 open two-seater in "MC" form in the USA. British-born Flight-Lieutenant John Bentley made his career as a motoring journalist in America after the war, he and his wife Ruth Sands Bentley were regular contributors to both US and UK magazines, and he had owned an XK 120.[10] For his road test of the new model for *Sports Illustrated* he borrowed a car from a private owner, George F Rolfe (which identifies it as chassis S 810507 DN). Perhaps in deference to Mr Rolfe, Bentley was a bit vague when it came to top speed, which he optimistically estimated as 145mph (233.4km/h) in overdrive: "a top speed close to that of a Formula II Grand Prix car" (*sic*). Remarkably, he stated that "The gearbox is a wonderful mechanism, rugged, silent and quick enough to make it almost

impossible to clash gears, no matter how fast you shift." The steering was "light, positive and accurate" but the brakes were "inadequate... Repeated hard applications at 80 or 100mph (129 or 161km/h)... induce brake fade" and he wished for Alfin drums. But the price of $3,905 (MC model with overdrive) made "the Jaguar one of the best sports car Dollar values on the market."[11]

Road & Track grumbled that their test car was not fitted with the hoped-for close-ratio gearbox, and while they noted that the car had "considerable roll on hard corners, for a sports car" they considered this as a useful indication of safe cornering speed, and that the XK 140 was "one of the easiest and safest automobiles to drive being built today." The gear change "objected to really brisk changes... it left the feeling that the synchronizers were not up to par" but they still equalled Bentley's 0-60mph (0-97km/h) time, of 8.4sec. The open car with hood and side screens in place was noisier than the fixed-head: "normal conversation ceases at about 75mph (121km/h)." In contrast to *The Autocar* they found the speedometer commendably accurate, reading 100mph (161km/h) at a true speed of 98.6mph (158.7km/h). They cheekily quoted the Cadillac slogan "Standard of the World" which they felt was represented by Jaguar in the sports car category.[12]

Sports Cars Illustrated, on the other hand, only published a full test of the XK 140 after production had ceased, despite which they still called it "The new Jag". The report was signed Ludvigsen who was none other than technical editor Karl Ludvigsen, the famous motoring writer and historian. He praised the handling and the fade-proof brakes – except if water got in through the cooling vents of the front drums, also noted by Mr Eyles in *The Motor* – and the fact that unlike the XK 120, the XK 140 did not overheat in traffic. On the other hand the synchromesh was "rudimentary" and "fallible", and the steering, which on the test car still had the original castor angle, was heavy at low speeds and road shocks were easily transmitted back to the steering wheel. A minor irritation, also expressed in other tests, was the lack of elbow room on the driver's outside. Ludvigsen summed up "If used in town it can be difficult to the point of being tiring, but this is not its purpose in life... it [is] a delight to drive at high speeds over long distances on fast, winding roads."[13]

One American article, in *Motor Life*, discussed a fixed-head with overdrive. This California-based publication did not quote specific performance figures but the article implied they had seen over 100mph (over 161km/h), even 120mph (192km/h) on the open road. They felt that the longer roof detracted from the car's appearance compared to the XK 120, but the interior was deemed tasteful: the wood trim might seem archaic but was nevertheless elegant. The writer would have preferred the instruments in front of him, and complained about the blind sports created by the wind-screen pillars.[14]

The following table gives the performance figures measured for the XK 140.

SE FHC with overdrive	Top speed	0-60mph 0-97km/h	0-100mph 0-161km/h	Std 1/4-mile Std 400m	Fuel consumption
Autosport 4 Nov 1955	121.6mph 195.7km/h	10sec	26.2sec	16.8sec	17.5mpg 16.1 l/100km
The Autocar 9 Dec 1955	129.25mph 208.2km/h	11sec	29.5sec	17.4sec	21.7mpg 13 l/100km
The Sunday Express 15 Jan 1956	133mph 214km/h		28.2sec		18-24mpg 15.7-11.8 l/100km
Motor World 7 Dec 1956	130mph 209.3km/h	11.4sec	30sec		22mpg 12.8 l/100km
Standard FHC					
Sports Cars & Specials Oct 1956	131.85mph 212.2km/h	8.9sec	26sec	16.8sec	18-24mpg 15.7-11.8 l/100km
SE/MC OTS					
Sports Illustrated 25 Apr 1955	113-145mph 182-233km/h (estimated)	8.4sec		16.2sec	12.7mpg* 18.5 l/100km
Road & Track Jun 1955	121-125mph 195-201km/h	8.4sec	26.5sec	16.6sec	16-18mpg* 14.7-13.1 l/100km
Sports Cars Illustrated Mar 1957	121-124mph 195-200km/h	9.1sec		16.9sec	11.5-18mpg* 20.5-13.1 l/100km

*assumed to be US gallons

This was one of the original XK 150 press cars; VDU 882 was road tested by The Autocar. (JDHT)

There were to be rather more road tests of XK 150s, because many journals in addition to having tried the normal car, chose to test the S model as well when that appeared. Again, almost without exception the British tests were of the fixed-head coupé model. This time there were two works press cars. VDU 882 chassis S 824046 DN in Mist Grey built in September 1957 was tested by *The Autocar*, and VVC 48 chassis S 824245 DN in Cotswold Blue built in February 1958 was used by *Motor Sport* and *Motor Racing*. The first road test only appeared in print during 1958.

There was consensus among the road testers as regards performance since all measured top speeds of around 125mph (201-202km/h): slower than the XK 140, reflecting the car's higher weight. Acceleration was better thanks to the improved torque characteristics of the engine. Flexibility was such that *The Autocar* this time did try the trick of accelerating from standing start to 100mph (161km/h) in top gear and accomplished this in 36.4sec; if the gears were used, the time came down to just over 25sec. The magazine was now openly critical of the synchromesh which was "scarcely adequate." The disc brakes merited fulsome praise, except for the handbrake whose "power was not up to the high standards of the foot-brakes" and "would not hold the car on a steep gradient." Other criticisms concerned the modest amount of lateral support offered by the seats, and it was suggested that the main instruments should have been placed in front of the driver. But the car overall was as impressive as ever, and *The Autocar* did not know "of any more outstanding example of value for money."[15]

Bill Boddy in *Motor Sport* agreed with *The Autocar* on the synchromesh but found the handbrake "absolutely effective" and was equally full of praise for the disc brakes. While the XK 150 "handles splendidly, especially in the hands of big-boned, bowler-hatted Britishers", "the hypercritical may perhaps feel that the Jaguar chassis is not so advanced as the splendid power unit" – indeed he felt it gave "a sense of vintage-style flexibility". He would have preferred independent rear suspension. The steering was heavy for parking and never really light, accurate if somewhat spongy, and transmitted some kick-back. A number of minor criticisms led Mr Boddy to state that "as a

connoisseur's fast car the Jaguar can be disappointing" but he made up for it by reminding the reader "of the very high performance offered... at what can only be regarded as a very modest price, and of the sheer pleasure to be derived from driving fast this very excellent motor car."[16]

Motor Racing, like *Motor Sport*, used VVC 48, the second Jaguar press car. The main impression was "the effortless manner with which it devoured the miles" which included overtaking a Police car "which was obviously in a hurry" – at about 105mph (169km/h)! However, the shallow boot would not take an ordinary suitcase, so the stowage space afforded by the rear seats was welcome. Neither the synchromesh nor the hand brake was commented upon, but "on fast bends a certain amount of body roll was felt... both driver and passenger would have appreciated more lateral support from the seats."[17]

Since the open two-seater was not yet available, in the USA *Road and Track* carried out a first test of a fixed-head. This was said to be "one of the prototype cars, reportedly no.2" with "A number of bugs [which] will be absent from production models." They complained of too-high pedal pressure, even with the brake servo, and amusingly attributed the disc brakes to Girling – a rare lapse for this publication, and one which they later admitted to. They regretted the loss of interior wood trim – but were to make a completely contradictory statement when they subsequently tested a two-seater, as mentioned in chapter 3. They made an interesting comment on the car's styling which it is worth quoting in full:

"...it is unmistakably a Jaguar... What is not so obvious is its newness. – Whether this conservatism in the face of the money spent for new dies has been a wise policy, only the years (nine?) will tell. From a distance of 6000 miles, it is easy to say that a little more should have been spent in order to introduce another sensation comparable to the first XK 120. But there is always the chance that an explosion will backfire."

This neatly sums up the dilemma of Jaguar designers then and for ever after! Worse was to come: "Its 4-inch width gain at shoulder height [reminds] one more of a mature mother cat than a lithe young huntress." The cat had indeed got fatter. The test car did not have overdrive which

Road and Track would have preferred. Among the minor changes they would like to see were doors lockable from the inside, instruments in front of the driver, and door checks, points which had also been criticized in some of the British reports.[18]

Nearly a year later *Road and Track* tried a two-seater, or actually two two-seaters, as they carried out a simultaneous test of the 3.4 and 3.4 S models. While they had only got their fixed-head test car up to 121.6mph (195.7km/h) they estimated that the standard two-seater, again a non-overdrive car, would reach 125mph (201km/h) which was the figure measured in British road tests, but they expected the S model to reach 136mph (219km/h), and measured significantly faster acceleration times for this car. The gearbox, for a change, behaved itself – "it shifts much easier and more smoothly than any previous Jaguar". Brakes and steering merited unstinted praise, and with the new RS4 tyres, "the former trait of total loss of adhesion in the wet has been completely overcome" which, in retrospect, makes worrying reading. Back in Coventry they would have been pleased to read that "the general quality level of paint, finish and trim are considerably improved". *Road and Track* approved of the roomier cockpit where it was "feasible to place a small child comfortably on the padded leather driveshaft tunnel, between driver and passenger."[19]

Sports Cars Illustrated and *Speed Age* also tried the 3.4 S two-seater but neither got quite the same performance out of their cars as *Road and Track*. John Bentley, the long-standing Jaguar devotee, was openly critical in *Speed Age* of the rear axle tramp: "Former XKs had this trouble, but it is now accentuated to a degree where you suspect the whole rear-end is coming apart." The car rode and handled well "but not well enough from the standpoint of the competition"; and "If the XK 150 S is merely intended as a Gran Turismo machine... then it has no peer in its price bracket... It is a splendid sports car... But it is not, by any stretch of the imagination, a racing machine as well."[20]

Sports Cars Illustrated begged to differ: "...the S is intended for SCCA's Production Sports Car category, where it should polish up Jaguar's glory". It didn't, as it happened. However, their test car, said to be the second S in the USA, failed to reach more than 120-122mph (193-196km/h), which left both the magazine and Jaguar Cars Inc unimpressed, and the car went back in the shop to find out why it did not reach the 125-135mph (201-217km/h) that had been expected.[21] Later that year, the magazine tried out an XK 150 S that had been prepared for SCCA racing by Bob Grossman. He had added an anti-roll bar and Koni shock absorbers – despite which fast cornering induced an "awe-inspiring roll angle" – and had also fitted Traction-Master trailing radius arms to reduce wheel spin and rear axle tramp, until disallowed by the SCCA. The reliability and flexibility of the car was such that apart from racing, Grossman also continued to use it quite happily as his everyday transport, and drove it to and from race meetings.[22]

All of the leading British journals tested the 3.4 S, predictably in fixed-head form, but only *Autosport* had a go in a 3.8 S (nobody seems to have tested a 3.8 non-S model), and also briefly tried a 3.4 S two-seater. The latter was a car which Bob Berry of Jaguar took to the test day of the Guild of Motoring Writers held at the Goodwood track at Motor Show time in 1958. The car was WWK 468, chassis S 837003 DN, which by October 1958 appeared as a two-seater with an S engine (see chapter 8). Its power filled Stuart Seager of *Autosport* "with sheer awe", its 250bhp was more than he had ever handled. He began gingerly but soon found that the acceleration was matched by the brakes, and "Of course, the whole performance takes place in the greatest comfort", with the hood down but side windows wound up: "none of this side-screen nonsense". American writers had also welcomed the wind-down side windows.[23]

Autosport was the first journal to conduct a full road test of the 3.4 S fixed-head press car, XDU 984 chassis T 824803 DN, a Carmen Red car built in March 1959. John Bolster measured a top speed of over 132mph (over 212km/h) which was about the average figure achieved in the four British tests of this car, but he measured the best acceleration times, and also suggested that over 135mph (217km/h) might be reached on racing tyres. He found acceleration "stupendous" but the car was also "sensationally lively" if top gear only was used, and the engine seemed "even more flexible than the normal Jaguar unit." There was again a question mark over the synchromesh. He found that the car handled best at the recommended tyre pressures

for high-speed driving – 40 lb front, 45 lb rear; for everyday motoring Jaguar recommended 23 lb front and 26 lb rear – and even at the higher pressures the car was comfortable at normal speeds. The XK 150 S was "An Ultra-High Speed car That Approaches Perfection", yet "it represents outstanding value for money."[24]

Likewise, to *The Motor* this was "An immensely impressive car which offers near-racing performance in complete touring comfort at a surprisingly moderate price" and "easily the fastest closed car ever subjected to a full-scale road test by *The Motor*." They, too, carried out performance tests on the highest recommended tyre pressures, which still "gave a surprisingly comfortable ride, even over Continental *pavé*". Only one serious shortcoming was high-lighted: "...the gearbox is the least pleasing feature of the car and cannot be regarded as reaching the very high standard of the rest."[25] This comment was echoed by *The Autocar* and this journal repeated their earlier criticism of the handbrake. Both magazines, incidentally, praised the Powr-Lok limited slip differential for reducing wheel spin and axle tramp. Just for fun, *The Autocar* again timed top gear acceleration from standstill to 100mph (161km/h) and managed this in 33.5sec.[26]

When Bill Boddy of *Motor Sport* got his hands on XDU 984 which he used to cover the RAC Rally in November 1959, the car was perhaps a little worse for wear and he had some slight

trouble with a blowing exhaust flange gasket, and worn splines on a rear wheel hub. Perhaps more seriously he reported oil consumption of less than 900 miles per gallon (approx. 300km/litre). In contrast to some road testers, Boddy found the boot capacious and the gear change excellent. He covered the recently-opened southernmost stretch of the M1 at an average of 114.5mph (184.3km/h) which took him about half an hour; happy days![27]

Around the same time that Boddy had the 3.4 S on loan, a 3.8 S was lent to Christopher Jennings, the editor of *The Motor* and the only journalist trusted to try out the first E-type prototype. The 3.8 S was YHP 791, chassis T 825028

The 3.4 S press car was this fixed-head. A GB plate was fitted in anticipation of the magazines wanting to take the car across the Channel for high-speed testing on the Continent. (JDHT)

This shot of XDU 984 with the door open was probably taken for the RAC homologation form. (JDHT)

DN, a fixed-head in British Racing Green which was one of the earliest examples built in September 1959, with the first engine, VAS 1001-9. Jennings used the car for a trip to cover the Scottish Motor Show and the RAC Rally in November 1959. He accomplished the 537-mile (864km) trip back from Scotland to his home in Wales comfortably in a day, and "Following a brief stop" went on to London – a further 228 miles (367km): a remarkable testimonial to the abilities of a car which "combined the essential merits of security and speed at a price which remains a source of envy and amazement to other makers of good motorcars all over the world."[28]

Later, John Bolster of *Autosport* had the same car on test, the only published full test of this most potent of all XKs. The top speed was a resounding 136.3mph (219.4km/h), the fastest ever reported for an XK, although not much more than claimed for the 3.4 S, while the 0-100mph (0-161km/h) time of 19sec was also the best ever. The extra torque of the bigger engine made itself felt in the way that the car continued to accelerate past 115mph (185km/h). Bolster speculated that with a little "cleaning up" 140mph (225km/h) might be reached. On the debit side, the car consumed a gallon of 100-octane petrol for every 13 miles (nearly 22 litres per 100km). He noted that the car "is of extremely solid construction and no attempt at weight reduction has been made": I don't quite know whether this was a compliment or not! Minor faults included steering which was heavy at parking speeds, the synchromesh which was not particularly potent, and seats which might provide more positive lateral location. But, "if £1000 were added to the price it would still represent excellent value."[29]

Only a single XK 150 3.4 S open two-seater found its way to Australia. This was chassis number T 820042 DN dating to May 1959. Destined to become a prize in a lottery to raise money for the War Veterans fund, it was briefly tried out by Doug Blain of *Sports Car World*. Out of deference to the newness of the car and its intended role, he did not exceed 3000rpm in any gear which was the equivalent of some 75mph (121km/h) in overdrive. He commented that "Road holding was not as inspiring as we had hoped, due in part to softish spring rates, but it was still mighty good for such a big car." Steering and brakes however passed muster,

Puzzle pictures. This car dates to between October 1959 when the large rear lamps were introduced and March 1960 when the handbrake was moved, yet it has the manual boot prop which was deleted in April 1959. More to the point this is an S model, probably by this time the 3.8-litre version, but it is not the press car YHP 391 which still had the small rear lamps. (JDHT)

and so for a change did the synchromesh, while he made the mistake of thinking the overdrive was operated electrically, when this car had the mechanical version.[30]

There seems to have been relatively few road tests in European magazines. The Swiss *Automobil Revue* tested the Mark VII and the 2.4-litre but not the XK; they did however test the two German competitors, the Mercedes-Benz 300 SL roadster and the BMW 507. I have not come across any French road tests and I doubt that the Italian magazines bothered, but there were at least two road tests of the XK 150 in German publications. The first was in the leading German motoring magazine *Das Auto, Motor und Sport* and the test was carried out by none other that the highly-respected Belgian journalist and racing driver Paul Frère who had driven for the Jaguar works team in 1956; he died at the age of 91 in February 2008. The car in question was a 3.4 fixed-head without overdrive, and was Belgian registered. It may have been S 834016 which was the 1957 demonstrator for the Belgian Motor Company; it had certainly covered 12,000km (7500 miles) by the time of his test.[31]

Frère found the car much improved and more rounded than previous XKs and in every respect it "met the expectations one has of a modern fast touring car." We are no longer surprised to learn that he complained about the lack of door checks, and the poor lateral support of the seats, but he also was unhappy that the angle of the seat backs could not be adjusted – except to be folded forward, which as far as the unoccupied passenger seat was concerned "happened automatically when braking hard." He noted that "By and large, the gearbox is not up to the high standards of the rest of the power train... the synchromesh is far from foolproof." Of course he had a unique perspective and was able to say that "It is unbelievable that the small but important improvements made to the basically identical D-type gearbox in the last few years have not been introduced in series production." But he was full of praise for the handling and road holding, the steering and the brakes and ended on the following note "There are sports cars which are faster than the XK 150 but hardly any... which are quite so civilised, and at such a relatively low price." The test car weighed 1390kg (3062lb), and Frère measured a top speed of exactly 200km/h (124.3mph). His 0-160km/h (0-99mph) time of 25.2sec was in line with most other road tests and the fuel consumption during the test was 18.7 litres per 100 km (15.1mpg). At the time, the German prices were DM 21,250 for the roadster or the fixed-head, DM 21,500 for the drophead which I think was then around £1930-£1955; overdrive was DM 750 extra and automatic DM 2000 extra. In 1958, a 300 SL roadster cost DM 32,500, and a BMW 507 DM 29,950.

The magazine *Hobby* carried out a less serious comparative test between the 300 SL roadster, a Swiss-owned XK 150 3.8 fixed-head – possibly an S model – and, of all things, a 1957 Ford Thunderbird of the model long since out of production by the time the article appeared. Other than the Thunderbird predictably failing to measure up to the standards of the two European cars, we learn relatively little. Thanks to its flexible engine Jaguar accelerated more quickly than the Mercedes-Benz up to around 145km/h (90mph), but then the 300 SL edged ahead and got to 160km/h (99mph) in 23.2sec rather than 24.1sec; on the other hand, the Jaguar's disc brakes were superior. The Mercedes had the more modest fuel consumption although I find the claimed figure of 10.8 litres per 100km (26.2mpg) a little hard to believe; the Jaguar used 12.3 litres per 100km, equivalent to nearly 23mpg, which is better than the British magazines managed. And as usual, the Jaguar gearbox was criticized: "one can not have any faith in the synchromesh."[32]

So the XK neared the end of its days, as far as road testers were concerned, with its reputation largely intact. If the XK was increasingly deemed to be less of a sports car and more of a Grand Touring car, it continued to be rated highly in this perhaps even more demanding category. The most-criticized aspect of the car was the gearbox. The performance was as impressive as ever, and would indeed only be decisively beaten in 1961 when both the leading weekly journals measured top speeds of 150mph (over 240km/h) for the new E-type. That new car also addressed the occasionally voiced opinions that the XK was getting a bit behind the times in respect of its chassis design. Above all, what continued to astonish commentators was the sheer value for money offered by the XK, and this tradition would certainly be upheld by its successor.

The table below sums up the performance measured in the most important road tests of the various XK 150 models.

3.4 FHC with overdrive	Top speed	0-60mph 0-97km/h	0-100mph 0-161km/h	Std 1/4-mile Std 400m	Fuel consumption
The Autocar 21 Feb 1958	125.5mph 202km/h	8.5sec	25.1sec	16.9sec	20.5mpg 13.8 l/100km
Motor Sport Oct 1958	125mph 201.2km/h	8.5sec	25.2sec		22mpg 12.8 l/100km
Motor Racing Nov 1958	125mph 201.2km/h		25sec	16.8sec	18mpg 15.7 l/100km
3.4 S FHC					
Autosport 5 Jun 1959	132.3mph 212.9km/h	7.4sec	20sec	15.8sec	18mpg 15.7 l/100km
The Motor 19 Aug 1959	132mph 212.4km/h	7.8sec	20.3sec	16.2sec	18.6mpg 15.2 l/100km
The Autocar 18 Sep 1959	134mph 215.7km/h	8.9sec	22.4sec	16.2sec	17mpg 16.6 l/100km
Motor Sport Jan 1960	130mph 209.3km/h	8.9sec	24.7sec		17.05mpg 16.6 l/100km
3.8 S FHC					
Autosport 17 Jun 1960	136.3mph 219.4km/h	7.6sec	19sec	16sec	13mpg 21.7 l/100km
3.4 FHC					
Road & Track Nov 1957	121.6mph 195.7km/h	9.5sec	25.8sec	17.1sec	16-21mpg* 14.7-11.2 l/100km
3.4 OTS					
Road & Track Sep 1958	125mph (est.) 201.2km/h	8.9sec	25sec	16.8sec	
3.4 S OTS					
Sports Cars Illustrated Aug 1958	125-135mph 201-217km/h	9.2sec		17.3sec	
Road & Track Sep 1958	136mph (est.) 218.9km/h	7.3sec	21.4sec	15.1sec	14-19mpg* 16.8-12.4 l/100km
Speed Age Oct 1958	125mph 201.2km/h	7.8sec			12.1mpg* 19.4 l/100km

*assumed to be US gallons

There is a postscript to be added to the story. In 1965 *Autocar* carried out a used-car test of a 1960 XK 150 3.8 fixed-head automatic with just over 70,000 miles on the clock which was then for sale at £565 as against a new price five years earlier of £2070 (including the auto 'box): a depreciation of almost 75 per cent. The car was registered TAP 66, chassis S 825312 BW. Slightly the worse for wear in some respects, it used a pint of oil for every 150 miles (equivalent of a litre for every 425km) and returned 14-18mpg (16-20 l/100km) but acceleration from 0-60mph (97km/h) of 10.5sec was still impressive, bearing in mind this was an automatic. An indicated 100mph (161km/h) came up easily. One is a little worried to learn that the car, still relatively young, had already been re-sprayed. But it is the concluding paragraph which is priceless: "Many believe that in years to come the Jaguar XK 150 will become a connoisseur's car, sought after and treasured. One such as this, which is structurally sound, certainly deserves to find an owner who will lavish care on it and restore it to impeccable condition." Someone did, as S 825312 BW survives today in Australia![33]

1. "La Vie en Rose", *The Motor* 23 Nov 1955
2. *Autosport* 7 Jan 1955
3. *Autosport* 4 Nov 1955
4. *The Autocar* 9 Dec 1955
5. "Black Jaguar", *The Autocar* 17 Aug 1956
6. *The Sunday Express* 15 Jan 1956
7. *The Motor World* 7 Dec 1956
8. *The Motor* 30 Oct 1957
9. *Sports Cars and Specials* Oct 1956;

Elmgreen & McGrath *The Jaguar XK in Australia* p.101
10. Clausager *Jaguar XK 120 in Detail* p.112
11. *Sports Illustrated* 25 Apr 1955
12. *Road & Track* Jun 1955
13. *Sports Cars Illustrated* Mar 1957
14. *Motor Life* Jul 1956
15. *The Autocar* 21 Feb 1958
16. *Motor Sport* Oct 1958
17. *Motor Racing* Nov 1958

18. *Road and Track* Nov 1957
19. *Road and Track* Sep 1958
20. *Speed Age* Oct 1958
21. *Sports Cars Illustrated* Aug 1958
22. *Sports Cars Illustrated* Dec 1958
23. *Autosport* 7 Nov 1958
24. *Autosport* 5 Jun 1959
25. *The Motor* 19 Aug 1959
26. *The Autocar* 18 Sep 1959
27. *Motor Sport* Jan 1960
28. *The Motor* 6 Jan 1960

29. *Autosport* 17 Jun 1960
30. *Sports Car World* Oct 1959; see also Elmgreen & McGrath p.117
31. *Das Auto, Motor und Sport* no.19, 1958; courtesy of Heiner Stertkamp
32. *Hobby* Nov 1960; courtesy of Terry McGrath
33. *Autocar* 9 Jul 1965; Elmgreen & McGrath p.135; information courtesy of David Bentley

Chapter Six

Rivals

What exactly constituted a rival for an XK 140 or XK 150, depended entirely upon your assessment of the Jaguars. Were they sports cars, or were they GT cars? I would argue that perceptions were also markedly different in the USA – which remained the biggest market – and in Europe, with the UK occupying a middle ground.

There was always greater readiness in the USA to consider an XK as a sports car, notwithstanding the fact that Jaguar's North American company advertised the XK 150 fixed-head as a "Grand Touring" car. To the American public, an open two-seater was a sports car, and even more so if it was an imported car. The XK 120 had established itself as a sports car in the USA, as had other British cars, notably of course the MG, the Austin-Healey and the Triumph. This foothold for imported sports cars led American manufacturers to investigate the possibility of producing rivals. We can probably disregard

such oddballs as the Kaiser-Darrin and the Willys-based Woodill Wildfire, as well as the limited production Nash-Healey and the later Arnolt-Bristol.[1] Far more important as competitors for the imported sports cars were the Chevrolet Corvette and the Ford Thunderbird. Chrysler stayed out of this game despite showing a Ghia-designed concept for a similar car called the Falcon in 1955.[2]

The Corvette came first, in 1953, but despite its beguiling styling, initially had only modest performance, with its six-cylinder engine and the hopeless two-speed Powerglide automatic transmission. The Thunderbird, new for 1955, had V8 oomph from the start, and there was the option of overdrive on second and third of its manual gearbox, giving the car effectively five speeds. Arguably, neither had the road holding or handling to match the imports, but they were home-grown, affordable, easily available and could be looked after by the mechanics at your

The second-generation Chevrolet Corvette had a styling update and, more importantly, was fitted with the firm's new overhead-valve V8 engine.

A rare example of an early Ford Thunderbird imported to the UK, against a backdrop of altogether more humble Ford products!

friendly neighbourhood dealership. As for prices, the 1953-54 Corvette cost around $3500, 1955-56 models were actually cheaper and they stayed below $4000 through the 1960 season. A 1955 Thunderbird was just under $3000 and was still under than $3500 in 1957 which was the final year for the two-seater. Mind you, these are list prices and do not include any options![3]

The original Corvette is thought to have had a top speed of around 103mph (165km/h) – I have not found a road test of this car in a British journal. A few examples of the Thunderbird did however reach these shores and *The Autocar* was able to carry out what they believed to be "the first full Road Test to be made on this side of the Atlantic". The car was not impossibly expensive for an import at £2536, although with extras as tested, including automatic transmission, the price was £3115. Top speed was 113mph (181.9km/h) and 0-60mph (0-97km/h) was accomplished in 10.2sec, after which progress was slower – not as quick as a Jaguar, but acceptable. Handling was not up to the best European standards, although with a sports car bias and slight understeer, but the brakes were extremely poor. The Thunderbird was summed up as a "clever compromise between comfort and very high performance indeed."[4]

Originally head-on rivals, the two American cars developed in very different ways. For 1955,

the Corvette adopted Chevrolet's new V8 engine as an alternative and was available in three-speed manual form but otherwise stuck to the two-seater formula. After a shaky start, with only 4629 cars made from 1953 to 1955, the Corvette began to sell in greater numbers than the Jaguar. Production figures increased sharply with the second generation body style which lasted from the 1956 model year through 1962, from 3467 in 1956 to 14,531 in 1962, for a total of over 64,000 over the seven years. The two-seater Ford Thunderbird reached 53,166 in three seasons. The 1958 Thunderbird went in another direction and became a bloated four-seater, of the type which the American industry considered a "personal car" and which was their idea of a GT. It outsold the Corvette by an enormous margin with over 64,000 cars in *each* model year from 1959 onwards.[5] These later T-birds were completely unsporting, but the V8 Corvette proved to be a serious competitor in American sports car racing.

The greatest rivals for the Jaguar in the USA were however other British sports cars. When the popularity of the MG and the Jaguar in export markets became obvious to other British car manufacturers, many of them responded by producing sports models which were aimed at plugging the very obvious gap in the market place between the two. The most successful of

these varied offerings came predictably from the mass manufacturers who apart from anything else already had well-established sales networks in North America. At the Earls Court Motor Show in October 1952, Standard-Triumph launched a sports car which after further gestation emerged as the TR2 in 1953. Fitted with a 2-litre version of the ubiquitous Standard Vanguard engine, this quickly established itself as the cheapest genuine 100mph (161km/h) car on the British market, although it took a few more years before it became a significant best-seller in TR3A form. However, in terms of price and performance, these Triumphs were always closer to the MGA, and can not be considered as Jaguar competitors.

At the same Motor Show, the small Healey company of Warwick launched the Healey 100 based on Austin components, which became the Austin-Healey 100 after Donald Healey did a deal with BMC. With a four-cylinder 2.6-litre engine it had superior performance to the Triumph and although more expensive, was initially the better seller. Of greater relevance to the Jaguar story, the Austin-Healey was also quicker to "up the ante" with the six-cylinder 100-Six of 1956: no six-cylinder engine was as yet available to Triumph. The first 100-Six however was a disappointment, with its two-plus-two body and underachieving engine, and

although matters were improved, a really satisfactory result was only achieved with the 3000 of 1959, with front disc brakes and more power. This cost £1176 and had a top speed of 114mph (183.5km/h), although acceleration was not its strongest suit as it took 11.4sec to reach 60mph (97km/h).[6] Never quite as potent as a Jaguar, it was never quite as expensive either, and established its own market niche below the Jaguar, both in the UK and the USA.

The following is a comparison of production figures, overall and for the USA, between the six-cylinder Austin-Healeys and the XK 150:[7]

	Austin-Healey, total	Austin-Healey, for the USA	Jaguar XK 150, total	Jaguar XK 150, for the USA
1958	6615	5427	4539	3148
1959	7900	6872	2171	1053
1960	7005	5379	1321	656

As one would expect, the cheaper car sold better, despite the lack of fixed-head or drop-head coupé versions. What is possibly more revealing is that the figures suggest that the popularity of the XK 150 after 1958 declined radically compared at least to this competitor. The Triumph TR3A and the MGA saw far higher production figures, with over 20,000 cars of either type made in the peak year of 1959 alone.

Most other British sports cars at the time were made in much smaller numbers. Allard and Frazer Nash had once offered cars which could compete with the XK 120 in terms of performance, if not in sophistication, but both were on the way out. Allard eventually had to go to Jaguar for its power units, and that they were allowed to buy XK engines speaks volumes for Jaguar's perception of Allard not being a competitor, much less a threat. Frazer Nash's final effort adopted a German BMW V8 unit, but the result was far too expensive at £3751 and got no further than a prototype shown at Earls Court in 1956. AC had a wonderful all-independently sprung chassis in the Ace and Aceca models but struggled to find an engine which was powerful enough, and the solution of using an American Ford V8 engine to make the Cobra was only found in the early 1960s. Meanwhile, the Bristol-engined Ace reached 116.5mph (187.5km/h), respectable for 1971cc, at a cost of £2095.[8] The longer wheelbase four-seater Greyhound of 1960 knocked on the door of the GT market but with the same engine size had a 104mph (167.4km/h) top speed, disappointing for £2892.

A final attempt of making a sports car for the American market came surprisingly from Daimler. By the mid-to-late 1950s this company

was in trouble, but their chief engineer Edward Turner came up with a pair of outstanding V8 engines, of 2½ and 4½ litres respectively. In contrast to AC, Daimler had the engines but was struggling to design cars to fit them into. By dint of copying a Triumph TR3A chassis, they came up with a sports car to use the smaller engine. It was cloaked in an outrageously-styled fibreglass body and launched at the 1959 New York Motor Show under the name of Daimler Dart, but since Dodge had registered this model name, the Daimler had to be re-named the SP250. Performance was good for the engine size, not in the XK league, but very comparable with the Austin-Healey. Top speed was 121mph (194.6mph), the 0-60mph (0-97km/h) time was 10.2sec, and the fuel consumption of 29.1mpg (9.7 l/100km) was remarkable. The home market price was £1395.[9]

The cars suffered from patchy build quality, and although Daimler tried hard to sell the cars in the USA – mostly through the organisation which handled BSA and Triumph motorcycles as Daimler was part of the BSA Group – many early cars were so poor that they had to be shipped back for re-work, and in any case 1960-61 saw the recession in the American car market with import sales dropping drastically. When Jaguar bought the Daimler company in 1960, some remedial work was undertaken to improve

The love-it-or-hate-it styling of the fibreglass body was not the greatest asset of the Daimler SP250; the engine, by contrast, was an absolute gem.

the structural deficiencies and build quality of the SP250, but the damage had been done, and although the SP250 lingered on until 1964, production only reached 2648 cars and Jaguar decided not to replace the model. That lovely engine actually found a worthier home in the Jaguar Mark II body shell.

The vast majority of Jaguar open two-seaters were sold in North America. In the UK, two-seater sales were negligible, and both here and in most other markets, the fixed-head and drop-head models were far more popular: a trend which had already manifested itself in the final years of the XK 120. This strongly suggests that in these markets, the Jaguars were now perceived more as GT cars. While high performance was as important in the GT market as it was in the sports car market, GT customers also expected comfort and sophistication, while open body styles were not necessarily sought-after or popular. On the other hand, occasional seating for four, and reasonable luggage accommodation, were welcome characteristics on a GT car. In the perfect GT car, you, your companion, and your luggage, would be able to travel the 600 miles (say 1000km) from Paris to the Riviera, at high speed, in a day, in comfort and safety, without feeling unduly tired at the end of your journey; even in pre-motorway days.

Of the UK offerings, the Jaguars always had the edge in terms of their combination of price and performance, yet price was not the only consideration in this class where some potential purchasers could just as easily buy a Bentley Continental and have done with it. Acceleration or ultimate top speed might not be as important as the ability to maintain a high cruising speed in a relaxed manner. Several British manufacturers offered admirable GT models in the late 1950s including Alvis, Aston Martin, Bristol, and Jensen, all of which were rather more expensive than an XK. The Alvis 3-litre Graber coupé and the Bristols, before this company adopted American Chrysler V8 engines, had top speeds around 105-110mph (170-180km/h), the later version of the Jensen 541 was quicker around 120mph (190km/h).

The most formidable performers came from Aston Martin, especially with the DB4 which was introduced at the 1958 London Motor Show. This was nearly a proper four-seater: "an ideal long-distance touring car… a Grand Tourer, in fact". With 267bhp from its 3.7-litre six-cylinder twin ohc engine and reasonably low weight thanks to the *Superleggera* construction it would reach 140.6mph (226.3km/h), and sprint to 100mph (161km/h) in 21.7sec.[10] Road behaviour was impeccable and the all-disc braking system outstanding. Looks were stunning, but so was

Jensen produced some interesting and powerful GT cars. This 541R benefited from four-wheel disc brakes, just like the Jaguars.

the price of £3755 when the most expensive XK 150 cost around £2200. A DB4 was for the privileged few, and production was measured in the hundreds. The supreme achievement of Jaguar was to offer comparable performance at a fraction of the cost of an Aston and its European peers.

European manufacturers had not quite neglected sports cars, but the most prominent manufacturer devoting itself to this market sector was Porsche which as yet offered nothing bigger than a 1.6-litre engine, although their small lightweight aerodynamic rear-engined cars were remarkably effective performers and already had an enviable competition record. The Carrera version with a quad-cam 1.6-litre engine had a top speed nudging 120mph (190km/h); later 2-litre versions were quicker. Furthermore, the 356 showed signs of combining the best of both worlds, as a sports car and a GT car. Porsche's day would come with the 911 which from its launch in 1963 developed into a competitor for the E-type, and whose popularity remains undiminished to this day, in its umpteenth reincarnation.

Further up the scale a similar status could be accorded to the Mercedes-Benz 300SL, a race-bred car with an impeccable sporting pedigree and a Le Mans win to its credit. This was an

engineering masterpiece, in most respects far in advance of what Jaguar or any British manufacturer could offer at the time. Furthermore, it had the looks, speed and glamour to take over from the XK as the must-have sports car for the international jet-set but at a price which was anything up to twice of a Jaguar (£4393 in Britain in 1955), and it was hardly suitable for large-scale production; only around 3000 were made altogether. Claims of a 260km/h (over 160mph) top speed for the early gull-wing coupés were unrealistic for standard cars, and for the later roadster from 1957 onwards were reduced to 215-225km/h (134-140mph).

These in fact were the sort of speeds which were recorded in British road tests of the original 300SL gull-wing coupé, by *Autosport* and *The Autocar* which managed 140.6mph (226.3 km/h) and 135mph (217.3km/h), with a significant difference in the times measured for 0-100mph (0-161km/h) acceleration of 16.2 and 21 sec.[11] Rob Walker who had the first 300SL imported to Britain claimed that 157-162mph (253-261km/h) had been obtained in Germany by similar cars with high axle ratios.[12] In Switzerland, *Automobil Revue* got a roadster with a 3.64:1 rear axle up to 237km/h (147.3mph).[13] Like the XK, the 300SL was reasonably quiet, comfortable and docile, with a flexible engine,

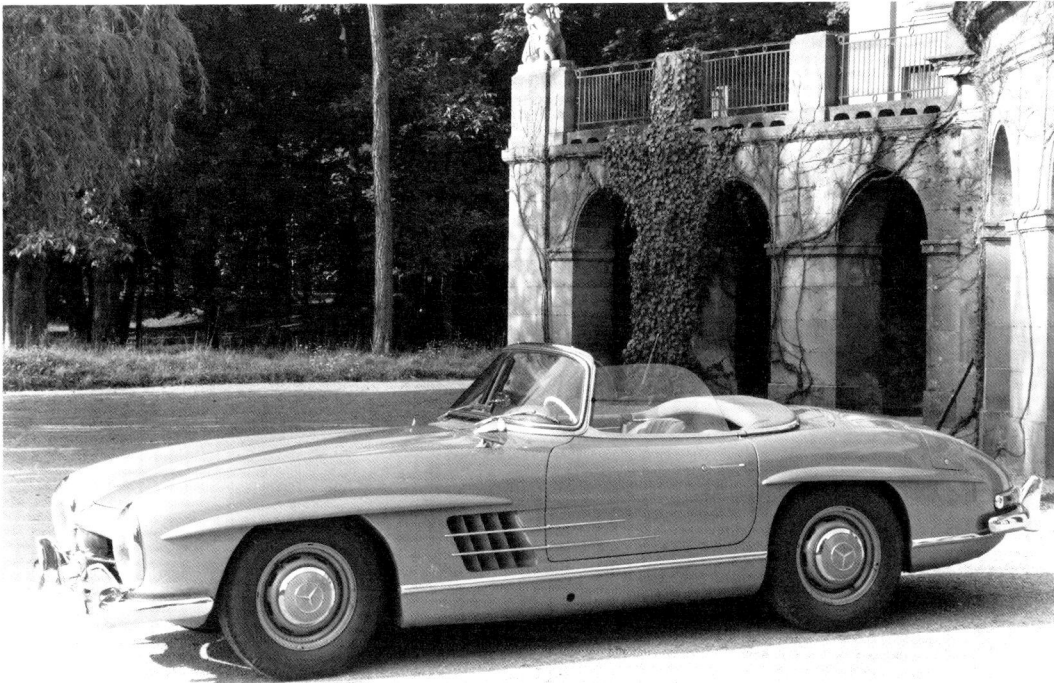

The roadster version of the Mercedes-Benz 300SL was probably developed with an eye to the American market. Performance was impressive.

but in the road test reports the Mercedes otherwise comes across as a machine for the initiated expert driver who could exploit the handling to the full without being caught unawares by its road behaviour, which could be wayward if the car was not handled with the care and respect it demanded and deserved.

BMW briefly tried to rival the 300SL with the Goertz-designed 507 roadster which was similar in terms of price and performance with a top speed around 221km/h (137.3mph), but lacked any competition pedigree and always had a rather more "boulevard" image. The pre-war Auto-Union racing driver Hans Stuck, by then BMW's sports car sales manager, bravely hill-climbed the 507 and had some good results. Very few came to the UK, although the racing driver John Surtees bought one. Among other famous customers were Elvis Presley and the Aga Khan. BMW made precisely 252 of them between 1955 and 1959.[14]

Most other large-engined European sporting cars tended more towards the GT class. For many years the yardstick was the Lancia Aurelia GT, but when that was discontinued in 1957 its Flaminia-based replacement never attracted a similar following, mainly I suspect since even the most sporting versions of the Flaminia – the short-wheelbase models such as the Zagato-

bodied coupé – did not have quite the same edge to their performance, despite the engine size being increased from 2.5 to 2.8 litres. They were however excellent cars, with all the contemporary elegance which you would expect from an Italian design.

Since Alfa Romeo throughout the 1950s made nothing bigger than a 2-litre four-cylinder car, the real Italian performance elite were repre-

Not as successful at the time as its Mercedes-Benz competitor, the stylish BMW 507 has since become somewhat of an icon.

sented by Ferrari and Maserati. Of this redoubtable pair, the lead undoubtedly belonged to Ferrari. They had the "unique selling point" of a V12 engine, they had a far more consistently successful record in motor sport, both in Grand Prix and in sports car racing, and they were ahead of their rivals in producing large-capacity road cars: by 1955 Maserati were rather grudgingly coming around to making a six-cylinder 2-litre road car, when your typical Ferrari had an extra litre and twice the number of cylinders. Five years later the balance had been somewhat restored with Maserati's 3½ and 5 litre V8 engines with 385bhp claimed for the latter, although Ferrari by then claimed 400bhp for their 4-litre V12. Both makes were bespoke and often fitted with special coachwork; as late as 1956 Ferrari built fewer than 100 cars per year.[15]

Maserati would not arrive in Britain until 1964 but Ferraris first came to these shores in 1958. Probably the only Ferrari that need concern us is the 250GT of which apparently precisely 11 were sold in the UK between 1958 and 1960. No wonder, as the original list price was £6469 (later reduced to below £6000): this was Rolls-Royce territory. The two-plus-two 250GTE model of 1960-62 did better in the UK, with 47 sales here of a total production of 950 units.[16] It

was of course a delectable piece of machinery with the Lampredi-designed 3-litre V12 engine producing 250bhp at a prodigious 7000rpm – but note, only one overhead camshaft per bank! I would have been happier to have had the claimed top speed of 145-150mph (233-241km/h) verified by an independent road test, but in 1961 Harry Mundy, then technical editor of *The Autocar*, drove a 250GT two-plus-two in Italy and reported a top speed of 137.2mph (220.8km/h) in overdrive top, together with a 0-100mph (0-161km/h) time of 19.1sec.[17] This was about what you would expect from an XK 150 S but not as quick as the E-type. To give Ferrari the benefit of the doubt, the short wheelbase two-seaters were lighter and would have been quicker. Bodies in either coupé or convertible form were Pininfarina at his supreme best, but of fragile aluminium construction.

The erstwhile *grandes routières* of France were on their uppers by the mid-1950s, with Bugatti, Delage, Delahaye, Hotchkiss, Salmson and Talbot-Lago all suffering lingering deaths. The two last-mentioned just about survived through the XK 140 era. Salmson was interestingly enough a long-standing devotee of engines with twin overhead camshafts, and their final fling was the lovely little 2300 GT coupé. On 110bhp it did quite well to reach 180km/h

At today's prices there are probably a few million Pounds' worth of Ferrari 250 GTs and GTEs in this contemporary factory shot.

The 2500 version of the handsome Talbot Lago was nearly the swansong for this old-established French manufacturer.

Salmson had similarly fallen on hard times when they introduced this GT model, just as pretty as the Talbot above, except for those wire wheels!

(112mph). Talbot had a thumping great 4.5-litre engine which was as near as you would get to a pre-war design but with an outstanding record in motor racing, including Grand Prix and Le Mans. They fitted this in the superb-looking GS coupé which later received a new, smaller 120bhp 2.5-litre engine and became the 2500 model, unfortunately with four rather than six cylinders, and performance similar to the Salmson. After frantically casting around for an alternative, they ended up briefly using the BMW V8 that Frazer Nash had also coveted. Neither of these French cars was available in the UK but they were not impossibly expensive in Switzerland. Production figures were tiny and the result was almost a foregone conclusion – they disappeared into the maws of mass-producers, Salmson fell to Renault and Talbot to Simca.

Surprisingly, in spite of a home market limited by exorbitant taxation on large-engined vehicles – which, perversely, seemed to allow a window of opportunity for imports such as Jaguar, Mercedes-Benz and many American cars – France produced a successor, of sorts. The Facel Vega had an extraordinary parentage, in the shape of the Comète, which was Ford-France's early attempt at a personal GT car, bodied by Jean Daninos's Facel concern which

also worked on chassis such as Bentley. When Ford sold out to Simca, Daninos and his stylist Brasseur came up with the Vega which in short order became the Facel Vega.

This was not quite the first "Euro-American" hybrid GT in the post-war period, as there was already the Allard, but by adopting the Chrysler V8 engine the Facel Vega nevertheless started a trend. The styling was quite outrageous with a wrap-around dogleg windscreen, in contrast to a complacently fake mock-traditional grille. The interior was remarkable with the first centre console on any car, and instruments and controls worthy of a light aircraft. Almost as

Facel Vega styling was by contrast an acquired taste. The HK 500 featured a Chrysler V8 engine and performance was more than adequate.

By Pegaso standards, the styling of this Z103 roadster is actually quite restrained, and, if the designer was not Italian, his inspiration clearly was.

extravagant as the Docker Daimlers, the Facel nevertheless combined substance with style. If prices were at the Aston Martin or Ferrari level, the performance was also comparable; *The Motor* testing an HK500 with a 6286cc 360bhp engine spoke of a top speed of approximately 140mph (225km/h) and quoted a 0-100mph (0-161km/h) time of 21.1sec. It was just as well that the Facel Vega had followed the Jaguar lead and adopted disc brakes. The price in the UK as tested was £4740.[18]

The car had a small but international following, the USA being predictably the biggest market. Sadly things soon began to wrong for Facel; questions were raised over the structural integrity of the Excellence long wheelbase four-door pillarless saloon, and allegedly for the

same reason the company declined orders for a convertible version once seen at the Paris Motor Show. Their effort to enter the British-dominated market for smaller sports cars with the twin-ohc engined Facellia was a disaster as the car was plagued by endless reliability problems. In the end they resorted to adopting Austin-Healey and Volvo engines, but gave up the unequal struggle in 1964.

Finally, the Pegaso, that all-but mythical Spanish beast. Designed by Wilfredo Ricart formerly of Alfa Romeo, this was truly a "jewel for the rich" and the most splendid piece of automotive theatre since the Mercedes-Benz 540K *Spezial-Roadster*, at least when bodied by Saoutchik or Touring; home-grown styling was humdrum in comparison. The recipe included a quad-cam V8 typically of 2.8 or 3.2 litres, and Pegaso was one of few at this time to espouse supercharging. There was also a "crash" five-speed gearbox mounted in unit with a limited-slip differential, and a deDion rear axle. The claims for power outputs and top speeds, up to 285bhp and 300km/h (186mph) for a "blown" 3.2-litre car, were equally extravagant but an alleged "stock" 2.8-litre supercharged roadster did reach 151mph (243km/h) over the flying kilometre on the Belgian Jabbeke motorway in 1953, inviting prompt retaliation from Jaguar. Factory prices in Barcelona started around £3000 but $15,000 was the lowest estimate for a Pegaso landed in New York, and a figure of £7800 was mentioned when the marque appeared at Earls Court in 1952. Little more than 100 cars had been built by the time Pegaso gave up the struggle and sought refuge in their traditional diesel-engined trucks in 1958.[19]

Bearing in mind that not all of the foreign competitors were available in the UK, and when they were, were priced out of sight because of the import duty of one-third of value, in the following tables I have also quoted the prices in the neutral Swiss market (there were then approximately 12 Swiss Francs to the £), which together with the technical data have been taken from the contemporary issues of that admirable annual publication, the catalogue issue of *Automobil Revue*. The only *caveat* is that they tended simply to report the top speed as stated by the manufacturer, and some of these were obviously not shrinking violets when it came to making extravagant claims!

Comparison between Swiss and UK markets, February 1955

	Price in Swiss francs	Price in UK incl. PT	Engine:cyl/cc/bhp (PS)	Top speed
AC Ace	n/a	£1439	6/1991/86	160km/h
Allard K3	n/a	£1559	V8/3622/96 (other engines available)	160km/h
Aston Martin DB2-4	34,950 (coupé) 36,450 (conv.)	£2728/£2870	6/2922/142	190-200km/h
Austin-Healey 100	14,500	£1064	4/2660/91	170km/h
Bristol	29,000 (403) 29,500 (404)	£2976/£3330	6/1971/107	165-170km/h
Chevrolet Corvette	n/a	n/a	6/3859/152	165km/h
Delahaye 235	38,750	n/a	6/3557/152	165-180km/h
Facel Vega	n/a	n/a	V8/4768/203	175km/h
Ferrari 250	52,000	n/a	V12/2953/220	190-218km/h
Ford Thunderbird	n/a	n/a	V8/4785/193 or 201	170-190km/h
Frazer-Nash	n/a	£3189	6/1971/142	200-215km/h
Jaguar XK 140	20,500 to 22,500	£1598 to £1644	6/3442/192 or 213	180-220km/h
Jensen 541	n/a	£1822	6/3993/131	170-180km/h
Lancia Aurelia B20	26,900 (GT) 29,500 (Spider)	£3472 (GT)	V6/2451/118	185km/h
Maserati 2000 A6 G54	n/a	n/a	6/1986/120	200km/h
Mercedes-Benz 300SL	33,500	£4393	6/2996/243	260km/h
Pegaso 102B/BS	n/a	n/a	V8/2816 or 3178/not quoted	240-300km/h
Salmson 2300 Sport	25,000	n/a	4/2328/110	180km/h
Talbot Lago GS	35,500	n/a	6/4482/210	185-200km/h

Comparison between Swiss and UK markets, February 1960

	Price in Swiss francs	Price in UK incl. PT	Engine:cyl/cc/bhp (SAE PS)	Top speed
AC Ace (Bristol)	23,350	£2045	6/1971/127	205km/h
AC Greyhound	31,200	£2891	6/1971/126	185km/h
Alfa Romeo 2000 spider	24,900	£3114	4/1975/133	175km/h
Allard Gran Turismo	n/a	£2409	6/3442/213	185-200km/h
Alvis TD21 coupe	29,900	£2827	6/2993/118*	165-175km/h
Aston Martin DB4	43,400	£3755	6/3670/267	225-238km/h
Aston Martin DB4 GT	47,500	£4534	6/3670/331	229-246km/h (or more)
Austin-Healey 3000	16,100	£1168	6/2912/132	173-184km/h
BMW 507	41,400	£4393	V8/3168/150 or 165*	205-221km/h
Bristol 406	45,400	£4244	6/2216/107	Over 160km/h
Chevrolet Corvette	31,100	£2905	V8/4637/233 to 319	190-220km/h
Daimler SP250	n/a	£1395	V8/2548/142	196km/h
Facel Vega HK500	43,250	£4534	V8/5907/335-360	205-235km/h
Ferrari 250GT	46,000	£5951	V12/2953/240-280**	225km/h (or more)
Ferrari 400	n/a	n/a	V12/3967/400**	Up to 300km/h
Ford Thunderbird	From 29,850	£3179	V8/5166 or 7045/304 or 355	180-200km/h
Jaguar XK 150	25,400 to 30,200	£1831 to £2176	6/3442 or 3781/213 to 268	220-225km/h
Jensen 541R	35,750	£2707	6/3993/152	193km/h
Lancia Flaminia GT or Sport	30,150	£3918	V6/2458/132	180-190km/h
Maserati 3500GT	From 41,500	n/a	6/3485/260	236km/h
Maserati 5000GT	61,000	n/a	V8/4975/385	275-290km/h
Mercedes-Benz 300SL	41,600	£5314	6/2996/240	215-225km/h

*DIN PS

** Measuring method not indicated

1. For accurate and often amusing thumbnail sketches of these and many other cars discussed in this chapter, I have extensively used and recommend Sedgwick *The Motor Car 1946-56*. Robson *Cars in the UK* – vol.1 1945 to 1970, Robson *A-Z British Cars 1945-1980* and Sedgwick/Gillies *A-Z of cars 1945-1970* are also handy reference books

2. *Autosport* 16 Sep 1955; *Automobil-Revue Katalog-Nummer* 1957 p.85

3. Anon *50 Years of American Automobiles from 1939* pp.476-77, 555

4. *The Autocar* 10 Feb 1956

5. Production figures from *50 Years of American Automobiles*

6. *The Autocar* 28 Aug 1959

7. Austin-Healey figures from Clausager *Original Austin-Healey* pp.88-91

8. *The Motor* 26 Aug 1959

9. *The Autocar* 2 Oct 1959

10. *The Autocar* 13 Oct 1961; until then the DB4 was the fastest production four-seater yet tested by this journal

11. *Autosport* 7 Jan 1955; *The Autocar* 25 Mar 1955

12. *Motor Sport* Aug 1955

13. *Automobil Revue* road test no.103 22 Jan 1959

14. *Automobil Revue* road test no.111 6 Aug 1959; Kittler *Essential BMW Roadsters & Cabriolets* pp.32-44

15. Ferrari press statement quoted in *Autosport* 9 Nov 1956

16. Robson *Cars in the UK...* pp.77, 86, 107; 160-61; 182-83

17. *The Autocar* 30 Jun 1961

18. *The Motor* 6 Apr 1960

19. Montagu *Lost Causes of Motoring: Europe* vol.2 pp.306-09; Franco "Pegaso: *El Caballo Volador de España* in *Automobile Quarterly* vol.6 no.2 1967

Chapter Seven

XK 140 and XK 150 in competition

The XK 140 and XK 150 were not to enjoy the same success in competition as their forerunner. The reasons for this were that they were not as competitive in first-line sports car racing as the XK 120 had been in its heyday, and that the new homologation system did not favour high-powered GT or production sports cars, whether in track or road events. As far as the cars themselves were concerned, rack-and-pinion steering and disc brakes must have been welcome improvements also for competition purposes, and while their performance was still remarkable, weight was beginning to tell against them. They were not as nimble as the XK 120s, which right through the 1950s and beyond often got the better of later cars, even E-types, in those races that were open to them.

The XK 120 had quickly made its mark, in racing with Johnson's win at Silverstone in 1949 and Moss's win in the 1950 Tourist Trophy, and in rallying, with Appleyard's performances in the Alpine and RAC rallies. However, from 1951 it was overshadowed by the C-type in racing. When the XK 140 appeared in 1954, the C-type had given way to the D-type, and neither the 140 nor the 150 could match the performance of these more specialised Jaguars. In rallying, the focus at the time was on saloon cars. In the Monte Carlo Rally open two-seaters were often barred from taking part, a ban extended to all rallies in France in 1956. It soon turned out that sports cars could be re-classified as GT cars, provided they had exterior door handles and

permanent side windows rather than removable side screens.[1] Instead, the Monte was won by Ronnie Adams's works-lent Jaguar Mark VII in 1956, and from 1957 onwards most Jaguars in rallies were 3.4-litre saloons.

Part of the problem facing the XKs in competition was the homologation system, then newly introduced by the *Commission Sportive Internationale* (the CSI) of the *Fédération Internationale de l'Automobile* (the FIA). In 1949, the organisers of the Le Mans 24-hour race, which had started out as an event for production touring cars, for the first time had admitted so-called "prototypes".[2] Eventually, this led to some cars taking part that were closer to Grand Prix racers than to any road-going car which the public could buy, such as the Talbot-Lago in 1950-51, or the Mercedes-Benz in 1955; in contrast, both the C-type and D-type were built in some numbers, and were on sale to the public. The new breed of highly specialised sports-racing prototypes, apart from the Jaguars mentioned, meant that normal production cars such as the XKs were quickly left behind in sports car racing.

When the World Championship for sports cars was inaugurated in 1953, qualifying races included Sebring (12 hours), Mille Miglia, Le Mans, Spa-Francorchamps (24 hours), the Nürburgring 1000km race, the Tourist Trophy and the Carrera Panamericana, all long-distance endurance events, but of hugely different character.[3] As the Championship became more

Guyot and Parsy finished 16th in the 1956 Tour de France with their XK 140 fixed-head. The location here is the Saint-Etienne circuit. (Paul Skilleter)

established it is likely that interest in this type of racing increased, and some of the manufacturers who contested the series made greater efforts to build competitive cars. Jaguar was never greatly interested in the Championship. Their main aim was to win at Le Mans, which in 1953 they duly did, but otherwise the works C-types only turned up for two championship races, Mille Miglia and the Tourist Trophy, and their scant reward was a third place in the latter, setting a pattern which was to be repeated over the following years.

Probably in response to the increasing number of prototype sports-racing cars, the FIA introduced the Appendix J of the International Sporting Code in February 1955 and for the first time this began to classify cars in various Groups, with limitations on permitted modifications, and stipulated minimum production figures. As the system evolved during the following years, both the XK 140 and the XK 150 were classified as Group 3 Grand Touring cars rather than Sports cars.[1] While they were clearly not competitive against prototype sports-racing cars, because they were GT cars (i.e. production sports cars), they were subject to handicapping in road rallies where they competed against production touring saloon cars.

Furthermore, in the late 1950s, racing for touring cars – again meaning saloons – was growing in popularity, but there were fewer races for production sports or GT cars. In the SCCA races in the USA, there were classes for such cars, but here the Chevrolet Corvette was rapidly becoming a formidable competitor, never mind the Mercedes-Benz 300SL. In Europe from 1957 onwards, the Jaguar of choice for motor sport was the 120mph (192km/h) 3.4-litre saloon, which was conveniently homologated as a standard touring car.

The FIA Appendix J was revised in 1956 and 1957 and the system of issuing formal homologation forms followed soon after. Previously, Jaguar had completed rather simple RAC "Recognition Forms" which were also used at first for the XK 150, but probably in 1960 official FIA forms were compiled for the XK 150 3.8 litre standard and S versions, two of them with the low FIA recognition numbers of 10 and 11.[5]

There were attempts at turning the clock back. The tragic disaster at Le Mans in 1955 led to some restrictions on sports-racing prototypes, including a limit on engine size to 2.5 and later 3 litres, minimum dimensions for windscreens and interior width, a requirement for two identical seats and two doors as well as a hood, and even in 1960 minimum boot size.[6] At Reims in 1957, the 12-hour race was run for GT cars but since this turned into a procession of Ferrari 250GTs "the public was frankly bored."[7] In Britain, *Autosport* magazine sponsored a championship for production sports cars from 1956 to 1961 which was contested, among others, by several XK 120s[8], but when a GT race was held as part of the International Trophy Race Meeting at Silverstone in May 1959 it was described as "the first event of its kind to be held at Silverstone."[9] Stirling Moss won in an Aston Martin DB4.

In 1960, the Tourist Trophy race then held at Goodwood was turned into a GT race, and the large-capacity class was predictably dominated by Aston Martin and Ferrari – Moss won in one of the latter – and Jaguars were completely absent.[10] While GT racing gained a toe-hold in the late 1950s and early 1960s, in Britain often as not the main beneficiary was the Lotus Elite. Ultimately, the compromise result was that endurance races came to be run for *both* categories together, sports-racing prototypes *and* GT production cars.

Therefore, as much as anything else for lack of opportunity, the career of the later XKs in motor sport, whether on road or track, was unremarkable, and the entrants and drivers of these cars were ever-hopeful privateers, who were occasionally given the opportunity to shine in the race meetings organised by the Jaguar Drivers' Club, formed in 1957. There are very few entries for the XK 140 and XK 150 in the appendix in Lord Montagu's *Jaguar – A Biography*. Apart from contemporary sources, notably *Autosport* magazine, of many other quoted references Viart's two books stand out for their coverage of Continental events which are less well-known in Britain, and my research in the *Car Record Books* has identified many cars, from the name of the first owner and the registration mark.

The XK 140

The most famous of all XK 140 race entries must be the car that took part in the 1956 Le Mans 24-hour race. In 1955, Hawthorn had won Le Mans with the D-type after the withdrawal of the Mercedes-Benz team which in turn had followed the disaster where Levegh's Mercedes had ploughed into spectators with horrendous loss of life. After the 1955 tragedy, the Le Mans track underwent considerable modification and in consequence, the 1956 race was delayed from its customary June date until the last weekend in July. As well as three works D-types in what was to prove the last race for the factory team, single D-types were entered by *Ecurie Ecosse* and *Ecurie Francorchamps*, with the most important competition coming from Aston Martin and Ferrari. And then there was an XK 140.

This was chassis number S 804231 DN, a Suede Green Special Equipment fixed-head coupé, which had been sold through Appleyard in Leeds, and was registered PWT 846. The first owner was Robert (Bob) Walshaw, who entered and ran the car at Le Mans with Peter Bolton as his co-driver. By the time of the race, the car had reputedly covered 25,000 miles (40,000km) and was in remarkably standard form, the most important mechanical modifications were 2in carburettors and supposedly an extra 36-gallon (164-litre) fuel tank – which is odd as the maximum allowed fuel capacity was 130 litres (28.6 gallons). The car ran like clockwork and was at one time in twelfth or even eleventh place, only to be disqualified after 20 hours for re-fuelling too early, after 33 rather than the 34 laps stipulated. The average speed for 212 laps had been 83mph (133.6km/h); for comparison, Flockhart and Sanderson averaged over 104mph (167.4km/h) in the winning *Ecurie Ecosse* D-type.

The disqualification was later disputed by

Peter Bolton who claimed the organisers had mixed up the race number 6 of the XK 140 with the number 4 carried by the winning D-type. It should be added that the Walshaw/Bolton team approached the race – their first Le Mans – in a happy-go-lucky spirit and might not even have got as far as they did, without some assistance from David Murray and *Ecurie Ecosse* with their pit work, but they won much praise from the press, and commiserations for their bad luck. Both drivers finished in the 1957 Le Mans race, Walshaw in a Lotus and Bolton in an AC-Bristol. Bolton indeed clocked up ten Le Mans entries until 1965, in a great variety of cars, and was seventh in an AC Cobra in 1963. Their XK 140 was later driven by Ivor Bueb who won a race in the *Daily Herald* Gold Cup meeting at Oulton Park in September 1956. It was at one time part of the Robert Danny collection of Jaguars, and happily still exists.[11]

Another famous French sports car race contested by an XK 140 was the fourth 12-hour race at Reims which as mentioned above for a change was for "Gran Turismo" cars and was held in connection with a Formula 1 race in July 1957. Ian Baillie and Peter Jopp very sportingly ran an XK 140, the only Jaguar entry. This was a Cream fixed-head which I think must have been PXU 643 which Baillie and Grennall ran in the 1958 Monte Carlo Rally. It was chassis S 804019 built in February 1955 and, according to the *Car Record Book*, sold by Henlys in London to one E

Dracakis. After Jopp was shunted by an Alfa and spun off, losing ten laps, they finished a lowly fourteenth in a race dominated by Ferrari 250GTs in first to fifth places, and they were also behind most of the smaller-engined Porsches and Alfa Romeos.[12] Ian Baillie later had an XK 150 (see chapter 9). An obviously wealthy officer and gentleman, he served in the Life Guards and is better known as the owner of D-type XKD 511 with which he set a number of Class C records at Monza in March 1957.[13]

One of few other entries of an XK 140 in a major European sports car race (but see also below) was that of John Heath of HWM who had an XK 140 fixed-head which I think was S 804007 DN (see chapter 9). He entered in the 1955 Mille Miglia and finished in 40th place. He also intended to enter the car in the 1955 Le Mans race, but it failed to appear.[14]

Miss Eunice Griffin drove an XK 140 drophead registered RXR 235 at Prescott in 1956, and also in the RSAC Rest-And-Be-Thankful hill climb in June 1957, where she set a time of 75 seconds which was the best performance by a lady.[15] Her car was chassis 807164, which went through Henlys in London, while the first owner was David Porter of Bishops Frome. Pantlin's XK 140 fixed-head was first in class E in the Snetterton Production Sports Car scratch race in May 1957 but he had lost to an XK 120 on this track in March. J Bekaert was third in the production sports car race at the BRSCC Brands

This is the XK 140 which ran at Le Mans in 1956, a Suede Green SE fixed-head coupé with many special modifications for racing.

The XK 140 wire wheels had 54 spokes, and were normally painted body colour, although they were also available part or fully chromed.

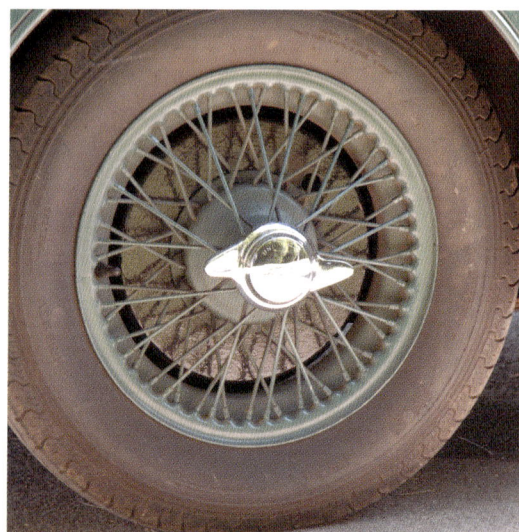

As discussed in the text, the Le Mans car had an extra large fuel tank, with this quick-release large filler cap mounted on the right-hand side of the car to make pit work easier.

The headlamps were the special high-efficiency Lucas Le Mans type.

The louvred bonnet was another non-standard feature of this car.

The Le Mans car was fitted with the sand-cast 2in carburettors which were available as special tuning equipment from Jaguar, but not fitted to production cars. The automatic starting carburettor was deleted when these were fitted, so a manual choke became necessary.

It was only the fixed-head coupé models which had sun visors, on the XK 140 of this type of dark green translucent plastic.

The dashboard of the Le Mans car was standard, but the car was later fitted with a brass plaque which gives this version of its history.

The Le Mans car had its bumpers removed and there were extra air intakes for the radiator and for keeping the front brakes cool.

The rear bumpers were also removed on the Le Mans car.

PWT 846

Unusually, the Le Mans car had the individual bucket seats, again offered by Jaguar. They had fixed back rests which wrapped well around.

The outsize fuel tank was mounted at the front of the boot, and the spare wheel was mounted at an angle, with a box for tools and spares below.

David Hobbs raced this drophead enthusiastically until crashing it so badly that it had to be completely rebodied. (Paul Skilleter)

Hatch meeting in August 1957, also in an XK 140. As neither name figures among the original owners in the factory records, I have not been able to trace these two cars.[16]

Then there was the David Hobbs car, an XK 140 drophead registered TAC 743, which was chassis S 807297, sold through SH Newsome in Coventry. The first owner was Howard Hobbs of Leamington Spa, the inventor of the Mechamatic automatic gearbox which it was intended to use on the still-born Lanchester Sprite of 1955-56. He fitted one of these gearboxes to a Lotus Elite, and another went into the XK 140 which was also given disc brakes. It was raced by Howard's son David, formerly a Daimler apprentice, who came first in the unlimited class of the touring and GT race at Snetterton in July 1960 and first in the GT race at Snetterton in August 1960, at a speed of 80.16mph (129km/h). He later wrote off the car at Oulton Park but it was re-bodied by Freddie Owen for Dick Tindell in the style of an E-type fixed-head coupé (see chapter 10).[17]

Further afield, in New Zealand Archibald finished second in the Christchurch sports car race in January 1956. Archibald was the name of the Christchurch-based Jaguar importer, and I suspect that the car was chassis S 800038, one of two open two-seaters consigned to this importer. This was a Personal Export Delivery car, registered in Coventry under NWK 185 for R J N Archibald. Presumably it was the same car that Ray Archibald raced at Christchurch in June 1957.[18] In Australia, John Bryson Junior who was the oldest son of the Jaguar importer ran an XK

140 fixed-head in the Australian TT in April 1957 but finished tenth behind smaller cars. His car was chassis number S 804502 and he also raced in a number of other events in 1956 and 1957, "with reasonable success".[19] Another slightly unexpected Australian XK 140 racer was N S Norway, better known as the novelist Nevil Shute, who raced a rare two-seater, chassis number S 800062, between 1956 and 1958, and was second in a race at Philip Island at Easter 1957 (see also chapter 9). The car was still in existence in Victoria in 2003.[20]

In the USA in March 1955, Dr Charles ("Charlie" or "Chuck") Wallace and Dr Richard Thompson finished tenth overall in 12-hour race at Sebring with their XK 140, entered by Jack Pry, the Jaguar dealer of Washington DC. Two other XK 140s finished 20th and 26th. Wallace's car was listed in the Sebring programme as a Jaguar "MC", and according to his article in *Sports Car Illustrated* he raced the XK 140 from then onwards, rather than his 1954 class-wining XK 120. He went on to win the 1955 SCCA C-production class (at that time, for cars of 3000cc to 5000cc) championship, and with 10,750 points was second in the championship overall, to the Mercedes-Benz 300SL (D-production class, 11,750 points) of Paul O'Shea whom Wallace beat at least once.[21] However, in 1956 Wallace raced a 300SL and then a Porsche RS. John Gordon Benett who became the sales manager of Jaguar in the USA occasionally flew the flag by racing various Jaguars, including an XK 140, at American tracks.[22]

As late as 1965, Ron McConkey of Iowa won

an SCCA National Championship in his XK 140, and in 1966 Paul Hammer was second in the Road Race of Champions at Riverside, California with a similar car.[23] Bob Smiley carried on racing his XK 140 in SCCA events even into the 1980s and in 1984 was rewarded with the American "Jaguar Driver of the Year" title.[24] At the Bonneville Speed Trials in August 1997, Mark Adams (driver) and Jerry Parkhill (crew chief) set an amazing class record of just over 180mph (290km/h) with a much modified 1955 XK 140.[25]

Jaguar was apparently in the process of preparing three XK 140 open two-seaters as a works rally team, with an eye on the 1955 Alpine Rally, where Ian Appleyard was one of the designated drivers. However, after the death of William Lyons's only son John in a road accident on his way to the 1955 Le Mans race, Appleyard who was John's brother-in-law withdrew from the team. After the major tragedy in the Le Mans race, many motor sports events were cancelled, and one casualty was the Alpine Rally. The three cars were chassis numbers S 800033 DN, S 800034 DN and S 800035 DN, although it seems odd that only the two first were British Racing Green and S 800035 DN was Cream.[26]

All three cars had interesting fates. The first, S 800033 DN, was built on 25 May 1955, and was registered SHP 575. It was modified by Jaguar's experimental department with extra bonnet louvres and air intakes in the front valance inboard and below the headlamps; a photo exists of the car being tested in this form.[27] It was then lent to Ronnie Adams who had just won the Monte Carlo Rally with a works-lent Mark VII, for him to drive in the 1956 RAC Rally, to some extent fulfilling Jaguar's ambition of fielding a rally car. Ronnie was far from happy with the car of which he said that "absolutely nothing [had been] done to it to prepare it for the rally... [it] was presumed to be a works car, but on closer inspection, was found to be nothing more than an old factory hack."

A letter of complaint to "Lofty" England had no result, and "Ronnie was left to prepare the car as best he could without factory assistance." The actual rally brought him no satisfaction either; due to a misunderstanding over clocking-in times, Adams was penalised and had to settle for a fourteenth place overall when he might have won his class. He returned the car to Jaguar and it was disposed of second-hand to

Imperial Motor Mart in Cheltenham in April 1956; the car still survives in the UK.[28]

When Jaguar's rally ambitions were thwarted, S 800034 DN and S 800035 DN, both built on 2 June 1955, were sold to Delecroix in Paris in July 1955. According to the *Car Record Book*, S 800034 DN was bought by one H J George of Paris. For S 800035 DN no first owner was recorded by Jaguar but it was presumably bought by Georges Guyot who went on to enter it in the Italian Mille Miglia road race in April 1956, under start number 245. The car was registered 1157 BF 59, so Guyot must have lived in the *département* of Nord. The 1956 Mille Miglia was a wet and miserable affair, and from the battered state of the car at the end, Guyot had more than his fair share of adventures, but he

This car is believed to be the XK 140 chassis number S 800033 DN later registered SHP 575, here on test to try out those extra air intakes. When the works rally programme was abandoned, it was lent to Ronnie Adams for the 1956 RAC Rally. (JDHT)

Guyot's XK140 at the start of the 1956 Mille Miglia. (Paul Skilleter)

Ian Appleyard briefly rallied this fixed-head registered VUB 140, and finished second in the 1956 RAC Rally. (Paul Skilleter)

strator. A car which was at one time registered VUB 140 now exists in Germany, but this is a case of "mistaken identity". Appleyard's VUB 140 was advertised for £50 "for breaking" in *Motor Sport* in 1967. Skilleter says that S 804340 DN no longer existed in 1975, but "its registration number was last seen decorating another XK 140 fixed-head" which is the car now in Germany, chassis 804753. That car was originally exported to Nigeria but came back to the UK, and in the 1970s was owned by Jim Patten, later editor of *Jaguar World* magazine.[30] In the 1958 RAC Rally, an XK 140 rally number 3 was driven by BF Mitten and GR Norton, who finished third in class. I think there were other XK 140s in this rally, and one of them, possibly the Mitten/Norton car, was a fixed-head registered HHH 422, chassis 804080.[31]

actually won his class, which was defined as the class for "open cars under £1100 over 2 litres" (!) at an average of 70.12mph (112.85km/h), and was 40th overall. It seems George's sister car ran in the same Mille Miglia under start number 244 but did not finish.[29]

Although Ian Appleyard had withdrawn from the planned works team of 1955, it was not quite the end of his rally career. He briefly rallied a fixed-head 140 registered VUB 140 in 1956, and was second overall in the 1956 RAC Rally. The car was S 804340 DN, which went to Appleyard, Leeds, officially as their demon-

Of other British drivers, Eric Haddon who had rallied XK 120s was pencilled in to take Appleyard's place in the 1955 works rally team and is said later to have rallied his own XK 140, which was a drophead, chassis S 807209 DN registered VAR 140, but I have not been able to trace this car in rallying unless the reference is to his XK 150 (see below). VAR 140 still exists, as a special, see chapter 10. Sleigh's XK 140 finished first in the big GT car class in the 1955 Scottish Rally. In the 1956 Scottish, Hally, Parkes and Kerr were first to third in this class, while a Miss C V Woodburne of Appleby in Westmor-

Parkes's XK 140 in the early stages of the 1958 Monte Carlo rally. The weather behaved in the UK; not so on the other side of the channel. (Paul Skilleter)

Stross and Pointing competing with the XK 140 drophead in the 1955 Liège-Rome-Liège Rally. They finished 17th and were second-highest placed British entry. (Paul Skilleter)

In the 1956 Tulip Rally Stross was accompanied by co-driver Whalley in the XK 140 drophead. (Paul Skilleter)

land won the Ladies' Touring Award in her fixed-head chassis 804421 registered CJM 936. G H "Bobby" Parkes went on to enter his fixed-head KFR 712 chassis S 804453 DN in the 1958 Monte Carlo Rally where he started from Glasgow with rally number 223. He did not manage to finish what turned out to be the toughest post-war Monte so far, with blizzards in France eliminating all but 38 of 303 starters; another retirement was the Baillie XK 140 mentioned above. Neither the Baillie nor the Parkes cars are listed by Viart. KFR 712 still exists in the UK.[32]

L S "Chippy" Stross of Leeds took part in a number of Continental rallies with his XK 140 drophead S 807078 DN which was sold through Appleyard. It carried the registration mark SUB 333, and with co-driver Pointing, Stross put up the second-best British performance in the 1955 Liège-Rome-Liège rally, coming seventeenth overall, while Mr and Mrs Stross were second in class in the MCC National Rally in 1955. Stross and Whalley finished 126th in the same car in the Tulip Rally in April 1956, where it was one of five XK 140s taking part.[33] To clarify matters, SUB 333 had previously been seen on an XK 120 drophead S 667178 which was Mrs Stross's car and which took part in the RAC Rally and

Wood and Booy with their XK 140 fixed-head in the 1956 Tulip Rally. (Paul Skilleter)

Arnold Burton was an enthusiastic but unsuccessful rally entrant with his XK 140, WUG 1, here in the Tulip Rally. (Paul Skilleter)

the Liège-Rome-Liège in 1954. It was probably this XK 120 that Stross and Pointing ran in the 1955 RAC Rally, winning their class, since at this time his new XK 140 had yet to be built.[31]

Also taking part in the 1956 Tulip Rally was Frank P Grounds of Birmingham and W C Johnson in a rather odd-looking fixed-head coupé registered LOE 3 but this was in fact a much-modified XK 120 which had started life as an open-two-seater 660337! For the record, they finished 75th. Another British entrant was an XK 140 fixed-head registered in Hull under SRH 399, driven by G Wood and J Booy, they finished 153rd. This car may have been S 804022 DN which was sold in Hull but neither first

owner nor registration mark were recorded by Jaguar. I think it must have been the same car that had already been entered by G Wood and E Batte in the 1955 Tulip Rally, but they do not appear to have finished.[35]

Going back to the 1956 Tulip Rally, Arnold Burton of Leeds entered his XK 140 fixed-head registered WUG 1 which was S 804592 DN sold through Appleyard. The car retired after it went off the road and damaged the front suspension. Burton went on to take part in the 1956 Alpine Rally and the 1957 Tulip Rally with the same car, again without success. Another British XK 140 in the 1956 Alpine Rally was a fixed-head registered WHT 888, which has turned out to be S 804557, sold through Henlys and the first owner was Inverest China Clays of St Austell, but the name of the driver in the rally does not seem to be known.[36]

Major A J Nuthall of the USAF stationed at Wiesbaden in Germany took delivery of a left-hand drive fixed-head XK 140 S 814195 DN sold through RM Overseas in Frankfurt; it bore the US Forces license plate 5C 62968. Together with another American serviceman Albrecht, he entered the 1956 Monte Carlo but could not finish any higher than 188th of 233. He tried his luck again in the 1956 Tulip Rally, now with Elliott C Tours as his co-driver, and was rewarded with a 74th place, which was the highest for a Jaguar XK in this event.[37] The fifth and last XK 140 in the 1956 Tulip was the drop-head of Dr W J van Rompu of Delft in Holland

who finished 173rd, with co-driver L J Mens. Their car was 817936 sold through the Dutch importers Lagerwij's.[38]

As mentioned, Georges Guyot ran an XK 140 in the 1956 Mille Miglia, but he also used a left-hand drive SE fixed-head registered 6937 MA 25 (in the *départément* of Doubs) in a number of rallies during the same year, often with Michel Parsy as his co-driver. These included the Lyon-Charbonnières in March, the Rallye de Picardie in June and the Tour de France in September where they finished sixteenth. Jacques Herzet also competed in this rally with his XK 140, with unknown result.[39]

Another seasoned French *Jaguariste* was Dr Maurice Rebatel of Lyon who had previously rallied the Barou special-bodied XK 120.[40] His next car was an XK 140 SE fixed-head chassis S 815069, exported to Delecroix in Paris, and registered 5234 AN 69. He used this car in two succeeding Lyon-Charbonnières rallies, in 1956 with Henri Peignaux – the Jaguar dealer in Lyon – as co-driver, and then in 1957, with co-driver Edouard Monnoyeur, he finished eleventh overall and second in class.[41] An equally keen competitor in the Lyon-Charbonnières rally was Robert Babolat. Together with Paul Babolat he took part in the 1955 event, possibly with an XK 140, finishing 34th and second in class, as the highest-placed British car.[42] In 1957 Robert finished 25th with Georges Sangan as his co-driver in an XK 140 SE fixed-head, and they were also recorded as taking part in the 1960

The XK 140 of Guyot and Parsy at Le Mans during the 1956 Tour de France. (Paul Skilleter)

Parsy and Guyot in the 1956 Picardie rally in an XK 140 fixed-head. (Paul Skilleter)

Dr Rebatel competed several times in the Lyon-Charbonnières Rally between 1954 and 1959. Here he is with co-driver Monnoyeur in his XK 140 fixed-head during the 1957 event. (Paul Skilleter)

the only SE two-seater exported to Belgium. Unfortunately they retired.[44]

A very unusual XK 140 drophead was entered by Papamichael and Mourtzopoulos in the 1958 Acropolis Rally. Apart from having Citroën 2CV seats and an improvised "hard top" the unusual aspect of the car was that it was alleged to have been owned originally by none other than HM King Paul of Greece. The car must have been S 817221 DN built in February 1955 which was the only drophead exported to Greece according to the *Car Record Book*, although the name of the first owner is not recorded. Originally Pearl Grey, by 1958 it was white and blue. In the rally, they finished in a splendid fourth place.[45]

At the time, the most important rally fixture in the USA was the Great American Mountain Rally where in November 1956 the XK 140 open two-seater of Florence and Donald Blackburn was third overall and convincingly won its class, and three XK 140s entered by Jaguar Cars North America took the team award. Judging from the owners' names in the *Car Record Book*, the Blackburn car was S 810089, originally black, but two-tone by the time of the 1956 rally; I last heard of it in Canada. The Blackburns continued to do rather well in American rallies and were credited with six first places during 1957. A company-supported three-car team of XK 140s was entered again in the 1957 Mountain Rally.[46]

Beaujolais-Charentes Rally with this car, registered 565 AP 69. Sangan and Chauviret contested the 1959 Rallye International de Limousin in another fixed-head, registered 2426 GN 75 in Paris.[45]

The Babolat and Sangan cars have defied identification, and so has the fixed-head SE that Tergoin from Paris used on the 1957 Mont Ventoux hill climb. The open two-seater registered 20 K 36 driven by the Belgian pair of Henry and Piret in the 1955 Liège-Rome-Liège was probably S 811043 in British Racing Green,

1957 Mont Ventoux hill climb. Tergoin takes his XK 140 fixed-head round the famous Saint-Estève curve. (Paul Skilleter)

An XK 150 two-seater at the Chamrousse hill climb near Grenoble in the French Alps in 1958. (Paul Skilleter)

The XK 150

In much the same way as the 140, the 150 was rarely seen on the race tracks, nor was it a frequent rally car. In the UK, it was mostly raced at club level. It was an equally unusual sight on American race tracks, although a few XK 150s were raced through 1959. Walt Hansgen had been racing Jaguars since 1951, and from 1956 to 1959, he regularly won the SCCA C-modified class championships in Cunningham team cars, D-types and later Lister-Jaguars. However, he did drive an XK 150 S open two-seater in the C-production class at Lime Rock in April 1958, and at Bridgehampton in June where he finished third. Charles Wallace won his race at Danville with another XK 150 S, where he "outclassed a field of Gran Turismo Ferraris, Mercedes 300SLs and Corvettes."[47]

In the UK, a relatively rare success, if in a minor event, was that of D Parker in the March 1960 Snetterton GT race where his XK 150 3.8 S was first in the over-2000cc class at a speed of 78.24mph (125.9km/h), and he also won his race at Oulton Park in May 1960. This car was presumably T 825141 DN, a fixed-head registered 1515 PX whose first owner was Don Parker of Bedfont, Middlesex. Similarly, Phil Scragg's XK 150 S which set fastest time in GT class on the Whit Monday meeting at Prescott in June 1960 must have been T 825215 DN, another 3.8 fixed-head which was supplied to E Scragg & Sons Ltd, Macclesfield although it was registered 5546 PX. Both of these cars were sold

by Fields Engineering of Crawley, hence the Sussex registrations. Jack Lambert's fixed-head registered XUE 234 was regularly seen in races and at hill climbs. This was S 824167 DN which was sold by P J Evans in Birmingham although the first recorded owner was Harry Shaw & Sons.[48] The car may later have been sold to Donald Smith who apparently drove it at Mallory Park in August 1961.[49] He seems to have had quite an active season in club racing during 1961 and *Autosport* frequently referred to his car as an "XK 150 S".[50]

There were two cars associated with Rosemary Massey who later married Dick Protheroe. Both were left-hand drive fixed-heads, regis-

This is Jean-Claude Cohade in his XK 150 hixed-head on his way to winning a wet Grand Prix de Staoueli in Algeria. This was actually a GT car race. (JDHT)

This 1960s shot is of the then Maharajkumar of Gondal, who later became the Maharajah, a keen sports car enthusiast who won an Indian Grand Prix with this no longer pristine-looking XK 150 drophead. (JDHT)

*FSN 1 was the
Dumbuck Garage
demonstrator and was
used by Jimmy Stewart
in a hill climb event.
(JDHT)*

*Andrew McCracken
ran his XK 150, V 150,
in the 1959 Monte
Carlo Rally, but did
not finish.
(Paul Skilleter)*

tered respectively UDU 491 and URW 782. The first was S 834201 DN, sold as a Personal Export Delivery car for Canada. She was the first owner, and raced this car with some success. The second was S 835628 DN, another PED car but this time supplied through Henlys; its engine had the 9:1 compression ratio although it was not an S model. She was again the first recorded owner. She won a handicap race at Goodwood in August 1958 and ran the car again in the 200-

mile relay race at Silverstone in May 1959, by which time it seems to have acquired right-hand drive. Indeed, I wonder whether the car photographed in this race was really URW 782 despite the number plate, as it also seems to be very dark for its original colour of Cornish Grey.[51]

Drivers of XK 150s in various races and other events included Jimmy Stewart, brother of Jackie, who entered a fixed-head registered FSN 1 in the Rest-And-Be-Thankful hill climb in 1958. This car was S 824092, an ex-Scottish Motor Show car serving as the demonstrator for Dumbuck Garage, the Stewart family firm. PH Dickinson of Gainsborough took his fixed-head KBE 1, chassis S 824292 DN, to the Yorkshire Autocross and finished second in class to of all things a C-type. Jonathan Sieff entered his two-seater in the GT race at Silverstone in May 1959 and was fourth in class but way down in the general classification. The Earl of Denbigh (William Rudolph Stephen Feilding, tenth Earl of Denbigh and ninth Earl of Desmond, 1912-1966) took part in some Jaguar Drivers' Club race meetings in his XK 150 S fixed-head which was said to be "his first appearance in racing since 1932". Robin Beck of Sutton Coldfield used his XK 150 3.8 S fixed-head 7219 NX, chassis T 825211 DN, to win the production sports car class at the Oulton Sprint in August 1960 but is of course better known for racing the much-modified ex-Ferodo XK 120, MXJ 954.[52]

The 3.4 S fixed-head chassis T 825009 DN built in September 1959 and originally registered AFD 250 was raced by its first owner AF (Tony) Davenport of Leek although not with any great results. Interestingly, this car was much modified and prepared for Davenport in Jaguar's service department during 1960, and the engine was bored out to 3.8 litres; Davenport later reckoned that he had clocked 152mph (244.6km/h) on the M1. When he changed to a new E-type (860002, the second FHC RHD) in 1961, not only was the personalised registration moved to the new car, but with so much effort put into tuning the XK 150 engine, this was swapped with the E-type engine. Both cars still exist.[53]

Andrew McCracken of Larkhall was a keen exponent of the XK 150 with his drophead S 827023 DN, sold through Rossleigh in Edinburgh and Murchiston Motors – the Ecurie Ecosse garage – and registered V 150. He started at the top, with an entry in the 1959 Monte Carlo

*The XK 150 of
Bowdage and Ozanne
in the 1959 Monte
Carlo Rally, avoiding
the fate of the
Borgward in front
which has gone over
the edge.*

Rally, rally number 92, but did not finish. In the
1959 RAC Rally he set best performance on the
Charterhall circuit, but was way down on the list
of finishers. In July 1960 in the RSAC Rest-And-
Be-Thankful hill climb he was first in class for
sports cars over 2000cc with a time of 65.47
seconds. His car in this event was said to be an
XK 150 S, but I have not found him as first
owner of an S, nor does the distinctive Lanark-
shire registration mark seem to have been
transferred to an S.[54]

Although neither survived to be classified as
finishing, there were two other XK 150s in that
1959 Monte Carlo, apart from McCracken's car.
The fixed-head coupé registered 910 SHX with
rally number 133 was S 824374 DN sold through
Henlys, the first recorded owner was Normand
Electric which must be a company name. The
Monte Carlo drivers were John Watkins Bowdage
and Patricia "Tish" Ozanne; she later joined the
BMC rally team. Their rally car was last heard of
in Switzerland. Rally number 23 was an XK 150
fixed-head registered VLO 574 which was S
824419 DN sold through Henlys in London, but
the first recorded owner was RM Merrick of
Birmingham, a Monte regular in many different
makes of car. His co-driver was called Bevan.
Finally, Viart says that an XK 150 driven by
Hugues and Conor registered 3000 U took part,

rally number 75, but this entry does not figure in
the contemporary lists. Viart also lists them as
taking part in the 1960 Alpine Rally with this car.
I have concluded that Viart in this instance is
wrong, and that the car was the 3.4-litre saloon
driven by Hugh O'Connor Rourke under number
90 in the 1959 Monte Carlo Rally and under
number 231 in the 1960 Monte; this car does
indeed seem to have been registered 3000 U.[55]

The best rally result for the XK 150 came in
the Tulip Rally of May 1960, where three XK

*The finest hour for the
XK 150 in rallying
came when Eric
Haddon finished tenth
in the 1960 Tulip Rally,
and won the GT class.
(Paul Skilleter)*

150s took part. The Dutch drivers Dr E A H Scholten of Aerdenhout and Janny W t'Eind entered a left-hand drive fixed-head 3.8, S 836628 DN. They were not classified at the end of the rally, but the car still exists in Holland. Another fixed-head, naturally with right-hand drive, registered SBD 453, was S 824607 DN sold through Henlys. Driven by E and J Whatton the car retired after breaking both rear springs, but was still in the UK in 2006. The success story was that of WLO 7, a rare right-hand drive 3.4 S open two-seater chassis T 820019 DN, sold through Henlys, first recorded owner Haddon Transformers Ltd of Wealdstone – which means Eric Haddon, a regular Jaguar rally driver in his earlier XK 120. Together with Charles Vivian, he won the GT class and finished tenth overall, with a remarkable performance in the Mont Ventoux hill climb. This car is also still in existence.[56]

Another well-known Jaguar driver who had a go at rallying an XK 150 was Peter Whitehead who had a fixed-head VDU 358, chassis S 824021, supplied through Henlys, although clearly factory registered with its Coventry mark, and fitted with what was in effect a prototype S engine (see chapters 3 and 9). Together with his half-brother Graham, Whitehead ran this car in the Tour de France in September 1957, but they retired with brake trouble. When they entered a 3.4-litre saloon in the 1958 Tour, Peter was tragically killed in an accident. In the Tour de France

Clearly in 1959 the Lorraine-Alsace rally made a detour across the German border to the Nürburgring. Barely visible in the foreground is an XK 120 two-seater, then XK 150 and XK 140 fixed-heads, while apart from the obvious Mercedes and Porsche opposition there is a Triumph and a Peugeot 403 saloon further down the line. (Paul Skilleter)

Galliet and Legourd and their XK 150 fixed-head in the 1959 Tour de France. They retired after an accident, only about 100km from the finish. (Paul Skilleter)

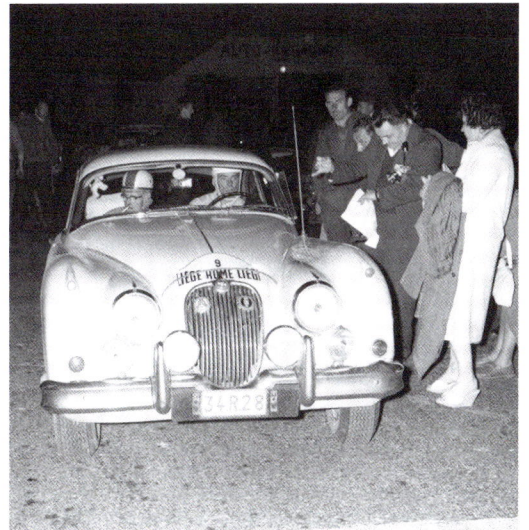

of September 1959, the XK 150 S fixed-head of French drivers Michel Legourd and Claude Gallier, registered 778 DV 64 (in the *départément* of Pyrénées Atlantiques) was eliminated by an accident, just 100km (62 miles) from the finish.[57]

The Lyon-Charbonnières rally was always a happy hunting ground for French Jaguar drivers, so it is no surprise that our old friend Dr Maurice Rebatel had another go with an XK 150 fixed-head in March 1959. The car which was registered 1515 AX 69 should have been chassis S 835422 as he is recorded as its first owner, but

The Belgian XK 150 in the Liège-Rome-Liège. (Paul Skilleter)

sadly that car was Black and photos clearly show his rally car to be a light colour. Strangely there is an identical problem with regard to identifying the fixed-head that the two American Servicemen Parker and Wallgreen ran in the 1960 Lyon-Charbonnières rally. Ake Wallgreen of the USAF who was stationed in Germany is the first owner recorded for S 835283 DN delivered through RM Overseas in Frankfurt, but this was Black, and the 1960 rally car was light in colour. It was registered 1CF 19328. They finished 34th in this event. In the same rally, two French drivers using the pseudonyms of "Yvons" and "Jane" entered an unidentified XK 150 open two-seater, with unknown result. The last recorded appearance for an XK 150 in a major rally came in the Liège-Rome-Liège of August 1960 where the Belgian drivers Durutte and van Maldeghem ran a fixed-head registered 34 R 28 but do not appear to have finished, and even in 1963 Barbier and Liagre ran a fixed-head in the Lyon-Charbonnières.[58]

1. *Autosport* 30 Mar, 6 Apr, 13 Apr 1956, covering the disqualification of Monnoyeur's XK 120 open two-seater from a third place in the Lyon-Charbonnières Rally. The optimistic Frenchman entered this car in the Mille Miglia in 1956 but failed to appear at the start, and again in 1957 but did not finish; Wimpffen *Time and Two Seats* pp.214, 237

2. Moity *The Le Mans 24-Hour Race* pp.37-39

3. Georgano (ed) *The Encyclopaedia of Motor Sport* p.21 *et passim*; Wimpffen pp.113-43

4. Skilleter *Jaguar Sports Cars* pp.155-56

5. Copy forms in JDHT archive; the numbers do not appear on all of the copies available to me of such forms

6. *Autosport* 18 Nov 1955; Wimpffen pp.252, 297; Parker *Jaguar at Le Mans* p.116, with a photo of an *Ecurie Ecosse* D-type with tall windscreen and improvised boot in the 1960 race

7. Gregor Grant in *Autosport* 13 Nov 1959; sentiments echoed by *The Motor* which found the race "dull, processional, and poorly attended", quoted in Montagu *Jaguar – A Biography* (first ed.) p.170

8. *Autosport* 4 Nov 1955. XK 120s were not successful; the 1956 championship was, controversially, awarded to an MGA, with Mike Salmon's XK 120 joint eighth; *Autosport* 28 Sep, 5 Oct 1956

9. *Autosport* 8 May 1959

10. Wimpffen pp.323-25

11. Harvey *The Jaguar XK* pp.105-06; Moity, appendices; Parker pp.74, 79; Skilleter *Sports Cars* pp.152-54, 156 and photos pp.138-39; Skilleter *The Jaguar XKs – A Collector's Guide* pp.99-100; Viart *Jaguar XK – le Grand Livre* pp.289-90

12. *Autosport* 19 Jul 1957, 31 Jan 1958; *Motor Sport* Aug 1957 p.449A; Baillie "A Year of Driving Jaguars", *The Autocar* 27 Jun 1958; Montagu p.170

13. Whyte *Jaguar... Competition Cars from 1954* p.546; Porter *Jaguar Sports Racing Cars* p.168

14. Skilleter *Sports Cars* p.153; Wimpffen p.181

15. Boyce *Jaguar XK Series* p.120; Montagu p.256

16. *Autosport* 5 Apr 1957; Montagu pp.256-57

17. Boyce pp.118-120; Harvey p.213; Montagu p.266; Skilleter *Sports Cars* p.156 and photos pp.138-39; Urban *Les Métamorphoses du Jaguar* pp.254-55; Whyte p.448; *XK Gazette* nos.44 May 2001, 63 Dec 2002, 109 Oct 2006

18. *Autosport* 12 Jul 1957; Montagu p.253

19. *Autosport* 12 Apr 1957; Elmgreen & McGrath *The Jaguar XK in Australia* p.104; the car was later owned by Terry McGrath

20. *Autosport* 12 Jul 1957; Elmgreen & McGrath p.98; JDHT correspondence with present-day owner

21. *Sports Car Illustrated* Jul 1955; Clausager *XK 120 in Detail* p.150; Harvey pp.103-05; Skilleter *Collector's Guide* p.100; Wimpffen p.176; www.etcerini.com for useful SCCA results lists

22. *Autosport* 29 Jul 1955; Dugdale *Jaguar in America* pp.57-58

23. Skilleter *Sports Cars* p.156

24. Boyce p.121

25. *Jaguar World* Jun 1998

26. Skilleter *Sports Cars* p.154; Whyte p.103 unfortunately quotes wrong and misleading registration marks; *XK Gazette* no.30 Mar 2000

27. Skilleter *Collector's Guide* p.62

28. *Autosport* 23 Mar 1956; Adams *From Craigantlet to Monte Carlo* pp.82-84; Boyce p.144; Skilleter *Collector's Guide* p.62; Skilleter *Sports Cars* p.154; Whyte p.118; *XK Gazette* no.121 Oct 2007

29. *Autosport* 4 May 1956; Skilleter *Sports Cars* p.155; Viart *Jaguar XK – la Compétition sur Route dans les Années* 1950 pp.204-05, 237; Viart *Grand Livre* p.289; Wimpffen pp.209, 213

30. *Autosport* 16 Mar 1956; Boyce pp.142-44; Montagu pp.147, 253; Skilleter *Sports Cars* p.156; Viart *Grand Livre* p.286; *Motor Sport* Aug 1967; *XK Gazette* nos.102 Mar 2006, 111 Dec 2006, 113 Feb 2007; JDHT correspondence with present-day owner

31. *Autosport* 28 Feb, 28 Mar 1958; Boyce p.119; Michael Griffiths in *XK Gazette* no.82 Jul 2004 lists three XK 150s taking part in this rally – Brinkman, Sopwith and Rowe – but these were 3.4 saloons, see *Autosport* 21 Mar 1958

32. Boyce p.113; Skilleter *Collector's Guide* p.100; Skilleter *Sports Cars* pp.154-56 and photos pp.138-39; Viart *Compétition* p.237 (this author seems to think there was a Monte in 1957); *Jaguar Quarterly* winter 1990; *XK Gazette* no.3 Dec 1997

33. *Autosport* 26 Aug, 2 Sep 1955, 18 May 1956; Skilleter *Sports Cars* pp.154-55

34. *Autosport* 18 Mar 1955; Boyce p.141; Viart *Compétition* pp.155, 157, 162-63, 172-73, 236; *XK Gazette* no.82 Jul 2004

35. *Autosport* 29 Apr 1955; Viart *Compétition* pp.172-73, 236

36. *Autosport* 5 Apr 1957, 17 May 1957; Skilleter *Sports Cars* p.155 and photos pp.138-39; Viart *Compétition* pp.174, 233, 236

37. *Autosport* 18 May 1956

38. Viart *Compétition* pp.185-86, 236; Viart *Grand Livre* p.288

39. Skilleter *Sports Cars* p.155; Viart *Compétition* pp.79, 107-10, 216, 234; Viart *Grand Livre* pp.290-91, 293 – where he says Herzet and Parsy shared 6937 MA 25

40. Clausager pp.149-50, 210-11

41. *Autosport* 29 Mar 1957, 5 Apr 1957

42. *Autosport* 25 Mar 1955 described the Babolat car as an XK 140; Viart thinks it was an XK 120, *Compétition* p.234

43. Viart *Compétition* pp.79-80, 213, 234; Viart *Grand Livre* pp.288-89, 291, 294

44. Viart *Compétition* pp.160-61, 164, 220, 236

45. *Autosport* 11 and 18 Apr 1958

46. *Autosport* 7 Dec 1956; Boyce p.144; Montagu p.152; Skilleter *Sports Cars* p.156; *The Jaguar Journal* Dec 1956, Nov-Dec 1957, courtesy of Mike Cook

47. Georgano *Encyclopaedia of Motor Sport* p.230; Skilleter *Collector's Guide* p.101; Skilleter *Sports Cars* p.205; Whyte pp.170-73, 433; *The Jaguar Journal* Apr-May 1958

48. Montagu p.264; Skilleter *Sports Cars* p.205, photos pp.210-11

49. *Autosport* 18 Aug 1961

50. *Autosport* 28 Apr, 28 Jul, 4 Aug and 15 Sep 1961

51. *Autosport* 29 Aug 1958, 25 Sep 1959; Boyce p.121; Skilleter *Collector's Guide* p.101; Skilleter *Sports Cars* p.205; Whyte p.446

52. *Autosport* 11 Jul, 22 Aug 1958; 8 May 1959; 12 Aug, 2 Sep, 23 Sep 1960

53. *Autosport* 23 Sep 1960, 19 May 1961; *XK Gazette* no.2 Nov 1997

54. Harvey p.103; Montagu p.265; Skilleter *Sports Cars* p.205; Viart *Compétition* pp.188, 237; Viart *Grand Livre* p.292

55. *Autosport* and *The Autocar* 16 Jan 1959; photo in *Autosport* 5 Feb 1960; Robson *Monte Carlo Rally The Golden Age* p.127; Skilleter *Sports Cars* photos pp.210-11; Viart *Compétition* pp.187, 233, 237; Viart *Grand Livre* p.292

56. Skilleter *Collector's Guide* p.100; Skilleter *Sports Cars* p.205, photos pp.210-11; Viart *Compétition* pp.175-79, 236

57. Skilleter *Jaguar Saloon Cars* p.448; Skilleter *Sports Cars* p.205; Viart *Compétition* pp.111-12, 235 (although he refers to *Alfred* Whitehead, and the Whitehead/Riley entry in the 1959 event was a 3.4-litre saloon, not an XK 150 as Viart claims); Whyte p.198; Cognet and Viart *Jaguar A Tradition of Sports Cars* p.207

58. Viart *Compétition* pp.82-3, 167, 234, 236; Cognet and Viart p.207

Chapter Eight

The prototypes and works cars

The cars dealt with in this chapter are those that were originally owned and used by Jaguar. The main source for this information are the *Car Record Books*, but I have been able to supplement these with information from the Coventry Registration Records, held in the archive of the Coventry Transport Museum.[1] However, some Jaguar experimental cars may not have been registered but could have been run on trade plates, and other cars may not have been registered before Jaguar sold them.

Development of the XK 140 began in 1952. The earliest clue that we have is that XK 120 chassis number 660971 built on 18 March 1952 was retained by Jaguar's experimental department and was fitted with rack-and-pinion steering.[2] It was also known as the "Mark III", which is believed to refer to a stage in the development of the XK 140. It may or may not have been registered under RHP 574 (see 811101 below). 660971 was fitted experimentally with Girling disc brakes. By early 1954, Norman Dewis was testing an XK 120 left-hand drive open two-seater with the forward-mounted engine and slanting radiator.[3] This car has defied identification, unless it is the car that became 811101.

Then there is the question of what happened to the very first XK 120, chassis 660001 which was registered HKV 455; the *Car Record Book* claims this car, or its chassis, or even just its chassis number, was used for the "Mark IV" fixed-head coupé prototype, and it is thought that the "Mark IV" designation relates to the XK 140 project.[4] This "Mark IV" prototype does not seem to have been XK 140 chassis number 804001 as the two cars existed side by side in 1955-56 (see below). We are on more certain ground when we look at the actual early XK 140 cars since eight of these had XK 120 engines as follows, quoted below with the dates of the engines:

W 9601-8 dating to August 1953 was fitted in 811101
F 1353-8 dating to December 1953 was fitted in 807002
F 1354-8 dating to December 1953 was fitted in 804002
F 1355-8 dating to December 1953 was fitted in 804001
F 1356-8 dating to December 1953 was fitted in 807001
F 1358-8 dating to December 1953 was fitted in 804004
F 2172-8 dating to February 1954 was fitted in 810001
F 2177-8 dating to February 1954 was fitted in 804003

It is entirely possible that some of these cars were built closer to the dates of their engines, than on the dates which were eventually listed in the *Car Record Book*.

Another curiosity is the car which Norman Dewis drove at Jabbeke to set the 172mph (277km/h) record in October 1953. In one photo with the bonnet open, this is seen to have an angled radiator apparently of the XK 140 type, from which it is possible to infer that this car may also have had the forward engine position and the rack-and-pinion steering of the later model – leading to speculation that the Jabbeke car may not have been MDU 524 at all![5]

XK 140 open two-seater right-hand drive:

S 800012 DN, S 800013 DN, S 800014 DN and S 800015 DN, all built in February 1955. These may have been built as Show Cars; they were all originally retained by Jaguar, and were only despatched some months later, between July and September 1955.

S 800033 DN, 15 May 1955, SHP 575. This car was one of three cars intended for the 1955 Alpine Rally, together with S 800034 DN and S 800035 DN, both of which went to Delecroix in Paris, whereas S 800033 DN was sold second-hand to Imperial Motor Mart in Cheltenham in April 1956. This British Racing Green car was fitted experimentally with extra bonnet louvres and air intakes, and had these extra air intakes when it was driven by Ronnie Adams in the 1956 RAC Rally (see chapter 7). It survives in the UK.[6]

XK 140 open two-seater left-hand drive:

810001 with engine number F 2172-8 and body number F 10001 (the first OTS body number), 29 September 1954, may be considered as one of the prototypes in that it had an XK 120 engine, but was despatched in the normal way to Hoffman in New York.

811101, Battleship Grey, with engine number W 9601-8, 22 February 1955, registered RHP

574. This car was built in the Experimental Department and was retained by Jaguar until sold second-hand to Duncan Hamilton in August 1955, by which time it had been converted to right-hand drive. There is a curious footnote to this in that in the *Car Record Book* I have also found RHP 574 quoted for XK 120 660971 referred to above. 811101 was later re-registered 78 GJH and was offered for sale, restored, in 1977. It had XK 120 bumpers and boot lid, but XK 140 grille and rear lamps, and had XK 140 running gear.[7]

XK 140 fixed-head coupé right-hand drive:

The first six cars were effectively the XK 140 prototypes or development cars.

804001, Black, with engine number F 1355-8, 11 February 1954, registered OWK 872. This car had the first fixed-head body, number J 4001, which in fact was an XK 120 fixed-head body. It went to the Dunlop Rim & Wheel Company, possibly for disc brake tests, and was later owned by John Pearson, John Harper and the XK restorer John May, before ending up with Hans Glaser in California (but see below).[8]

804002, Battleship Grey, with engine number F 1354-8, 11 February 1954, registered OVC 199. This car was used by "Lofty" England, but then also went to Dunlop.

804003, Battleship Grey, with engine number F 2177-8, 9 March 1954, registered PRW 477. This

car was allocated to the Experimental Department and was the 1954 Earls Court Motor Show demonstrator. It became a "road test car" and was used as one of the disc brake test cars. It still existed in 1958, but was finally scrapped and reduced to produce.[9]

804004, Dark Blue, with engine number F 1358-8, 3 September 1954, registered PKV 899. This car was allocated to the Experimental Department, and may later have been fitted with an overdrive. In 1955 it was sold second-hand to JT Thorpe, the Jaguar dealer at Wellesbourne near Stratford-on-Avon, who often bought ex-works cars. It is believed still to exist in the UK.[10]

804005 was apparently built in the Experimental Department, and no further details were entered in the *Car Record Book*, not even a build date or a registration mark, and I have not found this chassis number in the Coventry registration records.

These photos are rather curious, in that they are taken in the same location, at the same time, and should be of the same car. The fixed-head registered PRW 477 was chassis number 840003, which was later used for disc brake tests. It was a standard car yet the rear view shows a dual exhaust, and in the side view it has got wire wheels, but in the interior shot it has disc wheels. It may be that the wire wheels were simply propped against the car for a look-see. It still has some of the prototype features. (JDHT)

804006 DN, 7 October 1954, registered RHP 115 in April 1955. It was allocated to and possibly used by John Lyons, William Lyons's son. I believe it is the most likely candidate for having been one of the two 1954 Earls Court Motor Show cars, as it was Battleship Grey and had overdrive which fits the description of the fixed-head at the show. This car is seen in the background of the photos of the curious low-slung sports car mock-up taken at Wappenbury Hall which, judging from the profusion of tulips in bloom, must have been taken in the spring of 1955. RHP 115 was sold second-hand to the

racing driver Ivor Bueb in 1955.[11]

Some of these cars appeared on an inventory that Bob Knight compiled on 29 July 1955 of Experimental Department Cars, as follows (re-arranged here in chassis number order, with author's notes in italics in brackets):[12]

804001 Black Hard-top – Recently reduced to produce. (*But car exists; see above*)
804002 Battleship Grey Hard-top. (*See above*)
PRW 477 Battleship Grey – transferred to Sales dept. but on test. (*Chassis 804003*)
804004 Blue Hard-top – Sold. (*See above*)
(no number) Grey Open 2-str. Converted by Service Dept. to right hand drive for sale. (*This must be 811101, RHP 574, see above*)

Also on this list are the following XK 120s:
HKV 455, **660001** Gunmetal Hard-top on loan to Dunlop's. (*The first XK 120?*)
MHP 494, **667001** Black Drop-head Coupe – last used by Mr J Lyons? (*The first XK 120 DHC RHD, supposedly sold second-hand in April 1955*)
LWK 707, **669002** Bronze Hard-top – Service dept. (*The 1952 Montlhéry record car*)
JWK 675, **670172** Blue Written-off whilst on loan to Dunlop's. (*The first steel-bodied XK 120 from 1950*)

On the face of it, this seems to preclude the

hypothesis that 804001 was built on the chassis of 660001, as I have previously speculated[13], unless there were two cars with chassis number 660001. According to a similar list of company cars dated 31 August 1953, the "Prototype Mark IV XK 120 FHC has adopted Chassis No. 660001 HKV 455 and original Blue 660001 Open 2 Seater is to be broken up."[14] Therefore 804001 could have been built on the chassis of the first 660001. A car referred to as "Mark IV coupé" and "HKV 455" was in existence as late as 1956, when it is recorded that engine number W 5691 (an otherwise unused XK 120 engine from August 1952) was removed from this car.[15]

804127 DN, 5 May 1955, registered RHP 444. A Jaguar works car, it was used by Bill Heynes and was fitted with Alfin brake drums.[16] It was later sold to Duncan Hamilton and now survives in the USA.

S 804132 DN, 10 May 1955, registered RHP 576. Another works car, allocated to Bill Rankin as the press demonstrator. It was road tested by *Autosport*, by *The Autocar* and by the Scottish *Motor World*; it was also lent to Laurence Pomeroy of *The Motor* for his trip to the 1955 Frankfurt Motor Show (see chapter 5). It was finally sold second-hand to an owner in Manchester. In 1962 it was re-registered under XK 1, a registration which was later seen on an

XK 150 (see also chapter 9).[17]

804501 BW, 15 November 1955, registered TKV 10. The first right-hand drive fixed-head with automatic gearbox, it was used by the Experimental Department, and was eventually sold second-hand to Ivor Bueb. It may later have been re-registered in Lancashire under 99 HTC.[18]

S 804752 BW, 11 June 1956, registered SVC 44. This was a works car, again with automatic gearbox, and was used by Bill Heynes.

804807 BW, 3 October 1956, registered SKV 947. The 1956 Motor Show demonstrator, it was Battleship Grey, and was sold to Jaguar distributor W L Thompson of Hull in March 1957. Apart from the three cars listed here, there were only another four right-hand drive fixed-heads with the automatic gearbox.

XK 140 fixed-head coupé
left-hand drive:

814001, engine number and build date not recorded (but probably well before October 1954), the first left-hand drive fixed-head coupé chassis number, it went to Jaguar's Experimental Department as a bare chassis.

S 814004 BW, 26 January 1955, originally to the Experimental Department but was despatched to Jaguar Cars, New York in February 1956. It was the first car to be fitted with the automatic gearbox.

XK 140 drophead coupé
right-hand drive:

807001 with engine number F 1356-8 registered OWK 858 and **807002** with engine number F 1353-8 and body number P 3001 (the first DHC body) registered PRW 775, both February 1954. These were the two drophead coupé prototypes. 807001 was used by Bill Heynes. Both cars were disposed of second-hand to Coombs, Guildford. Both are believed to be still in existence and both are reported to have many XK 120 features including bumpers, rear lamps and boot lid, and in case of 807001 also a 120 grille.[19]

807004 DN, 5 October 1954, registered PRW

I believe this drophead with partly-painted hub caps may have been the 1954 Motor Show car, as the rear view shows the "XK 140" number plate. (JDHT)

476. This was Jaguar's "demonstrator" for the 1954 Earls Court Motor Show. It could have been the car on the Jaguar stand; the other possibility is that the actual stand car was **807003**. Both were Maroon with Biscuit trim and a Sand hood, the colour scheme of the show car. 807004 DN was later sold to Mike Hawthorn, while 807003 went through Henlys to Coombs of Guildford.[20]

807021, 1 February 1955, **807022** and **807023**, both 2 February 1955, as well as **S 807040 DN**, 21 February 1955, later registered FJX 450. These cars are marked as "Show Cars" in the *Car Record Book* and were only despatched to distributors in August or September 1955.

807312 BW, 15 November 1955. This was the first right-hand drive drophead coupé to be fitted with the automatic gearbox, and was built in the Experimental Department. It was subsequently sold second-hand to Coombs in Guildford. It was followed by only another three right-hand drive drophead coupés with automatic transmission.

XK 140 drophead coupé left-hand drive:

S 817378, 19 April 1955, registered RWK 700. This became a "works car" for the most trivial of reasons. It was intended for Hoffman in New York but was damaged either before despatch or while in transit. The car was then rebuilt with right-hand drive and registered by Jaguar, before being sold second-hand.

It seems more sensible to deal with the XK 150 cars in more or less chronological order, because of the staggered release date of the different models. Surprisingly, there are only two cars with low chassis numbers which according to the *Car Record Books* were used by Jaguar's Experimental Department. It is possible that much of the development of the XK 150 was carried out on those 120 or 140 cars which were used by Jaguar and the Dunlop Company for disc brake development.

One of the XK 150 prototypes was given the unusual chassis number of **XB 1001**. This was a fixed-head coupé which was painted Sherwood Green and was fitted with engine number KE 1005-8. Oddly enough this was an engine for a 3.4-litre saloon and this engine number can be dated to late 1956; otherwise we do not know

the build date. The car was registered WDU 493 and was sold to Ivor Bueb in July 1958. It was advertised for sale in *Thoroughbred & Classic Cars* in September 1976 and is still in existence.[21]

The car that has defied identification, is the light grey fixed-head which has been described as "the first XK 150 S". Its unique recognition point is the cut-away rear spats, although it had wire wheels. We are not helped by the published photos which show it as both as a right-hand drive and a left-hand drive car, but without a number plate. The Experimental Department notebooks confirm that there was a light grey prototype dating to December 1956 which over time had several different engines, possibly starting with KE 1005-8 (see above) but in April 1957 a three-carburettor engine D 5173-9 was fitted. This engine number is for a late 1954 Mark VIIM engine, which originally would have had neither three carburettors, nor a 9:1 compression ratio. The notebook entries finish in December 1958 with the statement "Complete car sold to Mr Mike Hawthorn", but since another notebook entry states that D 5173-9 was fitted to WWK 468, chassis S 837003, which according to the *Car Record Book* was sold to Hawthorn's company at this time (see below), there is scope for confusion. The grey fixed-head prototype "number 4" is also stated to have been fitted with engine V 1002-8, which was the original engine in WWK 468. I am left with a feeling that Jaguar played a game of "musical chairs" with experimental engines.[22]

XK 150 fixed-head coupé left-hand drive:

S 834001, 3.4, 5 March 1957. The first left-hand drive fixed-head, it may also be described as an XK 150 prototype. It was originally allocated to Jaguar's Experimental Department, and later went to the Service Department. The colour was Claret which ties in with references to a "maroon" car in the experimental department notebooks. It was scrapped in 1962, but had long before given up its original engine V 1001-8, which was then fitted to a right-hand drive fixed-head, S 824021 which became Peter Whitehead's car (see chapters 3 and 9). The first fixed-head body, J 7001, was fitted to an early production car, S 834013, 8 April 1957, which was exported to the USA.

XK 150 drophead coupé left-hand drive:

S 837003 DN, 3.4, 6 May 1957, registered WWK 468. Curiously, it was only this car, the third drophead with the fourth body P 6004, which was allocated to Jaguar's Experimental Department; the two first cars were exported to the USA. It was originally Cream. However, the registration mark WWK 468 was seen on the car which Jaguar's press officer Bob Berry took along to the Guild of Motoring Writers' Test Day at Goodwood in October 1958, by which time the car was a Carmen Red open two-seater XK 150 S with, I think, right-hand drive! I have concluded that WWK 468 became the prototype S two-seater. According to the *Car Record Book*, S 837003 DN was sold second-hand to the Tourist Trophy Garage at Farnham in December 1958 (Mike Hawthorn's company). It was at a Coys' auction in 2002 and presumably still exists in the UK.[23]

Same car as below, different setting; this may be the park at Compton Verney near Stratford which was used for several Jaguar photo shoots. (JDHT)

On this red XK 150 drophead, the body colour wire wheels show up particularly well, as does the red piping on the hood cover. (JDHT)

This grey XK 150 drophead was apparently taken to Norfolk on a winter's day. (JDHT)

This is a left-hand drive drophead in a darker red colour, with whitewall tyres and a fawn hood cover, the setting may be the River Avon near Stratford. (JDHT)

A left-hand drive XK 150 drophead in black with red trim; this car has the later rear lamp units. (JDHT)

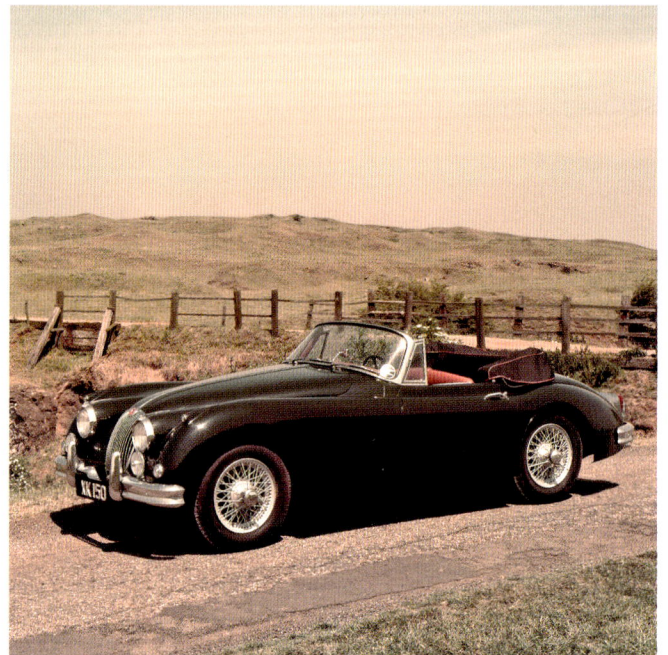

XK 150 fixed-head coupé right-hand drive:

S 824046 DN, 3.4, 9 September 1957, registered VDU 882. Jaguar Cars Limited show and press car, later sold second-hand to J T Thorpe at Wellesbourne. It was road tested by *The Autocar*.[24]

S 824245 DN, 3.4, 21 February 1958, Jaguar Cars Limited, registered VVC 48. Jaguar's demonstrator for the Geneva Motor Show, and road tested by *Motor Sport* and *Motor Racing*. It may be noted that this car had the second-type boot lid with the greater slope to the rear number plate, supporting the theory that this had been introduced by this time. Jaguar's press officer Bob Berry is supposed to have had an accident in this car, but it survived to be sold second-hand, and is believed to exist in the UK.[25]

T 824803 DN, 3.4 S, 5 March 1959, Jaguar Cars Limited, registered XDU 984. This was Jaguar's demonstrator for the 1959 Geneva Motor Show, it was road tested by *Autosport*, *The Motor*, and *Motor Sport*.[26] It was sold second-hand to Keith N Balisat in 1960.

T 825028 DN, 3.8 S, 18 September 1959, Jaguar Cars Limited demonstrator and press car, registered YHP 791. This was possibly the first of all

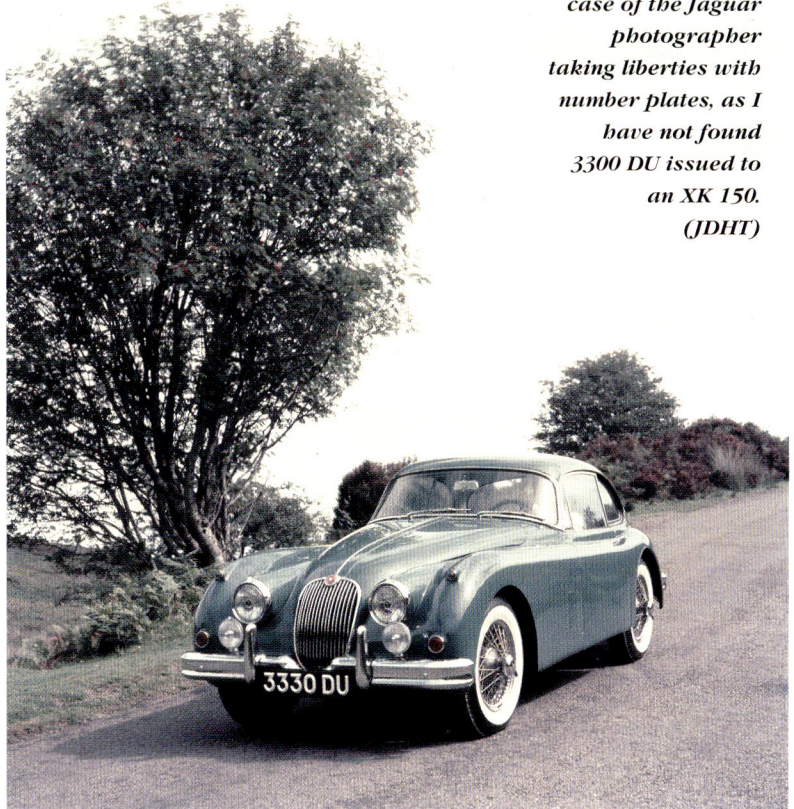

Possibly another case of the Jaguar photographer taking liberties with number plates, as I have not found 3300 DU issued to an XK 150. (JDHT)

A lovely setting, possibly somewhere in Scotland, for an XK 150 fixed-head. (JDHT)

The setting for this XK 150 fixed-head looks familiar, I think it must have been taken somewhere along the River Severn. (JDHT)

The setting for this XK 150 fixed-head looks familiar, I think it must have been taken somewhere along the River Severn. (JDHT)

the 3.8 S models and it had the first engine of this type, VAS 1001-9. It was road tested by *Autosport.*[27] It was last reported in the ownership of Jac Nasser, some time CEO of Ford Motor Company.

XK 150 open two-seater left-hand drive:

S 830001, 3.4, 13 September 1957. I should make a note of this car here, as I think this was the car with the early-type boot lid photographed in the factory before the introduc-

There were far more colour shots of the XK 150s, of several different cars in a variety of locations. It is probably the River Avon which forms the background for this two-seater in Carmen Red with red trim. (JDHT)

Not surprisingly, this Carmen Red XK 150 two-seater with black trim is also a left-hand drive car. This setting is probably Stratford-on-Avon. (JDHT)

Taken during a winter visit to Norfolk, this white two-seater sports chrome wire wheels. (JDHT)

This grey two-seater is a later car, as is evident from the rear lamp units. The wheels seem to be painted a lighter grey colour. (JDHT)

tion of the two-seater, see chapters 3 and 9, and could be described as the prototype two-seater. It had the first two-seater body, number F 15001, and the colour was changed from Sherwood Green to Cream before it was despatched to New York on 26 February 1958.[28]

XK 150 open two-seater right-hand drive:

S 820046 DN, 3.4 S, 19 June 1959, registered YDU 455. This is a real oddity in that it was converted from a left-hand drive car T 832016 DN which had been built 14 February 1959. Furthermore, in June 1959 another LHD car was built and given the chassis number S 832016, and this second car was exported to France in the normal way. The converted car S 820046 DN had the same engine and body numbers as the original T 832016 DN and was registered on 20 August 1959. The record does not explain why this happened, or what the car was used for by

Jaguar, but it was eventually sold second-hand to Coombs, Guildford.

It is interesting that the only four XK 150 cars which were used by the company as home market demonstrators and press cars were all fixed-head coupés. This probably tells us a great deal about the way in which Jaguar wanted to position the XK 150 in the market: as a GT car, rather than a sports car. By contrast, there were several road tests of the open two-seater in American magazines (see chapter 5). Similarly, with one exception, the Earls Court Motor Show Cars were all fixed-head coupés, whether of the XK 140 or XK 150 type. The following is an attempt at a list of the Motor Show cars, as they are known from contemporary press reports, the actual official Motor Show Catalogues, or photos of the Jaguar stand.

1954: There were two XK 140s on the Jaguar stand; both were right-hand drive standard cars with disc wheels. One was a Battleship Grey fixed-head with overdrive, probably 804006 DN;

the other was a drophead in Maroon with Biscuit trim and Sand hood, and must have been either 807003 or 807004 DN (see above).[29]

1955: The only XK 140 on the Jaguar stand was a Pearl Grey fixed-head right-hand drive car with Blue trim. This car has defied identification, but the most likely candidates are S 804463 or S 804464, both built 12 October 1955. These cars were eventually sold through Henlys in London and Rossleigh in Edinburgh respectively.[30]

1956: Again there was only a single XK 140 on the stand, a fixed-head right-hand drive car with overdrive. It was a light colour, possibly Cream, and may have been 804802 DN, which is listed in the *Car Record Book* as having been despatched only on 1 November 1956, and then went through Parkers, Bolton, to Bamber of Southport.[31]

1957: The sole example of an XK 150 on the Jaguar stand was a fixed-head right-hand drive car with overdrive and chrome-plated wire wheels; according to *The Autocar*, it was the "first time since the introduction of the original XK 120 that Jaguars have not displayed an open sports car" – in fact I think the last time that Jaguar had shown an open two-seater version of the XK at Earls Court was in 1953. The 1957 show car may have been S 824046 DN registered VDU 882, see above.[32]

1958: Again, there was only one XK 150 on the stand, a dark-coloured right-hand drive fixed-head, probably with chrome-plated wire wheels. It was a 3.4-litre non-S car. In their London show coverage, *The Autocar* published a photo of an open two-seater at a motor show, but other photos confirm that there was only the single fixed-head on Jaguar's Earls Court stand in 1958, and the photo in *The Autocar* has turned out to have been taken at the Paris Motor Show in the previous week.[33]

1. With thanks to Lizzie Hazlehurst
2. Clausager *XK 120 in Detail* p.190; Whyte *Jaguar* (first ed.) p.220
3. Skilleter *Norman Dewis of Jaguar* pp.239, 242
4. Clausager p.156
5. Clausager p.178; Skilleter *Dewis* p.162
6. Adams *From Craigantlet to Monte Carlo* p.83; Boyce *Jaguar XK Series* p.144; Skilleter *Jaguar XK – A Collector's Guide* p.62; Viart *Jaguar XK - la compétition sur route dans les années* 1950 pp.204-05; *XK Gazette* no.121 Oct 2007; information courtesy of David Bentley
7. *XK Bulletin* no.3 1976; information courtesy of David Bentley and Terry McGrath
8. Probably the car shown in Harvey *The Jaguar XK* p.13 bottom; information courtesy of John May and David Bentley; *XK Gazette* no.6 Mar 1998, no.33 Jun 2000
9. "Road Test Cars" and "Experimental Cars – Work Progress Book II" experimental department notebooks, JDHT archive; Skilleter *Dewis* p.247
10. "Road Test Cars" experimental department notebook, JDHT archive; www.xkdata.com
11. *The Autocar* 22 Oct 1954 p.607; Skilleter *Collector's Guide* p.67; Skilleter *Dewis* p.246
12. Porter *Jaguar Scrapbook* (2006) p.59
13. Clausager p.156
14. Porter *The Jaguar Scrapbook* (1989) p.65; Skilleter *Dewis* p.238
15. "Experimental Cars – Work Progress Book II" p.20, JDHT archive
16. Skilleter *Dewis* p.245
17. *Autosport* 4 Nov 1955; Pomeroy *"La Vie en Rose" The Motor* 23 Nov 1955; *The Autocar* 9 Dec 1955; *The Motor World* 7 Dec 1956; information courtesy of Terry

McGrath; Skilleter *Jaguar Sports Cars*, cover photo
18. Information courtesy of David Bentley
19. David Bentley in *XK Gazette* no.80 May 2004; Terry McGrath in *Jaguar Driver* Aug 1993; Paul Skilleter in *Jaguar Quarterly* autumn 1988
20. *The Autocar* 22 Oct 1954 p.607; *Autosport* 4 Mar 1955; Skilleter *Jaguar Sports Cars* photos pp.138-39
21. *Jaguar Driver* Jun 1988 front cover, Sep 1988 letter from former owner I D Brawn; *Jaguar World* vol.9 no.5 May/Jun 1997 pp.38, 42; information courtesy of Terry McGrath
22. Skilleter *Dewis* p.252; Skilleter *Collector's Guide* p.75; "Experimental Cars – Work Progress Book II" and "Book III"
23. *Autosport* 7 Nov 1958; Porter *Scrapbook* (1989); JDHT correspondence with owner 1996; www.xkdata.com
24. 21 Feb 1958
25. *Motor Sport* Oct 1958; *Motor Racing* Nov 1958; information from Richard Hassan via Terry McGrath; www.xkdata.com
26. Issues for 5 Jun 1959, 19 Aug 1959 and Jan 1960 respectively
27. 17 Jun 1960
28. *The Autocar* 21 Mar 1958; *The Motor* 26 Mar 1958; Skilleter *Collector's Guide* p.72; information from present-day owner via Terry McGrath
29. *The Autocar* 22 Oct 1954 p.607
30. *The Autocar* 21 Oct 1955 p.609, photo p.599
31. *The Autocar* 19 Oct 1956 p.551, photo p.544
32. *The Autocar* 18 Oct 1957 p.568; Clausager p.199
33. *The Autocar* 24 Oct 1958 p.597, compare with Cognet & Viart *Jaguar A Tradition of Sports Cars* p.199

Chapter Nine

Some famous XK 140 and XK 150 cars

This chapter contains an admittedly eclectic selection of those cars which are of more than passing interest, for instance because they had a famous first owner, or they can be identified as being for motor shows abroad, or were the first or last of their model. The cars used in competition which can be identified are mostly mentioned in chapter 7. This is not by any means a complete list and I have omitted some titled first owners, and at least three MPs. Similarly, many cars were bought by companies, and most of these have been omitted; more and more Jaguars were now being bought as company cars for senior executives, and the list would simply become too long. However, companies which bought XKs and which are still well-known include Ansells Brewery, Brook Street Bureau, C&A Modes, Calorgas, Decca, Ever Ready, Fisons, Fox's Glacier Mints, GKN, Jet Petroleum, Johnson Matthey, Liptons, Mecca, Sir Robert McAlpine, Shell, Sketchley, and Taylor Woodrow, to name some of them. Finally, I admit that some of my conclusions about the identity of first owners as their names appear in the *Car Record Books* are slightly speculative...

XK 140 open two-seater right-hand drive:

S 800001 DN, 1 October 1954, to Henlys, London, registered PLH 988. The first OTS RHD, sold in London.

S 800010 DN, 2 February 1955, to Henlys,

London, registered PYU 7. The first owner was the Earl of Brecknock. John Charles Henry Pratt, fifth Marquess Camden and fifth Earl Brecknock (1899-1983), had been a director of Darracq Motor Engineering Co Ltd, of Bayard Cars, and later of the Rootes-owned Clément-Talbot Ltd.[1] However, the owner of this XK 140 may have been his son David (born 1930), later the sixth Marquess, since Earl of Brecknock is used as a courtesy title for the eldest son and heir.

800032 DN, 10 May 1955, to Parkers, Bolton, registered JFV 263. The first owner was Jack Hylton, the dance band leader and impresario (1892-1965), who later owned a DHC, see below.

S 800062, 29 November 1955, exported to Bryson in Melbourne. The first owner was Nevil Shute Norway, the aircraft engineer and best-selling author (1899-1960). The car still exists in Victoria. A few months after having suffered a heart attack in November 1955, Shute wrote to a friend: "I suddenly went crazy the other day and ordered an open two-seater Jaguar XK 140 so you will probably see my obituary before long." In the words of Shute's biographer, "He had decided to take up road racing, feeling that he had reached the age when he was calm enough to do so, that he had lived his life and learned something of patience." With this car, Shute had a brief career as a racing driver in Australia between 1956 and 1958. Some of this experience found its way into his last novel *On the Beach* (1957), set in Australia during the aftermath of apocalyptic nuclear war, where one of the characters, nerdy scientist John Osborne, takes part in the Australian Grand Prix as a rookie driver, and wins, although Osborne drives a Ferrari! In the film version, Osborne was played rather improbably by Fred Astaire, and Shute in the XK 140 may have appeared in some of the racing scenes. Shute is thought to have part-exchanged the 140 against a new XK 150 fixed-head, S 824004 DN built 21 August 1957, in 1958.[2] Not many people can have taken up motor racing at the age of 57 and made a reasonable job of it…

S 800074, 16 October 1956, exported to Thailand where it still exists. The last OTS RHD.

XK 140 open two-seater left-hand drive:

810001, 29 September 1954, to Hoffman, New York. The first OTS LHD.

S 810154, 9 November 1954, to Hornburg, Los Angeles. This Cream car had White trim, and all its chrome parts were gold plated! – presumably for the Los Angeles Motor Show. It was featured on the cover of *Road & Track* when they tested another XK 140.[3]

S 812181 DN, 6 March 1956, Personal Export Delivery through Henlys in London, registered NVC 278. The first owner was Swedish-born Hollywood star Anita Ekberg (born 1931), who starred in Fellini's 1960 film *La Dolce Vita*.

S 812270 DN, 27 March 1956, to Jaguar Cars, New York. The first owner was the thriller-writer Mickey Spillane (1918-2006) who had previously owned an XK 120. He later claimed to have been given the car by John Wayne, as a thank-you for re-writing a film script.[4]

S 812506 DN, 24 May 1956, to Saad in Beirut, Lebanon, but Personal Export Delivery in the UK and registered NVC 811. The first owner was one Hussein Ali who may have been Prince Sharif Al-Hussein bin Ali, a cousin of the Iraqi King Feisal I, who had previously owned an XK 120 drophead.[5] It should be noted that A 817530 DN, DHC LHD, 8 June 1955, to Delecroix in Paris, was sold to ALS Hussein Ali, Nice, who could be the same owner.

812683, 19 July 1956, to Jaguar Cars, New York. The first owner was James Stewart of San Clemente, California, who may have been the Hollywood actor of that name (1908-97).

S 813282, 30 January 1957, to Jaguar Cars, New York. The last OTS LHD.

I do not think that Bill Hayley ever had an XK but when he visited the Jaguar factory in 1956, he was photographed at the wheel of an XK 140 two-seater. (JDHT)

XK 140 fixed-head coupé right-hand drive:

804001, the first FHC RHD; see chapter 8 on works cars.

S 804007 DN, 26 January 1955, through Henlys, London, to HWM Motors, registered WPH 500. The first owner in the *Car Record Book* was George Heath of HWM Limited. This should probably be John Heath, the Surrey Jaguar dealer and, together with George Abecassis, maker of the HWM racing cars. I think this must

The 1954 Motor Show saw the debut of the XK 140, with a fixed-head and a drophead on the stand, together with two Mark VIIs and a D-type. (JDHT)

The 1955 stand gave pride of place to the 2.4 and there was but a single XK 140 on the stand, a fixed-head SE model. (JDHT)

In 1956, the Mark VIII was Jaguar's Motor Show debutante. The sole representative of the XK 140 this year was a standard fixed-head model. That's the Rover T3 gas turbine car on the stand behind. (JDHT)

have been the car that John Heath drove into 40th place in the 1955 Mille Miglia, see chapter 7.[6] Tragically, Heath was killed in the 1956 Mille Miglia driving one of his own HWM-Jaguars.

804045 DN, 10 March 1955, to C H Truman in Nottingham, registered UAU 812. The first owner was George Brough of Brough Superior Motors, the motorcycle manufacturer who was an old friend of William Lyons and a long-standing Jaguar customer.

804068, 24 March 1955, Personal Export Delivery through Henlys in London, registered RGT 801. The first owner was The Maharajah of Bahawalpur. This must be Lt-General Sir Sadiq Muhammad Khan Abbasi V GCSI, GCIE, KCVO, Nawab of Bahawalpur (1904-66). When in 1955 the Nawab allowed his state to be merged with Pakistan, he was given special privileges, including the right to import several cars duty-free every year. This Jaguar was unusually supplied in primer. It was sold through Christies in 1996 and is now thought to exist in Germany. Many of the late Nawab's cars were only auctioned in 2004 and a Jaguar was then said to have fetched Rs 0.5 million.[7]

804082 DN, 7 April 1955, through Henlys to Jarvis of Wimbledon, registered XPT 1. The first owner was Captain George Eyston (1897-1979), the racing driver and record-breaker famous for his association with MGs. He also owned a Riley Pathfinder and an MG Magnette.[8]

804209 DN, 14 June 1955, to SH Newsome, Coventry. The first owner was the Abbey Panels company in Coventry, long-standing supplier to Jaguar.

804237 DN, 20 June 1955, through Henlys to Wadham Bros, registered OOW 625. The first owner was A J Harmsworth, Lyndhurst, Hampshire, possibly a member of the Associated Newspapers press dynasty who were then the publishers of the *Daily Mail* and the *Evening News*. Later, there were also two XK 150s originally owned by Associated Newspapers Ltd; 3.4 DHC RHD S 827001 29 November 1957 registered UXB 113, see below, and 3.4 FHC RHD S 824857 16 April 1959 registered XYH 278.

S 804340 DN, 19 August 1955, to Appleyard, Leeds, registered VUB 140. Officially the Appleyard demonstrator, it was rallied by Ian Appleyard who came second in the 1956 RAC Rally (see chapter 7).

804390, 8 September1955, through Henlys, London to Murketts, Peterborough, registered EEG 525. The first owner was Jaguar racing driver George Howorth who later had two XK 150s, see below.

804622 DN, 1 February 1956, to Henlys, London, registered SLU 927. The first owner was Iliffe & Sons, publishers of *The Autocar* magazine. It was the company car of Michael Brown of *The Autocar* who wrote about it in the magazine (see chapter 5).[9]

S 804635 DN, 27 February 1956, to Henlys, London, registered SLU 815. The first owner was Lord Curzon, High Wycombe. Richard Nathaniel Curzon, second Viscount Scarsdale (1898-1977), was the nephew of the Lord Curzon who was viceroy of India.

S 804668 DN, 13 March 1956, through Henlys, London, to Ken Rudd, registered UPX 939. The first owner was famous woman racing and rally driver Betty Haig. It was also one of very few cars painted in the rare colour of Mediterranean Blue. Ms Haig later remembered it as "A lovely car on the *autostrada*, it was too much like a lorry in towns – I preferred the XK 120."[10]

S 804671, 21 March 1956, to Henlys, London, registered SXK 313. The first owner was The fifth Marquess of Cholmondeley GCVO (1883-1968), soldier and land owner, of Houghton Hall, Norfolk, and Cholmondeley Castle, Cheshire.

804674, 24 March 1956, through Henlys to Mann Egerton, Norwich, registered UPW 750. The first owner was Lady Elizabeth Mary Yorke, Countess of Leicester (born 1912), wife of the fifth Earl, of Holkham Hall, near Wells in Norfolk.

804728, 15 May 1956, through Henlys to Coombs, Guildford, registered 329 BPG. The first owner was The Rt. Hon. Lord Latymer, Mayfield, Sussex. Thomas Burdett Money-Coutts, seventh Baron Latymer (1901-87), was a member of the Coutts banking dynasty.

S 804760, 2 June 1956, to Charles Attwood, Wolverhampton, registered 870 LRF. The first owner was H V Bamford, Uttoxeter, Staffordshire; although these initials are less familiar, surely this was a member of the family behind the JCB company?

804843 DN, 30 November 1956, through Charles Attwood to Burton Autos, registered FFA 248. The last FHC RHD car, it was sold in Burton-on-Trent.

XK 140 fixed-head coupé left-hand drive:

814001, the first FHC LHD; see chapter 8 on works cars.

S 814096 DN, 23 March 1955, chassis only, direct sale to the automotive and industrial designer Raymond Loewy in Paris, see chapter 10 on special-bodied cars.

S 814399, 17 June 1955, to Delecroix, Paris. The first owner was the Martell cognac company.

S 814550 DN, 5 July 1955, Personal Export Delivery through Henlys in London, registered RXU 827. The first owner was the German Prince Wittgenstein. This could be Richard, Prince of Sayn-Wittgenstein-Berleburg (born 1934) who later married HRH Princess Benedikte of Denmark, but there are other possible Prince Wittgensteins, including Prince Ludwig (1915-62)![11]

S 814773 DN, 6 September 1955, to Delecroix, Paris. The 1955 Paris Motor Show car, it was later sold in the Lyon area.

S 815069, 26 October 1955, to Delecroix, Paris. The first owner was Dr Rebatel of Lyon who had previously owned a XK 120 with a special coupé body by Barou.[12] He rallied both of these cars, see chapter 7, and later owned an XK 150, see below.

S 815164, 9 November 1955; S 815197, 15 November 1955; S 815198 DN, 15 November 1955; and S 815424, 14 March 1956, registered NVC 808. All were sold directly by Jaguar apparently to HM King Hussein of Jordan. At least S 815197 still exists in Germany.

A 815551 BW, 13 April 1956, and A 815619 BW, 1 May 1956. It appears that both of these cars were used by Charles Hornburg, the original Jaguar importer in Los Angeles.

S 815922 BW, 22 November 1956, to Jaguar Cars, New York. The first owner was Billy Wilder (1906-2002), director of – among many other films – *Sunset Boulevard* and *Some Like It Hot*. Incidentally, I have not been able to verify that Marilyn Monroe owned a Jaguar XK. Wilder and his wife, the actress Audrey Long, had already bought a Jaguar in Paris in 1951, and drove it through France and Italy, before shipping it back to the USA.[13]

S 815966 BW, 9 January 1957, to Jaguar Cars, New York, sold in New York State. The last FHC LHD.

XK 140 drophead coupé right-hand drive:

807001, the first DHC RHD; see chapter 8 on works cars.

807207 DN, 29 June 1955, through Parkers, Bolton, to Imperial Garages, Blackpool, registered JFV 825. The first owner was Jack Hylton, who also had 800032 DN, see above.

807224 DN, 5 July 1955, to Ritchies in Glasgow, registered PGE 246. The first owner was the commercial vehicle manufacturer Albion Motors.

807355, 18 January 1956, to Henlys, London, registered SXK 270. The first owner was Lord Camrose, c/o *The Daily Telegraph*. John Seymour Berry, the second Viscount Camrose (1909-95), was some time chairman of the *Daily Telegraph*. He had been the Conservative MP for Hitchin from 1941 to 1945, and served in the army in North Africa and Italy.

807417 DN, 1 June 1956, to Henlys, London, registered SXX 8. The first owner was Harry Mundy, some time technical editor of *The Autocar* magazine, who later became Jaguar's engine designer.

S 807420 DN, 2 June 1956, through Henlys to F English, registered TRU 140. The first owner was Colonel R J "Ronnie" Hoare, later the British

Ferrari importer and owner of several Jaguars including a D-type. He also had an XK 150, see below.

807442 DN, 9 July 1956, through Henlys to Brooklands of Bond Street, registered LG 2. The first owner was Lew & Leslie Grade Ltd, but who of the famous brothers drove the car?

807479 DN, 27 November 1956, Personal Export Delivery through Henlys, London, registered NKV 664. The first owner was the Nawab of Bhopal. This must have been Air Vice-Marshal and Major-General Sir Muhammad Hamidullah Khan Bahadur, GCSI, GCIE, CVO, ADC (1894-1960).

807480 DN, 1 January 1957, to Sagers, Bulawayo, Rhodesia. The last DHC RHD, it survives in Switzerland, owned by the well-known XK expert and author Urs Schmid.

XK 140 drophead coupé left-hand drive:

817001, 5 October 1954, to Hoffman in New York, although the first owner of record was in San Francisco. The first DHC LHD.

817031, 1 December 1954, to Hornburg. The first owner was Dean Martin, the singer and Hollywood actor (1917-95). It appears that he later had an XK 150, S 837975 BW, see below.

S 817337 DN, 31 March 1955, to Hornburg. The first owner was John F Dugdale, at the time Jaguar's representative on the West Coast, who went on to head Jaguar PR in the USA and wrote the book *Jaguar in America*.

S 817604, 29 June 1955, to Hornburg. The first owners were Mr and Mrs Ronald Colman, he was the British-born romantic actor (1891-1958), who made his career in Hollywood.

S 817609, 30 June 1955, to Hornburg. The first owner was Stanley Kubrick (1928-99), the film maker famous for *Spartacus*, *Lolita*, *Dr Strangelove*, *2001 A Space Odyssey* and *A Clockwork Orange*, who lived in England from 1962 until his death.

817676, 18 July 1955, to Budd & Dyer in Montreal but Personal Export Delivery, registered NWK 566. The first owner was P E Trudeau, Montreal; this is believed to have been the future Canadian Prime Minister Pierre Elliott Trudeau (1919-2000), who apparently also at one time owned a Mercedes-Benz 300SL.

A 817828, 2 September 1955, to Delecroix. For the 1955 Paris Motor Show.

S 817877 DN, 16 September 1955, to Hoffman. The first owner was Walter Hill, Miami, Florida, the Jaguar collector *extraordinaire* until he disposed of his collection in 2004.

818530, 24 April 1956, to Delecroix in Paris. The first owner was Marcel Breuer, presumably the Hungarian-born architect and furniture designer (1902-81), who, although by then based in New York, undertook several projects in France.

S 818631, 8 June 1956, to Abolhassan Diba, Teheran, Iran, but Personal Export Delivery in the UK, registered NKV 79. The first owner was one F Diba in South Kensington, possibly c/o the Iranian Embassy; it is tempting to think that could this have been Farah Diba who later married the last Shah of Iran but she was only born in 1938 and was a student in Paris at this time. I suppose the owner might have been her mother, Farideh Diba, and were they related to the Iranian Jaguar importer?

S 818673 BW, 21 June 1956, to Jaguar Cars New York. The first owner was Charles Hornburg, although he also seems to have had two FHC models around this time, see above. May be these cars were simply Hornburg demonstrators.

S 819311 BW, 9 January 1957, to Jaguar Cars New York, sold in New York. The last DHC LHD.

XK 150 open two-seater right-hand drive:

S 820001, 3.4, 9 October 1958, to St Helier Garage, Jersey. The first OTS RHD, one of only 23 with the standard 3.4-litre engine.

S 820003 DN, 3.4 S, 30 October 1958, through Henlys to Coombs, Guildford, registered 971 JPE. The first 3.4 S; there were 44 cars of this type.

T 820019 DN, 3.4 S, 30 December 1958, through Henlys to Rose & Young, London, registered WLO 7. The first owner was Eric Haddon who rallied this car, see chapter 7.

T 820056 DN, 3.8 S, 14 October 1959, to Victor, Belfast. The first 3.8 S, of only 24 cars of this type.

S 820065 DN, 3.4, 15 December 1959, to Henlys, London, registered YYF 168. The first owner was The Marchioness of Bute, presumably Beatrice Nicola (born 1933), wife of the sixth Marquess.

S 820081, 3.8, 19 May 1960, Personal Export Delivery to Accra, Ghana, registered 5395 DU. The first of only two 3.8-litre models; this one was actually converted from a 3.4-litre model.

T 820093 DN, 3.8 S, 19 October 1960, through Henlys to Boorers Garage, Worthing, registered 9787 PX. The last OTS RHD, it still exists, now registered JAG 150.

XK 150 open two-seater left-hand drive:

S 830001, 3.4, 13 September 1957, to Jaguar Cars, New York. The first OTS LHD, and effectively the prototype; regular production commenced with S 830002 DN in January 1958 (see chapters 3 and 8).

S 830073 DN, 3.4 S, 7 March 1958, to Jaguar Cars, New York. The first 3.4 S model, probably for the New York Motor Show, together with S 830074 DN, which had the first 3.4 S engine, VS 1001-9.

S 830756, 3.4, 20 June 1958, to Jaguar Cars, New York. The first owner recorded was one R Moore, Los Angeles. It is natural to assume that this was the British actor Roger Moore (born 1927) who was photographed with just such a car.[14] Of course in his later professional life he was mostly linked with a Volvo P1800 and with Aston Martins!

Six cars in August-September 1958 are marked as "Show Cars" in the records, they are: **S 831138**, **S 831139 DN**, and **S 831348 BW** (all 3.4); **T 831280 DN**, **T 831301 DN**, and **T 831383 DN** (all 3.4 S). The first five were all Black, with special White trim piped Black, and all went to the USA, possibly for the Los Angeles Motor Show. T 831383 DN was Cream with Black trim and went to Delecroix; it was probably the 1958 Paris Motor Show car.[15]

T 832012 DN, 3.4 S, 12 February 1959, to Jaguar Cars, New York. The first owner was Paul Newman, possibly the Hollywood film star (born 1925) who was also a competent racing driver and was co-driver of the Porsche which finished second at Le Mans in 1979. The car was finished in a special colour, "Crushed Strawberry Red".

S 832108, 3.4, 19 November 1959, to Saudi Arabia. The first owner was HRH Prince Mansour Bin Saud.

T 832109 DN, 3.4 S, 20 November 1959, to Jordan. The first owner was possibly HM King Hussein, or the car was intended for him, his name is in the *Car Record Book* but was crossed out. The car, curiously, had disc wheels.

T 832110 DN, 3.8 S, 27 November 1959, to Fendler & Luedemann, Hamburg, Germany. The first 3.8 S model, of only fourteen OTS LHD with this engine.

S 832112, 3.8, 14 December 1959, to Panama. The first 3.8 litre model.

S 832174 DN, 3.8, 24 November 1960, to Jaguar Cars, New York. The last OTS LHD.

XK 150 fixed-head coupé right-hand drive:

S 824001, 3.4, 20 August 1957, to Delecroix, Paris. The first FHC RHD.

S 824021, 3.4, 24 August 1957, to Henlys, London, registered VDU 358. The first owner was the racing driver Peter Whitehead. The car was specially prepared for the Tour de France with an experimental S cylinder head with three 2in carburettors, see chapters 3 and 7. It is now owned by Terry McGrath.

S 824076, 3.4, 9 October 1957, through Henlys

There were two new models on the Jaguar Motor Show stand in 1957, the 3.4 litre which got a turntable, and the XK 150 – which did not. (JDHT)

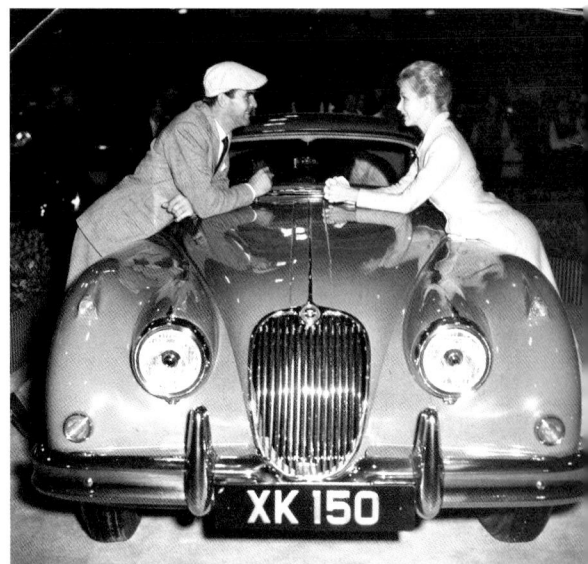

The two actors Stanley Baker and June Laverick from the Rank Organisation found time to stop by the XK 150 on the Jaguar stand at the 1957 Motor Show. (JDHT)

to Mann Egerton, Norwich, registered BB 14. The first owner was Major Ian B Baillie, Norfolk, the well-known Jaguar racing driver. He later also had **T 825012 DN**, 3.4 S, 3 September 1959, registered 3266 DU as a Personal Export Delivery car.[16]

S 824092, 3.4, 22 October 1957, through Ritchies, Glasgow to RP Stewart of Dumbuck Garage, registered FSN 1. This was probably one of the Scottish Motor Show cars, and went on to become the demonstrator for Dumbuck Garage, the family firm of the racing Stewart brothers, Jimmy and Jackie. Jimmy used this car at least once in a competitive event, see chapter 7. There were three or four other cars which may have been Scottish Motor Show cars, as follows: **S 824089 DN**, **S 824090 DN**, **S 824093** (doubtful), and **S 824094 DN**, all built in October 1957, and all despatched to either of the two Scottish distributors.

S 824114, 3.4, 7 November 1957, direct sale from Jaguar to the Ministry of Supply. A black disc-wheeled car registered UXR 271, it was was used for testing the friction of road surfaces.

S 824330, 3.4, 26 March 1958, through Henlys to Murketts, Huntingdon, registered HEG 58. The first owner was the well-known Jaguar racing driver George Howorth. He later also owned **T 824839 DN**, 3.4 S, 26 March 1959,

The 1958 show was the last occasion when an XK 150 was shown at Earls Court. This fixed-head which shared floor space with a Mark VIII and a 2.4, with a Mark IX and a 3.4 on turntables (which Jaguar used for several shows), and the sectioned engine in a glass case which also made several appearances. (JDHT)

A number of well-known Jaguar personalities with a famous customer and an XK 150 fixed-head – from left to right "Lofty" England, Norman Dewis, HRH The Duke of Kent, and William Heynes. (JDHT)

registered VEW 966.

S 824476 DN, 3.4, 9 June 1958, through Henlys to Harold Radford, Kensington, registered DC 7. The first owner was the world land speed record holder Donald Campbell (1921-67). His car was of course Cotswold Blue, to match his *Bluebirds*.

S 824617 DN, 3.4, 10 September 1958, to Henlys, London, registered UXY 552. The first owner was the much-married playboy and bobsleigh-runner Lord Kimberley (1924-2002), in his obituary described as a "as a rackety motorist, [who] was frequently fined by the police. He also killed a pedestrian he claimed not to have seen crossing the road in Piccadilly." He had previously owned an MG Magnette.[17]

S 824624 BW, 3.4, 17 September 1958, through Henlys to Jack Barclay, London, registered VXA 295. The first owner was the actor Sir Ralph Richardson (1902-83), a great motorcycle enthusiast who still rode a BMW when in his seventies.

S 824649 DN, 3.4, 28 October 1958, through Rossleigh, Aberdeen to P S Nicholson, registered ESO 600. The first owner was Lord Doune, later the 20th Earl of Moray (born 1928), who until 1998 exhibited his collection of cars at the Doune Motor Museum.

S 825110 BW, 3.8, 3 December 1959, through Henlys to Elmbridge Motors, Tolworth, registered 785 MPH. The first owner was a certain S Moss. We should not be surprised that Stirling Moss used a car with automatic transmission for road use; in fact he once claimed to prefer this system. Shortly before, he had bought a Facel Vega for use on the Continent.[18] His XK 150 now exists in Switzerland.

T 824789 DN, 3.4 S, 17 February 1959, to Henlys, London, registered 977 JPE. The first 3.4 S model.

S 825041 DN, 3.8, 16 October 1959, to Rossleigh, Edinburgh. The first 3.8 model.

S 825275 DN, 3.4, 16 June 1960, through Henlys to Motorworks, Chalfont, registered 11 PBH. The first owner was Cecil Clutton, the well-known veteran and vintage motorist and writer. He subsequently wrote a letter to *Motor Sport* bitterly complaining about the inaccuracy of its speedometer, and also found that Koni shock absorbers greatly improved the handling.[19]

At the end of production, the following cars were converted from LHD to RHD:

T 825363 DN converted from S 847042
T 825364 DN converted from S 847048 BW
S 825365 DN converted from S 847041 BW
S 825366 DN converted from S 847067 BW
S 825367 BW converted from S 847062 BW
S 825368 DN converted from S 847070 BW
S 825369 BW converted from S 847039 BW, built 24 October 1960 as a LHD car, converted 3 July 1961, through Henlys to Chipstead Motors, London, registered 606 CXW. This was the last FHC RHD.

XK 150 fixed-head coupé left-hand drive:

S 834001, the first FHC LHD; see chapter 8 on works cars.

S 834911, 3.4, 13 December 1957, to Delecroix, Paris. The first owner was the Jaguar dealer and rally driver Henri Peignaux in Lyon.

S 835422, 3.4, 27 March 1958, to Delecroix, Paris. The first owner was another French Jaguar rally driver, Dr Maurice Rebatel of Lyon, who had previously owned both XK 120 and XK 140 cars, see above and chapter 7.

S 835530 DN, 3.4, 29 April 1958, to Belgian Motor Company, Bruxelles, but a Personal Export car delivered in the UK. The first owner was Peter Townsend (1914-95), the RAF Group Captain and Royal Equerry who had a famous romance with Princess Margaret, but as he was divorced they could not marry. He was air attaché to the British Embassy in Bruxelles between 1953 and 1955, and in 1959 married a Belgian lady, described as a "wealthy tobacco heiress", later settling in France.

The following cars in September 1958 are all marked as "Show Cars" in the *Car Record Book*: **S 835769 BW, S 835770 BW, S 835773 BW, S 835779 BW, S 835784, S 835785 BW, S 835789, S 835791 BW**, which all went to the USA; also **S 835786 DN**, which went to Delecroix in Paris and could have been the Paris Motor Show car. Of the eight cars which went to the USA, the first four were Black with special White trim piped Black, the other four were Cream with Black trim piped Red.

T 835897 DN, 3.4 S, 20 November 1958, to Jaguar Cars, New York. The first 3.4 S model, it now survives in Canada.

T 835997 DN, 3.4 S, 12 January 1959, to Jaguar Cars, New York. The first owner was the British-born Hollywood actor and long-time Jaguar enthusiast Ray Milland (1907-86) who previously owned an XK 120.[20] This car still exists in the USA.

T 836311 DN, 3.4 S, 10 July 1959, to Jaguar Cars, New York. The first owner was W N Reynolds II of Winston Salem, North Carolina, a member of the tobacco dynasty.

S 836399 BW, 3.8, 27 August 1959, to Jaguar Cars, New York. The first 3.8 model.

In January 1960, there were three cars marked "Show Car" in the *Car Record Book*: **S 836657 DN, S 836658 DN**, and **S 836659 BW**. They all had 3.8-litre standard engines with the 9:1 compression ratio, and all had chrome wire wheels. All went to the USA and could have been New York Motor Show cars.

T 836438 DN, 3.8 S, 15 September 1959, to RM Overseas, Frankfurt. The first 3.8 S model; one car with a lower chassis number was converted from a 3.4 S after delivery.

S 836970 BW, 3.8, 21 September 1960, to Jaguar

Cars, New York. The first owner was Leyland Motors (USA) Inc, of Long Island City. At this time, Jaguar handled the importation and distribution of Leyland vehicles in the USA (see chapter 4).

S 847044 BW, 3.8, 25 October 1960, to Jaguar Cars, New York. The first owner was Hollywood actress Kim Novak (born 1933) who starred in Hitchcock's 1958 film *Vertigo*; the car is now owned by the Swiss XK expert Urs Schmid.

S 847095 DN, 3.4, 18 November 1960, Personal Export through Henlys, registered 7582 DU. The last FHC LHD.

XK 150 drophead coupé right-hand drive:

S 827001, 3.4, 29 November 1957, to Henlys, London, registered UXB 113. The first RHD DHC; the first owner was Associated Newspapers Ltd.

S 827186 DN, 3.4, 23 July 1958, to Henlys, Bournemouth, registered XEL 150. The first owner was Colonel R J "Ronnie" Hoare, Jaguar enthusiast who had several XKs and a D-type, and who became the Ferrari importer.

S 827196 DN, 3.4, 21 August 1958, through Henlys to P Pike, Plymouth, registered HRH 118. The first owner was Prince Chula Chakrabongse of Thailand (1908-63), cousin of the racing driver "Bira" and until 1948 manager of Bira's "White Mouse" team. It was painted a special Blue colour. The car was later re-registered 66 VCV and now survives in Germany.[21]

S 827216 BW, 3.4, 11 September 1958, through Appleyard, Leeds, to Hoyland Motors, registered PKW 350. The first owner was Terry-Thomas Enterprises Ltd, the company of the comedy actor (1911-90) who starred in *School for Scoundrels*, *Those Magnificent Men in Their Flying Machines*, and more appropriately in this context, *Monte Carlo or Bust*. It is believed that one or two XK 140 dropheads, 807212 and 807426 DN, were used in some Terry-Thomas films.[22]

S 827299 DN, 3.4, 18 February 1959, through Henlys to Lex, London W1, registered WLY 150. A later owner of this car was Dr Stephen Ward (1912-1963). Ward introduced showgirl Christine Keeler to the Secretary of State for War, John Profumo who then had an affair with Keeler, but she also had an affair with the Soviet Naval Attaché. When this was exposed, Profumo was forced to resign and the scandal contributed to the fall of the Conservative Government in the 1964 election. Ward was charged with living off immoral earnings but committed suicide on the last day of the trial. The jury found him guilty.[23]

S 827332, 3.4, 25 March 1959, through Ritchies, Glasgow, to McQuistton, Ayr. The first owner was one M Richmond of Maybole, who obtained for this car the famous registration mark JAG 1, which is now on the XK-SS once owned by Campbell McLaren and later by Allen Lloyd.

T 827334 DN, 3.4 S, 3 April 1959, to P J Evans, Birmingham, as their demonstrator, registered YOE 890. The first 3.4 S model.

T 827461 DN, 3.8 S, 21 September 1959, to Charles Attwood, Wolverhampton, registered 170 WU. The first 3.8 S model, it survives in the UK.

S 827467 DN, 3.8, 9 November 1959, through Parkers, Bolton, to R Bamber, Southport, as their demonstrator, registered KWM 707. The first 3.8 model.

T 827468 DN, 3.4 S, 13 November 1959, Personal Export Delivery, registered 3594 DU. The first owner was Sahadevji, Maharajah of Dharampur. The car is said to have been raced and still survives in the Gondal collection in India.[24]

T 827622 DN, 3.8 S, 18 July 1960, through Henlys to Clarke & Simpson. The first owner was Sir Alan Cobham (1894-1973), the pioneering long-distance aviator of "Flying Circus" fame whose company later pioneered in-flight re-fuelling.

S 827663 DN, 3.4 converted from DHC LHD T 838974 DN 3.8 S, built in LHD form 27 September 1960, converted 25 May 1961, to Henlys, London. The last DHC RHD car.

XK 150 drophead coupé left-hand drive:

S 837001, 3.4, 27 March 1957, to Jaguar Cars, New York. The first DHC LHD.

S 837407, 3.4, 29 April 1958, to Delecroix, Paris. The first owner was Henri Peignaux, Jaguar dealer of Lyon, see S 834911 above.

S 837425 BW, 3.4, 6 April 1958, to Jaguar Cars, New York. The first owner was the songwriter Irving Berlin (1888-1989), whose most famous and enduring title is "White Christmas" sung by Bing Crosby.

S 837550, 3.4, 4 July 1958, to Jaguar Cars, New York. The first owner was Spencer Tracy, Los Angeles; presumably the Hollywood character actor (1900-67).

S 837599, 3.4, 24 July 1959, Personal Export Delivery, registered UWK 79. The first owner was Count Victor Emmanuel de Sarde, presumed to be the exiled heir to the Italian throne (born 1937) who became a wealthy businessman and returned to Italy in 2002.

S 837658 DN, 3.4, 29 August 1958, to Delecroix, Paris. Marked "Show Car" in *Car Record Book*, it was presumably the 1958 Paris Motor Show car. In September 1958 three cars for the USA are marked "Show Car" in the *Car Record Book*, as follows: **S 837692 BW**, **S 837693 BW**, and **S 837697 BW**. They were all Black, trimmed in White with Black piping which seems to have been a preferred colour scheme for show cars around this time, compare the OTS and FHC cars discussed above. A fourth car in this colour scheme, **S 837700**, is however *not* marked "Show Car".

S 837975 BW, 3.4, 30 December 1958, to Jaguar Cars, New York. The first owner was D Martin of Beverly Hills, presumably the Hollywood actor Dean Martin, whom I have already mentioned as the owner of an XK 140 DHC.

S 837993 DN, 3.4 S, 2 January 1959, to Jaguar Cars, New York. The first 3.4 S model, still with the S rather than the T prefix.

S 838072, 3.4, 20 January 1959, to Jaguar Cars, New York, but Personal Export Delivery in the UK, registered UVC 484. The first owner was CS Peck, who might be Cameron Peck, the extraordinary car collector who previously had owned an XK 120 fixed-head.[25]

S 838392 BW, 3.8, 27 August 1959, to Jaguar Cars, New York. The first 3.8 model.

T 838454 DN, 3.8 S, 2 October 1959, to Jaguar Cars, New York. The first 3.8 S model.

S 839010 BW, 3.8, 25 October 1960. The last DHC LHD.

Apart from specific sources mentioned in the notes, much of the data and information on XK owners can be found on web sites, including Wikipedia and thePeerage.com both of which I have used extensively.

Occasionally, there are cars mentioned in the literature which would justify inclusion in this list, but which have defied identification, typically because the first owner's name and registration mark were not reported back to Jaguar and therefore did not get entered in the *Car Record Books*. For instance, Hollywood star Jayne Mansfield (1933-67) is supposed to have had an XK 140 which was damaged by fire in the workshop of customiser Barris, but it may have been her XK 120.[26] French novelist Françoise Sagan (1935-2004) had an XK 140 drophead.[27] It is also rumoured that Steve McQueen as well as his XK-SS, may have had an XK 150.

Apart from JAG 1 mentioned above, many cars registered in Britain had distinctive numbers. XK 1 was originally issued in London in January 1922, but forty years later appeared on at least three XKs; first XK 140 chassis S 804132 DN originally registered RHP 576 (see chapter 8), then XK 150 3.8 S T 820092 DN, and later XK 120 660446. The registration XK 140 was on XK 140 drophead S 807257 (originally registered RYO 140) owned by L R P Landsberg, and he later moved it to his XK 150 S 827320 DN. Quite a few cars had either "140" or "150" on the number plate, including some of the demonstrators used by various dealers. The Ayrshire mark JAG 140 was on the XK 140 fixed-head 804636 DN originally sold to Lt-Col. Mackie-Campbell of Monkton, Ayrshire in March 1956, but this car – or its registration – seems to have been acquired by John Coombs, the well-known Jaguar dealer of Guildford. JAG 140 was later transferred to XK 140 two-seater S 800011. JAG 150 was at one time on T 825143 DN but was later transferred on to T 820093 DN, the very last right-hand drive two-seater.[28]

One of the advantages of having the records as a computer database is that it becomes much easier to spot owners who over the years had more than one XK. Apart from HM King Hussein of Jordan, whose four or five cars are detailed above, at the top of this list is the family-owned building and property company of A&J Mucklow at Halesowen,[29] with no less than five XK 150 fixed-heads, four of them bought in the spring of 1958, followed by a 3.8 model in late 1959. Not far away, John Moore in Worcestershire had an XK 140 drophead registered SON 140, while TUY 917 graced his three XK 150 fixed-heads, two 3.4 models and a 3.4 S model between 1957 and 1959. He later had an E-type but is said to have been unhappy with the headroom in this car, so he changed back to his last XK 150.[30]

G Mason-Styrton in Surrey had four cars – two XK 140s, two XK 150s, all fixed-heads.

One of several cars bearing SVM 779 and owned by Mr Corser of Shrewsbury, this is believed to be his 1958 car S 824174 DN, with disc wheels and unusual wheel trims, extra lamps, an array of club badges, and "leaper" mascot. (JDHT)

Ernest W Birkett of Suffolk had three XK 150 fixed-heads, two 3.4 models and a 3.8 S, between 1957 and 1959, all registered RT 1. This registration mark also appeared on a fourth car which had Mann Egerton of Norwich as its recorded first owner; there must have been a connection. Quite a few names appear three times in the records. My favourite is Dr Doreen Hayes of Cheshire who had three XK 150 fixed-heads between 1958 and 1961, all of which carried the number plate VXJ 860; the first was a 3.4, the two later were 3.8 S models. Similarly, AH 250 was found on three XK 150 dropheads owned by Anthony Hopkins of London, a 3.4, a 3.4 S and a 3.8 S, between 1958 and 1960, and SVM 779 on three cars owned by GB Corser, Shrewsbury: an XK 140 drophead and two XK

150 fixed-heads. The cars owned by Ian Baillie, "Ronnie" Hoare and George Howorth have been detailed individually above.

In the USA, the XK 150 records show at least one triple owner, Frank Granat of San Francisco, all of his cars were dropheads, a 3.4, a 3.4 S and a 3.8 in that order from 1957 to 1960. Howard C Walker of San Antonio in Texas may have had three fixed-heads; he certainly had two. In the XK 140 records, JW Snowden, Rockville, Indiana, is listed as owner of three dropheads in 1955-56, but two of these are so close together that it may be an error in the records, or perhaps one of his cars met with a swift and unhappy demise. Many more private owners had two cars in succession, as did some of the companies mentioned at the beginning of this chapter.

1. Nickols and Karslake *Motoring Entente* pp.276, 280
2. delarue.net/norway.htm; Julian Smith *Nevil Shute*; *Autosport* 12 Jul 1957; Elmgreen & McGrath *The Jaguar XK in Australia* pp.98, 120, 211-17
3. *Road & Track* Jun 1955, courtesy of Terry McGrath
4. Clausager *XK 120 In Detail* p.194; *XK Gazette* no.5 Feb 1998, no.6 Mar 1998
5. Clausager *XK 120* p.199
6. Wimpffen *Time and Two Seats* p.181
7. www.dawn.com/2004/05/10/local28.htm, report by Majeed Gill
8. Clausager *MG Saloon Cars* p.129
9. *The Autocar* 17 Aug 1956
10. "The Cars of Betty Haig", *Motor Sport* Jan 1965
11. www.sayn.de
12. Clausager *XK 120* pp.149, 210
13. *New York Times* 15 Apr 1951, from their web site
14. Photo by Eric Skipsey dated 1958, on www.imdb.com
15. Cognet & Viart *Jaguar A Tradition of Sports Cars* p.199
16. Baillie "A Year of Driving Jaguars" *The Autocar* 27 Jun 1958
17. *The Daily Telegraph* 29 May 2002; Clausager *MG Saloon Cars* p.129; Lord Kimberley with Charles Roberts *The Whim of the Wheel, the Memoirs of the Earl of*

Kimberley
18. *Autosport* 15 May 1959
19. *Motor Sport* Apr 1961
20. Clausager *XK 120*, p.111
21. *XK Gazette* no.33 Jun 2000 where the car is mistakenly said to have been owned by "Bira"
22. *XK Gazette* nos.5 Feb 1998, 114 Mar 2007
23. *XK Gazette* no.119 Aug 2007
24. Article by Srinivas Krishnan on www.bsmotoring.com, posted 21 Jun 2002
25. Clausager *XK 120* p.197
26. Mansfield photo by Gabi Rona dated 1956 on www.imdb.com; letter from Bruce Carnachan in *XK Gazette* no.82 Jul 2004
27. *Independent on Sunday* 5 Jul 1998
28. XK 1: Information courtesy of Terry McGrath; Skilleter *Jaguar Sports Cars*, cover photo; XK 140: *The Autocar* 27 Jan 1956; JAG 140: *Autosport* 2 Aug 1957; in all cases, additional information courtesy of David Bentley
29. www.mucklow.com
30. Porter *Jaguar E-type* p.241

Chapter Ten

Special bodies

By the second half of the 1950s, most of the diminishing number of special bodies on British chassis were made by Italian and Swiss rather than British coach-builders, typically on high-grade GT chassis, including Alvis, Aston Martin and Bristol. In case of Jaguar, there were twenty XK 140 and XK 150 cars which were delivered in chassis-only form, most of them with left-hand drive, and most of them destined to be bodied by European coach-builders. In addition, some other cars which had left the factory complete with standard body-work, were subsequently re-bodied, or were turned into "specials".

It is easy to produce a list of cars supplied in chassis form, but very difficult to match all of them to the known special bodies. Much of the groundwork was done by the two French Jaguar historians Roland Urban and Bernard Viart with their books *Les Métamorphoses du Jaguar* and *Jaguar XK – Le Grand Livre*, as well as by the research of Terry McGrath for whose help with this chapter I am greatly indebted, but some cars still defy identification.

There were eleven XK 140 cars supplied in chassis form.

The first of these, **814001** which was the first FHC LHD chassis number, was retained by Jaguar's experimental department (see chapter 8). No engine number is recorded, and the like-lihood is that it never became a complete car.

Three of the chassis listed were bodied by

Ghia of Torino in Italy, with coupé bodies of similar design. Ghia had already bodied three XK 120s, two of which had a connection with the French importer Delecroix, and the first Ghia XK 140 may also have been commissioned by Delecroix, as it was on their stand at the 1955 Paris Motor Show. This was **810827 DN**, which in December 1955 was sold to a Mr Altweg who was "known for his taste in beautiful cars", and subsequently entered the car in *concours d'élégance*. At the Paris Show, the car had a curved line to the top of the grille, and was most likely white. It had an air intake on the bonnet, a round badge, and recessed head-lamps. There seemed to be chromed air vents to the rear wings. It had chrome wire wheels although it was not an SE model.

However, the car that Urban says was the Altweg car with this chassis number (registered in Lyon under 7434 AN 69) had a flatter line to the top of the grille, although it still had the air intake on the bonnet, the recessed headlamps and other distinguishing features, and was also white. It is possible that the car had the front end and grille re-worked after the show. After it had been in an accident in 1959, the front end was "modernised", supposedly by Ghia, and air vents were added to the front wings, but it still kept the air intake on the bonnet, and the same registration mark. Urban bought the car in 1963, and used it extensively in competition. He still owned it in 2008, by which time the car was nearing completion of a long restoration.[1]

XK 140 cars supplied in chassis form

Chassis no.	Type	Date	Destination (agent)	Body fitted
814001	FHC LHD	1954	Jaguar experimental department	Not known
810827 DN	OTS LHD	25 Jan 1955	Delecroix, Paris	Ghia
S 814096 DN	FHC LHD SE	23 Mar 1955	Loewy, Paris	Loewy; Boano
S 814437	FHC LHD SE	24 Jun 1955	Martins & Almeida, Lisbon	Not known
S 814937 DN	FHC LHD SE	5 Oct 1955	Trad, Beirut, Lebanon	Ghia
814942	FHC LHD	5 Oct 1955	Trad, Beirut, Lebanon	Not known
S 804578	FHC RHD SE	20 Dec 1955	Delecroix, Paris	Not known
S 800067 DN	OTS RHD SE	24 Jan 1956	Henlys, London	Rixon Bucknall special
S 815315	FHC LHD SE	27 Jan 1956	Erwin Lutz, Switzerland	Ghia-Aigle or Allemano?
S 815404	FHC LHD SE	6 Mar 1956	Hornburg, Los Angeles	Ghia
S 804650	FHC RHD SE	7 Mar 1956	No destination recorded	Not known

The second Ghia car was **S 814937 DN**, which was consigned to Robert M Trad, the importer in Lebanon. It has an air intake to the bonnet but not to the rear wings, flatter grille top, trapezoidal badge, and normal headlamps. It was for many years in Switzerland, then came to the UK in the 1990s wearing the remains of metallic red paint, and by 2001 had been restored and was owned by a Belgian collector. I think this may be the red car that was photographed in the Gene Ponder collection in Texas in February 2005, but when this collection was auctioned in April 2007, there was no XK 140 Ghia in the sales list. It is probably the Ponder car that was reported at a concours event in Connecticut in June 2007, unless there was a *fourth* Ghia car – which would solve a few puzzles.[2]

The third Ghia car **S 815404** was ordered through Hornburg, by R W Martin of La Jolla, California. This may be the car pictured in Burgess-Wise's Ghia book, which lacks the air intake to the bonnet but is otherwise similar to the second car; it seems to be white. Ricardo Montalban bought it in 1967, he was the third owner, but he believed that the car was red from new, as it is today. It was auctioned in Japan in 1991, and was later in the famous Behring collection at the Blackhawk Auto Museum, Danville, California. Like the car in the Ghia book, the Behring car has no air intake to the bonnet. It appeared at the Pebble Beach concours in 1992. It was offered at a Barrett-Jackson auction in the USA in 1998 with a reserve of $250,000 but apparently attracted no bids.[3] Incidentally, Ghia had used the same design for an Alfa Romeo 1900 in 1954, but the proportions were somewhat different; such a car

exists in the USA.[4]

Raymond Loewy (1893-1986) was a Franco-American pioneering industrial and automotive designer who worked on everything from Lucky Strike cigarette packets and the Coca-Cola bottle to railway locomotives. He designed bodies for Hupmobile and Studebaker cars in the 1930s, was a consultant to the Rootes Group in Britain and achieved real fame with his 1947 and 1953 Studebakers. In the 1950s and 1960s he designed and had built one-off bodies on a variety of chassis, including BMW, Cadillac and Lancia, as well as on a Jaguar.[5] In fact, he ordered **S 814096 DN** directly from Jaguar, and commissioned Boano in Italy to build the body to his design. In October 1955, Loewy showed the car to the press before the Paris Motor Show, where it was displayed on the Boano stand, and it is said to have been also at the 1956 Torino Show. Loewy took the car to the USA where it was photographed in Central Park

This is possibly the third Ghia-bodied XK 140, chassis S 815404, photographed in Torino when new; unless this is a fourth unidentified car. (Paul Skilleter)

187

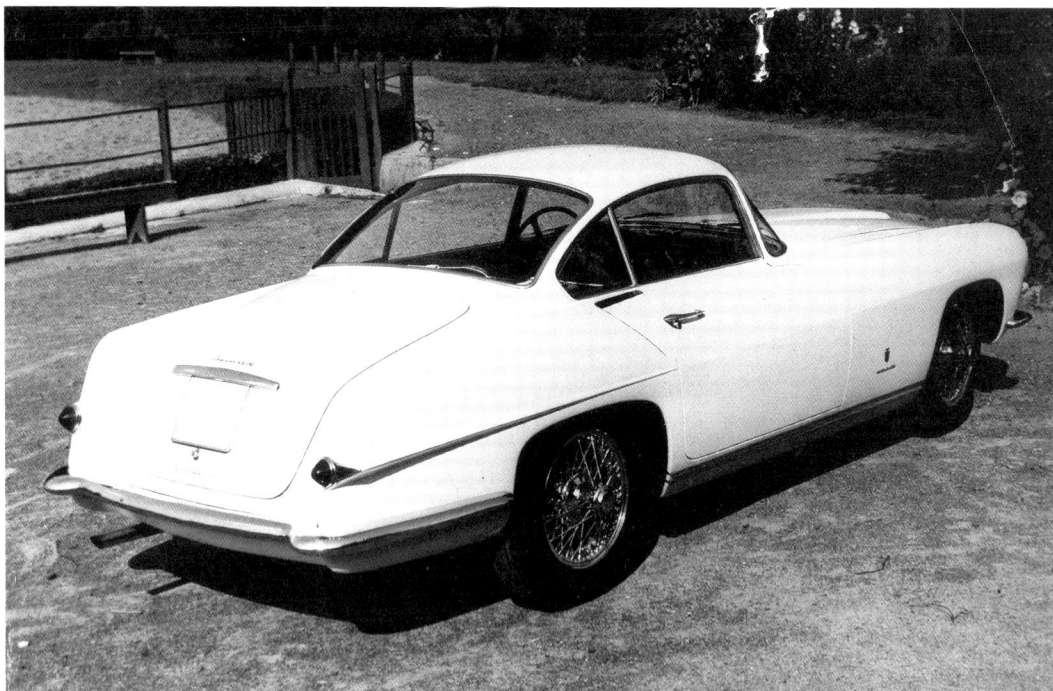

The boot badges obligingly read "Jaguar XK 140" above and "Ghia Special" below the number plate area. (Paul Skilleter)

That goldfish bowl-like rear window of the Loewy-designed XK 140 must have cost a fortune to have made. (Paul Skilleter)

in New York. As if the original style was not flamboyant enough, Loewy by then had added huge external trumpet horns. It has mysteriously disappeared, but we live in hope![6]

To return to the chronological order, there are three chassis which have not been conclusively identified. **S 814437** went to Martins & Almeida, the Jaguar importers in Portugal, but nothing seems to be known about which body was put on it. **814942** went to Trad in Lebanon. Since it is so close to **S 814937 DN** and went to the same agent, one wonders whether this could be a *fourth* Ghia car? **S 804578** which was a right-hand drive car went to Delecroix, and according to the *Car Record Book* was sold to Faime Darley in Paris. Yet there is also a note that this chassis first went to Jaguar's experimental department…

We are on safer ground with the next car which is very well known, and was the only XK 140 fitted with a special body in the UK. **S 800067 DN** went to Henlys, to the order of Colonel Rixon Bucknall, late of the Coldstream Guards. It became better known as the Rixon Bucknall special and was registered RB 1903, as the Colonel was born in that year. He had very specific ideas about what constituted his ideal touring car, and apart from anything else wanted a car which combined the best of modern technology with a vintage look. His choice of chassis fell on an XK 140, as a Bentley was too big and the waiting list for an Aston Martin too long. In any case he claimed to have been one of Lyons's first customers, for a Swallow sidecar in his motorcycling youth, and had owned a number of Jaguars. Casting around for a coachbuilder to put his ideas into practice, he began with Hooper but after no less than 38 refusals finally ended up with Hastings Motor Sheet Metal Works.

The body shape was loosely based on an MG 18/80 the Colonel had once owned, but what made the Jaguar such a remarkable car was that the bodywork was equipped with almost every imaginable form of accessory, each carefully stowed in its own compartment – but "no frills, like wireless sets or tape recorders". The colour scheme of Scarlet and Black was a reminder of the Coldstream Guards dress uniform. The body originally cost around £570. The car gave every satisfaction on a number of long Continental trips, and already during the Colonel's ownership was modified in a number of respects, with magneto ignition, disc brakes, and a three-carburettor straight-port head. The original flowing front wings and running boards were replaced by helmet-type wings, and the wind-down side windows by loose side screens. The Colonel kept "the red car" (as he called it) for many years, but later also commissioned a four-seater MGB and a specially-modified Austin/MG 1800. His Jaguar was sold at auction in 1972, shortly before the Colonel died. The car still exists and has been beautifully restored.[7]

Apart from the Italian Ghia, there was a Swiss branch of Ghia, known variously as Ghia-Aigle or Ghia Suisse. They had customised a couple of XK 120s, and had bodied a number of Mark VIIs, mostly as drophead coupés. At this time,

This extraordinary creation on an XK 140 chassis was designed by Raymond Loewy, who is here photographed with the car on its public debut before the 1955 Paris Motor Show.

This is how Loewy's XK 140 design appeared on the Boano stand at the 1955 Paris Motor Show. (Paul Skilleter)

In complete contrast to the Continental extravaganza on XK chassis, this was one traditionally-minded Britisher's idea of the perfect touring car: the Rixon Bucknall special on an XK 140 chassis. (JDHT)

The bucket seats in the Rixon Bucknall car were quite possibly supplied by Jaguar. The doors had large pockets for the side screens, with map pockets on the outside of these, and the Colonel must have been a pioneer in adopting side repeater flashers. (Paul Skilleter)

Giovanni Michelotti was their chief designer. They bodied an XK 140 which was exhibited at the Geneva Motor Show in 1956. I feel this is possibly chassis number **S 815315**, although I accept that the timing is very tight: this chassis left Jaguar on 9 February 1956, leaving less than a month to build the body, as the show opened on 8 March. However, this chassis did go to Switzerland; it was consigned to Erwin Lutz, but according to the sales statistics it was sold to Emil Frey, the Jaguar importer in Zürich. Lutz figures occasionally in the Jaguar records and also handled some Austin-Healeys, but I have never been able to pin down who, what or where he was.

Anyway, if the Ghia-Aigle XK 140 is not S 815315, the question is what chassis number is it? The Ghia-Aigle car is believed to be the car that was offered for sale by Christophe Pund of *La Galerie des Damiers* in 2000 as a "1956 Jaguar XK 140 Ghia ex Geneva M/Show", unless the car for sale was one of the cars with an *Italian* Ghia body – but if so, which one, and was an XK 140 with an Italian Ghia body ever exhibited at Geneva?[8] Another possibility is that chassis number S 815315 is the Allemano XK 140 (see below), in which case the Ghia-Aigle car remains to be identified.

For the last XK 140 chassis **S 804650** there is no destination or further details known. This chassis does not seem to be included in the sales statistics either, so it may not have been despatched or sold. There was actually a twelfth chassis, as S 815446 built on 20 March 1956 was originally a chassis only but this was fitted with a standard fixed-head body in July 1956, before being despatched to Jaguar Cars, New York, on 3 August 1956.

The three-carburettor engine and cropped wings were among the later modifications to the Rixon Bucknall special. This must be the Colonel himself. (Paul Skilleter)

Chassis numbers are known for some of the cars that left the factory in standard form but were later re-bodied. **S 814286** was a fixed-head with left-hand drive built 25 May 1955, it went to Delecroix, and was originally owned by Mme Jeanne Gaymard, Paris. It is supposed to have been damaged in an accident in 1957, and was later re-bodied by Michelotti as a fastback coupé, in a style which is clearly of the 1960s. The suggestion that it was commissioned, even owned, by actress Brigitte Bardot, has not been confirmed. By 1983 the car was in the hands of the British classic car dealer Stephen Langton and then for a time ended up in the Urban collection, although it seems to have changed hands by 1999.[9]

The Zagato XK 140 was **814537**, another FHC LHD built 13 July 1955, exported to Compagnia Generale Auto in Milano, and originally owned by Guido Modiano who may have been a Jaguar dealer. The story again goes that the car was damaged in an accident and was re-bodied by Zagato, for an Italian playing card manufacturer. It was fitted with wire wheels and

Ghia Aigle bodied at least two Xks. This was their XK 140, designed by Michelotti, which was displayed at the 1956 Geneva Motor Show. (Paul Skilleter)

was registered MI 290760. There are photos of the car with this number plate with two different front ends, both of which have a truncated XK 140 grille in the centre. It is believed that the original design had large, chrome side grilles with vertical bars similar to the centre grille, but that it was quickly re-worked to have smaller side grilles with horizontal bars. It was bought by an American Serviceman in Italy in 1967 and taken to the USA, by which time it was metallic green and had yet a third arrangement of side grilles. Over the next 30-odd years the car passed through a number of owners before restoration was completed by Scott Gauthier, who showed the car at the Pebble Beach concours in 2003. The front end treatment has been restored to the second type, and the car is now dark blue, while the interior trim in tan suede is believed to be original.[10]

Unusually, one car was re-bodied in Spain. This was FHC LHD **S 815518**, dating to 5 April 1956, which had been exported to Hornburg. It is believed to have been brought to Spain by its American owner, and nothing much seems to be known about the coachbuilder Galo Mateos, but the car is said to have been completed in 1960. It looks like an oversized Austin-Healey, even down to the shape of the windscreen, but has a large oval egg-crate grille, like a 1950s Ferrari. In the USA, the engine was fitted with Iskenderian

racing camshafts and a McCulloch supercharger which together boosted power to a claimed 300bhp. In 1985 Ramon Magriñá found the car in a Madrid garage, and he has owned it ever since.[11]

Much closer to home, another re-bodied XK 140 was the DHC RHD **S 807297** registered TAC 743 which was David Hobbs's racing car (see chapter 7). After Hobbs wrote it off at Oulton Park, it was re-bodied by Freddie Owen in the Isle of Wight, in a style probably inspired by the E-type fixed-head coupé. More recently the car was acquired by Trevor Groom who had the Owen body restored, and who has continued the car's racing career in the XK Championship and at the Goodwood Revival Meeting.[12]

The Allemano XK 140 has not been identified, unless this car after all was chassis **S 815315**, see the Ghia Aigle car discussed above. It was not a particularly inspired design, one might call it stock second-rate 1950s Italian, and had some very peculiar air vents in the front wings just behind the wheel arches. There is another mystery here; in 1958, Allemano bodied what is often described as an XK 150, yet photos seem to show that car with drum brakes behind the wire wheels. This second body was much better looking. One possibility is that Allemano re-bodied the first car for a second time; one clue is that both cars had a similar two-tone colour

Michelotti Later designed this fastback body for an XK 140 in France. (Paul Skilleter)

scheme, and both had a Swiss owner; the second car was registered in Zürich under ZH 282518.[13]

A remarkable American transformation was the Royale, an XK 140 fixed-head which after a racing career in the hands of Rod Carveth was heavily customized by Joe Wilhelm for Charles "Andy" Anderson in California, with chopped roof, Frenched lights, a low wide mouth-organ grille, a purple paint job, and much more. Mechanical modifications included a McCulloch supercharger. In this form it won more than 60 concours awards, including class wins at Pebble Beach in 1957 and 1958. The car re-surfaced at the American RM Auction in January 2005 in immaculate original condition with 6700 miles on the clock; it sold for $68,200. The auctioneers quoted a "chassis number" of G 2273-8 which of course is the engine number; this engine was fitted in fixed-head **A 814071** on 15 March 1955, a car which went to Hornburg.[14]

The Blythe car may have been built on an XK 120 chassis but experts are now more inclined to think it was fitted to an XK 140. John Blythe was apparently based in Canada and the car is thought to survive in the USA. It was a quite good-looking fibreglass fastback coupé, of a style which suggests it was probably built in the

1970s, and the design was really too modern for the chassis.[15]

There were nine XK 150 chassis only deliveries, listed below in chronological order.

The first chassis **S 834361** went to Delecroix, Paris, where it languished, unbodied, for nearly two years. In July 1959, Jaguar supplied Delecroix with a standard open two-seater body (F 17140 for the record) which they then fitted to this chassis. It was some time registered under

Zagato's interpretation of an XK 140 in a contemporary Italian photo. Their XK 150s were in fact very similar. (Paul Skilleter)

The second Allemano body fitted to an XK, but is it a 140 or a 150? (Terry McGrath)

150 RQ 16 (Charente). When the car turned up on the internet in 2006 it caused some fluttering in the XK dovecotes, because the chassis number was for a fixed-head but the body was a two-seater.[16]

There were three chassis bodied by Bertone, and while they look nothing like a Jaguar apart from the radiator grille, they are to me the best-looking of all special-bodied XKs, not to say Jaguars. They were to the same basic design, which Bertone also used for two Aston Martins around this time, but there are enough detail differences for one to be able to tell them apart. I can not identify the chassis number of the first Bertone Jaguar. It is known to have been displayed at the Torino Motor Show in

November 1957, in company with a light-coloured Aston Martin with a similar body design. This first Jaguar was a left-hand drive car, with a rather curious "scallop" just behind each front wheel arch. It had three wipers, and the interior mirror was above the windscreen. It may have been dark red or black.[17]

The second Bertone car was **S 834365** which went to CGA in Milano, the first owner was Fratelli Ingegnoli – probably a company name as I think it means "Ingegnoli Brothers" – and it carried a Milano (MI) registration. This is the easy one to tell because it has large air vents, Mercedes-Benz 300SL-style, in the front wings. It also has two wipers and the interior mirror is below the windscreen. It was originally metallic

XK 150 chassis only deliveries

Chassis no.	Type	Date	Destination	Body fitted
S 834361	FHC LHD 3.4	14 Aug 1957	Delecroix, Paris	Standard OTS body
S 834365	FHC LHD 3.4	15 Aug 1957	CGA, Milano	Bertone
S 834369	FHC LHD 3.4	15 Aug 1957	Claparede, Geneva; USA	Zagato
S 834831 DN	FHC LHD 3.4	28 Nov 1957	RM Overseas, Frankfurt; for Switzerland	Ghia Aigle (Frua)
S 824166 DN	FHC RHD 3.4	31 Dec 1957	Delecroix, Paris	Possibly Motto
S 835227	FHC LHD 3.4	13 Feb 1958	Metaucol, Italy; for Germany	Zagato
S 835235	FHC LHD 3.4	14 Feb 1958	Metaucol, Italy; for the USA	Zagato
S 835381	FHC LHD 3.4	14 Mar 1958	No destination recorded	Not known
S 824439 DN	FHC RHD 3.4	19 May 1958	Via Henlys, London, to Coombs, Guildford	Bertone

Bertone's first left-hand drive XK 150 was on their stand at the 1957 Torino Motor Show, in company with a very similar body on an Aston Martin chassis, the white car glimpsed on the right. (Photo courtesy of Bertone)

green. For many years this car was owned by Ettore Mariano of the Lido of Venice and was registered VE 576493. It then turned up in the Behring collection at the Blackhawk museum in California and was at the Pebble Beach concours in 1992, by which time it was red. In 2000 it was bought by the Dutch Jaguar collector Tom Zwakman, but has since changed hands again although it is believed to be still in Holland. It now has a 3.8-litre engine.[18]

The third Bertone car was definitely **S 824439 DN**, with right-hand drive. According to the *Car Record Book*, it went via Henlys to Coombs of Guildford, the first owner was Anthony Strickland Hubbard, and it was originally registered 953 HPH on 1 January 1959. Apart from the right-hand drive, this car can be identified by the flattened top to the rear wheel arches, and hockey-stick chrome trims coming off the rear, as well as off the front wheel arches. Bertone displayed the car at the Torino Motor Show in November 1958, together with another almost-twin Aston Martin. The car at one time went up to Browns Lane for Jaguar to have a look at. It had an engine change from 3.4 to 3.8 litres early in life, and its original engine found its way into an XK 120 owned by Coombs. It was later registered under 6 APC. Originally metallic red, during the late 1960s it was repainted in a lighter colour. According to Urban, in 1993 the car was in the process of a

total restoration, and it is now believed to live in Essex. By the way, an amusing fact is that Bertone called his XK 150 design the "XKE", and another curiosity is that when they published a leaflet for the Jaguar it was illustrated with a side view of the Aston Martin![19]

Zagato is almost as famous as Bertone, and they are also thought to have bodied three XK 150s. The basic design was similar to their XK

The nicely-executed interior of the first Bertone car with the standard XK 150 instruments placed in front of the driver. (Photo courtesy of Bertone)

A contemporary Bertone publicity shot of the first left-hand drive car. (Photo courtesy of Bertone)

In 1958, Bertone had a very similar car on their Torino show stand, but this had right-hand drive and other differences.

140, but there were subtle variations, not least in the front end design. The first was **S 834369**, which originally went to Claparede, Geneva, and despite the fact that it was only despatched on 15 January 1958, may have been the car that was displayed at the Geneva Motor Show in March 1958, where it was dark blue and, like the XK 140, had suede trim. The grille had a heart-shaped centre section with vertical bars, flanked by side extensions with horizontal bars. The first owner recorded is one H H Johnson, of Chula Vista in California, but he only took delivery in January 1960! This car exists in the USA, awaiting restoration. However it should be noted that the present owner of S 834369, whose father bought it in 1964, believes his car

was originally white.[20]

An otherwise unknown business in Milano called Metaucol Italiana then had the idea of commercialising the Zagato Jaguar. They published a four-page leaflet in English with photos of probably the first car – unfortunately not showing the front end, or may be Zagato was redesigning this, or may be the photos were of the XK 140 – and ordered two chassis from Jaguar, **S 835227** and **S 835235**, which were despatched together on 4 March 1958. Both the completed cars found owners, the first one went to Carl Hans Graser in Munich, the second to N Pensker & Co, Hempstead, New York. The red car with just a heart-shaped centre grille and a Swiss registration TI 90236 (Ticino) is perhaps

197

The interior shot of the right-hand drive car reveals that this car had a centre console. (JDHT)

1957, it was re-exported to Switzerland. Here it was bodied by Ghia-Aigle, to a design by the Italian Pietro Frua who had taken over from Michelotti as chief designer to this company. It was originally silver-grey and is now a very light metallic green, and sports later Mercedes head-lamps. The car still exists in a private collection in Switzerland but is reported to be in poor condition.[22] There are subtle detail differences in the various photos of the Ghia-Aigle XK 150, so it has quite naturally been speculated that there might have been at least two cars built to this design, which is entirely possible. Indeed **S 835381**, another left-hand drive car, is not accounted for as the records do not quote the original destination for this chassis.

Since chassis **S 824166 DN** had right-hand drive, it can not be a Ghia-Aigle car, and in any case it went to France. The only other known special-bodied XK 150 with right-hand drive is the Motto coupé, which furthermore was photographed with a temporary French registra-tion 3806 TT 75. Carozzeria Rocco Motto (or Ca-Mo) is so obscure that it does not rate an entry in the *Beaulieu Encyclopaedia – Coach-building* but was active in Torino between 1931 and 1965, and afterwards built motor caravans. Motto apparently did quite a lot of sub-contract work to better-known coachbuilders but also bodied cars under his own name, including the Motto-MG and allegedly the Biondetti special based on an XK 120; many of his designs were

most likely to be the car originally sold in Munich. This car was photographed at the Eber-bach hill climb in Germany in March 1961 where it was driven by Ernst Lautenschlager.[21]

It seems that only one car went to a Swiss coachbuilder. This was **S 834831 DN** which was originally consigned to RM Overseas, but imme-diately on arrival in Germany in December

This Zagato-bodied car is believed to be the 1958 Geneva Motor Show XK 150, which is probably the car which now exists unrestored in the USA. (Paul Skilleter)

Motto was one of the more obscure Italian coachbuilders. Looking at their XK 150 we can guess why. (Paul Skilleter)

primarily intended for racing. He did quite a lot of work for French clients, was associated with the Grand Prix driver Louis Rosier, and has been credited with the design of the Brissonneau Renault 4CV. The most prominent feature of his Jaguar was a large oval grille. The car is believed to have been raced between 1958 and 1962 but has disappeared.[23]

This completes the list of XK 150 chassis-only deliveries, except for noting that Philip Porter quotes S 834483 as a chassis delivery, but it was in fact a complete car exported to Belgium, and was reported in existence in Germany in 2005.[24]

Quite a number of cars were re-bodied, either more or less "in period" or later. A very well-known car is **T 825146 DN** registered RPM 935. This was a fixed-head 3.8 S which the original owner A E Richardson had re-modelled as a fastback coupé by Hartin Panels of Hanwell in London, who were also associated with the construction of many Cooper racing cars. The result was rather attractive, and the car happily still exists in this form.[25]

Following the great British tradition of putting practicality before style, inevitably there were some estate cars based on the XK 150. One of these was **S 825043 DN** sold in Manchester and registered 6797 N. From 1965 to 1968 it was owned by Douglas Hull who carried out the

conversion, and raced it, both before and after. It was later in Holland and Germany, until it was auctioned by Bonhams in June 2004 and is now in Switzerland.[26]

Another estate car was built on the basis of **S 825106** which was sold by Bellamy in Grimsby and registered VBE 438, but later re-registered 558 NOT. It was last reported in France, although it may now have come back to the UK. Affectionately known as the "Foxbat", this car was converted by Geoffrey Stevens in the 1970s, mainly so that he and his wife could transport their two Labrador dogs. It made use of the rear end of a Morris Minor Traveller, and may be the only half-timbered XK in existence.[27]

Truly horrible was an extraordinarily primitive estate car conversion of a fixed-head with a box-like contraption fitted in the boot aperture, covering up the centre part of the rear window, allegedly to carry the owner's golf trolley. In one photo the car bears the number plate CRO 150, but the real registration was 150 CRO which makes it **S 824200 DN**, and which incidentally was one of few XK 150s fitted with disc wheels. The car looked as if it would be fairly easy to restore back to original, which has probably happened. It was last reported when sold by Coys in 1996.[28] Another estate car, this time in New Zealand, was based on XK 150 drophead chassis **S 827405 DN** and made use of the rear bodywork from a Holden, but was being restored back to original in the 1990s.

The drophead XK 140 chassis **S 807209 DN** registered VAR 140 was rebuilt after an accident with a narrow two-seater sports body with cycle type wings. Around 1997 it migrated to Canada where it was for sale in 2006. By that time, under the bonnet was a very modern-looking plate claiming that it had been prepared by H.W. Motors Ltd. What is potentially more interesting is that the first owner of this car was the Jaguar rally driver Eric Haddon, although I can not confirm that he rallied this car (see chapter 7).[29]

Quite a number of other cars have been turned into "specials" and appear from time to time. Among them are **S 830432** (with a question mark as this number has also been reported on a car now in New Zealand) found in California with a body said to be in the style of the Napier-Railton, and **S 835252 BW** in Wisconsin with a body described as in the style of a vintage Mercedes-Benz SS. The bodies on these two cars are in fact very similar and are believed to have been the work of one Bruce Adams who planned small-scale production of this "BA Special" in the 1970s. In Europe there is **S 824547 DN** originally sold in Surrey but now in France or Belgium with a body in the style of a Citroën *Traction Avant* roadster; it is reported that it will be fitted with an aluminium replica of an XK two-seater body in Argentina. Finally, **S 834783 DN** with a mock D-type fibreglass body, formerly in Texas, now in Scotland.[30] No doubt more will continue to crop up on www.xkdata.com, on e-bay, or in the pages of *XK Gazette* and other magazines.

Terry McGrath's favourite – but not mine! – is an unknown XK 150 which in the 1960s had its chassis shortened by 12in (305mm) and was fitted with a modified Triumph Vitesse body. It was claimed to have been conceived by Downton which is probably a slur on their reputation, but was said to have been re-bodied by its then owner, Thomas Wood. Inevitably the engine protruded well into the front passenger compartment. While the engine was left in standard tune, the car was much modified in many other respects, and a top speed of over 130mph (209km/h) was claimed, together with a 0-60mph (0-97km/h) time of 9secs: about what you would expect from an XK 150. The car was re-registered in Wiltshire in 1965 under DWV 431 C, and still exists in this form. Another special based on an XK 140 fixed-head was created by Bill Hodge; it featured a body which was a cross between the famous tulip-bodied Hispano-Suiza and Chitty-Chitty-Bang-Bang (the film version) but had the windscreen of a two-seater XK 140. Its registration mark XLT 849 was a London issue of 1959-60, so the car must have been re-registered.[31] To me, these specials are a reminder of that period in the 1960s when XKs were of so little value that they tempted customisers and special-builders in search of performance, much as do early Jaguar V12s today!

This is Douglas Hull's XK 150 estate car conversion which now survives in Switzerland. (Bonhams)

1. *The Autocar* 14 Oct 1955; *Autosport* 14 Oct 1955; *Motor Sport* Nov 1955; *XK Gazette* no.124 Jan 2008; Frostick *The Jaguar Tradition* p.85; Harvey *The Jaguar XK* p.209; Mennem *Jaguar An Illustrated History* p.112; Skilleter *Jaguar Sports Cars* photos between pp.66-67; Urban *Les Métamorphoses du Jaguar* pp.177-78; Viart *Jaguar XK Le Grand Livre* p.311

2. Urban p.179 bottom right; *XK Gazette* no.119 Aug 2007, citing www.xkdata.com; www.rmauctions.com, 2007 results; www.msemc.org/events_021205ponder.html, information courtesy of Stefan Dierkes

3. Burgess-Wise *Ghia – Ford's Carozzeria* p.67; Urban pp. 97, 179; *XK Gazette* no.82 Jul 2004

4. *The Autocar* 12 Oct 1954, 18 Mar 1955; *Annual Automobile Review* 1954-55 photo opp. p.188; *The Beaulieu Encyclopaedia of the Automobile – Coachbuilding* p.167

5. Jodard *Raymond Loewy* pp.133-36

6. *The Autocar* 14 Oct 1955; *The Motor* 9 May 1956; Frostick p.85; Harvey p.214; Skilleter p.135; Urban pp.114-15 who says the car was at the 1955 Torino show which is impossible; Viart pp.313-15; *XK Gazette* no.54 Mar 2002 citing web site www.westnet.com/~mfrank/LoewyJaguar.html, which credits the photos shown to the Library of Congress

7. Rixon Bucknall in *Autosport* 15 Feb 1957; *High Road* Aug 1970; *XK Gazette* no.7 Apr 1998; *Classic & Sports Car* Sep 2006; Urban p.317

8. *The Autocar* 16 Mar 1956; advertisement in *Thoroughbred & Classic Cars* Dec 2000; Frostick p.84; Harvey p.213; Skilleter p.135; Urban p.168; information courtesy of Stefan Dierkes of www.ghia-aigle.info

9. Urban pp.242-44; Viart p.317; *XK Gazette* no.23 Aug 1999

10. Fagiuoli *Zagato* p.81; Urban pp.300-01; Viart p.320; *Classic & Sports Car* Dec 1998; story by Richard Owen and photos on www.supercars.net

11. Urban pp.236-38; www.cocheclasico.com/ramonmagrina/rm3.php

12. Boyce pp.118-120; Harvey p.213; Skilleter photos pp.138-39; Urban pp.254-55 (and on p.313 where the car is wrongly attributed to Freddie *Dikon*); *XK Gazette* nos.44 May 2001, 63 Dec 2002, 105 Jun 2006, 109 Oct 2006

13. *Quattroruote* Aug 1956, May 1958; Terry McGrath in *Jaguar World* vol.9 no.5 May/Jun 1997; Viart p.299

14. Urban p.319; *XK Gazette* nos.92 May 2005, 94 Jul 2005; www.rmauctions.com, 2005 results

15. Harvey p.210; Urban p.306; information courtesy of John Elmgreen

16. Terry McGrath in *Jaguar World* vol.9 no.5 May/Jun 1997; www.xkdata.com; www.carclassic.com

17. Greggio *Bertone 90 Years – Forma e progetto – Il catalogo* p.67; Harvey p.215 bottom; Skilleter photos between pp.210-11; Urban p.96 bottom, Viart p.303; www.bertone.it, section "Storia – Prototipi" and information courtesy of Elisabetta Farmeschi of Bertone

18. Pfannmüller *Jaguar Coupés* p.63; Urban pp.94, 97-98; Viart p.305; www.zwakmanjaguar.com or www.zwakmanmotors.com; information courtesy of Tom Zwakman

19. *The Motor* 12 Nov 1958; *Autosport* 14 Nov 1958; *The Autocar* 14 Nov 1958; Frostick p.90; Harvey p.215 top; Urban pp.96, 98; Viart p.304; information courtesy of John May; story by Graham Gauld on www.historicmotorracing.co.uk although he mixes up the RHD car with the Behring LHD car

20. *The Motor* 19 Mar 1958; *Autosport* 21 Mar 1958; *The Autocar* 21 Mar 1958; Skilleter photos between pp.210-11; Viart p.321; Urban p.302; *XK Gazette* no.111 Dec 2006; www.xkdata.com

21. Urban p.302; www.jag-lovers.org, brochures, for images of the Metaucol brochure

22. *Automobile Year* 6, 1958-59 p.87; Ghia-Aigle advertisements in *Automobil Revue – Katalog-Nummer* between 1959 and 1964; Pfannmüller p.63; Urban p.169; Viart p.312; www.pietro-frua.de and www.ghia-aigle.info; www.classic-sportcars.ch where the chassis number is quoted incorrectly as S 83 434 DN; information courtesy of Stefan Dierkes

23. *Quattroruote* Sep 1958; Viart pp.316-17; information on Motto from various web sites

24. Porter *Original XK* second edition p.140; www.xkdata.com

25. Urban p.332; *XK Gazette* nos.8 Mar 1998, 112 Jan 2007, 113 Feb 2007; www.xkdata.com

26. Skilleter *The Jaguar XK – A Collector's Guide* p.76; Harvey p.110; Urban p.331; Michael Ware in *Classic Cars* Jun 1997; *XK Gazette* nos.59 Aug 2002, 82 Jul 2004, 84 Sep 2004, 98 Nov 2005, 120 Sep 2007, 121 Oct 2007

27. Harvey p.212; Urban p.331; *XK Gazette* nos.98 Nov 2005, 100 Jan 2006 (Les Hughes); www.xkdata.com; information courtesy of Derek Hood, J D Classics

28. Urban p.332; information courtesy of David Bentley

29. *XK Gazette* nos.89 Feb 2005, 97 Oct 2005, 99 Dec 2005

30. *Jaguar Driver* Feb 1980 for Adams special; *XK Gazette* nos.62 Nov 2002, 101 Feb 2006, 103 Apr 2006, 120 Sep 2007

31. *Hot Car* May 1969, Sep 1969

Afterword

XK present and future

As I did in my XK 120 book, I stress that I have no personal experience of the Jaguar XKs. This is reflected in the character of this book: it is not about practical aspects of ownership, restoration or using these cars. It is written from the point of view of a historian and archivist, although I accept that I have occasionally allowed personal opinions to appear, rather than maintain complete impartiality. Well, maybe XKs are simply not the sort of car that you can be entirely dispassionate

about. But other than missing out on the present-day ownership experience, I hope that I have covered most aspects of the cars.

At the time of writing in 2008, there has been solid interest in the XKs as what we now call classic cars for thirty-five to forty years. As far as I can judge, the XK range is that of the classic Jaguars which in relation to its original production figure has the highest survival rate and generates most interest. It is commonly estimated that maybe half of all XKs survive. Sure, there are a lot more E-types around, but then Jaguar made 72,000 of those, compared to around 30,000 XKs. The third most popular model is the Mark II but survival rates are much lower.

The XK interest is supported by an extensive international network. There are specialists for parts and restoration; there are dealers who mainly or exclusively handle XKs and other Jaguars. There are clubs world-wide. In Britain, Jaguar and especially XK owners are spoilt for choice, since in addition to the Jaguar Drivers' Club and the Jaguar Enthusiasts' Club, the respected Jaguar historian and author Phillip Porter now for more than ten years has run the XK Club which enjoys a steadily growing membership. While all of the clubs publish excellent magazines, the XK Club's monthly *XK Gazette* in particular is a treasure trove of XK lore, of which I have made extensive use. Another very useful publication is the *Jaguar World* magazine, and then there are all the general classic car magazines. In the USA the local Jaguar Clubs are gathered under the umbrella of the Jaguar Clubs of North America which publishes the *Jaguar Journal*, and there will be at least one club in almost any country where classic Jaguars are found.

There are plenty of books about various aspects of Jaguar and XK history, and then there is the internet. One of the most interesting web sites to the XK enthusiast is the appropriately-named xkdata.com which is a growing list of preserved XKs, with an amazing resource of photos of surviving cars, all submitted by their owners.

I am pleased to be able to say that XK owners and enthusiasts rather defy categorization or classification; there are simply too many different views and opinions, but that's all to the good. In my XK 120 book I discussed the apparent dichotomy between the purists for whom an all-original matching number car is the Holy Grail, and those enthusiasts who espouse various modifications, to adapt their cars for modern driving conditions. Because the XK 140 and especially the XK 150 are more modern in some fundamental aspects than the XK 120, there are perhaps not so many modifications being made to the later cars, except that the much-maligned Moss gearbox is often replaced by a modern five-speed all-synchro 'box, and some XK 140s are converted to disc

brakes. Incidentally there are still owners who like to think that their XK 140 really had its disc brakes originally… But you could go the whole hog and have an XK 150 fitted with a modern Jaguar V8 engine. I suspect you would simply be storing up trouble for the future.

For some years, on average classic car values have held reasonably steady, although the very best cars have seen increases. Most XK 140s and XK 150s are not as highly valued as XK 120s, and you can probably still get a car in need of attention for under £10,000. The XK 140 fixed-head is the best value for money, since closed cars are less sought-after than open cars, and the 140 generally speaking seems less in demand than the 150. On the other hand, the right-hand drive XK 140 two-seater is almost at the other end of the scale, as you would expect of a car of which only 74 were made. Other short-run production models similarly tend to be highly valued.

Naturally, the XK 150 two-seaters command the highest prices within this range, especially the S models, and S models with other body styles are not far behind – but beware forgeries. Incidentally I am a little bemused by the fascination with the XK 150 S; in this day and age, how important can a hypothetical extra 10mph (16km/h) on the top speed be? The very best cars, whether restored or original, will be knocking on the door of £100,000, may be more if there is any interesting history or provenance. As far as special-bodied cars, assuming that they are original and attractive, it is anyone's guess, but in 2007 one of the three Ghia-bodied XK 120s became the first XK to break through the one million barrier; admittedly of the somewhat depressed US Dollars. This was the ex-Urban car 679768 sold by Bonhams at Monaco on 21 May 2007; the actual hammer price was 680,000 Euros or 753,000 Euros including premium and tax, and *Classic & Sports Car* (August 2007) reported that it was bought by a Swiss collector. We hope his investment is safe for the time being…

This book was timed to appear in print more or less on the sixtieth anniversary of the debut of the first XK, an event which had already been celebrated earlier in 2008 with the "XK 60" event held at Goodwood. All other things being equal, the XKs are likely to continue to hold the affection of enthusiasts and the public for the next sixty years, at least.

Appendix 1:

All the XK 150 3.8 S cars

Ref	Body type	Date man.	Chassis no	Paint colour	Trim colour	Destination	UK reg. mark(s)	Remarks, status
1	OTS RHD	14/10/1959	T 820056 DN	British Racing Green	Suede Green	Victor, Belfast	6969 IA, XK 1505	Exists in the UK
2	OTS RHD	20/10/1959	T 820057 DN	Carmen Red	Red	Henlys, London	4824 PO	Exists in the UK
3	OTS RHD	26/10/1959	T 820059 DN	Cream	Red	Sturgess, Leicester	WTF 1	
4	OTS RHD	30/10/1959	T 820060 DN	Cream	Red	Henlys, London	XYH 720, 257 CYN	Exists in the UK
5	OTS RHD	12/11/1959	T 820062 DN	Pearl Grey	Red	Henlys, London	YLK 773, FSU 951	Exists in the UK
6	OTS RHD	04/12/1959	T 820063 DN	Cream	Red	Henlys, London	RAH 112, OTS 999 (and four others)	Exists in the UK
7	OTS RHD	08/12/1959	T 820064 DN	Carmen Red	Red	Henlys, London	RNJ 325	Exists in the UK
8	OTS RHD	04/01/1960	T 820067 DN	Shell Grey	Suede Green	Henlys, London	MP 63	Exists in the UK
9	OTS RHD	18/02/1960	T 820068 DN	Black	Red	Independent, New Zealand	n/r	Exists in New Zealand
10	OTS RHD	25/02/1960	T 820069 DN	Cornish Grey	Red	Henlys, London	LXO 1, 906 YNY, AAB 42 B	Exists in the UK
11	OTS RHD	08/03/1960	T 820070 DN	Pearl Grey	Black	Henlys, London	EOM 702 C, 111 XKK	Exists in the UK
12	OTS RHD	15/03/1960	T 820071 DN	Black	Red	Bryson, Australia	n/r	Exists in Australia
13	OTS RHD	14/04/1960	S 820073 DN	Cream	Red	Henlys, London	190 AXM	Converted to S in Service Dept 3 Jun 1960; exists in Italy
14	OTS RHD	21/04/1960	T 820074 DN	Carmen Red	Red	Henlys, London	263 AXT	Exists in the USA
15	OTS RHD	26/04/1960	T 820075 DN	Cornish Grey	Red	Henlys, London	4988 PX	Exists in the UK
16	OTS RHD	04/05/1960	T 820076 DN	Cotswold Blue	Dark Blue	Appleyard, Leeds	8759 UB	
17	OTS RHD	04/05/1960	T 820077 DN	Carmen Red	Black	Evans, Birmingham	333 BOB, 144 COH	Exists in the USA
18	OTS RHD	09/05/1960	T 820078 DN	Cream	Red	Henlys, London	WSJ 399, XKK 150	Exists in the UK
19	OTS RHD	12/05/1960	T 820079 DN	Cream	Light Blue	Henlys, London	191 PPL	Exists in South Africa
20	OTS RHD	25/05/1960	T 820082 DN	Pearl Grey	Black	Henlys, Manchester	YNE 111, 1 LUM	Exists in Switzerland
21	OTS RHD	15/06/1960	T 820086 DN	Pearl Grey	Red	Rossleigh, Edinburgh	PWG 434	Exists in the UK
22	OTS RHD	15/06/1960	T 820087 DN	Pearl Grey	Red	Sturgess, Leicester	VUT 583	Exists in the UK
23	OTS RHD	30/08/1960	T 820092 DN	Cream	Red	Henlys, London	666 SPA, XK 1, 186 WNK	Exists in Japan
24	OTS RHD	19/10/1960	T 820093 DN	British Racing Green	Suede Green	Henlys, London	9787 PX, JAG 150	Exists in the UK
25	FHC RHD	18/09/1959	T 825028 DN	British Racing Green	Suede Green	Jaguar Cars Ltd press car	YHP 791	Exists in the USA
26	FHC RHD	22/10/1959	S 825042 DN	Cream	Red	Evans, Birmingham	AFD 444	Exists in Australia, converted to DHC in UK pre-1996
27	FHC RHD	23/10/1959	T 825047 DN	Pearl Grey	Dark Blue	Attwood, Wolverhampton	RDA 877	
28	FHC RHD	23/10/1959	T 825048 DN	Carmen Red	Black	Henlys, London	GR 24	Exists in the UK
29	FHC RHD	27/10/1959	T 825050 DN	Mist Grey	Red	Henlys, Manchester	7576 N, PSU 984	Exists in the UK
30	FHC RHD	02/11/1959	S 825054 DN	Carmen Red	Red	Appleyard, Leeds	n/r	
31	FHC RHD	02/11/1959	T 825055 DN	Carmen Red	Red	Appleyard, Leeds	LJX 360	
32	FHC RHD	06/11/1959	T 825056 DN	Cotswold Blue	Dark Blue	Evans, Birmingham	6007 RE	In UK ca. 1988
33	FHC RHD	09/11/1959	T 825058 DN	Imperial Maroon	Biscuit	Anderson, Australia	n/r	Exists in Australia
34	FHC RHD	17/11/1959	T 825061 DN	Cornish Grey	Dark Blue	Ashton, Preston	150 LTJ	Exists in South Africa
35	FHC RHD	19/11/1959	T 825063 DN	Mist Grey	Light Blue	Bellamy, Grimsby	OFE 977	Exists in the UK
36	FHC RHD	19/11/1959	T 825064 DN	Cornish Grey	Red	Henlys, London	YDF 678	Exists in the UK
37	FHC RHD	19/11/1959	T 825065 DN	Cornish Grey	Light Blue	Henlys, London	XYH 643	
38	FHC RHD	20/11/1959	T 825069 DN	Pearl Grey	Blue	Henlys, London	VJJ 399	Exists in Australia
39	FHC RHD	23/11/1959	T 825072 DN	Cream	Red	Parkers, Bolton	384 LTJ, 700 FS	Exists in Australia
40	FHC RHD	24/11/1959	T 825073 DN	Pearl Grey	Red	Henlys, London	YLK 483	

Ref	Body type	Date man.	Chassis no	Paint colour	Trim colour	Destination	UK reg. mark(s)	Remarks, status
41	FHC RHD	24/11/1959	T 825076 DN	Pearl Grey	Grey	Henlys, London	XYN 555	Exists in the UK
42	FHC RHD	24/11/1959	T 825077 DN	Cream	Red	Henlys, London	656 GHU	
43	FHC RHD	25/11/1959	T 825081 DN	Indigo Blue	Biscuit	Attwood, Wolverhampton	4777 DA	Exists in the UK
44	FHC RHD	26/11/1959	T 825085 DN	Cream	Black	Henlys, London	YJJ 280	
45	FHC RHD	26/11/1959	T 825086 DN	Imperial Maroon	Grey	Evans, Birmingham	LEW 95	Exists in the UK
46	FHC RHD	26/11/1959	T 825088 DN	Indigo Blue	Light Blue	Henlys, London	n/r	Exists in South Africa
47	FHC RHD	27/11/1959	T 825091 DN	Imperial Maroon	Maroon	Sanderson & Holmes, Derby	RRC 675	Exists in the UK
48	FHC RHD	30/11/1959	T 825092 DN	British Racing Green	Biscuit	Henlys, London	XYR 83	Exists in the UK
49	FHC RHD	30/11/1959	T 825094 DN	British Racing Green	Suede Green	Henlys, London	3100 NG	Exists in the UK, is now DHC
50	FHC RHD	30/11/1959	T 825095 DN	Sherwood Green	Suede Green	Evans, Birmingham	n/r	Exists in the UK
51	FHC RHD	30/11/1959	T 825096 DN	British Racing Green	Suede Green	Henlys, London	n/r	Exists in Holland
52	FHC RHD	01/12/1959	T 825098 DN	Sherwood Green	Suede Green	Henlys, London	7232 PO	
53	FHC RHD	03/12/1959	T 825111 DN	British Racing Green	Suede Green	Henlys, London	YJJ 278	Exists in New Zealand
54	FHC RHD	04/12/1959	T 825113 DN	Cream	Red	Anderson, Australia	n/r	Exists in Australia
55	FHC RHD	09/12/1959	T 825119 DN	Cream	Dark Blue	Appleyard, Leeds	3970 UB	Exists in the USA
56	FHC RHD	09/12/1959	T 825120 DN	Cream	Red	Evans, Birmingham	7290 RE	Exists in the UK
57	FHC RHD	04/01/1960	T 825127 DN	Regal Red	Biscuit	Henlys, London	YLY 299	Exists in Australia
58	FHC RHD	11/01/1960	T 825128 DN	Sherwood Green	Suede Green	Henlys, London	XOR 150	Exists in the UK
59	FHC RHD	08/02/1960	T 825129 DN	Cotswold Blue	Dark Blue	Henlys, London	n/r	
60	FHC RHD	10/02/1960	T 825134 DN	Cotswold Blue	Red	Henlys, London	8362 PO	Exists in the UK
61	FHC RHD	10/02/1960	T 825135 DN	Indigo Blue	Dark Blue	Sanderson & Holmes, Derby	n/r	
62	FHC RHD	12/02/1960	T 825138 DN	Pearl Grey	Red	Henlys, Manchester	VXJ 680, YVS 713	Exists in the UK
63	FHC RHD	12/02/1960	T 825139 DN	Indigo Blue	Light Blue	Glovers, Harrogate	UVY 1	Exists in Japan
64	FHC RHD	15/02/1960	T 825141 DN	Carmen Red	Red	Henlys, London	1515 PX	
65	FHC RHD	16/02/1960	T 825143 DN	Black	Red	Henlys, London	1823 PX, JAG 150	Exists in the UK
66	FHC RHD	16/02/1960	T 825144 DN	Black	Biscuit	Henlys, London	YLR 479	Exists in the UK
67	FHC RHD	16/02/1960	T 825145 DN	Indigo Blue	Dark Blue	Evans, Birmingham	BMS 145, 228 DXN	Exists in the UK
68	FHC RHD	17/02/1960	T 825146 DN	Black	Red	Henlys, London	RPM 935	The Hartin fastback coupé; exists in the UK
69	FHC RHD	17/02/1960	T 825148 DN	Indigo Blue	Grey	Henlys, Manchester	n/r	
70	FHC RHD	19/02/1960	T 825151 DN	Carmen Red	Red	Henlys, London	YYU 484	Exists in the UK
71	FHC RHD	26/02/1960	T 825157 DN	Black	Red	Henlys, London	660 NPJ	Exists in the UK
72	FHC RHD	29/02/1960	S 825158 DN	Cornish Grey	Red	Henlys, London	5550 PX	
73	FHC RHD	01/03/1960	T 825159 DN	Cornish Grey	Red	Henlys, Manchester	MDJ 182	
74	FHC RHD	01/03/1960	T 825160 DN	British Racing Green	Suede Green	Henlys, London	n/r	
75	FHC RHD	01/03/1960	T 825163 DN	Pearl Grey	Light Blue	Henlys, London	608 KKJ	Exists in the UK
76	FHC RHD	07/03/1960	T 825170 DN	Cotswold Blue	Dark Blue	Henlys, London	1691 MV	
77	FHC RHD	08/03/1960	S 825173 DN	Cotswold Blue	Grey	Henlys, London	150 HHW	
78	FHC RHD	10/03/1960	T 825175 DN	Sherwood Green	Suede Green	Evans, Birmingham	n/r	Exists in the UK
79	FHC RHD	16/03/1960	T 825180 DN	British Racing Green	Suede Green	Henlys, London	YYF 126	
80	FHC RHD	17/03/1960	T 825181 DN	Indigo Blue	Light Blue	Henlys, London	6 SPC	Exists in the USA
81	FHC RHD	17/03/1960	T 825183 DN	British Racing Green	Suede Green	Henlys, London	YYR 333	Exists in the UK
82	FHC RHD	17/03/1960	T 825184 DN	Pearl Grey	Red	Parkers, Bolton	RBN 376	Exists in the UK, is now DHC
83	FHC RHD	18/03/1960	S 825185 DN	Cotswold Blue	Light Blue	Rossleigh, Edinburgh	VSC 899, SN 3, YBR 511, VVS 544	Exists in the UK
84	FHC RHD	24/03/1960	T 825192 DN	Mist Grey	Red	Bryson, Australia	n/r	Exists in Australia
85	FHC RHD	24/03/1960	T 825194 DN	Mist Grey	Red	Henlys, London; PED	4746 DU	Exists in Australia
86	FHC RHD	25/03/1960	T 825195 DN	Cream	Red	Henlys, London	2 HYA, 999 FAR	Exists
87	FHC RHD	30/03/1960	T 825203 DN	Indigo Blue	Red	Henlys, London	YYU 437	
88	FHC RHD	04/04/1960	T 825206 DN	Pearl Grey	Light Blue	Henlys, London	n/r	Exists in Switzerland
89	FHC RHD	06/04/1960	T 825207 DN	Pearl Grey	Light Blue	Henlys, London	11 TVX	Exists in the UK
90	FHC RHD	07/04/1960	T 825211 DN	Imperial Maroon	Maroon	Evans, Birmingham	7219 NX	Converted from 3.4 S; exists in the UK
91	FHC RHD	08/04/1960	T 825212 DN	Imperial Maroon	Biscuit	Henlys, London	WVW 56, 9364 AP	Exists in the UK
92	FHC RHD	13/04/1960	T 825215 DN	Carmen Red	Red	Henlys, London	5546 PX	Exists in the UK
93	FHC RHD	20/04/1960	T 825222 DN	Cream	Red	Evans, Birmingham	4858 RF	
94	FHC RHD	21/04/1960	T 825224 DN	Indigo Blue	Light Blue	Henlys, London	8835 PX	

Ref	Body type	Date man.	Chassis no	Paint colour	Trim colour	Destination	UK reg. mark(s)	Remarks, status
95	FHC RHD	22/04/1960	T 825225 DN	Black	Red	Independent, New Zealand	n/r	Written off in New Zealand
96	FHC RHD	25/04/1960	T 825226 DN	Cotswold Blue	Grey	Henlys, London	700 PPE	Exists in the UK, is now DHC
97	FHC RHD	25/04/1960	T 825227 DN	Cream	Black	Henlys, London	145 AXM	Exists in the UK
98	FHC RHD	27/04/1960	T 825229 DN	Imperial Maroon	Black	Africa Motores	n/r	Exists in South Africa
99	FHC RHD	27/04/1960	T 825230 DN	British Racing Green	Biscuit	Bryson, Australia; PED	4756 DU	Exists in Australia
100	FHC RHD	27/04/1960	T 825231 DN	Cotswold Blue	Grey	Henlys, London	8188 CR	Exists in Australia
101	FHC RHD	05/05/1960	T 825236 DN	Cotswold Blue	Black	Henlys, London	3423 PX	Exists in the UK
102	FHC RHD	12/05/1960	T 825240 DN	Cotswold Blue	Grey	Henlys, London	569 AXT	Exists in Australia
103	FHC RHD	13/05/1960	T 825242 DN	Sherwood Green	Biscuit	Henlys, London	5552 PX, CU 22, JKS 24	Exists in the UK
104	FHC RHD	17/05/1960	T 825247 DN	British Racing Green	Suede Green	Henlys, London	188 JHU, JSV 840	Exists in the UK
105	FHC RHD	23/05/1960	T 825251 DN	British Racing Green	Suede Green	Bellamy, Grimsby	PFE 150	Exists in the UK
106	FHC RHD	26/05/1960	T 825255 DN	Mist Grey	Red	Evans, Birmingham	222 BOM, CKC 942 B	Stolen in the UK 1991, not recovered
107	FHC RHD	27/05/1960	T 825256 DN	Claret	Maroon	Henlys, London	WHR 484	
108	FHC RHD	27/05/1960	T 825257 DN	Black	Tan	Henlys, London	285 AXT	Exists in the UK
109	FHC RHD	30/05/1960	T 825258 DN	Indigo Blue	Light Blue	Henlys, London	n/r	
110	FHC RHD	08/06/1960	T 825262 DN	British Racing Green	Tan	Independent, New Zealand	n/r	Exists in New Zealand
111	FHC RHD	09/06/1960	T 825266 DN	Pearl Grey	Red	Bellamy, Grimsby	ODO 428	Exists in the UK
112	FHC RHD	10/06/1960	T 825268 DN	Black	Red	Henlys, London	300 JYA	Exists in the UK
113	FHC RHD	13/06/1960	T 825270 DN	Pearl Grey	Red	Bellamy, Grimsby	SFW 2, 893 BFW	Exists in the UK
114	FHC RHD	15/06/1960	T 825273 DN	Pearl Grey	Red	Henlys, London	TSU 186	Exists in the UK
115	FHC RHD	23/06/1960	T 825282 DN	British Racing Green	Suede Green	Evans, Birmingham	7258 TU	Exists in the UK
116	FHC RHD	24/06/1960	T 825284 DN	Sherwood Green	Suede Green	Rothwell & Millbourne, Malvern	682 BNP	
117	FHC RHD	05/07/1960	T 825288 DN	British Racing Green	Suede Green	Evans, Birmingham	n/r	Exists in the UK
118	FHC RHD	08/07/1960	T 825292 DN	Sherwood Green	Tan	Henlys, London	3 LKP	
119	FHC RHD	11/07/1960	T 825293 DN	Pearl Grey	Red	Henlys, London	151 AXM	Exists in South Africa
120	FHC RHD	11/07/1960	T 825294 DN	Cotswold Blue	Light Blue	Byatts, Stoke-on-Trent	992 NEH	Exists in the UK
121	FHC RHD	11/07/1960	T 825296 DN	Imperial Maroon	Biscuit	Henlys, London	686 BGK	
122	FHC RHD	12/07/1960	T 825297 DN	British Racing Green	Biscuit	Henlys, London	TY 1, YSU 209, 880 EXK	Exists in the UK
123	FHC RHD	13/07/1960	T 825302 DN	Mist Grey	Dark Blue	Henlys, London	n/r	
124	FHC RHD	13/07/1960	T 825304 DN	Black	Red	Henlys, London	FCJ 76	Exists in the UK (or the USA?)
125	FHC RHD	14/07/1960	T 825305 DN	Mist Grey	Red	Henlys, London	86 PPP	
126	FHC RHD	14/07/1960	T 825306 DN	Battleship Grey	Red	Rossleigh, Edinburgh	VSG 2	
127	FHC RHD	15/07/1960	T 825307 DN	Carmen Red	Biscuit	Henlys, London	AGM 500	Exists in New Zealand
128	FHC RHD	15/07/1960	T 825308 DN	Cream	Red	Henlys, London	595 RPD (?)	
129	FHC RHD	15/07/1960	T 825309 DN	Cotswold Blue	Dark Blue	Appleyard, Leeds	8895 WW	Exists in the UK
130	FHC RHD	20/07/1960	T 825313 DN	Carmen Red	Black	Henlys, London	7788 PX	
131	FHC RHD	22/07/1960	T 825316 DN	Pearl Grey	Dark Blue	Henlys, London	674 BGK	
132	FHC RHD	09/08/1960	T 825318 DN	Carmen Red	Red	Glovers, Harrogate	JHR 685, 689 AVN	Exists in the UK, is now DHC
133	FHC RHD	18/08/1960	T 825320 DN	Carmen Red	Biscuit	Bryson, Australia	n/r	Exists in Australia
134	FHC RHD	24/08/1960	T 825324 DN	Sherwood Green	Suede Green	Henlys, London	BS 150, OSU133	Exists in the UK
135	FHC RHD	30/08/1960	T 825335 DN	Indigo Blue	Light Blue	Byatts, Stoke on Trent	586 PVT (?)	
136	FHC RHD	15/09/1960	T 825348 DN	British Racing Green	Suede Green	Evans, Birmingham	1 BON, 770 MOL	Exists in the UK
137	FHC RHD	16/09/1960	T 825350 DN	Cotswold Blue	Grey	Henlys, London	YUD 931	Exists in the UK
138	FHC RHD	28/09/1960	T 825351 DN	Cream	Red	Bryson, Australia	n/r	Exists in Australia
139	FHC RHD ex-LHD	25/10/1960	T 825363 DN converted from S 847042	Indigo Blue	Light Blue	Sanderson & Holmes, Derby	VXJ 860	Exists in the UK
140	DHC RHD	21/09/1959	T 827461 DN	British Racing Green	Biscuit	Attwood, Wolverhampton	170 WU	Converted from 3.4 S; now FHC? Exists in the UK or Switzerland

Ref	Body type	Date man.	Chassis no	Paint colour	Trim colour	Destination	UK reg. mark(s)	Remarks, status
141	DHC RHD	25/11/1959	T 827476 DN	Cream	Light Blue	Henlys, London	YXD 851	
142	DHC RHD	27/11/1959	T 827482 DN	British Racing Green	Suede Green	Rossleigh, Edinburgh	n/r	Converted from 3.4 S
143	DHC RHD	30/11/1959	T 827485 DN	British Racing Green	Suede Green	Henlys, London	YJJ 276	
144	DHC RHD	02/12/1959	T 827488 DN	Carmen Red	Black	Ashton, Preston	NRN 6	Chassis for sale in UK c.1970
145	DHC RHD	02/12/1959	T 827489 DN	British Racing Green	Tan	Henlys, London	n/r	Exists in South Africa
146	DHC RHD	03/12/1959	T 827491 DN	Indigo Blue	Red	Henlys, London	150 MPH	
147	DHC RHD	03/12/1959	T 827492 DN	Indigo Blue	Light Blue	Henlys, London	164 DUO	
148	DHC RHD	08/12/1959	S 827495 DN	Cream	Black	Henlys, London	1453 CD	
149	DHC RHD	09/12/1959	T 827497 DN	Cream	Dark Blue	Henlys, London	260 NPA	
150	DHC RHD	09/12/1959	T 827499 DN	Cotswold Blue	Maroon	Appleyard, Leeds	2 MTD	
151	DHC RHD	10/12/1959	T 827502 DN	Mist Grey	Red	Bellamy, Grimsby	OVL 150	Exists in the UK
152	DHC RHD	05/02/1960	S 827507 DN	British Racing Green	Black	Rossleigh, Edinburgh	SSV 861	Exists in the UK
153	DHC RHD	09/02/1960	T 827510 DN	Pearl Grey	Red	Henlys, London	YUW 903	Exists in Holland
154	DHC RHD	09/02/1960	T 827512 DN	Cream	Red	Henlys, London	n/r	Exists in the UK
155	DHC RHD	11/02/1960	T 827518 DN	Cream	Red	Henlys, London	GW 444	Exists in the UK or Switzerland
156	DHC RHD	12/02/1960	T 827521 DN	Maroon	Biscuit	Henlys, Manchester	300 HYR, 1 DUF	
157	DHC RHD	16/02/1960	T 827525 DN	British Racing Green	Suede Green	Evans, Birmingham	605 AAB, TPN 1	Exists in the UK
158	DHC RHD	17/02/1960	T 827528 DN	Sherwood Green	Tan	Henlys, London	416 CKR	
159	DHC RHD	24/02/1960	T 827530 DN	Cotswold Blue	Dark Blue	Henlys, London	150 LBH	Exists in Switzerland
160	DHC RHD	29/02/1960	T 827531 DN	Pearl Grey	Red	Henlys, London	n/r	Exists in South Africa(?)
161	DHC RHD	08/03/1960	T 827536 DN	Cotswold Blue	Light Blue	Henlys, London	1829 PX	
162	DHC RHD	17/03/1960	S 827541 DN	British Racing Green	Suede Green	Henlys, London	585 PPF	Exists in the UK
163	DHC RHD	18/03/1960	T 827543 DN	Imperial Maroon	Biscuit	Henlys, London	DAH 50	Exists, in Bahrain 1983
164	DHC RHD	21/03/1960	T 827546 DN	British Racing Green	Biscuit	Henlys, London	YYU 414	
165	DHC RHD	29/03/1960	T 827551 DN	Carmen Red	Red	Henlys, London	JJW 446	
166	DHC RHD	30/03/1960	T 827553 DN	Carmen Red	Biscuit	Henlys, London	155 MKX	
167	DHC RHD	07/04/1960	T 827555 DN	Cotswold Blue	Dark Blue	Henlys, London	n/r	
168	DHC RHD	08/04/1960	T 827556 DN	Indigo Blue	Dark Blue	Glovers, Harrogate	TWU 2	Converted from 3.4 S
169	DHC RHD	08/04/1960	T 827559 DN	Imperial Maroon	Maroon	Victor, Belfast	1246 AZ	
170	DHC RHD	13/04/1960	T 827561 DN	Cream	Red	Evans, Birmingham	XAC 333	Exists in the UK
171	DHC RHD	15/04/1960	T 827564 DN	Cream	Red	Henlys, London	n/r	
172	DHC RHD	15/04/1960	T 827566 DN	Cream	Red	Sturgess, Leicester	n/r	
173	DHC RHD	25/04/1960	T 827569 DN	Sherwood Green	Biscuit	Henlys, London	5555 PX, 6462 PP	Exists in the UK
174	DHC RHD	27/04/1960	T 827570 DN	Sherwood Green	Suede Green	Appleyard, Leeds	2181 WW	Exists in the UK (ex New Zealand)
175	DHC RHD	28/04/1960	T 827572 DN	Indigo Blue	Dark Blue	Henlys, London	219 PPD	Exists in the UK (or Italy?)
176	DHC RHD	02/05/1960	T 827576 DN	Cream	Biscuit	Henlys, London	XK 155	Exists in Australia
177	DHC RHD	09/05/1960	T 827577 DN	Pearl Grey	Dark Blue	Henlys, London	YLO 599	Exists in the UK
178	DHC RHD	16/05/1960	S 827582 DN	Carmen Red	Black	Henlys, London	n/r	
179	DHC RHD	24/05/1960	T 827585 DN	Pearl Grey	Dark Blue	Henlys, London	150 PPJ	Exists in the UK
180	DHC RHD	24/05/1960	T 827586 DN	Pearl Grey	Red	Henlys, London	AH 250, 599 HYX	Exists in the UK
181	DHC RHD	26/05/1960	T 827588 DN	Carmen Red	Black	Henlys, London	SH 2710, VSJ 273	Exists in the UK
182	DHC RHD	30/05/1960	S 827589 DN	British Racing Green	Suede Green	Appleyard, Leeds	n/r	
183	DHC RHD	30/05/1960	T 827590 DN	Sherwood Green	Suede Green	Henlys, London	LPV 757	
184	DHC RHD	10/06/1960	T 827593 DN	Indigo Blue	Grey	Jaguar Cars Ltd; PED	7181 DU	
185	DHC RHD	10/06/1960	T 827595 DN	British Racing Green	Suede Green	Henlys, London	n/r	
186	DHC RHD	14/06/1960	T 827597 DN	Pearl Grey	Dark Blue	Henlys, London	HBF 478	Exists in the UK
187	DHC RHD	15/06/1960	T 827598 DN	Carmen Red	Black	Henlys, London	PUC 1, 638 DYH	
188	DHC RHD	15/06/1960	T 827599 DN	Cotswold Blue	Light Blue	Henlys, London	AET 9, 160 HPO, TRF 707	Exists in the UK
189	DHC RHD	21/06/1960	T 827604 DN	British Racing Green	Suede Green	Henlys, London	6319 PX	
190	DHC RHD	05/07/1960	T 827610 DN	British Racing Green	Suede Green	Ritchies, Glasgow	400 BGD	Exists in Germany
191	DHC RHD	14/07/1960	T 827616 DN	Sherwood Green	Suede Green	Newsome, Coventry	5345 HP	Exists in the UK
192	DHC RHD	15/07/1960	T 827619 DN	Imperial Maroon	Biscuit	Henlys, London	865 SBP, YSU 593	Exists in the UK
193	DHC RHD	18/07/1960	T 827622 DN	British Racing Green	Tan	Henlys, London	n/r	
194	DHC RHD	19/07/1960	T 827623 DN	Indigo Blue	Light Blue	Henlys, London	567 AYU	Exists in the UK
195	DHC RHD	08/08/1960	T 827627 DN	Cream	Red	Henlys, London	n/r	Exists in the UK
196	DHC RHD	15/08/1960	T 827630 DN	Pearl Grey	Red	Ritchies, Glasgow	27 JAC	Exists in the UK
197	DHC RHD	17/08/1960	T 827632 DN	Carmen Red	Red	Henlys, London	8827 PX	

Ref	Body type	Date man.	Chassis no	Paint colour	Trim colour	Destination	UK reg. mark(s)	Remarks, status
198	DHC RHD	17/08/1960	S 827633 DN	Carmen Red	Black	Henlys, London	n/r	Exists in Australia
199	DHC RHD	25/08/1960	T 827640 DN	Black	Biscuit	Henlys, London	445 AYN	
200	DHC RHD	26/08/1960	T 827641 DN	Pearl Grey	Red	Henlys, Manchester	NDJ 847	Exists in the UK
201	DHC RHD	26/08/1960	T 827643 DN	Pearl Grey	Red	Henlys, Manchester	6552 K	Exists in Australia
202	DHC RHD	31/08/1960	T 827645 DN	Sherwood Green	Suede Green	Henlys, London	8833 PX	Exists in the UK
203	DHC RHD	31/08/1960	T 827646 DN	Cream	Red	Henlys, Manchester	XCA 989	Exists in New Zealand
204	DHC RHD	01/09/1960	T 827647 DN	Cream	Black	Henlys, London	78 PP	Exists in Holland
205	DHC RHD	06/09/1960	T 827649 DN	Silver	Red	Ritchies, Glasgow	452 BBG, XXK 150, GFN 581	Exists in Belgium
206	DHC RHD	08/09/1960	T 827652 DN	Cotswold Blue	Dark Blue	Henlys, London	323 AUW, KXK 1	Exists in the UK
207	DHC RHD	16/09/1960	T 827654 DN	Sherwood Green	Suede Green	Henlys, London	268 AUW	
208	DHC RHD	19/09/1960	T 827657 DN	Sherwood Green	Suede Green	Henlys, London	468 BLO	Exists in the UK
209	OTS LHD	27/11/1959	T 832110 DN	Cream	Tan	Fendler & Luedemann, Germany	n/r	Exists in the UK
210	OTS LHD	17/12/1959	T 832113 DN	Carmen Red	Biscuit	Belgian Motor Company	n/r	Exists in the USA
211	OTS LHD	20/01/1960	T 832117 DN	Carmen Red	Black	Jaguar Cars Ltd; PED	3851 DU, XHL 251	Exists in the UK
212	OTS LHD	25/02/1960	T 832118 DN	Cream	Tan	Fendler & Luedemann, Germany	n/r	
213	OTS LHD	08/04/1960	T 832120 DN	Cotswold Blue	Light Blue	Fendler & Luedemann, Germany	n/r	Exists in Holland
214	OTS LHD	22/04/1960	T 832122 DN	Carmen Red	Black	Belgian Motor Company	n/r	
215	OTS LHD	25/04/1960	T 832123 DN	Cream	Black	Trad, Lebanon	n/r	Exists in Switzerland
216	OTS LHD	26/05/1960	T 832126 DN	Cream	Red	Jaguar, Canada	n/r	Exists in Holland
217	OTS LHD	16/06/1960	T 832128 DN	British Racing Green	Tan	Henlys, London; PED	5751 DU	
218	OTS LHD	19/07/1960	T 832132 DN	Cornish Grey	Red	Trad, Lebanon		Exists in the UK or Denmark
219	OTS LHD	20/07/1960	T 832133 DN	Cream	Black	Tabbaa & Salameh, Jordan	n/r	
220	OTS LHD	09/08/1960	T 832134 DN	Indigo Blue	Grey	Trad, Lebanon	n/r	Exists in Holland
221	OTS LHD	29/08/1960	T 832137 DN	Cream	Red	Martins & Almeida, Portugal	n/r	Exists in Portugal
222	OTS LHD	31/08/1960	T 832138 DN	Pearl Grey	Grey	Baxter, Okinawa	n/r	
223	FHC LHD	14/05/1959	T 836237 DN	Mist Grey	Red	RM Overseas, Germany	n/r	Converted from 3.4 S in Service Dept?
224	FHC LHD	15/09/1959	T 836438 DN	Cream	Red	RM Overseas, Germany	n/r	Exists; in Christie's auction 1989
225	FHC LHD	18/09/1959	T 836448 DN	Pearl Grey	Red	Frey, Switzerland; PED	3316 DU	Converted from 3.4 S
226	FHC LHD	21/09/1959	T 836450 DN	Cream	Red	Jaguar, USA	n/r	Converted from 3.4 S
227	FHC LHD	24/09/1959	T 836460 DN	Carmen Red	Red	Jaguar, USA	n/r	Exists in Holland
228	FHC LHD	25/09/1959	T 836466 DN	Carmen Red	Black	Jaguar, USA	n/r	
229	FHC LHD	30/09/1959	T 836479 DN	Cream	Red	Jaguar, USA	n/r	Exists in the USA
230	FHC LHD	19/10/1959	S 836513 DN	Cream	Red	Jaguar, USA	n/r	Exists
231	FHC LHD	13/11/1959	T 836590 DN	Cream	Black	RM Overseas, Germany	n/r	
232	FHC LHD	16/11/1959	T 836593 DN	Cornish Grey	Red	Delecroix, France	n/r	
233	FHC LHD	17/11/1959	T 836596 DN	Cream	Black	Delecroix, France	n/r	Exists in Switzerland
234	FHC LHD	08/12/1959	T 836614 DN	Cream	Red	Belgian Motor Company	n/r	Exists in Holland
235	FHC LHD	09/12/1959	T 836616 DN	Cream	Red	Jaguar, USA	n/r	
236	FHC LHD	16/12/1959	T 836626 DN	Pearl Grey	Dark Blue	CGA, Italy	n/r	
237	FHC LHD	22/12/1959	T 836637 DN	Black	Red	RM Overseas, Germany	n/r	
238	FHC LHD	23/12/1959	T 836638 DN	Black	Black	Jaguar Cars Ltd; PED	3729 DU	Exists in France or Switzerland
239	FHC LHD	23/12/1959	T 836640 DN	British Racing Green	Tan	Jaguar, USA	n/r	
240	FHC LHD	29/12/1959	T 836645 DN	Cotswold Blue	Red	Jaguar, USA	n/r	
241	FHC LHD	01/01/1960	T 836656 DN	Cotswold Blue	Red	Jaguar, USA	n/r	
242	FHC LHD	13/01/1960	T 836675 DN	Black	Black	Jaguar, USA	n/r	
243	FHC LHD	22/01/1960	T 836696 DN	Carmen Red	Black	SAMDACO, Brazil; PED	4019 DU	

Ref	Body type	Date man.	Chassis no	Paint colour	Trim colour	Destination	UK reg. mark(s)	Remarks, status
244	FHC LHD	19/02/1960	T 836730 DN	Pearl Grey	Black	Jaguar, USA	n/r	Exists in Germany
245	FHC LHD	08/03/1960	T 836739 DN	Pearl Grey	Red	SAMDACO, Brazil	n/r	Exists in Brazil
246	FHC LHD	04/04/1960	T 836755 DN	Pearl Grey	Red	Frey, Switzerland; PED	4999 DU	Exists in Holland
247	FHC LHD	14/04/1960	T 836761 DN	Carmen Red	Black	Jaguar, USA	n/r	Exists in the USA
248	FHC LHD	25/05/1960	T 836802 DN	Cream	Red	Henlys, London; PED	5589 DU	
249	FHC LHD	08/06/1960	T 836819 DN	Cotswold Blue	Grey	Juhan, Guatemala	n/r	
250	FHC LHD	15/06/1960	T 836827 DN	Carmen Red	Black	Jaguar, USA	n/r	
251	FHC LHD	24/06/1960	T 836839 DN	Cream	Red	Juhan, Guatemala	n/r	
252	FHC LHD	13/07/1960	T 836856 DN	British Racing Green	Beige	Jaguar, USA	n/r	Exists in New Zealand
253	FHC LHD	15/07/1960	T 836858 DN	Cream	Black	Jaguar, USA	n/r	
254	FHC LHD	19/07/1960	T 836861 DN	Black	Red	Jaguar, USA	n/r	
255	FHC LHD	21/07/1960	T 836869 DN	Carmen Red	Black	Jaguar, USA	n/r	Exists in the USA
256	FHC LHD	22/07/1960	T 836870 DN	Cream	Tan	Jaguar, USA	n/r	
257	FHC LHD	12/08/1960	T 836888 DN	Carmen Red	Black	Jaguar, USA	n/r	
258	FHC LHD	17/08/1960	T 836900 DN	Sherwood Green	Suede Green	Delecroix, France	n/r	Exists in France
259	FHC LHD	22/08/1960	T 836909 DN	Carmen Red	Black	Jaguar, USA	n/r	
260	FHC LHD	24/08/1960	T 836916 DN	British Racing Green	Suede Green	Jaguar, Canada	n/r	Exists in New Zealand
261	FHC LHD	26/09/1960	T 836984 DN	British Racing Green	Tan	Sanderson & Holmes, Derby; PED	7184 DU	
262	FHC LHD	29/09/1960	T 836994 DN	Pearl Grey	Light Blue	Belgian Motor Company	n/r	Exists in the UK
263	FHC LHD	17/11/1960	T 847091 DN	Cotswold Blue	Grey	DIFMA, Morocco	n/r	Exists
264	DHC LHD	02/10/1959	T 838454 DN	Cream	Red	Jaguar, USA	n/r	
265	DHC LHD	13/10/1959	T 838464 DN	Cream	Red	Jaguar, USA	n/r	
266	DHC LHD	26/10/1959	T 838495 DN	Cream	Red	Jaguar, USA	LVS 428	Exists in the UK
267	DHC LHD	16/12/1959	T 838581 DN	Pearl Grey	Black	CAPIMA, Algeria	n/r	
268	DHC LHD	18/01/1960	T 838651 DN	Black	Red	Jaguar, USA	n/r	Exists in the UK
269	DHC LHD	25/01/1960	T 838665 DN	Carmen Red	Black	Jaguar, USA	n/r	
270	DHC LHD	03/02/1960	T 838685 DN	Cream	Black	Jaguar, USA	n/r	Exists in the UK
271	DHC LHD	16/02/1960	T 838703 DN	Cream	Black	Delecroix, France	n/r	
272	DHC LHD	18/02/1960	T 838705 DN	Cream	Red	Jaguar, Canada	n/r	Exists in the USA
273	DHC LHD	19/05/1960	T 838856 DN	Black	Red	Jaguar, Canada	n/r	
274	DHC LHD	27/05/1960	T 838870 DN	Cream	Maroon	Jaguar, Canada	n/r	Exists in the UK
275	DHC LHD	30/05/1960	S 838872 DN	British Racing Green	Tan	Jaguar, Canada	n/r	Exists in Canada
276	DHC LHD	08/07/1960	S 838901 DN	Carmen Red	Black	Jaguar, USA	n/r	Exists
277	DHC LHD	14/07/1960	S 838905 DN	Cream	Red	Jaguar, USA	n/r	
278	DHC LHD	19/07/1960	T 838908 DN	Black	Red	Jaguar, USA	n/r	Exists in France
279	DHC LHD	09/08/1960	T 838915 DN	Cream	Red	Jaguar Cars Ltd direct sale to Shell Petroleum	n/r	
280	DHC LHD	24/08/1960	T 838934 DN	Black	Black	Jaguar, USA	n/r	
281	DHC LHD	30/08/1960	S 838939 DN	Cream	Black	Jaguar Cars Ltd; PED	6986 DU	Exists in USA
282	DHC LHD	08/09/1960	T 838950 DN	Cotswold Blue	Dark Blue	Belgian Motor Company	n/r	
283	DHC LHD	27/09/1960	S 838974 DN converted to S 827663 DN	Cream	Dark Blue	Henlys, London	n/r	Converted to RHD with 3.4 non-S engine, finally despatched 16/06/1961

Notes to this table:
PED = Personal Export Delivery.

Registration marks have been taken where available from the Car Record Books but some have been supplied by owners. Many cars have been re-registered, or have been given age-related registration marks.

Information on cars known to exist has partly been based on JDHT certificates issued since 1991. Some information on the location of surviving cars may be out of date. I thank David Bentley of the XK Club, John Elmgreen and Terry McGrath for helping me to complete information on registration marks and cars that are known to exist.

It would appear that at least around 165 of the 282/283 cars are known to exist. A few have been confirmed to have been lost. A few 3.8 S engines are now claimed to be fitted in other XK 150 cars. Unfortunately there are also cars out there with engines whose numbers have been faked to show the VAS prefix, but which were originally VA (3.8 litre) or VS (3.4 litre S) engines.

Appendix 2:
Change points

Over the years there has been much useful information published on the changes to the XK cars made during their production, for instance in Philip Porter's *Original Jaguar XK* (second or later edition), Paul Skilleter's *The Jaguar XKs – A Collector's Guide* and Bernard Viart's *Jaguar XK – Le Grand Livre*, apart from numerous magazine articles. Ultimately of course all of these derive from the original *Spare Parts Catalogues* published by Jaguar; J.15 for the XK 140 (with supplements J.18 for overdrive cars and J.19 for automatic cars), J.29 in two volumes for the XK 150, as well as the individually numbered *Service Bulletins* and *Spare Parts Bulletins*. The *Service Manual* originally covered the Mark VII and XK 120 but was updated with supplements for later models which make it slightly confusing. Much of the original factory literature has been reprinted, and is included on CDs which are available from the JDHT.

In the lists below, I have re-arranged all of the changes in chronological order by year and month, and have checked all the chassis and engine numbers against the actual production records.

XK 140:

Feb 1954 First cars, 804001 FHC RHD with regular production from 804004 in Sep 1954, 807001 DHC RHD with regular production from 807003 in Oct 1954

Sep 1954 First OTS LHD, 810001

Oct 1954 First OTS RHD, 800001; first FHC LHD, 814001; first DHC LHD, 817001

Oct 1954 Overdrive option introduced, from 800001 (OTS RHD), 810002 (OTS LHD), 804006 (FHC RHD), 814002 (FHC LHD), 807004 (DHC RHD), 817002 (DHC LHD), and engine number G 1015

Dec 1954 Clutch pedal return spring on LHD open cars, from 810430 (OTS LHD), 817051 (DHC LHD)

Dec 1954 Boot lid with handle and trim, from 800009 (OTS RHD), 810549 (OTS LHD), 807005 (FHC RHD), 817091 (FHC LHD), 804008 (DHC RHD), 814004 (DHC LHD)

Dec 1954 OTS shorter tonneau cover with "Durable Dot" fasteners, from 800009 (OTS RHD) and 810476 (OTS LHD)

Jan 1955 "Lift the Dot" fasteners re-introduced for OTS tonneau cover, from 800010 (OTS RHD) and 810729 (OTS LHD)

Jan 1955 Modified steering pinion housing and steering rack tube, from 800025 (OTS RHD), 810859 (OTS LHD), 804058 (FHC RHD), 814010 (FHC LHD), 807056 (DHC RHD), 817189 (DHC LHD)

Jan 1955 Oil pump of rotor type introduced, with associated changes, including oil filter with relief valve in filter head, circular oil seal at front of crankshaft, new sump and dipstick, from engine number G 1908 which was fitted in 811017 (Feb 1955); at this point the cylinder block part number changes from C.4820 to C.8610 (*Service Bulletin* no.161 Feb 1955)

Feb 1955 FHC radiator and fan, radiator mounting brackets on chassis, from 804020 (FHC RHD), 814035 (FHC LHD)

Mar 1955 Lock straps for crown wheel set screws, from 800022 (OTS RHD), 811093 (OTS LHD), 804031 (FHC RHD), 814053 (FHC LHD), 807047 (DHC RHD), 817268 (DHC LHD)

Mar 1955 Diaphragm assembly front wing/dash on open cars, from 800023 (OTS RHD), 811114 (OTS LHD), 807052 (DHC RHD), 817275 (DHC LHD)

Mar 1955 Dust cover for adjustable steering column on coupé models, from 804067 (FHC RHD), 814098 (FHC LHD), 807069 (DHC RHD), 817302 (DHC LHD)

Mar 1955 Common prop shaft tunnel introduced on both LHD and RHD cars, from 800025 (OTS RHD), 811257 (OTS LHD), 804069 (FHC RHD), 814133 (FHC LHD), 807070 (DHC RHD), 817337 (DHC LHD), with associated trim changes

Apr 1955 Modified rear brake cylinders, from 800025 (OTS RHD), 811284 (OTS LHD), 804080 (FHC RHD), 814153 (FHC LHD), 807080 (DHC RHD), 817356 (DHC LHD)

Apr 1955 Distributor protection shield added on open cars, from 800030 (OTS RHD), 811335 (OTS LHD), 807096 (DHC RHD), 817389 (DHC LHD)

Apr 1955 New carburettor needles on engines with C-type cylinder head, from engine number G 3250-8S which was fitted in S 811381 (May 1955)

May 1955 Relay incorporated in overdrive circuit, from 800031 (OTS RHD), 811382 (OTS LHD), 804121 (FHC RHD), 814216 (FHC LHD), 807113 (DHC RHD), 817426 (DHC LHD)

May 1955 Petrol pump with two points, from 800032 (OTS RHD), 811422 (OTS LHD), 804140 (FHC RHD), 814240 (FHC LHD), 807126 (DHC RHD), 817458 (DHC LHD)

May 1955 New rev. counter with higher red line, from 800033 (OTS RHD), 811417 (OTS LHD), 804140 (FHC RHD), 814237 (FHC LHD), 807133 (DHC RHD), 817461 (DHC LHD)

May 1955 New radiator with fluted top, from 800037 (OTS RHD), 811424 (OTS LHD), 804142 (FHC RHD), 814241 (FHC LHD), 807128 (DHC RHD), 817460 (DHC LHD), coinciding with revised water outlet pipe for inlet manifold from engine number G 3550 which was fitted in 814479 (Jul 1955), and tie rod to inner wing

Jun 1955 New type of grease gun in tool kit, from 800049 (OTS RHD), 811527 (OTS LHD), 804270 (FHC RHD), 814454 (FHC LHD), 807207 (DHC RHD), 817604 (DHC LHD)

Jul 1955 Castor angle reduced from 2½-3 degrees positive to 1½-2 degrees positive to reduce steering kick back, from 800052 (OTS RHD), 811562 (OTS LHD), 804308 (FHC RHD), 814532 (FHC LHD), 807237 (DHC RHD), 817653 (DHC LHD)

Jul 1955 Renold hydraulic tensioner for camshaft drive chain introduced, from engine number G 4431 which was fitted in 811568, also on engine numbers G 4411-4420; cylinder block part number becomes C.8610/1

Aug 1955 Clip added to retain stop button on inner steering column, from 800053 (OTS RHD), 811590 (OTS LHD), 804326 (FHC RHD), 814604 (FHC LHD), 807241 (DHC RHD), 817708 (DHC LHD)

Aug 1955 Hexagon type ball housing on steering tie rod inner ball joints, from 800054 (OTS RHD), 811595 (OTS LHD), 804328 (FHC RHD), 814616 (FHC LHD), 807243 (DHC RHD), 817716 (DHC LHD)

Sep 1955 Change to windscreen washer connection and introduction of check valve, from 800061 (OTS RHD), 811698 (OTS LHD), 804426 (FHC RHD), 814854 (FHC LHD), 807288 (DHC RHD), 817896 (DHC LHD)

Oct 1955 Depth of holes for inlet manifold studs reduced and studs shortened, from engine number G 5789 which was fitted in 815175 (Nov 1955)

Nov 1955 Overdrive cars: Throttle switch incorporated in the electrical operation of the overdrive, to prevent change from overdrive to direct top if decelerating with closed throttle, and two relays; chassis plate moved, from 800062 (OTS RHD), 811866 (OTS LHD), 804523 (FHC RHD), 815252 (FHC LHD), 807319 (DHC RHD), 818193 (DHC LHD)

Nov 1955 Modified oil filter (Tecalemit FA 2708), from engine number G 6233 which was fitted in 818187

Dec 1955 Cylinder head modified, from engine number G 6407-8S which was fitted in S 804526, and G 6912 which was fitted in 818294 (Jan 1956); cylinder head part numbers changed from C.6733 to C.6733/1 (standard head) and from C.7707 to C.7707/1 (C-type head)

Dec 1955 Modified exhaust valves and guides on engines with C-type cylinder head, from engine number G 6678 S which was fitted in S 807479

Jan 1956 Automatic gearbox introduced on LHD coupés, from 815285 (FHC LHD), 818256 (DHC LHD), coinciding with engine number G 6591, apart from five earlier prototypes, and an earlier batch of 30-odd engines mostly numbered from G 3079 to G 3111

Jan 1956 Carmen Red and Arbour Green colours introduced on LHD cars; Carmen Red from 812033 (OTS LHD), 815285 (FHC LHD), 818192 (DHC LHD; Dec 1955); Arbour Green from 812052 (OTS LHD), 815286 (FHC LHD), 818257 (DHC LHD).

Jan 1956 Engine drive plate for torque converter increased in size from 7.5in (190.5mm) to 11.1875in (284.2mm) and revised converter assembly on automatic cars, from engine number G 6615 which was fitted in 815290 BW

Feb 1956 Nylon insert to end of inner rev. counter cable on coupé models, from 804640 (FHC RHD), 815395 (FHC LHD), 807367 (DHC RHD), 818385 (DHC LHD)

Mar 1956 Pistons fitted with tapered periphery compression rings and modified oil control ring, from engine number G 7229 which was fitted in 815415

Apr 1956 FHC LHD with automatic gearbox, new selector controls, from 815532 (FHC LHD)

Apr 1956 Larger bolts for drive gear to differential case, from 800071 (OTS RHD), 812311 (OTS LHD), 804676 (FHC RHD), 815528 (FHC LHD), 807389 (DHC RHD), 818488 (DHC LHD)

Jun 1956 Automatic gearbox introduced on RHD coupés, from 804749 (FHC RHD), 807439 (DHC RHD)

Jul 1956 Fly-off handbrake re-introduced, from 800072 (OTS RHD), 812647 (OTS LHD), 804767 (FHC RHD), 815755

	(FHC LHD), 807441 (DHC RHD), 818729 (DHC LHD)
Jul 1956	Steel doors instead of aluminium doors on coupés, from 804781 (FHC RHD), 815773 (FHC LHD), 807447 (DHC RHD), 818796 (DHC LHD) (*Service Bulletin* no.198 Oct 1956)
Jul 1956	Modified speedometer cable with nylon insert, from 800072 (OTS RHD), 812707 (OTS LHD), 804781 (FHC RHD), 815778 (FHC LHD), 807447 (DHC RHD), 818801 (DHC LHD) (earlier on automatic cars)
Oct 1956	Last OTS RHD, 800074
Nov 1956	Last FHC RHD, 804843
Jan 1957	Last OTS LHD, 813282; FHC LHD, 815966; DHC RHD, 807480; DHC LHD, 819311

XK 150:

Mar 1957	First FHC LHD, 834001; first DHC LHD, 837001
Jun 1957	Conical filter gauze fitted to oil feed hole for hydraulic chain tensioner in cylinder block, from engine number V 1191 in 834119
Jun 1957	Longer inlet valve guides 1 13/16 in instead of 1½ in, from engine number V 1281 in 834198
Aug 1957	Wiper motor bracket changed on coupé models, from 834395 (FHC LHD), 837157 (DHC LHD), and RHD models from start
Aug 1957	First FHC RHD, 824001
Aug 1957	Rear disc brake calipers with 1 5/8 in pistons rather then 1¾ in, from start of OTS models and DHC RHD, 824023 (FHC RHD), 834454 (FHC LHD), 837014 (DHC LHD)
Aug 1957	New smaller grease gun in tool kit, from start of OTS models and DHC RHD, 824025 (FHC RHD), 834458 (FHC LHD), 837017 (DHC LHD)
Sep 1957	Smaller dynamo pulley and shorter fan belt, from engine number V 1599 in 837017
Sep 1957	Larger diameter anti-creep solenoid valve for auto gearbox, from start of OTS models and DHC RHD, 824046 (FHC RHD), 834491 (FHC LHD), 837030 (DHC LHD)
Sep 1957	Block rear cover and sealing ring, from engine number V 1631 in S 824048 DN
Sep 1957	First OTS LHD, 830001; regular production from 830002, Jan 1958
Oct 1957	Modifications to upper steering column to provide more positive locking of the steering wheel, from start of OTS models and DHC RHD; 824076 (FHC RHD), 834600 (FHC LHD), 837071 (DHC LHD)
Oct 1957	Carpet quality changed from ref.1185 to ref.1763, from start of OTS models and DHC RHD; 824079 (FHC RHD), 834596 (FHC LHD), 837082 (DHC LHD)
Oct 1957	Timing cover attached with five set screws of equal length, from engine number V 1921 in 834654
Oct 1957	50 amp fuses fitted to some electrical circuits instead of 35 amp fuses, from start of OTS models and DHC RHD; 824096 (FHC RHD), 834658 (FHC LHD), 837090 (DHC LHD)
Oct 1957	Front bumper, brackets, and plinth panels behind front bumper changed to OTS type to enable fitting of fog lamps (now standard on SE models, except cars for USA), from start of OTS models and DHC RHD, 824097 (FHC RHD), 834682 (FHC LHD), 837104 (DHC LHD)
Nov 1957	Stop pin added to oil pressure relief valve with longer and lighter spring, 2 1/16 in instead of 1¾ in, from engine number V 2011 in 837111
Nov 1957	Timing chain dampers changed from nylon to synthetic rubber, from engine number V 2029 in 834733
Nov 1957	First DHC RHD, 827001
Jan 1958	(approx.) Gradual introduction of British-made automatic gearbox, JBX series; actual first 'box JBX 1001 in 824319 (Mar 1958); US made 'boxes continued to be used intermittently on some cars through to the end of 1958, and a few cars built in 1959
Jan/Feb 1958	Believed to be approximate date for introduction of new boot lid with greater slope to number plate, and boot lid handle finishing on number plate lamp housing, see for instance OTS LHD 830009 and FHC LHD 835189 both with new boot lid (www.xkdata.com)
Feb 1958	Brake master cylinder body now of cast iron instead of aluminium, with unhardened piston (*Service Bulletin* no.238, Feb 1958)
Feb 1958	New gear lever, gear lever knob and gear selector lever; new transmission covers on manual cars, from start of OTS RHD, 830016 (OTS LHD), 824240 (FHC RHD), 835254 (FHC LHD), 827008 (DHC RHD), 837320 (DHC LHD)
Feb 1958	Pull-type armrests to doors, from start of OTS models, 824253 (FHC RHD), 835301 (FHC LHD), 827011 (DHC RHD), 837332 (DHC LHD)

Mar 1958   First 3.4 S model, 830073 (OTS LHD); regular production from 830336, 29 Apr 1958

Apr 1958   Dunlop RS4 tyres instead of Road Speed tyres, from start of OTS RHD, 830227 (OTS LHD), 824348 (FHC RHD), 835452 (FHC LHD), 827050 (DHC RHD), 837381 (DHC LHD)

May 1958   Indicator switch on dash replaced by steering column stalk with changes to steering column, change to rev. counter, from start of OTS RHD and OTS LHD, 824414 (FHC RHD), 835548 (FHC LHD), 827069 (DHC RHD), 837415 (DHC LHD)

May 1958   Thermometer bulb moved to top water outlet pipe

May 1958   Modifications to brake master cylinder to reduce pedal travel when brakes first applied after car has been standing, from start of OTS RHD, 830438 (OTS LHD), 824420 (FHC RHD), 835566 (FHC LHD), 827072 (DHC RHD), 837434 (DHC LHD)

May 1958   New instrument panel with heater control moved, rheostat for heater fan control, from start of OTS RHD, 830439 (OTS LHD), 824420 (FHC RHD), 835566 (FHC LHD), 827072 (DHC RHD), 837434 (DHC LHD)

May 1958   New unique boot floor mat on OTS and spring-loaded boot hinges introduced, non-telescopic boot lid prop, from start of OTS RHD, 830457 (OTS LHD)

May 1958   Petrol filler box, and larger diameter vent pipe to petrol tank, from start of OTS RHD, 830560 (OTS LHD), 824453 (FHC RHD), 835589 (FHC LHD), 827094 (DHC RHD), 837468 (DHC LHD); different change points for S models

Jun 1958   New solenoid for intermediate speed hold on auto cars, from start of OTS RHD, 830692 (OTS LHD), 824463 (FHC RHD), 835610 (FHC LHD), 827118 (DHC RHD), 837486 (DHC LHD)

Jun 1958(?)   60-spoke wire wheels introduced instead of 54-spoke wheels

Jun 1958   Drophead coupé instrument board changed from aluminium finish (part numbers BD.18868/18869) to grey leather trim in common with other models (part numbers BD.13574/18870), from 827133 (DHC RHD), 837517 (DHC LHD)

Jul 1958   Redesigned rear springs with thicker top leaf and nylon interleaf etc, from start of OTS RHD, 830960 (OTS LHD), 824551 (FHC RHD), 835671 (FHC LHD), 827168 (DHC RHD), 837573 (DHC LHD)

Aug 1958   New heater of fresh-air type introduced, with water valve control from slide lever in cockpit; bonnet changed to accommodate this; central heater control and new instrument board; changes to automatic gear selector; new front wing ventilators (etc); larger petrol filler box, with rearwards-opening flap and change to left-hand rear wheel arch (with associated trim changes); floorboards on LHD cars; casings to side of facia and LH/RH top of dash panels on coupé models; new battery connecting cable; bracket holding reversing lamp switch superseded; new vacuum hose for brake servo unit; from start of OTS RHD, 831140 (OTS LHD), 824585 (FHC RHD), 835719 (FHC LHD), 827194 (DHC RHD), 837628 (DHC LHD); probably at this point, check straps added to doors (Terry McGrath in *Jaguar World* vol.9 no.5 May/Jun 1997)

Aug 1958   New kick-down controls on cars with automatic gearbox, from start of OTS RHD, 831267 (OTS LHD), 824592 (FHC RHD), 835751 (FHC LHD), 827207 (DHC RHD), 837655 (DHC LHD)

Aug 1958   New dipstick, from engine numbers V 5060 in 835719, VS 1304 in 831140

Aug 1958   Centre and front petrol pipes; bracket for second petrol pump added to chassis (second pump fitted only on S models); new pedal assemblies, from start of OTS RHD, 831143 (OTS LHD), 824610 (FHC RHD), 835718 (FHC LHD), 827213 (DHC RHD), 837629 (DHC LHD)

Sep 1958   Rear bumper with overriders closer together, new bumper irons, from start of OTS RHD, 831250 (OTS LHD), 824607 (FHC RHD), 835745 (FHC LHD), 827209 (DHC RHD), 837662 (DHC LHD)

Oct 1958   Changed crankshaft, water pump and dynamo pulleys for new ½ in fan belt, and new dynamo adjusting link, from engine numbers V 5733 in 831595, VS 1523 in 831621

Oct 1958   First OTS RHD, 820001; first 3.4 S OTS RHD, 820003

Oct 1958   Single instead of two-piece Hardura panel to LH side of boot, from 820002 (OTS RHD), 831620 (OTS LHD), 824644 (FHC RHD), 835867 (FHC LHD), 827236 (DHC RHD), 837796 (DHC LHD)

Oct 1958   Changes to DHC soft top, from 827229 (DHC RHD), 837799 (DHC LHD)

Nov 1958   Brake calipers of bridge type with quick-change square pads, new handbrake calipers, from 820004 (OTS RHD), 831712 (OTS LHD), 824669 (FHC RHD), 835886 (FHC LHD), 827236 (DHC RHD), 837836 (DHC LHD), and on S models from 820005 (OTS RHD), 831703 (OTS LHD), 824789 (FHC RHD), 835961 (FHC LHD), 827334 (DHC RHD), 837993 (DHC LHD)

Nov 1958   New front suspension top ball joint assemblies with large diameter balls, from 820004 (OTS RHD), 831968 (OTS LHD), 824668 (FHC RHD), 835882 (FHC LHD), 827234 (DHC RHD), 837831 (DHC LHD)

Nov 1958   Rear parcel tray changed on coupé models as mounting for radio power supply and amplifier moved to left-

	hand rear wheel arch; spring-loaded boot hinges introduced with non-telescopic boot lid prop, as already found on OTS, from 824677 (FHC RHD), 835893 (FHC LHD), 827240 (DHC RHD), 837846 (DHC LHD)
Nov 1958	First 3.4 S FHC LHD, 835897; regular production from 835968 (1 Jan 1959)
Nov 1958	Door ash trays replaced by single ash tray on tunnel, from 820014 (OTS RHD), 831825 (OTS LHD), 824702 (FHC RHD), 835905 (FHC LHD), 827258 (DHC RHD), 837865 (DHC LHD)
Dec 1958	Mudshield protecting LH battery box (etc); inlet manifold and air balance pipe changed, also windscreen washer check valve on inlet manifold, new carburettor bodies; glass bowl petrol filter introduced on standard models (found on S models from start) and petrol pipes changed; bracket for holding bonnet prop on OTS models; Reservac vacuum reservoir added to brake servo unit; from 820017 (OTS RHD), 831899 (OTS LHD), 824742 (FHC RHD), 835935 (FHC LHD), 827272 (DHC RHD), 837941 (DHC LHD)
Dec 1958	Tonneau cross member, from 820019 (OTS RHD), 831910 (OTS LHD), 824677 (FHC RHD), 835893 (FHC LHD), 827240, (DHC RHD), 837846 (DHC LHD); also modified boot lid casing on OTS model
Jan 1959	Mechanical overdrive operation fitted on XK 150 S model, from 831963 (OTS LHD) and start of production of other types, and available to special order on non-S cars; it could be fitted only on gearboxes of the JLS-JS type but it seems not all later S models had the mechanical overdrive, which has been described as rare
Jan 1959	First 3.4 S DHC LHD, 837993
Feb 1959	First 3.4 S FHC RHD, 824789
Feb 1959	Drophead hood frame and toggle clamps changed, from 827292 (DHC RHD), 838138 (DHC LHD)
Mar 1959	Lead indium bearings introduced to replace white metal type, from engine number V 6709 in 838215
Apr 1959	First 3.4 S DHC RHD, 827334
Apr 1959	Improved boot hinges, boot lid prop deleted, from 820038 (OTS RHD), 832074 (OTS LHD), 824863 (FHC RHD), 836184 (FHC LHD), 827349 (DHC RHD), 838238 (DHC LHD); also modified boot lid casing on coupé models, as already found on OTS models
Apr 1959	New adjustable interior mirror, of Mark II type on FHC models, from 820039 (OTS RHD), 832071 (OTS LHD), 824900 (FHC RHD), 836219 (FHC LHD), 827340 (DHC RHD), 838231 (DHC LHD)
Apr 1959	Air box with single paper element instead of three wire-mesh filters and changes to petrol pipes on S models, from 820039 (OTS RHD), 832076 (OTS LHD), 824864 (FHC RHD), 836187 (FHC LHD), 827355 (DHC RHD), 838246 (DHC LHD)
Apr 1959	Changes to petrol pipes on standard models, from 820040 (OTS RHD), 832081 (OTS LHD), 824885 (FHC RHD), 836192 (FHC LHD), 827359 (DHC RHD), 838247 (DHC LHD)
May 1959	Blanking plate between oil filter and block deleted, with associated changes, from engine number V 6861 in 827363; cylinder block part number becomes C.15951
May 1959	New 25 amp dynamo with different armature etc, new control box and voltage regulator with revised setting, from 820043 (OTS RHD), 832088 (OTS LHD), 824900 (FHC RHD), 836222 (FHC LHD), 827273 (DHC RHD), 838259 (DHC LHD)
May 1959	Electronic rev. counter introduced, associated changes to cylinder head and inlet camshaft etc, dash panel modified to suit, with changes to wiring harness, from 820043 (OTS RHD), 832088 (OTS LHD), 824905 (FHC RHD), 836233 (FHC LHD), 827373 (DHC RHD), 838272 (DHC LHD); cylinder head part number becomes C.14956 (non-S models, also found on 3.4-litre saloon) or C.14957 (S models)
May 1959	Strengthened clutch slave cylinder bracket, from 820043 (OTS RHD), 832089 (OTS LHD), 824903 (FHC RHD), 836227 (FHC LHD), 827379 (DHC RHD), 838273 (DHC LHD)
Jun 1959	Stiffener added to bearing support bracket on accelerator cross shaft, from 824964 (FHC RHD)
Jul 1959	Glass instead of steel brake fluid reservoir on cars for some European markets, from 832093 (OTS LHD), 836293 (FHC LHD), 838311 (DHC LHD)
Aug 1959	New throttle anti-creep switch on automatic cars, from engine number V 7247 in 838357
Aug 1959	First 3.8-engined cars, from 836399 (FHC LHD), 838392 (DHC LHD); followed by 825041 (FHC RHD) in Oct 1959, 827467 (DHC RHD) in Nov 1959, 832112 (OTS LHD) in Dec 1959, and 820081 (OTS RHD) in May 1960
Sep 1959	First 3.8 S models, from 836438 (FHC LHD), 825028 (FHC RHD) and 827461 (DHC RHD), followed by 838454 (DHC LHD) and 820056 (OTS RHD) both in Oct 1959, and 832110 (OTS LHD) in Nov 1959
Sep 1959	Overdrive relay changed, from 820055 (OTS RHD), 832104 (OTS LHD), 825035 (FHC RHD), 836457 (FHC LHD), 827463 (DHC RHD), 838432 (DHC LHD)
Sep 1959	New Girling front shock absorbers, from 820055 (OTS RHD), 832106 (OTS LHD), 825038 (FHC RHD), 836471 (FHC LHD), 827463 (DHC RHD), 838444 (DHC LHD)

Oct 1959   New larger rear lamp units with separate lenses for flashing indicators and separate reflectors, and changes to body wiring harnesses, from 820056 (OTS RHD), 832106 (OTS LHD), 825039 (FHC RHD), 836490 (FHC LHD), 827464 (DHC RHD), 838458 (DHC LHD)

Nov 1959   New jack, black rather than red, from 820063 (OTS RHD), 832111 (OTS LHD), 825092 (FHC RHD), 836608 (FHC LHD), 827483 (DHC RHD), 838562 (DHC LHD)

Dec 1959   Modified crankshaft rear cover assembly and oil seal, from engine numbers V 7460 in 827506, VS 2183 in 832102 (both earlier car which had an engine change), VA 1399 in 838582, VAS 1085 in 836645

Dec 1959   New type of brake master cylinder, from 820066 (OTS RHD), 832113/832114 (OTS LHD), 825125/825127 (FHC RHD), 836635 (FHC LHD), 827505/827506 (DHC RHD), 838590 (DHC LHD)

Jan 1960   8:1 pistons part number C.14806/1 as used on 3.8 S engine now also used on 3.8 engine, from engine number VA 1543 in 838661; the previous 3.8 piston C.14806 was not compatible with 3.8 S cylinder head which is not chamfered at the bottom of the combustion chambers (*Service Bulletins* B.1 Jan 1960 and B.14 Jan 1962, *Spare Parts Bulletins* A.28 and A.29 Mar 1960)

Jan/Feb 1960   Notched fan belt, from engine numbers V 7464 in 838706, VS 2188 in 836725, VA 1449 in 838624, VAS 1097 in 825128 (*Spare Parts Bulletin* P.27 Nov 1960)

Feb/Mar 1960   Carpet changed from curly pile (ref.1763) to straight-cut pile (ref.1201), depending on carpet colour from approx. 820069 (OTS RHD), 832118 (OTS LHD), 825131 (FHC RHD), 836687 (FHC LHD), 827508 (DHC RHD), 838661 (DHC LHD)

Feb 1960   Longer handbrake connecting link, from 836727 (FHC LHD), 827510 (DHC RHD)

Mar 1960   Handbrake lever moved from passenger's side to driver's side of the prop shaft tunnel (but possibly not on all LHD cars), old RHD tunnel covers now used on LHD cars and vice versa, warning light introduced for handbrake and low brake fluid level with change to wiring harness; all cars now have polythene brake fluid reservoir; Mintex M.33 brake pad material instead of Ferodo DS.5, new handbrake pads of Mintex M.34, various changes to rear brakes; new Girling rear shock absorbers, with 1 3/8 in diameter piston to rear shocks; exhaust tail pipes now clipped rather than welded to silencers (*Service Bulletin* N.1 Jan 1960, *Spare Parts Bulletin* M.5 Apr 1960), from 820071 (OTS RHD), 832120/832121 (OTS LHD), 825179 (FHC RHD), 836744 (FHC LHD), 827540 (DHC RHD), 838754 (DHC LHD)

Mar 1960   New type of converter assembly and other changes to automatic gearbox, from engine numbers V 7463 in 838789, VA 1675 in 838773

Jul/Aug 1960   New headlamps on American export cars, from 832138 (OTS LHD), 836855 (FHC LHD), 838904 (DHC LHD)

Sep 1960   Big end bearings changed to the same material specification as used on 3.4 S engine from start, part number C.16295, from engine numbers V 7640 in 838956, VA 2054 in 836941, VAS 1284 in 827647

Sep 1960   Last 3.4 S car, 836988 (FHC LHD) except one later car which was converted later

Oct 1960   Last OTS RHD 820093, and last DHC cars 827663 RHD, 839010 LHD

Nov 1960   Final cars (except conversions), 832174 (OTS LHD), 825369 (FHC RHD), 847095 (FHC LHD); the last 3.8 S was 847091 (FHC LHD)

The following late changes are not quoted in the *Spare Parts Catalogue* and may only be found in the *Service Bulletins* or *Spare Parts Bulletins*, so I have included individual references below.

Mar 1960   One tab washer instead of two shake-proof washers for the two set screws holding intermediate timing chain damper, from engine numbers V 7496 in 825200, VA 1708 in 825208, VS 2197 (engine not used), VAS 1160 in 827553 (*Spare Parts Bulletin* A.32 Apr 1960)

Mar 1960   New type of piston for 3.4 litre engines with 9:1 compression ratio with domed crown (part number C.16339) rather than flat top (part number C.10649), from engine numbers V 7524 in 832124, VS 2195 in 827544; also around this time, TDC mark on front of crankshaft damper continued on the edge of the damper to facilitate Crypton tuning (*Service Bulletin* B.3 May 1960, *Spare Parts Bulletin* A.33 Apr 1960)

May 1960   Longer set screws attaching automatic gearbox torque converter to drive plate, from engine number VA 1838 in 838867 (*Service Bulletin* FF.1 May 1960, *Spare Parts Bulletin* E.8 Jun 1960)

Jun 1960   Overdrive units on 3.8 cars fitted with magnetic ring, modified drain plug and filter, from engine numbers VA 1882 in 827625, VAS 1225 in 827599 (*Spare Parts Bulletin* D.4 Jun 1960)

Jul 1960   Champion N8 spark plugs instead of N5 for 8:1 compression ratio engines for North America (*Service Bulletin*

B.6 Jul 1960)

Aug 1960   New rev. counter drive generator to eliminate noise, from engine numbers V 7612 in 825322, VA 2004 in 836902, VS 2207 in 836927, VAS 1268 in 827627 (*Spare Parts Bulletin* A.35 Nov 1960)

Sep 1960   Boss for fitting engine heater moved from LH to RH side of cylinder block, from engine numbers VA 2053 in 836925, VAS 1285 in 827654; 3.8-litre cylinder block part number becomes C.17212; this change does not appear to have been introduced on the 3.4-litre cylinder block (*Service Bulletin* B.8 Nov 1960, *Spare Parts Bulletin* A.41 Feb 1961)

Oct 1960   Pressure die-cast timing cover introduced; modified small end bearings to con rods, from engine numbers V 7656 in 825362, VA 2202 in 847030 (NB small end bearings from VA 2204 in 847020), VS 2212 (engine not used), VAS 1293 (engine not used) (*Spare Parts Bulletin* A.41 and A.42 Feb 1961)

Nov 1960   Studs with longer thread at bottom of timing cover for attachment of oil sump, from engine number VA 2251 in 847088 (*Spare Parts Bulletin* A.43 Feb 1961)

Nov 1960   Dipstick guide tube fitted, block modified to suit, from engine number VA 2260 in 847082 (25 cars from end of production) (*Spare Parts Bulletin* A.44 Feb 1961); 3.8-litre cylinder block part number now C.17212/1; also introduced on 3.4 litre engine, probably for replacement engines only, 3.4-litre cylinder block part number with this modification C.17568

Appendix 3: **Dating and Identification**

For the post-war cars in 1945-46, Jaguar introduced a new system of chassis numbering. Where pre-war cars had five-digit chassis numbers, the post-war models had six-digit chassis numbers which started with 4 on a 1½-litre, 5 on a 2½-litre and 6 on a 3½-litre. This system was followed for the Mark V models, and for the XK 120, so all XK 120 chassis numbers started with 6, as these cars had "3½-litre" engines. However, "6" numbers were running out, so when the new Mark VII model was introduced, it was given chassis numbers starting with 7, with the Mark VIII and Mark IX also having numbers in the "7" series.

When the XK 140 was introduced in 1954 it was given numbers starting with 8. The XK 150 and later the E-type Series 1 3.8-litre also had numbers starting with 8, while in 1955 the 2.4-litre model began the "9" series which was used for the 3.4-litre model as well. So in the period 1955-59 Jaguar chassis numbers starting with 7 were for large saloons, numbers starting with 8 were for sports cars and numbers starting with 9 were for compact saloons.

Chassis numbers:

Each of the XK 140 and XK 150 models was allocated a starting chassis number depending on the type of bodywork and whether the car had right-hand or left-hand drive. The following two tables give the batches of chassis numbers, and show the first chassis number allocated in each calendar year:

XK 140:

from	OTS RHD Oct 1954	OTS LHD Sep 1954	FHC RHD Feb 1954	FHC LHD Oct 1954	DHC RHD Feb 1954	DHC LHD Oct 1954
1954	800001	810001	804001	814001	807001	817001
Jan 1955	800009	810618	804007	814004	807007	817112
Jan 1956	800063	811988	804592	815269	807343	818240
Jan 1957	n/a	813122	n/a	815962	807480	819305
last	800074	813282	804843	815966	807480	819311
in	Oct 1956	Jan 1957	Nov 1956	Jan 1957	Jan 1957	Jan 1957

XK 150:

from	OTS RHD Oct 1958	OTS LHD Sep 1957	FHC RHD Aug 1957	FHC LHD Mar 1957	DHC RHD Nov 1957	DHC LHD Mar 1957
1957		830001	824001	834001	827001	837001
Jan 1958		830002	824167	834985	827002	837214
Oct 1958	820001					
Jan 1959	820020	831924	824744	835966	827274	837984
Jan 1960	820067	832114	825127	836654	827506	838613
Oct 1960				To 836999		
Oct 1960				From 847000		
last	820093	832174	825369*	847095	827663*	839010
in	Oct 1960	Nov 1960	Oct 1960	Nov 1960	Oct 1960	Oct 1960

*Chassis numbers 825363 to 825369 and 827663 were converted from left-hand drive cars post production.

The anomaly here is the XK 150 FHC LHD model where the allocated batch of numbers ran out in October 1960, so to avoid duplication with the DHC LHD model, the chassis number series "jumped" by 10,000.

Many cars had either a prefix letter or suffix letters to the chassis numbers, as follows:

XK 140 standard – no prefix letter
XK 140 Special Equipment without C-type cylinder head ("XK 140 M") – prefix letter A
XK 140 Special Equipment with C-type cylinder head ("XK 140 MC") – prefix letter S
XK 150 "Standard" with disc wheels – no prefix letter, but this may not have been applied consistently
XK 150 "Special Equipment" with wire wheels – prefix letter S
XK 150 S models – prefix letter T, *except* that early S models until August 1958 had the prefix letter S, as did a few later cars, even including some 3.8 S models

On both models, suffix letters indicate various types of gearbox:
Manual gearbox without overdrive – no suffix letters
Manual gearbox with overdrive – suffix letters DN for (Laycock) De Normanville
Automatic gearbox – suffix letters BW for Borg Warner

Engine numbers:

On the XK 140s, there is only one series of engine numbers but there were four different series on the different versions of the XK 150, as follows:

Model	Engine no. prefix	Engine no.s from	Engine no.s to	Notes
XK 140	G	1001	9980	S suffix on engines with C-type cylinder head
XK 150 3.4 litre	V	1001	7660	
XK 150 3.4 litre S	VS	1001	2210	
XK 150 3.8 litre	VA	1001	2297	
XK 150 3.8 litre S	VAS	1001	1291, and 1312	

Apart from the S suffix found only on XK 140 engines with the C-type cylinder head, all engine numbers were suffixed with the compression ratio, which was 8:1 as standard on all models, *except* the on the XK 150 S where it was 9:1, but 9:1 (and 7:1) could be found on non-S engines. Typical engine numbers might be G 9876-8S on an XK 140 with the C-type head, V 5432-8 on an XK 150 3.4 litre and VAS 1234-9 on an XK 150 3.8 litre S engine. In all engine number series there were a few engine numbers which were not issued to production cars, and there are a few instances of numbers being duplicated in the records.

Body numbers:

The body number prefix letters were different on OTS, FHC and DHC models, and were the same as found on these body styles on the XK 120. The numerical series of the body numbers continued from those found on the XK 120 but in all cases there were gaps in the number series, clearly indicating the split between the three different XKs.

| Body type | XK 140 | | XK 150 | |
	Body no.s from	Body no.s to	Body no.s from	Body no.s to
Open two-seater	F 10001	F 13353	F 15001	F 17270
Fixed-head coupé	J 4001	J 6808	J 7001	J 11455
Drophead coupé	P 3001	P 5796	P 6001	P 8675

A few body numbers were not issued in production, and as for the engine numbers there are some instances where a body number is duplicated for two cars in the records.

Gearbox numbers:

These are by far the most confusing and difficult to sort out, and are also those numbers which are most likely to be inaccurate or duplicated in the records. Broadly speaking, on both models there were two types of manual gearboxes, with either a one-piece or a built-up gear cluster (discussed in chapters 2 and 3), one type of manual gearbox with overdrive, always with a built-up gear cluster, and one or more types of automatic gearbox.

The following can be identified:

Model	Gearbox type	Prefix	No.s from approx.	No.s to approx.
XK 140	Manual, one-piece gear cluster, possibly always close ratio gears	OSL, suffix B	1001	4400
XK 140	Manual, built-up gear cluster, normal or close ratio gears	JL	20000	37000
XK 140	Manual o/d, built-up gear cluster, normal or close ratio gears	JLE	20000	37000
XK 140	Automatic	None	3000	14000
XK 150	Manual, one-piece gear cluster, close ratio gears	M, suffix J	4400	5400
XK 150	Manual, built-up gear cluster, normal or close ratio gears	JL	36000	47000
XK 150	Manual o/d, built-up gear cluster, normal or close ratio gears	JLS	36000	47000
XK 150	Automatic, US made	None, suffix 15R	3000	14400
XK 150	Automatic, British made	JBX*	1001	1800

*Prefixes JB4, JB8 or JBC also found, although more rarely

The most common gearboxes are the various manual boxes with or without overdrive of the JL family. These all share a common series of numbers, with in practice a bit of an overlap between XK 140 and XK 150 'boxes. It also seems likely that the XK 140 OSL 'boxes and the XK 150 M 'boxes shared one number series. On all JL family manual gearboxes with or without overdrive, the gearbox numbers may have the suffix letters CR for Close-Ratio gear sets, while a few XK 140 JL or JLE boxes have the suffix MS for Moss-shaved gears and on the XK 150, the suffix letters JS for Jaguar-shaved are commonly found on boxes with normal gear ratios. One point to bear in mind with the gearbox numbers is that gearboxes of the same type and with the same prefix letters, or at least with numbers in the same number series, could be found on Mark VII, VIII and IX saloons, which explains why the numerical series are some times so much greater than the number of cars produced.

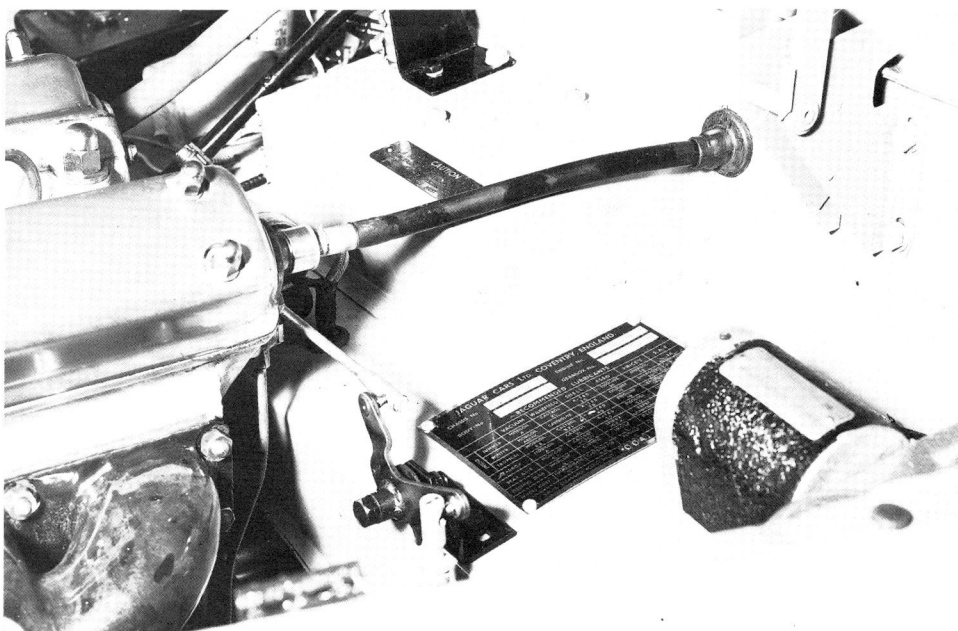

This is guaranteed to be an original identification plate, as the photo was taken in the factory in 1954. By enlarging the photo I was just able to make out some of the numbers, and it appears to be from the left-hand drive two-seater with chassis number 810295, a car which still exists. (JDHT)

Identifying a car:

Somewhere under the bonnet, each XK had a nice big rectangular brass or aluminium plate, about 5.75in by 3.75in (145mm by 95mm) stamped with the four numbers discussed above, with a chart of recommended lubricants and the valve clearances stamped at the bottom. The only exception may be the few cars that were supplied in chassis form (see chapter 10); these are known to have been sent out with such an ID plate, with a blank space for the body number, but the plate may not always have been fitted to the finished car. The exact location of the plate does vary. Please note that reproduction plates are (have been?) made, but with a bit of practice they can be distinguished from originals.

However, it is always useful as far as possible to check the numbers where they are actually stamped in. The following information has been based on Philip Porter's book *Original Jaguar XK* (second edition) pages 138-143, *Jaguar World* vol.9 no.5 May/Jun 1997, and Jaguar's original technical literature.

On the XK 140 and XK 150, the chassis number should be stamped on top of the left-hand chassis side member near the rear engine mounting, opposite the flywheel and clutch housing, and at least some times also on top of the front chassis cross member. The engine number is stamped on the right-hand side of the cylinder block, on the horizontal surface on top of the oil filter mounting, and on the vertical face at the front of the central valley in the cylinder head. These locations are common to virtually all XK engines. There appears to be no information on the numbering of factory replacement engines, but I believe that such engines simply had numbers in the normal engine number series.

The body number was stamped on a small aluminium tag pop-riveted to the bulkhead or firewall behind the engine, and may also be found on the back of the dashboard, or the back of trim panels and carpets which of course will often have been replaced on a restored car. It is some times stamped on the left-hand valance panel integral with the bonnet behind the grille. The gearbox number on manual gearboxes was stamped on a boss at the rear on the left-hand side of the casing, and on the top cover in the circle around the core plug. Automatic gearboxes should have the number on a plate on the left-hand side of the casing. In all cases it will be jolly difficult to read the gearbox number with the 'box still in the car.

Rear axles were numbered, although Jaguar did not enter the axle number in the *Car Record Books* and did not quote it on the main identification plate. A tag with the number of teeth of respectively the crown wheel and the pinion was attached under the head of one of the set screws holding the rear cover plate in place. On an XK 150 car with a limited slip differential there should be a separate tag stamped "P/L".

The 3.8 S engine numbers have the prefix VAS, as can be seen stamped here in the cylinder head.

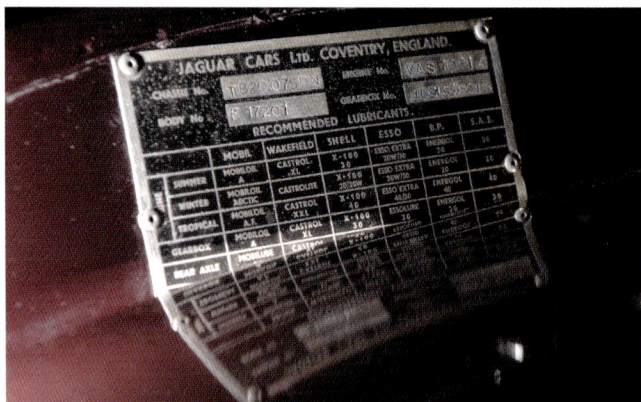

A nice example of an original plate of the later aluminium type.

Another original brass ID plate, this time with the original black infill still intact. Note this is fitted with screws rather than rivets, and I find the slight paint overspray curious.

Here is the engine number of an Xk 140 at the front of the cylinder head valley; it will also be stamped in the cylinder block, on top of the flange where the oil filter is attached.

XKs typically have the body number stamped on a tag riveted to the firewall behind the engine. Since it was fitted before the car was painted, it ended up body-coloured as it is here. The "F" prefix indicates that the body is an open two-seater.

A very important thing to check on any XK is the chassis number stamped in the chassis frame, near the rear engine mount on the left-hand side (nearside). Here, this number is particularly clear but it can be obscured by paint or just dirt. On an XK 140, the S prefix indicates that it is an SE model with the C-type cylinder head.

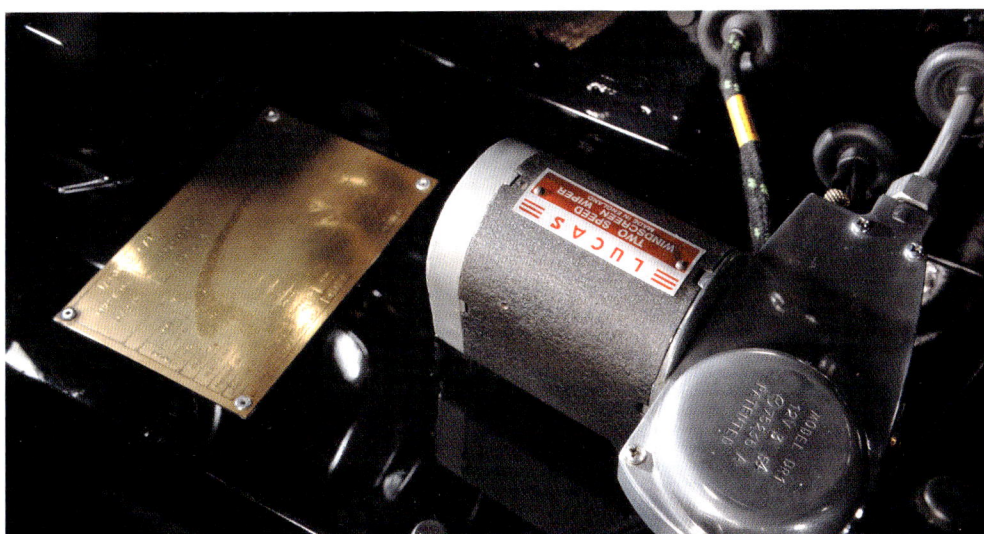

The main ID plate was at this time still of brass, although it was not originally as highly polished as it appears here. The wiper motor with its Lucas label and date stamp "3 54" is also worth noting

Appendix 4:

Colour schemes

The XK 140 initially featured many paint colours which were found on the XK 120, but there were some new shades as well. Colours shared with XK 120 were Battleship Grey, Birch Grey, Black, British Racing Green, Cream, Dove Grey (which was rare), Lavender Grey, Light Grey (which was short-lived and only found on 19 left-hand drive open two-seaters; it seems this was not the same colour as Pearl Grey), Pastel Blue, Pastel Green, Red, and Suede Green. The new colours were Maroon, Pacific Blue, and Pearl Grey, as well as Mediterranean Blue which, although quoted as a standard colour, was used only on five cars.

In 1956, two further colours were introduced, Arbour (or "Arbor") Green and Carmen (or "Carmine") Red, but these were found exclusively on left-hand drive cars, and have been quoted as being for the US market only. Curiously, the introduction of these colours coincided more or less with the introduction of the automatic gearbox.

At the very end of production in 1956, small numbers of left-hand drive open two-seaters were finished in the new colours which were introduced generally on the XK 150, these being Claret, Cornish Grey, Cotswold Blue, Imperial Maroon, Indigo Blue, Mist Grey and Sherwood Green. These colours were however found on only 46 XK 140 cars altogether.

The normal trim colours on the XK 140 were Biscuit, Black, Blue, Dark Blue, Duo-Blue (i.e. seats in two different blue colours), Grey, Red, Suede Green and Tan. Furthermore, used on such small numbers of cars that they may not qualify for the description "standard" were Biscuit and Red (two-tone combination), Light Blue, and White. So, two-tone interiors were found on the XK 140!

Many cars had trim with a contrast piping colour, the one most frequently found being Dark Blue piped Light Blue, but there were many others. It should be noted while that the *Car Record Books* appear to distinguish between *three* blue trim colours, i.e. Blue, Dark Blue, and Light Blue, it is entirely possible that there was some confusion here, and that Blue and Light Blue may be the same colour, and indeed the same as the Pale Blue trim colour which was featured on some XK 140 colour charts.

The standard hood colours were Black, Blue, Fawn, French Grey, Gunmetal and Sand, which had all been found on the XK 120.

XK 140 OTS

Paint colour	Trim colour	Black	Blue	Fawn	French Grey	Gunmetal	Sand	Other or n/r	Total
Arbour Green	Biscuit			4	8		16		28
Arbour Green	Black	6		1	1		2		10
Arbour Green	Suede Green				7		26		33
Battleship Grey	Grey	6				6			12
Battleship Grey	Red	21			1	49		1	72
Birch Grey	Black	18							18
Birch Grey	Red	62			58	2		1	123
Black	Biscuit	1					20		21
Black	Black	30				4			34
Black	Grey	25			1	4			30
Black	Red	256			45	22	48		371
British Racing Green	Biscuit	4	19						23
British Racing Green	Suede Green	8	10		6	18		1	43
British Racing Green	Tan	9	9		1	17	1		37
Carmen Red	Black	115							115
Carmen Red	Red	11	1						12

Paint colour	Trim colour	Hood colours							Total
		Black	Blue	Fawn	French Grey	Gunmetal	Sand	Other or n/r	
Cream	Black	317	2	7	6	1			333
Cream	Dark Blue		51					1	52
Cream	Red	457		50			1	1	509
Dove Grey	Suede Green			2	17				19
Lavender Grey	Biscuit			18					18
Lavender Grey	Red	3		4	7				14
Lavender Grey	Suede Green			4			23		27
Light Grey	Dark Blue		12						12
Maroon	Biscuit	6		23			15		44
Maroon	Grey	11			3				14
Pacific Blue	Blue	1	14		5	1			21
Pacific Blue	Grey	1	8		2	1			12
Pacific Blue	Red	1	31		2		3		37
Pastel Blue	Blue	25	17	50	18	4	3		117
Pastel Blue	Dark Blue		67		2			2	71
Pastel Blue	Duo-Blue		8	16	28			1	53
Pastel Blue	Red	60	26	3	32	3	2		126
Pastel Green	Biscuit			25				1	26
Pastel Green	Red	8		5					13
Pastel Green	Suede Green	6		19	16		3		44
Pastel Green	Tan	1		1	2		25		29
Pearl Grey	Black	74	1		1	6		1	83
Pearl Grey	Blue	2	6		2				10
Pearl Grey	Dark Blue	1	45			14			60
Pearl Grey	Red	109			20	39	4		172
Red	Biscuit	12		23	2		3		40
Red	Black	162			9	6			177
Red	Grey	11				2			13
Red	Red	16		6			1		23
Suede Green	Suede Green				31	1		2	34
		1856	288	300	333	200	196	12	3185

This accounts for 95 per cent of all XK 140 two-seaters. Of the remaining 171 cars, 80 cars were finished in "non standard" combinations of standard paint and trim colours, none of which was used on more than seven cars, 46 were LHD cars finished in the new XK 150 colours at the end of production, four of these as well as 38 others had special trim colours (see below), two were finished in the supposedly standard colour of Mediterranean Blue, both with Blue trim and a Black hood, three were in special paint colours (see below; one of these also had special trim) and the last two cars were chassis-only deliveries.

XK 140 FHC
Paint colour

Paint colour	Biscuit	Black	Blue	Dark Blue	Duo-blue	Grey	Red	Suede Green	Tan	Total
Arbour Green	12	8				1		32		53
Battleship Grey	7		3	3		26	147		2	188
Birch Grey	3	2	6			8	166			185
Black	24	11	1			24	319	3	22	404
British Racing Green	23					2	6	132	57	220
Carmen Red	3	42				2	5			52
Cream	5	138	4	42	2		314	6	1	512
Dove Grey	4						9		11	24

Paint colour	Trim colours									
	Biscuit	Black	Blue	Dark Blue	Duo-blue	Grey	Red	Suede Green	Tan	Total
Lavender Grey	3	1					24	14	3	45
Maroon	66	11	1			7	20			105
Mediterranean Blue			1	1						2
Pacific Blue	4	1	29	8		33	31		1	107
Pastel Blue	1	1	129	72	4	2	92			301
Pastel Green	11					1	4	67	2	85
Pearl Grey		46	29	25		4	179	1	2	286
Red	36	71				4	23	1		135
Suede Green	10					1		62	3	76
	212	332	203	151	6	115	1339	318	104	2780

This table includes all of the XK 140 fixed-heads finished in combinations of standard paint and trim colours. Of the remaining 29 cars, 12 had standard paint colours with special trim (see below), while for one car the trim colour is not recorded, nine were chassis-only deliveries, six cars were finished in special paint colours (see below; two of these also had special trim), and for one car the colour scheme was not recorded at all, this was 804005 allocated to the Experimental Department.

XK 140 DHC

Paint colour	Trim colour	Hood colours							
		Black	Blue	Fawn	French Grey	Gunmetal	Sand	Other, or n/r	Total
Arbour Green	Biscuit			3	8		14		25
Arbour Green	Suede Green						22		22
Battleship Grey	Red	34	1			59	2	1	97
Birch Grey	Red	56		2	41	3			102
Black	Biscuit	15	1	8	1		14	1	40
Black	Black	19		1			1	1	22
Black	Grey	9			1	1	1		12
Black	Red	237		1	36	14	53	1	342
Black	Tan	22		2			1		25
British Racing Green	Biscuit	2		8	2	1	3		16
British Racing Green	Suede Green	35		7	1	15	2		60
British Racing Green	Tan	12		7	1	15	11		46
Carmen Red	Black	82							82
Carmen Red	Red	10	1						11
Cream	Black	228		1	1		1	1	232
Cream	Blue	3	12	3					18
Cream	Dark Blue		33	1					34
Cream	Red	344	1	29	1		1	1	377
Cream	Suede Green	1		1	11		1		14
Lavender Grey	Red			20	1		4		25
Lavender Grey	Suede Green	2		5	2		1		10
Maroon	Biscuit	5		23	2		44	1	75
Maroon	Red	9					4		13
Pacific Blue	Blue		17		5	3	1		26
Pacific Blue	Grey	3	28	1	3	2			37
Pacific Blue	Red	3	41		8				52
Pastel Blue	Blue	20	56	8	39	4	3		130
Pastel Blue	Dark Blue		63		2			2	67
Pastel Blue	Duo-Blue	1	4		18				23
Pastel Blue	Red	51	28	2	34	1	3		119

XK 140 DHC

Paint colour	Trim colour	Black	Blue	Fawn	French Grey	Gunmetal	Sand	Other, or n/r	Total
					Hood colours				
Pastel Green	Biscuit			11			1	1	13
Pastel Green	Suede Green	6		23	15				44
Pearl Grey	Black	38	1			2			41
Pearl Grey	Blue	3	15		1	2		1	22
Pearl Grey	Dark Blue		27		2	3			32
Pearl Grey	Red	94	3	4	11	41			153
Red	Biscuit	8		23			2		33
Red	Black	97							97
Red	Red	7		1			5		13
Suede Green	Suede Green	5		2	37		1		45
		1461	332	197	284	167	195	11	2647

As for the open two-seaters, this table includes 95 per cent of all dropheads. Of the remaining 144 cars, 108 had non-standard combinations of otherwise standard paint and trim colours, 21 had special trim colours and for one car the trim colour is not recorded, eleven cars were in very rare paint colours (ten in Dove Grey and a single Mediterranean Blue car) and the last three cars were in special paint colours (see below).

The twelve XK 140 cars finished in special paint colours were as follows:

Model	Chassis no	Paint	Trim	Hood
OTS RHD	S 800010 DN	Ault & Wiborg Blue	Blue	Black PVC
OTS RHD	800021 DN	Special Red	Red	Fawn
OTS RHD	S 800073	Italian Racing Red	Biscuit and Red	Fawn
FHC RHD	804004	Dark Blue	n/r	
FHC RHD	804068	Primer	n/r	
FHC RHD	804082 DN	Winchester Green, Parsons	Special Biscuit	
FHC RHD	S 804193	Pastel Green metallic	Suede Green	
FHC RHD	S 804635 DN	Valentine's Blue	Biscuit	
FHC LHD	815414 BW	Canary Yellow	Black piped Yellow	
DHC RHD	807112	Dual Grey	Grey	Black
DHC RHD	S 807368 DN	Valentine's Blue	Biscuit	Black
DHC RHD	S 807400	Circassian Blue, Rolls-Royce	Grey	Blue

The cars with special trim, apart from those with Light Blue (27 cars), Biscuit and Red duo-tone (22 cars) and White trim (21 cars), were as follows:

Model	Chassis no	Paint	Trim	Hood
OTS LHD	S 810276	Cream	Black and White	Black
OTS LHD	S 810277	Cream	Black and White	Black
OTS LHD	811404	Cream	Black and White	Black
OTS LHD	S 811976 DN	Black	Black and White	Black
FHC RHD	804082 DN	Winchester Green, Parsons	Special Biscuit	
FHC RHD	S 804304	Cream	Special Green	
FHC LHD	815414 BW	Canary Yellow	Black piped Yellow	
DHC LHD	S 817486 DN	Cream	Black and White	Black

Hoods in special colours or materials were found on the following cars:

Model	Chassis no	Paint	Trim	Hood
OTS RHD	S 800001 DN	Cream	Duo-Blue	Dark Blue
OTS RHD	S 800010 DN	Ault & Wiborg Blue	Blue	Black PVC
OTS RHD	800063 DN	Cream	Red	White PVC
OTS LHD	811893	Pastel Blue	Blue	Dark Blue
DHC RHD	S 807019 DN	Black	Biscuit	Biscuit GOJ PVC no.2
DHC RHD	807110	Cream	Red	Black vynide
DHC RHD	807132 DN	Pearl Grey	Dark Blue piped Red	Dark Blue
DHC RHD	807167 DN	Cream	Red	Black PVC
DHC RHD	807180 DN	Cream	Red	White tonneau cover material
DHC RHD	S 807190 DN	Black	Red	Black PVC
DHC RHD	807200 DN	Suede Green	Suede Green	Fawn PVC
DHC LHD	S 818506	Pastel Blue	Blue	Dark Blue
DHC LHD	818817	Red	Black piped White	Black piped White
DHC LHD	S 818957	Black	Black piped Red	Tan

Finally it is worth listing those few XK 140s which were finished in Mediterranean Blue:

Model	Chassis no	Paint	Trim	Hood
OTS RHD	800007	Mediterranean Blue	Blue	Black
OTS RHD	800018	Mediterranean Blue	Blue	Black
FHC RHD	804183	Mediterranean Blue	Blue	
FHC RHD	S 804668 DN	Mediterranean Blue	Dark Blue	
DHC LHD	S 817380	Mediterranean Blue	Blue	Blue

Summary of XK 140 colours:

Paint colours	OTS RHD	OTS LHD	FHC RHD	FHC LHD	DHC RHD	DHC LHD	Total
Arbour Green		73		53		57	183
Battleship Grey	2	88	113	76	42	67	388
Birch Grey	3	142	91	94	36	82	448
Black	5	460	120	285	60	391	1321
British Racing Green	17	90	160	60	70	58	455
Carmen Red		136		52		100	288
Claret		6					6
Cornish Grey		4					4
Cotswold Blue		20					20
Cream	15	901	68	447	73	607	2111
Dove Grey		21	15	9	5	5	55
Imperial Maroon		7					7
Indigo Blue		2					2
Lavender Grey	1	60	15	30	16	24	146
Light Grey		19					19
Maroon		72	27	78	41	56	274
Mediterranean Blue	2		2			1	5
Mist Grey		4					4
Pacific Blue		86	19	91	8	114	318
Pastel Blue	9	365	60	243	42	308	1027
Pastel Green	1	112	13	72	8	56	262
Pearl Grey	4	322	75	212	45	211	869

Paint colours	OTS RHD	OTS LHD	FHC RHD	FHC LHD	DHC RHD	DHC LHD	Total
Red	7	253	12	125	9	141	547
Sherwood Green		3					3
Suede Green	4	35	45	31	22	33	170
Specials	3		5	1	3		12
n/a (chs only) or n/r	1	1	3	7			12
	74	3282	843	1966	480	2311	8956

Trim colours	OTS RHD	OTS LHD	FHC RHD	FHC LHD	DHC RHD	DHC LHD	Total
Biscuit	3	211	58	155	58	171	656
Bisc & Red (special)	7	10	0	2	2	1	22
Black	1	788	4	328	7	486	1614
Blue	6	151	88	115	61	147	568
Dark Blue	1	214	10	141	8	130	504
Duo-Blue	7	53	0	6	2	24	92
Grey	1	90	49	66	20	64	290
Light Blue (special)		17	1	4	1	4	27
Red	26	1479	390	949	208	1101	4153
Suede Green	11	192	158	161	77	121	720
Tan	10	67	76	28	35	49	265
White (special)		5	1	3		12	21
Other specials		4	2	1		1	8
n/a or n/r	1	1	6	7	1		16
	74	3282	843	1966	480	2311	8956

Hood colours	OTS RHD	OTS LHD	DHC RHD	DHC LHD	Total	
Black	31	1903	189	1322	3445	Incl. Black PVC or Vynide
Blue	9	314	44	301	668	Incl. Dark Blue
Fawn	9	313	53	174	549	Incl. Fawn PVC
French Grey	10	342	67	245	664	
Gunmetal	12	195	71	107	385	
Sand	1	203	50	156	410	
Other	1		2	1	4	Incl. Biscuit, Tan, White
n/a or n/r	1	12	4	5	22	
	74	3282	480	2311	6147	

Matters were simplified for the XK 150, in that the same range of twelve paint colours was used from 1957 to 1960, without any variations for individual models. They were: Black, British Racing Green, Carmen Red, Claret, Cornish Grey, Cotswold Blue, Cream, Imperial Maroon, Indigo Blue, Mist Grey, Pearl Grey and Sherwood Green. The only exception was Claret, always a rare colour, which, depending on body style, was discontinued before the end pf production. That Claret, and Imperial Maroon, were not found on any right-hand drive open two-seaters, was as much to do with the limited production figure for this model as anything else.

On the whole, the colour range was now rather sombre, with three greys and a blue-grey, two dark reds, two dark greens and a dark blue, apart from Black; only Carmen Red and Cream were bright sports car colours. The explanation is that the XK 150 used the standard Jaguar colour range, which was now geared to the luxury saloon car market. Two-tone colour schemes were theoretically available, but it does not appear that any cars were finished in two-tone schemes.

Trim colours were mostly the same as found on the XK 140, with the addition of Beige and Maroon (neither of which was common), while on the XK 150 it is almost certain that Blue and Light Blue in the *Car Record Books* now refer to the same colour. Two-tone trim was no longer offered. Again, many cars are listed with a contrast colour for the piping. More cars were now fitted with White trim, without this ever being quoted as a standard colour; it is possible that White was favoured as a trim colour for show cars. Hoods were available in the same six colours as on the XK 140.

XK 150 OTS

Paint colours	Trim colours	Hood colours							
		Black	Blue	Fawn	French Grey	Gunmetal	Sand	Other, or n/r	Total
Black	Black	34		1		2	8		45
Black	Red	193		3	11	3	19		229
Black	Tan	7					36		43
British Racing Green	Suede Green	20		2		14	14		50
British Racing Green	Tan	4		5		14	25		48
Carmen Red	Biscuit	8					2		10
Carmen Red	Black	186		2	2	1	8	1	200
Carmen Red	Red	85		10	4		3		102
Claret	Red	12	1				4		17
Cornish Grey	Dark Blue	3	7		2				12
Cornish Grey	Light Blue		11		2				13
Cornish Grey	Red	50			14				64
Cotswold Blue	Dark Blue	4	55		2				61
Cotswold Blue	Grey	4	16		2				22
Cotswold Blue	Light Blue	4	32		4		1	1	42
Cotswold Blue	Red	15	66	1	14		7		103
Cream	Black	176		28	3				207
Cream	Dark Blue		30	1	4				35
Cream	Light Blue	3	21	4	2				30
Cream	Red	313	4	75	3		6	1	402
Imperial Maroon	Black	14			1		1		16
Imperial Maroon	Maroon	10		1					11
Imperial Maroon	Red	8					2		10
Indigo Blue	Dark Blue	3	3			2	2		10
Indigo Blue	Grey	2	6		2	2			12
Indigo Blue	Light Blue		8			2	1	1	12
Indigo Blue	Red	3	20		2		3		28
Mist Grey	Black	11			2				13
Mist Grey	Dark Blue	2	11		2				15
Mist Grey	Light Blue	4	3		2				9
Mist Grey	Red	49		1	18				68
Pearl Grey	Black	23			6	4			33
Pearl Grey	Dark Blue	4	15		3				22
Pearl Grey	Grey	8					2		10
Pearl Grey	Light Blue	4	3		6				13
Pearl Grey	Red	83	1	1	26	12			123
Sherwood Green	Suede Green	1		2	2	1	18		24
Sherwood Green	Tan	1			1		12		14
		1351	313	137	142	57	174	4	2178

This accounts for 96 per cent of all open two-seaters. Of the remaining 89 cars, 56 were finished in non-standard combinations of standard paint and trim colours, none of which was used on more than seven cars. Seven cars were finished in special paint colours, of which one also had special trim in white. The remaining 26 cars had special trim, of which 24 had white trim.

XK 150 FHC
Paint colours   **Trim colours**

	Beige	Biscuit	Black	Blue	Dark Blue	Grey	Light Blue	Maroon	Red	Suede Green	Tan	Total
Black	12	12	52			27	1		489	2	55	650
British Racing Green	19	24	2			2			8	249	120	424
Carmen Red	3	17	169			6			78		1	274
Claret		1	11			3		1	15			31
Cornish Grey		1	8	21	27	25	7		166		1	256
Cotswold Blue		1	4	29	178	117	22		122		1	474
Cream	4	7	282	6	52	2	18	1	596	2	8	978
Imperial Maroon		13	13			11		25	44		1	107
Indigo Blue		6	1	12	22	25	27		43			136
Mist Grey			10	23	35	21	21		232	1	2	345
Pearl Grey		1	39	21	77	17	33		313	1		502
Sherwood Green	5	6	1			10			1	135	59	217
	43	89	592	112	391	266	129	27	2107	390	248	4394

Of the remaining 63 fixed-heads, 28 were in special paint colours of which one also had special (white) trim, 26 others had special trim including 23 with white trim, and finally there were nine chassis only deliveries.

XK 150 DHC
Paint colours   **Trim colours**   **Hood colours**

Paint colours	Trim colours	Black	Blue	Fawn	French Grey	Gunmetal	Sand	Other, or n/r	Total
Black	Biscuit	4		2			4		10
Black	Black	30		1		1	2		34
Black	Grey	7				1		1	9
Black	Red	186		11	11	10	51	1	270
Black	Tan	16		1			14		31
British Racing Green	Biscuit	1		4		1	5		11
British Racing Green	Suede Green	67		4	10	37	19	1	138
British Racing Green	Tan	17		2		18	30		67
Carmen Red	Biscuit	8		1			1		10
Carmen Red	Black	144	1		3	1	1		150
Carmen Red	Red	74		7			2	1	84
Cornish Grey	Grey	5			3	1			9
Cornish Grey	Light Blue	2	3		3				8
Cornish Grey	Red	42	1	1	14	9			67
Cotswold Blue	Blue		3		6				9
Cotswold Blue	Dark Blue	7	66		2				75
Cotswold Blue	Grey	19	20		1	2			42
Cotswold Blue	Light Blue	4	22		2		1		29
Cotswold Blue	Red	17	68	4	7		8		104
Cream	Biscuit	2		5			1		8
Cream	Black	191		1	2		1	2	197
Cream	Dark Blue	10	48	3					61
Cream	Light Blue	3	29	3	1				36
Cream	Red	394	3	32	1	1	13	2	446
Imperial Maroon	Biscuit			2			6		8
Imperial Maroon	Black	14					1		15
Imperial Maroon	Maroon	8					10		18
Imperial Maroon	Red	6					8	1	15
Indigo Blue	Dark Blue	1	10		1		1	1	14

Paint colours	Trim colours	Hood colours							
		Black	Blue	Fawn	French Grey	Gunmetal	Sand	Other, or n/r	Total
Indigo Blue	Grey	3	15		3	3			24
Indigo Blue	Light Blue	7	16		1	1			25
Indigo Blue	Red	14	11		4	1	3		33
Mist Grey	Dark Blue	6	2		2	1			11
Mist Grey	Grey	6	1		3		1	1	12
Mist Grey	Light Blue	3	1		9				13
Mist Grey	Red	56	1		20	9	1	1	88
Pearl Grey	Black	13			4		1	1	19
Pearl Grey	Dark Blue	9	21		6	1		1	38
Pearl Grey	Light Blue	1	12		11		1		25
Pearl Grey	Red	125	2	2	28	2			159
Sherwood Green	Suede Green	21		4	19	5	21	1	71
Sherwood Green	Tan	2			6	1	10		19
		1545	356	90	183	106	217	15	2512

This accounts for 94 per cent of all dropheads. Of the 160 other cars, there were 109 in other combinations of standard paint and trim colours which includes all the eight dropheads in Claret and the 16 cars with Beige trim, as none of these combinations of paint and trim were found on more than at the most seven cars. There were 30 in special paint colours of which two had special trim including one with white trim, and there were 21 others which had special trim, of which 19 had white trim. (Chassis 837003 changed from Cream to Carmen Red and has been counted as Carmen Red.)

The next table lists all of the 65 XK 150s which were finished in special paint colours:

Model	Chassis no	Exterior paint colour	Interior trim colour	Hood colour
OTS RHD	T 820015 DN	Larch Green cellulose	Biscuit	Fawn
OTS RHD	S 820017 BW	Red (Old XK 140 Red)	Red	Red
OTS RHD	T 820032 DN	Speedwell Blue (Austin?)	Grey	Black
OTS RHD	T 820037 DN	Lavender Grey	Red	French Grey
OTS RHD	T 820066 DN	Post Office Red	White piped Red (front seats), Red (rest) (special)	Black
OTS RHD	T 820067 DN	Shell Grey (Rolls-Royce?)	Suede Green	Black
OTS LHD	T 832012 DN	Crushed Strawberry Red	Red	Black
FHC RHD	S 824010 BW	Pacific Blue	Grey	
FHC RHD	S 824084 DN	Horizon Blue (Austin?)	Red	
FHC RHD	S 824208 DN	Silver Grey	Blue	
FHC RHD	S 824332 DN	Pastel Blue	Blue	
FHC RHD	S 824346 DN	Dove Grey	Tan	
FHC RHD	S 824411 DN	Pastel Blue	Dark Blue	
FHC RHD	S 824473	Circassian Blue (Rolls-Royce)	Grey	
FHC RHD	S 824504 BW	Velvet Green (Rolls-Royce)	Grey	
FHC RHD	S 824644 DN	Metallic Silver cellulose	Light Blue	
FHC RHD	S 824706 BW	Pacific Blue	Dark Blue	
FHC RHD	S 824735 BW	Kensington Blue (Aston Martin)	White piped Dark Blue (special)	
FHC RHD	S 824757 DN	Pastel Blue	Light Blue	
FHC RHD	S 824787 DN	Pure White cellulose	Red	
FHC RHD	T 824897 DN	Red (XK 140 Red)	Light Blue	
FHC RHD	S 824947 DN	Apricot	Black	
FHC RHD	T 824980 DN	Ferrari Red	Black	
FHC RHD	S 825016 BW	Smoke Green (Rolls-Royce)	Suede Green	
FHC RHD	T 825087 DN	Lavender Grey	Red	
FHC RHD	T 825127 DN	Regal Red, Belco	Biscuit	

Model	Chassis no	Exterior paint colour	Interior trim colour	Hood colour
FHC RHD	S 825132 DN	Pastel Blue	Light Blue	
FHC RHD	T 825179 DN	Primrose Yellow (Austin?)	Black	
FHC RHD	S 825232 DN	Metallic Blue	Light Blue	
FHC RHD	S 825267	Pippin Red	Black	
FHC RHD	S 825287 DN	Lavender Grey	Red	
FHC RHD	S 825303 BW	Turquoise, Dockers	Tan	
FHC RHD	T 825306 DN	Battleship Grey	Red	
FHC LHD	S 836628 DN	Pastel Blue	Biscuit	
FHC LHD	S 836633 DN	Pastel Blue	Grey	
DHC RHD	S 827018 DN	Pastel Green	Suede Green	Fawn
DHC RHD	S 827064 BW	Beige Metallic	Red	Fawn
DHC RHD	S 827068 DN	Red (Old XK 140 Red)	Grey	Black
DHC RHD	S 827078	Lavender Grey	Red	French Grey
DHC RHD	S 827139 DN	Empress Blue	Grey	Black
DHC RHD	S 827193 DN	Pure White	Black	Black
DHC RHD	S 827196 DN	Blue	Light Blue	Gunmetal
DHC RHD	S 827225 DN	Pure White	Dark Blue	Blue
DHC RHD	S 827245 DN	Battleship Grey	Red	Gunmetal
DHC RHD	S 827268 BW	Battleship Grey	Red	Gunmetal
DHC RHD	S 827279	Pastel Blue	Dark Blue	Blue
DHC RHD	S 827317	Pastel Blue	White (special)	Black
DHC RHD	S 827320 DN	Corsican Blue, Valentines	Grey Vaumol (special)	Grey (special)
DHC RHD	S 827328 DN	Pastel Blue metallic	Dark Blue	Blue
DHC RHD	T 827345 DN	Pastel Blue	Dark Blue	Blue
DHC RHD	S 827357 DN	Pure White cellulose	Dark Blue	Blue
DHC RHD	S 827373 BW	Pastel Blue	Black	Black
DHC RHD	827378 DN	Lavender Grey	Suede Green	Sand
DHC RHD	S 827454 DN	Midnight Blue, Belco	Grey	Blue
DHC RHD	T 827471 DN	Primrose Yellow (Austin?)	Black	Black
DHC RHD	S 827517 DN	Blue, Domolac	Biscuit	Black
DHC RHD	T 827521 DN	Maroon	Biscuit	Black
DHC RHD	S 827554	Pastel Blue	Light Blue	Blue
DHC RHD	S 827601	Banff Blue	Biscuit	Black
DHC RHD	S 827617	Pastel Blue	Light Blue	Blue
DHC RHD	T 827649 DN	Silver, Zofelac	Red	Black
DHC LHD	S 837872 BW	Alice Blue	Light Blue	French Grey
DHC LHD	S 838235 BW	Birch Grey	Grey	Blue
DHC LHD	T 838317 DN	Silver Grey metallic	Biscuit	Gunmetal
DHC LHD	S 838937 DN	Bronze	Biscuit	Sand

There are colours here from the XK 120 or XK 140, colours from other makes ranging from Rolls-Royce to Austin, and many other colours which I have not been able to pin down. It is interesting that many more customers wanted XK 150s in special colours, than XK 140s or XK 120s.

The next table lists the special trim colours, except for the cars with White trim:

Model	Chassis no	Exterior paint colour	Interior trim colour	Hood colour
OTS RHD	T 820051 DN	Mist Grey	Dark Blue and Grey	Fawn
OTS LHD	T 831834 DN	Carmen Red	Red roll, Biscuit pleating	Fawn
FHC RHD	S 824074	Carmen Red	Cream piped Red	
FHC RHD	T 825227 DN	Cream	Connolly Brushed Black piped White	

Model	Chassis no	Exterior paint colour	Interior trim colour	Hood colour
FHC LHD	S 834145 DN	Cream	Blue pleats and Dark Blue roll	
DHC RHD	S 827117 DN	Pearl Grey	Light Grey	French Grey
DHC RHD	S 827146 BW	Imperial Maroon	Red and Dark Blue piped White	Blue
DHC RHD	S 827320 DN	Corsican Blue, Valentines (special)	Grey Vaumol	Grey (special)

Of 69 cars with White trim, 40 were painted Black, eleven Carmen Red and seven Cream. Eight were various other standard colours (British Racing Green, Cotswold Blue, Indigo Blue and Sherwood Green) while the last three were in special paint colours (see above). 40 cars have trim simply described as "White". 24 had White trim piped Black, and one each had White trim with Dark Blue piping or Red piping. For the last three cars, trim was described as "White Morocco", and one of these had Light Blue piping.

Finally, the cars with special hood colours or materials:

Model	Chassis no	Exterior paint colour	Interior trim colour	Hood colour
OTS RHD	S 820017 BW	Red (Old XK 140 Red) (special)	Red	Red
OTS RHD	S 820072 DN	Indigo Blue	Light Blue	White PVC
OTS RHD	S 820088 DN	Cream	Red	Off-white PVC
OTS LHD	S 830495 DN	Cream	Dark Blue	Dark Blue
DHC RHD	S 827034	Cream	Red	Black PVC
DHC RHD	S 827252 DN	Cream	Red	Blue PVC
DHC RHD	S 827320 DN	Corsican Blue (special)	Grey Vaumol (special)	Grey
DHC RHD	S 827330	British Racing Green	White (special)	White plastic
DHC RHD	S 827346 DN	Mist Grey	Red	Grey
DHC RHD	T 827426 DN	Mist Grey	Grey	Grey PVC no. 4
DHC LHD	S 837384 DN	Sherwood Green	Suede Green	Tan
DHC LHD	T 838167 DN	Black	Red	White plastic
DHC LHD	S 838403 DN	Black	Black	Sand piped Black

Summary of XK 150 colours:

Paint colours	OTS RHD	OTS LHD	FHC RHD	FHC LHD	DHC RHD	DHC LHD	Total
Black	3	337	72	592	24	345	1373
British Racing Green	10	95	243	182	108	123	761
Carmen Red	17	305	50	228	43	211	854
Claret	0	19	3	28	2	6	58
Cornish Grey	3	95	106	150	31	70	455
Cotswold Blue	6	227	158	318	56	204	969
Cream	29	655	167	815	140	625	2431
Imperial Maroon	0	40	51	56	26	36	209
Indigo Blue	3	63	59	78	38	63	304
Mist Grey	4	108	150	195	48	87	592
Pearl Grey	10	193	177	325	84	171	960
Sherwood Green	2	36	105	112	37	64	356
Special	6	1	26	2	26	4	65
n/a or n/r	0	0	2	7	0	0	9
	93	2174	1369	3088	663	2009	9396

Trim colours	OTS RHD	OTS LHD	FHC RHD	FHC LHD	DHC RHD	DHC LHD	Total
Beige	0	0	0	43	0	16	59
Biscuit	4	14	34	58	29	33	172
Black	12	506	41	555	41	393	1548

Trim colours	OTS RHD	OTS LHD	FHC RHD	FHC LHD	DHC RHD	DHC LHD	Total
Blue	0	13	29	84	1	23	150
Dark Blue	4	151	157	236	86	125	759
Grey	4	59	133	137	59	64	456
Light Blue	7	112	75	59	54	86	393
Maroon	0	11	20	7	15	7	60
Red	47	1103	537	1575	231	1046	4539
Suede Green	11	64	241	150	106	109	681
Tan	2	116	95	155	35	90	493
White (special)	1	24	3	21	3	17	69
Other special	1	1	2	1	3	0	8
n/a or n/r	0	0	2	7	0	0	9
	93	2174	1369	3088	663	2009	9396

Hood colours	OTS RHD	OTS LHD	DHC RHD	DHC LHD	Total	
Black	64	1348	349	1266	3027	Incl. Black PVC
Blue	8	317	118	263	706	Incl. Dark Blue, Blue PVC
Fawn	6	136	32	70	244	
French Grey	4	142	86	119	351	
Gunmetal	4	53	36	84	177	
Sand	3	177	34	200	414	Incl. Sand piped Black
Special	3	0	4	2	9	Grey, Red, Off-white, Tan and White; see above
n/a or n/r	1	1	4	5	11	
	93	2174	663	2009	4939	

Paint colour references:

All XK 140s and XK 150s were finished in synthetic paint which had been introduced by Jaguar in late 1952. The original paint suppliers were British Domolac (BD) or Pinchin Johnson (PJ). The table below gives the original Jaguar paint codes, and equivalents from paint suppliers. The ICI and Glasso codes are still widely recognised today. Several of the paints underwent slight changes during the production run, indicated by a suffix to the original code, or an alternative code number; it is thought these were changes to chemical composition, rather than shade changes. Other paint manufacturers will use their own codes but most publish a catalogue indexed by make of car and group/name of colour. Many colours will also be available from American paint manufacturers (PPG/Ditzler, Dupont, and Glasso/Rinshed Mason).

Colour name	BD code	PJ code	ICI code(s); PPG/Nexa	Glasso GIP code
Arbour (Arbor) Green	Q.1191, Q.1191/1		3098	
Battleship Grey	Q.1075, Q.1075/1	J.875	2378 (2677, 3159?)	16203
Birch Grey	Q.1079, Q.1079/1	J.865	2396	
Black	Q.1073	J.869	122	1073, 5030
British Racing Green	Q.1076	J.860	2539	16712
Carmen (Carmine) Red	Q.1190		3097	21948
Claret	Q.1230, Q.1230/1	J.1015	5176	19227
Cornish Grey	Q.1236		4178	19164
Cotswold Blue	Q.1234		3318	19224
Cream (Old English White)		J.863, J.863/C	2680 (5619?)	18442
Dove Grey		J.861	2395 (2879, 2929?)	
Imperial Maroon	Q.1229, Q.1229/1	J.1011	3311 (2280, 2473?)	18475
Indigo Blue	Q.1233		3312	19226, 27153
Lavender Grey	Q.1072, Q.1072/1	J.871	2377 (2926, 3402?)	

Colour name	BD code	PJ code	ICI code(s); PPG/Nexa	Glasso GIP code
Light Grey			3152	30829 (?)
Maroon (XK 140)	Q.1135, Q.1135/1, Q.1135/2			3152 (2925?)
Mediterranean Blue			2927	
Mist Grey	Q.1235	J.809	3154	19180
Pacific Blue	Q.1132, Q.1132/1		2928	
Pastel Blue (non metallic)		J.867	2674	17069
Pastel Green (non metallic)	Q.1081, Q.1081/1	J.877	2656	
Pearl Grey	Q.1129, Q.1129/1, Q.1129/2		2931 (3108?)	18043
Red (XK 140 red)	Q.1089		2798 (3097?)	18431 (?)
Sherwood Green	Q.1231		3146	19225
Suede Green	Q.1080, Q.1080/1	J.873	2397	16256

See Jaguar *Service Bulletin* nos.113, 136, 185 (Apr 1956), 205 (Jan 1957), 238 (Feb 1958), N.4 (May 1960); Roger Mills in *XK Gazette* nos.84, 85, Sep and Oct 2004; John Elmgreen in *XK Gazette* nos.33 Jun 2000, 63 Dec 2002

An XK 140 two-seater, photographed in the factory with stacks of new bodies in the background, just to prove the existence of two-tone trim on this model.

Appendix 5:

Coventry registration marks 1954-60

The following is a list of the letter combinations issued for Coventry-registered motor vehicles during the XK 140 and XK 150 years:

Letters	From	To	Notes	Letters	From	To	Notes
NRW	1954/06	1955/04	HDES*	UWK	1958/07	1959/07	HDES
NWK	1955/04	1955/12	HDES	UVC	1958/12	1959/05	HDES
NVC	1955/12	1956/06	HDES	UKV	1959/05	1959/07	HDES
NKV	1956/06	1957/03	HDES	VDU	1957/08	1957/10	
PRW	1954/09	1954/11		VHP	1957/10	1957/11	
PWK	1954/11	1954/12		VRW	1957/11	1958/01	
PVC	1954/12	1955/02		VWK	1958/01	1958/03	
PKV	1955/02	1955/03		VVC	1958/03	1958/04	
RDU	1955/03	1955/04		VKV	1958/04	1958/05	
RHP	1955/04	1955/06		WDU	1958/05	1958/06	
RRW	1955/06	1955/07		WHP	1958/06	1958/08	
RWK	1955/07	1955/08		WRW	1958/08	1958/09	
RVC	1955/08	1955/10		WWK	1958/09	1958/11	
RKV	1955/10	1955/11		WVC	1958/11	1958/12	
SDU	1955/11	1956/01		WKV	1958/12	1959/02	
SHP	1956/01	1956/03		XDU	1959/01	1959/03	
SRW	1956/03	1956/04		XHP	1959/03	1959/04	
SWK	1956/04	1956/06		XRW	1959/04	1959/05	
SVC	1956/06	1956/07		XWK	1959/05	1959/06	
SKV	1956/07	1956/10		XVC	1959/06	1959/06	
TDU	1956/10	1956/12		XKV	1959/06	1959/07	
THP	1956/12	1957/02		YDU	1959/07	1959/09	
TRW	1957/02	1957/04		YHP	1959/09	1959/10	
TWK	1957/04	1957/05		YRW	1959/10	1959/11	
TVC	1957/05	1957/07		YWK	1959/11	1959/12	
TKV	1957/07	1957/08		YVC	1959/12	1960/01	
UDU	1957/03	1957/08	HDES	YKV	1960/01	1960/02	
UHP	1957/08	1958/03	HDES	DU reversed**	1959/07	1961/09	HDES
URW	1958/03	1959/05	HDES	HP reversed	1960/02	1961/02	

*HDES: Home Delivery Export Scheme, relating to new vehicles sold tax-free to overseas visitors (or UK residents moving abroad), on the condition that these cars were exported within 12 months, also known as "Personal Export Delivery". In such cases, a pink rather than a buff Log Book was issued.
**Reversed: Numbers (from 1 to 9999) before the letters.

Cars registered locally by Jaguar Cars Limited fell mostly in two categories: Firstly the cars used by the company itself (prototypes, experimental cars, press cars and demonstrators, and finally company cars for senior management). Secondly, cars sold directly by Jaguar to private customers, but these were almost inevitably Personal Export Delivery cars; ordinary home market customers would place an order in the usual way through a dealer or distributor, and the cars would be registered in the locality of the selling dealer, or the first owner.

The PED cars were often delivered to their first owners at the factory, but some were ordered and delivered through Henlys in London, or provincial distributors, or in case of the frequent sales to US Service Personnel, via the US Forces Post Exhange UK Exchange Service. Some PED cars were direct sales, others were consigned to the overseas importer or distributor through whom the order had been placed, even if the point of delivery was in the UK.

Jaguar in common with other motor manufacturers and traders was pre-allocated batches of registration marks, which means that the dates of first registration for individual cars do not completely follow the sequence of numbers from 1 to 999. The Jaguars sold through the local distributor S H Newsome were also registered in Coventry, but there were far fewer of these than there were cars registered by the company.

There are two sources for details of Coventry registered cars. One is the Coventry Transport Museum, which keeps the original issue ledgers of Coventry registrations from 1949 to 1975. The other is the Coventry City Archive, which keeps the "cancellation cards" for Coventry registrations for the period 1921 to 1963. A "cancellation card" was the final (and only) record kept by the registration authority, once a vehicle was declared exported or scrapped, and the log book returned (if it was), or if the vehicle had not been taxed for five years. If a vehicle continued to exist and to be taxed, there will not be a cancellation card. On the other hand, there are cancellation cards for most of the PED cars, which were exported before their year of grace was out.

These original registration records are interesting as they contain the chassis number and engine number, and (on the cancellation cards) colour, first registered owner, last known owner, and date of expiry of the last tax disc. If you have a Jaguar with a Coventry registration or have any interest in these records, you can make an appointment to visit the archive or museum to have a look at the record for your car.

The sources for the information above are *Glass's Index of Registration Numbers 1929-1965* (1965), Philip Riden's *How to trace the History of Your Car* (second edition 1998) and L H Newall's *A History of Motor Vehicle Registration in the United Kingdom* (third edition 2008).

Bibliography

Primary unpublished sources:
In the JDHT archive: *Car Record Books*; Experimental Department notebooks; Jaguar sales statistics; photographic department negative registers; SS Cars Limited board minutes; RAC and FIA recognition and homologation forms; in Coventry City Archives: Registration cards for cancelled registrations; in Coventry Transport Museum: Coventry Registration Ledgers.

Primary printed sources – contemporary newspapers, journals and annuals:
Annual Automobile Review (Automobile Year) (Switzerland); *Auto Age* (USA); *Automobil Revue – Katalog-Nummer* (Switzerland); *Automobile Quarterly* (USA); *Autosport*; *Das Auto Motor und Sport* (Germany); *High Road*; *Hobby* (Germany); *Hot Car*; *Jaguar Journal* (USA); *Motor Life* (USA); *Motor Racing*; *Motor Sport*; *New York Times* (USA); *News Exchange* (Nuffield Exports magazine); *Road and Track* (USA); *Speed Age* (USA); *Sports Car World* (Australia); *Sports Cars and Specials* (Australia); *Sports Illustrated* (USA); *Sportscar Illustrated* (USA); *Quattroruote* (Italy); *The Autocar*; *The Motor*; *The Motor Industry of Great Britain* (SMM&T annual handbook); *The Motor World*; *The Sunday Express*; *The Times Survey of the British Motor Car Industry*

Published papers:
W M Heynes "The Jaguar Engine" (published in *The Autocar* 24 Apr 1953, *The Motor* 15 and 22 Apr 1953); W M Heynes "Milestones in the Life of an Automobile Engineer" (1960)

Jaguar Cars Limited publications:
Jaguar XK 120 and Mark VII Service Manual (with supplements for later models); *Spare Parts Catalogues* for Jaguar XK 140 and XK 150 models; *Service Bulletins*; *Spare Parts Bulletins*; price lists and dealer lists; XK 140 and XK 150 sales brochures and handbooks

Secondary sources – published books:
Adams, Ronnie *From Craigantlet to Monte Carlo* (Newtownards n.d.)
Anon *50 Years of American Automobiles from 1939* (Yeovil 1989)
Bellamy, Roland C *Who's Who in the Motor Industry* (Grimsby or London, various years)
Boyce, Jeremy *Jaguar XK Series – The Complete Story* (Marlborough 1996)
Burgess-Wise, David *Ghia – Ford's Carozzeria* (London 1985)
Clausager, Anders *MG Saloon Cars* (Bideford 1998)
Clausager, Anders *Original Austin-Healey* (Bideford 1990 and later editions)
Clausager, Anders *The Jaguar XK 120 in Detail* (Shebbear, Devon 2006)
Clausager, Anders "The Swinging Sixties" in *Britain's Motor Industry* (Yeovil 1995)
Cognet, Michel and Viart, Bernard *Jaguar A Tradition of Sports Cars* (Yeovil 1985)
Dugdale, John *Jaguar in America* (Otego, NY 1993 and later edition)
Dussek, Ian *H.R.G. The Sportsman's Ideal* (Croydon 1985)
Dunnett, Peter *The Decline of the British Motor Industry* (London 1980)
Elmgreen, John and McGrath, Terry *The Jaguar XK in Australia* (Sydney 1985)
Fagiuoli, Gianfranco and Gerosa, Guido *Zagato* (Rome 1969)
Frostick, Michael *The Jaguar Tradition* (London 1973)
Harvey, Chris *The Jaguar XK* (Oxford 1978)
Georgano, GN (ed.) *The Beaulieu Encyclopaedia of the Automobile – Coachbuilding* (London 2001)
Georgano, GN (ed.) *The Encyclopaedia of Motor Sport* (London 1971)

Glass's Index of Registration Numbers 1929-1965 (Weybridge, Surrey 1965)
Greggio, Luciano *Bertone 90 Years* (Vimodrone, Milano 2002)
Jodard, Paul *Raymond Loewy* (London 1992)
Kimberley, Earl of (Wodehouse, John), with Roberts, Charles *The Whim of the Wheel* (London 2001)
Kittler, Eberhard *Essential BMW Roadsters & Cabriolets* (Bideford 1996)
Mennem, Patrick *Jaguar – An Illustrated History* (Marlborough 1991)
Moity, Christian and Tubbs, D B *The Le Mans 24-hour Race 1949-1973* (Lausanne 1974, and Radnor, PA 1975)
Montagu of Beaulieu, with Sedgwick, Michael *Jaguar – A Biography* (London 1961 and later editions)
Montagu of Beaulieu, with Sedgwick, Michael *Lost Causes of Motoring, Europe vol.2* (London 1969)
Newall, L H with Harrison, J *A History of Motor Vehicle Registration in the United Kingdom* (third edition, Scarborough 2008)
Newcomb, T P, and Spurr, R T *A Technical History of the Motor Car* (Bristol and New York 1989)
Nickols, Ian and Karslake, Kent *Motoring Entente* (London 1956)
Parker, Paul *Jaguar at Le Mans* (Yeovil 2001)
Porter, Philip *Original Jaguar XK* (second edition, Bideford 1998)
Porter, Philip *The Jaguar Scrapbook* (Yeovil 1989)
Porter, Philip *Jaguar E-type – The definitive history* (Yeovil 1989 and later editions)
Porter, Philip *Jaguar Scrapbook* (Tenbury Wells 2006)
Porter, Philip and Skilleter, Paul *Sir William Lyons* (Yeovil 2001)
Pfannmüller, Matthias *Jaguar Coupés* (Bruckmühl, Germany 2005)
Riden, Philip *How to trace the History of Your Car* (second edition, Cardiff 1998)
Robson, Graham *A to Z British Cars 1945-1980* (Shebbear, Devon 2006)
Robson, Graham *Cars in the UK Vol. 1 1945-1970* (Croydon 1996)
Robson, Graham *Monte Carlo Rally – The Golden Age* (Shebbear, Devon 2007)
Sedgwick, Michael *The Motor Car 1946-1956* (London 1979)
Sedgwick, Michael and Gillies, Mark *A-Z of cars 1945-1970* (Twickenham, Middlesex 1986)
Shute, Nevil *On the Beach* (London 1957)
Skilleter, Paul *Jaguar Saloon Cars* (Yeovil 1980 and later editions)
Skilleter, Paul *Jaguar Sports Cars* (Yeovil 1975 and later editions)
Skilleter, Paul *Norman Dewis of Jaguar* (Barton on Sea, Hampshire 2007)
Skilleter, Paul *The Jaguar XKs – A Collector's Guide* (London 1981, and later editions)
Smith, Julian *Nevil Shute* (London 1976; Kerthonkson, NY 2002)
Urban, Roland *Les Métamorphoses du Jaguar* (Cannes and Paris 1993)
Viart, Bernard *Jaguar XK – Le Grand Livre* (Paris 1993)
Viart, Bernard *Jaguar XK – la compétition sur route dans les années 1950* (Boulogne-Billancourt, France 2006)
Whyte, Andrew *Jaguar Sports Racing and Works Competition Cars to 1953* (Yeovil 1982)
Whyte, Andrew *Jaguar Sports Racing and Works Competition Cars from 1954* (Yeovil 1987)
Whyte, Andrew *Jaguar – The History of a Great British Car* (Cambridge 1980 and later editions)
Wimpffen, János L *Time and Two Seats – Book 1* (Redmond, WA 1999)

Later newspapers and journals:
Car; Classic & Sports Car; Independent on Sunday; Jaguar Driver (JDC publication); *Jaguar Enthusiast* (JEC publication); *Jaguar Heritage (Archive); Jaguar Journal* (USA); *Jaguar Quarterly*, later *Jaguar World; The Daily Telegraph; The XK Gazette* (XK Club publication); *(Thoroughbred &) Classic Cars; XK Bulletin* (JDC XK Register)

Web sites (see notes for some more detailed references):
bertone.it, books.google.co.uk, bsmotoring.com, carclassic.com, classic-sportcars.ch, cocheclasico.com, dawn.com, delarue.net, etcerini.com, ghia-aigle.info, historicmotorracing.co.uk, hornburg.com, icfah.org, imdb.com, jag-lovers.org, msemc.org, mucklow.com, nevilshute.org, pendragonplc.com, pietro-frua.de, rmauctions.com, sayn.de, supercars.net, theP-eerage.com, westnet.com, Wikipedia, xkdata.com, zwakmanjaguar.com or zwakmanmotors.com, and others

Apart from the authors and editors of the works listed above, I would also like to acknowledge and thank the following who have been quoted directly or indirectly or who have assisted in writing this book:

At the JDHT: Derek and Margaret Boyce, Den Carlow, Penny Graham, Siân Moore, François Prins, Julia Simpson, and my predecessor Ann Harris; at the Jaguar Cars North America archive: Mike Cook, Gloria Pedati, and the late Karen Miller; at the BMIHT, Gaydon: Gillian Bardsley and the archive team; at the Coventry Transport Museum: Lizzie Hazlehurst; of the XK Club and *XK Gazette*: David Bentley, Peter Ingram.

As well as: Ronnie Adams, Ian Appleyard, Tony Bailey, Major Ian Baillie, Mrs Annabelle Beaty, John and Ruth Sands Bentley, Bob Berry, Doug Blain, William Boddy, John Bolster, ID Brawn, Guy Broad, Jeremy Broad, Michael Brown, Colonel Rixon Bucknall, Bruce Carnachan, Coventry City Archives staff, Stefan Dierkes, Barry Dixon, John Dowdeswell, FRW "Lofty" England, Elisabetta Farmeschi (Bertone), Nicolàs Franco junior, Paul Frère, Graham Gauld, Majeed Gill, Gregor Grant, Michael Griffiths, Betty Haig, Richard Hassan, Mike Hawthorn, William Munger Heynes, Derek Hood (JD Classics), Les Hughes (*Jaguar Magazine*, Australia), Dr James Hull, Bruce and Robert Kneale, Srinivas Krishnan, Karl Ludvigsen, Sir William Lyons, Ramon Magriñá, John May, John Morgan, Stirling Moss, Harry Mundy, Philip Oag and colleagues, Richard Owen, Jim Patten (*Jaguar World*), Laurence Pomeroy junior, Ernest "Bill" Rankin, Mike Riedner (*JagMag*, Germany), Urs Schmid, Heiner Stertkamp (Jaguar Association Germany), Jeremy Wade, Michael Ware, John Woods, Gordon Yardley (Woodmanton Classics), Tom Zwakman, and probably others to whom I apologise for forgetting to mention them by name, including JDHT clients.

Photographic acknowledgements:

Many of the photos used in this book came from the JDHT archive, thanks to the invaluable assistance of Karam Ram. The colour photos specially taken for this book are by Simon Clay, and feature cars owned by Dr James Hull. Photos were also taken by François Prins of Mrs Beaty's XK 140 FHC, and by Karam Ram of the XK 140 DHC then owned by Gordon Yardley. Other archive photos came from Paul Skilleter (including the former Bernard Viart collection), Mike Cook of the archives of Jaguar Cars North America, Terry McGrath, and the collection of Herridge and Sons (including the collection of the late David Hodges). Where possible, individual photos have been acknowledged also to the original source, but the author and publisher apologise if individual photos remain unattributed or incorrectly attributed. We thank all contributors for allowing images to be used.

I have included this picture in homage to the late Andrew Whyte, since it was the cover photo of the first 1980 edition of his classic Jaguar history. This was the XK 140 right-hand drive two-seater S 800024, which was actually originally cream, but had been restored in red when this photo was taken in 1979. (JDHT)